The Perspective of the Acting Person

Martin Rhonheimer

The Perspective of the Acting Person

Essays in the Renewal of Thomistic Moral Philosophy

Edited with an introduction by
William F. Murphy Jr.

The Catholic University of America Press
Washington, D.C.

The paper used in this publication meets the minimum requirements of American National Standards for Information Science—Permanence of Paper for Printed Library Materials, ANSI Z39.48-1984.
∞

LIBRARY OF CONGRESS CATALOGING-IN-PUBLICATION DATA
Rhonheimer, Martin, 1950–
The Perspective of the acting person : essays in the renewal of thomistic moral philosophy / by Martin Rhonheimer ; edited with an introduction by William F. Murphy, Jr.
p. cm.
Includes bibliographical references and index.
ISBN 978-0-8132-1511-2 (pbk. : alk. paper) 1. Thomas, Aquinas, Saint, 1225?–1274. 2. Ethics, Medieval. I. Murphy, William F. II. Title.
BJ255.T5R46 2007
171'.2—dc22

2007015719

Contents

Acknowledgments

"Is Christian Morality Reasonable? On the Difference between Secular and Christian Humanism" originally appeared in *Annales Theologici* 15, no. 2 (2001): 529–49, and is reprinted by permission.

"'Intrinsically Evil Acts' and the Moral Viewpoint: Clarifying a Central Teaching of *Veritatis Splendor*" originally appeared in *The Thomist* 58, no. 1 (1994): 1–39, and is reprinted by permission.

"Intentional Actions and the Meaning of Object: A Reply to Richard McCormick" originally appeared in *The Thomist* 59, no. 2 (1995): 279–311, and is reprinted by permission.

"Practical Reason and the 'Naturally Rational': On the Doctrine of the Natural Law as a Principle of Praxis in Thomas Aquinas" was originally published as "Praktische Vernunft und das 'von Natur aus Vernünftige.' Zur Lehre von der Lex naturalis als Prinzip der Praxis bei Thomas von Aquin," *Theologie und Philosophie* 75 (2000): 493–522. It was translated by Gerald Malsbary.

"The Moral Significance of Pre-Rational Nature in Aquinas: A Reply to Jean Porter (and Stanley Hauerwas)" was originally published in *The American Journal of Jurisprudence* 48 (2003): 253–80, and is reprinted by permission.

"The Cognitive Structure of the Natural Law and the Truth of Subjectivity" originally appeared in *The Thomist* 67, no. 1 (2003): 1–44, and is reprinted by permission.

"The Perspective of the Acting Person and the Nature of Practical Reason: The 'Object of the Human Act' in Thomistic Anthropology of Action" was originally published in *Nova et Vetera* 2, no. 2 (2004): 461–516, and is reprinted by permission. It was translated from the Italian by Joseph T. Papa.

"Practical Reason and the Truth of Subjectivity: The Self-Experience of the Moral Subject at the Roots of Metaphysics and Anthropology" was translated

Gerald Malsbary from the Italian manuscript "Ragione practica e verità della soggettività: l'autoesperienza del soggeto morale alle radici della metafisica e dell'anthropologia."

The review of Jean Porter's *Nature as Reason: A Thomistic Theory of Natural Law* was originally published in *Studies in Christian Ethics* 19, no. 3 (2006), and is reprinted by permission of SAGE publications.

Abbreviations

All works are cited according to the Marietti edition (Turin); the only exception is the Commentary on the Sentences, which is cited according to the edition used in the *Index Thomisticus: S. Thomae Aquinatis Opera Omnia,* vol. 1, ed. Roberto Busa (Stuttgart-Bad Cannstatt: Frommann-Holzboog, 1980).

In Sent.	*In Quattuor Libros Sententiarum Petri Lombardi (Commentary on the Sentences)*
ST I	*Summa Theologiae, Prima pars*
ST I-II	*Summa Theologiae, Prima secundae*
ST II-II	*Summa Theologiae, Secunda secundae*
ST III	*Summa Theologiae, Tertia pars*
In Ethic.	*In Decem libros Ethicorum Aristotelis ad Nicomachum expositio (In I Ethic.—Commentary on the First Book of Aristotle's Nicomachean Ethics)*
In de Anima	*In Aristotelis librum de Anima commentarium*
Super Ioannem	*Super Evangelium S. Ioannis Lectura*
Ad Rom.	*Super Epistolam S. Pauli ad Romanos Lectura*
Super Psalmos	*In psalmos Davidis expositio*
In duo Praecepta	*In duo praecepta caritatis et in decem legis praecepta expositio (Opuscula Theologica, vol. II)*
In Post. Anal.	*In Aristotelis libros Posteriorum Analyticorum expositio*
De Malo	*Quaestiones disputatae de Malo*
De Anima	*Quaestiones disputatae de Anima*
De Veritate	*Quaestiones disputatae de Veritate*

Preface

I would like to take this opportunity to express my thanks to Prof. Bill Murphy, for his conception and execution of this project, for his careful editing of the enclosed essays, and for his thoughtful introduction, which will not only help readers grasp their place in the context of my broader work, but will also facilitate the understanding of some of their basic contents. This is particularly important because, in the Anglo-Saxon world, scholarly discussion of my work has sometimes evidenced a lack of familiarity with my main treatments of philosophical ethical theory. With exception of my *Natural Law and Practical Reason,* these works have been published so far only in German, Italian, and Spanish. For this reason, I am delighted that these related essays are here gathered and thereby made more readily accessible for both scholars and students, who will appreciate the detailed index and bibliography. Moreover, I am pleased that those previously published in English are now complemented by related and perhaps overlooked works that are now available for the first time in English. Although I am a philosopher offering primarily philosophical arguments, much of the present work concerns questions raised in the context of moral theology, so I hope these essays will be useful to scholars and students in both moral philosophy and theology. Besides Prof. Murphy, to whom I am especially thankful for ongoing support of my work, I also wish to thank Drs. Gerald Malsbary and Joseph T. Papa for having so competently translated some of the essays from German and Italian, respectively. Finally, I wish to express my thankfulness to the staff of the Catholic University of America Press for publishing the volume.

Martin Rhonheimer
April 2007

Introduction

Over the past few decades, Swiss philosopher Martin Rhonheimer has developed an impressive body of work ranging from the most fundamental questions of ethical theory to more applied areas including political philosophy, sexual ethics, and biomedical ethics. His work provides one of the leading contemporary examples of the ongoing fecundity of the Aristotelian-Thomistic moral tradition when placed in dialogue with present-day alternatives, and in response to current questions. Since these works have been published primarily in German, Italian, and Spanish, however, relatively few English readers have grasped either the contours or the significance of Rhonheimer's work. Moreover, his corpus continues to grow rapidly, with several major books now available in German, Italian, and Spanish, along with several dozen substantial articles. Not surprisingly, over the last several years, these works have begun to appear in English translations. Because these initial translations have been parts of a larger whole, one that continues to develop, however, and because they have often been occasioned by particular questions, there remains a pressing need for a volume in English that presents his thought, especially that in fundamental ethics, in a more comprehensive and up-to-date manner.

The present introductory essay is intended to facilitate interaction with the essays by providing (i) a brief personal and intellectual biography, (ii) a sketch of the development of Rhonheimer's thought in fundamental ethics, (iii) a brief overview of his three major works, and (iv) an introduction to some of the key themes addressed in the essays here included. By doing so in some depth, this introductory essay seeks to provide a broad introduction to Rhonheimer's work in fundamental ethics.

A Short Personal and Intellectual Biography

The following biographical remarks are intended to facilitate understanding of Martin Rhonheimer's work in philosophical ethics.[1] He was born in 1950 in Zurich, Switzerland, and grew up in a family of converts, surrounded by both Jewish and Protestant members of his extended family. From the age of thirteen to twenty, he studied at a boarding school run by the Benedictines. Here, during his high school years, his love for philosophy was nurtured through a full two-year program of Thomistic philosophy. He then studied history, philosophy, and political science and did his Ph.D. in political philosophy at the University of Zurich. For six years he was an assistant to Professor Hermann Lübbe, who is one of the more prominent contemporary German philosophers. Therefore, although he has distinguished himself in recent decades through his work in what we might call fundamental ethics (i.e., action, virtue, and natural law theories), his primary interest remains political philosophy, including the history and theory of liberalism, questions regarding constitutional democracy and the common good, and those concerning the secular state, religious freedom, and pluralism.

Rhonheimer was ordained a Catholic priest in 1983, and he is incardinated in the personal prelature of the Holy Cross and Opus Dei. He is currently professor of ethics and political philosophy at the School of Philosophy of the Pontifical University of the Holy Cross in Rome. In addition, he spends several months per year in Fribourg, Switzerland, doing pastoral work with university students. Rhonheimer is a member of the editorial boards of *The American Journal of Jurisprudence* and the Fordham Series in Moral Philosophy and Moral Theology, a member of the scientific board of *Acta Philosophica,* and a corresponding academician to the Pontifical Academy of St. Thomas Aquinas.

The Development of Rhonheimer's Thought in Fundamental Ethics

Rhonheimer built upon his early acquaintance with Thomism through his later ecclesiastical studies in philosophy and theology in Rome. Both before and especially after his 1983 ordination to the priesthood, he focused his efforts on the ethics of Aristotle and Aquinas. As indicated above, this has

1. The following information was obtained from correspondence with Fr. Rhonheimer, and from his personal Web page, http://www.pusc.it/html/php/rhonheimer/.

led to the publication of various books, one of which has been translated into English.[2] His reading of Aquinas draws upon not only primary texts but also a wide range of primarily twentieth-century interpreters; indeed, his grasp of primary and secondary literature is perhaps unrivaled, especially by English-speaking moralists. The first decisive influence upon his work in Thomistic ethics was a series of writings by Servais Pinckaers, O.P., from which Rhonheimer learned (i) the importance of the end or *finis,* (ii) the need to understand objects as goals of the will, (iii) the need to overcome the object/subject dichotomy, and (iv) the importance of understanding human actions as "intentional actions"—something that he also learned from the writings of G. E. M. Anscombe. Another important influence was the work of Theo G. Belmans on the objective meaning of human acts, from whom Rhonheimer first learned to understand the "object" of a human act as a chosen action and not merely a thing of the physical order. From the work of Joseph de Finance, he came to see in Thomas a notion of human moral autonomy and to articulate it as "participated theonomy." From Giuseppe Abbà, he learned to better understand how Aquinas shifted from an ethical outlook centered on law to one more centered on the virtues. Rhonheimer also credits the scholarship of Angel Rodríguez Luño with enriching his understanding of Thomistic virtue ethics, especially regarding moral virtue as a *habitus electivus.* In these emphases, the reader should note a strong affinity between Rhonheimer's retrieval of Aquinas and the approach taken by Pope John Paul II in his 1993 encyclical, *Veritatis Splendor,* in the decisive section dealing with moral acts (cf. nos. 78ff.).

Rhonheimer originally learned and accepted the traditional interpretation of Aquinas on the relation between nature and morality, which presupposed that practical judgments are grounded in theoretical judgments about the order of nature. He later came to see a fundamental incompatibility between this reading of Thomas and the texts themselves, however, and between their sources in Aristotle's theories of action and the virtues. A decisive shift in Rhonheimer's reading of Aquinas began when he encountered the article by Germain Grisez entitled "The First Principle of Practical Reason," which convinced him that practical reason has its own starting point. This shift was reinforced by the deepening insight that our understanding of human nature—and thus the moral good—is not originally derived from metaphysical speculation, but is rather gained through the subject's practi-

2. Those of primary interest to this volume will be introduced below.

cal insight as embodied in the inner experience of his natural inclinations. In this, Rhonheimer's reading of Jacques Maritain's *Neuf leçons sur les notions premières de la philosophie morale* and John Finnis's *Fundamentals of Ethics* were also crucial. From this new perspective, Rhonheimer was able to appreciate greatly Wolfgang Kluxen's work in Thomistic ethics, especially his insistence that ethics should not be understood as methodologically subordinated to metaphysics, that is, derived from it. Similarly, because he had come to see in Thomas an understanding of natural law as a theory of the practical reason, and not primarily one of speculative judgments that were then applied to practice, Rhonheimer became convinced that subsequent thought had imposed upon Thomas a viewpoint that was not his own.

Because of his emphasis on natural law as belonging essentially not to what we might call "pre-rational nature" but to practical reason,[3] and his emphasis on natural law theory as being a theory of practical reason, some readers have misunderstood and greatly overestimated the extent to which Rhonheimer follows the "new natural law theory" of Grisez and Finnis. On the contrary, Rhonheimer has expressed various criticisms against (i) certain aspects of their action theory, (ii) their understanding of practical reason, (iii) their neglect of virtue, and (iv) their treatment of particular questions such as contraception. Moreover, Rhonheimer's interpretation of Thomistic ethics as a rational virtue ethics in the Aristotelian tradition is fundamentally distinct from their new natural law theory. Therefore, although he thinks Grisez and Finnis made important contributions to a more adequate reading of Aquinas, and although these contributions contributed to an important shift in his thought, Rhonheimer does not seek to develop a new theory, as they do, or a natural law ethics. Instead, he tries to remain firmly grounded in the teaching of Aquinas himself, which he understands as a rational virtue ethics in the Aristotelian tradition.

Similarly, although he studied the work of Wolfgang Kluxen and takes from him the understanding that Thomas does not subordinate ethics to metaphysics but rather upholds its distinctive scope, Rhonheimer does not take any other significant positions primarily from Kluxen. Moreover, as will be seen in chapter 5, some of his most serious disagreements are with former students of Kluxen, whose revisionist divergences from Aquinas have no direct grounding in Kluxen's work, although they stem from certain ambiguities in his interpretation of Aquinas. Most significantly, however, these for-

3. Recall that, for Thomas, reason specifies human nature.

mer students of Kluxen have introduced into their interpretation of Aquinas a "Kantian turn," for which Rhonheimer explicitly criticizes their work. Because of this, Rhonheimer is actually known and sometimes criticized in the German-speaking world as an outspoken anti-Kantian. Especially in his *The Perpsective of Morality: Philosophical Bases of Thomistic Virtue Ethics,*[4] he has extensively emphasized the difference between a Kantian and a Thomistic approach to ethics and he systematically rejects any reading of Aquinas that is "contaminated" by Kantianism. Surprisingly, some Thomists have come to believe that Rhonheimer's understanding of practical reason and intentionality are influenced by Kant, thereby reflecting a "subjectivist" turn. This, however, is far off the mark because Rhonheimer holds that the human intellect is essentially a truth-attaining capacity, so that the morally upright subjectivity of which he writes is one rooted in the truth. So, unlike Kant, his emphasis is not simply on subjectivity (or the subject) but on the *truth* of subjectivity, which is clear in the remarks below on the seventh and ninth chapters, and is reflected in this collection as a whole.

The various interpretative elements identified above are important components of Rhonheimer's broader project in fundamental ethics, which can be understood as an attempt to better articulate and to develop Thomistic virtue ethics as an explicitly first-person account of moral action. As noted above, however, this should not be understood as something like a new theory. Instead, as his extensive references to primary and secondary sources demonstrate, Rhonheimer seeks to be a faithful interpreter of Aquinas, and one who is particularly well informed by the tradition of interpretation. He also, however, seeks to make more explicit certain elements that, as he is convinced, are largely implicit in the writings of Thomas himself. Indeed, one can view his work as benefiting from various important clarifications and developments in Thomistic studies, as well as integrating what is true in the more traditional interpreters (such as Ralph McInerny), who emphasize metaphysics and nature, with more recent developments (such as the work of Grisez and Finnis), which seek to recover the emphasis of Thomas on reason (and not "nature") as the "proper principle," the "rule and measure" of human acts. Therefore, in light of the widespread renewal of interest in Thomis-

4. This is the tentative title of the English translation, forthcoming from the Catholic University of America Press. The original German edition is *Die Perspektive der Moral: Philosophische Grundlagen der Tugendethik* (Berlin: Akademie Verlag, 2001), which is available in an Italian translation as *La Prospettiva Della Morale: Fondamenti Dell'Etica* (Rome: Armando Editore, 2006).

tic ethics, this work should be of great interest to philosophers and theologians who want to be informed about developments and important debates in this tradition.

Overview of Rhonheimer's Major Works in Fundamental Ethics

In this section, I will offer a brief overview of Rhonheimer's three primary works in Thomistic ethics, which will help us to situate the essays included in this volume in light of his broader body of work. These three primary works include *Natural Law and Practical Reason: A Thomist View of Moral Autonomy*[5]; *The Perspective of Morality: Philosophical Bases of Thomistic Virtue Ethics*; and a yet-untranslated work that might be rendered in English as *Practical Reason and the Rationality of Praxis: Thomistic Action Theory in the Context of its Origin in Aristotelian Ethics.*[6]

Natural Law and Practical Reason

Rhonheimer suggests that *Natural Law and Practical Reason* should be read as the documentation of a process of reflection.[7] It serves as an invaluable resource for those who seek to evaluate his broader articulation of Thomistic ethics, precisely because it documents his initial analysis of the primary texts in light of the tradition of interpretation as reflected in the secondary literature, his assessment of the problems requiring resolution, and his initial efforts toward a comprehensive articulation of a rational virtue ethic in the Aristotelian/Thomistic tradition. The primary contributions of this volume include argumentation addressing (i) the distinctive character of practical reason, (ii) the natural law as a law of this practical reason, (iii)

5. *Natural Law and Practical Reason* (hereafter *NLPR*) was published by Fordham University Press (New York, 2000), was originally published in German as *Natur als Grundlage der Moral* (Innsbruck-Vienna: Tyrolia-Verlag, 1987), and is also available in Italian and Spanish translations.

6. This work is available only in the original German as *Praktische Vernunft und Vernünftigkeit der Praxis: Handlungstheorie bei Thomas von Aquin in ihrer Entstehung aus dem Problemkontext der aristotelischen Ethik* (Berlin: Akademie Verlag, 1994). Readers of this volume will also be interested in his forthcoming work in sexual ethics, *Ethics of Procreation: Contraception, Artificial Fertilization, and Abortion.* This is published in Italian as *Etica della procreazione: Contraccezione, Fecondazione artificiale, Aborto* (Mursia, Milan: Edizioni PUL, 2000) through the Pontifical John Paul II Institute for Studies on Marriage and Family at the Lateran University.

7. I will offer relatively brief remarks on this complex work; those interested in a detailed review can refer to my "Martin Rhonheimer's Natural Law and Practical Reason," *Sapientia* 56 (2002): 517–48, upon which I draw.

the implications of Thomas's metaphysics of participation for anthropology and "autonomy," (iv) the dynamics of the natural reason as the epistemological substructure of natural law, (v) Thomas's doctrine about reason as the rule and standard of human morality, (vi) a basic account of the object of the moral act, and (vii) an application of this basic reading of Thomistic ethics to the crucial test case of contraception.

Because it is not treated in the other works we will consider, let us note some of the key features of the fourth theme, his account of the dynamics of the natural reason as the epistemological substructure of natural law. Rhonheimer builds upon his retrieval of Aquinas's teachings regarding (i) the natural reason as a participation in the divine power of knowing, and (ii) the *inventio* or explication of our originally intuitive understanding (the *intellectus*) by means of discursive reasoning *(ratio)* to explain how the secondary principles of the natural law are an explication of what is implicit in the primary principles. He shows how these secondary principles are "discovered" in the first and universal principles through the discursive process of the natural reason so that they are able to direct human action. The basic movement that initiates this process of discovery is grounded in *synderesis*, the *habitus* of our intuitive knowledge of these first principles of natural law, which provides a natural source of intellectual light and the seeds of all subsequent practical knowledge. However, it is important to note that Rhonheimer sees this discovery as dependent upon the experience of particular kinds of action. The principles guide the process of discovery, but not without concrete moral experience since the universal is always known in and through the particular and concrete. He would even grant that the principles are first grasped in the particular. From this emphasis on the need for concrete experience, he would deny that we can simply "deduce" more particular norms from the principles of natural law.

The Perspective of Morality

The Perspective of Morality presents and argues for a systematic account of a rational virtue ethic in the Aristotelian/Thomistic tradition.[8] In so doing, it both engages recent work in moral philosophy and is open to a theological

8. The following comments on *The Perspective of Morality* are adapted from the longer synopsis provided on Fr. Rhonheimer's personal Web page as cited above. I will also keep this section relatively brief, as the work is available not only in German but also in Italian and Spanish, and the English translation is forthcoming.

completion.[9] It also functions as an introduction to moral philosophy by, for example, including a critique of rival ethical conceptions structured around moral norms, rules, or duties such as utilitarianism, consequentialism, and Kantianism.

More specifically, "the book sets out to demonstrate rigorously the rational structure, the anthropological presuppositions and the normative relevance of virtue ethics." It first "argues that the viewpoint proper to a virtue-centered conception of morality"—and "presupposed by an adequate approach to resolving concrete moral questions"—is the "first-person" perspective of the acting person who perceives goods to be pursued and acts freely through reason and will. To address concrete moral questions from this properly moral perspective of distinctively human acts—those understood by reason and intended/deliberately chosen by the will of the agent—the book includes an account of human agency in terms of "intentional" actions. Here, the central topic is the object of the moral act, where Rhonheimer introduces his concept of the "intentional basic action."[10] Because a credible contemporary account of Thomistic ethics must do more than offer a fragmented treatment of particular themes such as natural law or the moral object, he seeks also to show the connections between these key topics and others such as happiness, reasonableness, practical principles, moral norms, conscience, and freedom—all within an ethical conception centered on the virtues and conducive to a theological completion.

Along with an account of intrinsically evil acts, the final chapter sets forth a theory about the "structures of reasonableness," which Rhonheimer considers an indispensable element of a complete account of virtue ethics, although it is generally neglected in the literature on virtue. This theory treats the meaning of and relationship between practical principles, conscience, moral norms, and the virtue of prudence. While the ultimate "structure of reasonableness" is the eternal law, Rhonheimer's theory seeks to show how the right practical reason that guides human acts is seen not merely in human inclinations and

9. As discussed more fully in the first essay of this collection, Rhonheimer insists that the truth claims of the Catholic moral tradition are inherently intelligible and accessible to human reason and philosophy, although in a qualified sense, since the light of human reason is darkened by human weakness and often by vice. On the other hand, he affirms the "intrinsic incompleteness of the purely philosophical viewpoint," which calls for completion—and indeed rescue—through Christian theology.

10. The eighth essay of the present volume offers a recent and detailed account of Rhonheimer's approach to this central topic, in support of and close affinity with the central teaching of *Veritatis Splendor* nn. 78ff.

their natural ends—as for many post-Tridentine and neo-Thomistic interpretations—but in the practical reason of the good and virtuous agent who is perfectly subject to the eternal law *(ST* Ia-IIae, q.93, a.6, *corpus).*

Practical Reason and the Rationality of Praxis

Practical Reason and the Rationality of Praxis proceeds from the thesis that "Aristotle's ethics limits itself to a study of the affective conditions of reasoned behavior (i.e., the moral virtues), but does not include a (normative) doctrine of principles of the practical reason, which reveals a certain lacuna in Aristotle's action theory."[11] Rhonheimer's objective in this book is to argue—through an extensive "analysis not only of Aristotelian passages but also of Thomas's appropriation, interpretation, and completion of these texts"—that Thomistic action theory fills this lacuna, while resolving various other problems. He wants to show that Thomas remains genuinely Aristotelian while integrating the work of "the philosopher" into a higher synthesis.

For our purposes, I will now summarize some of the key conclusions of *Practical Reason and the Rationality of Praxis* to alert readers of this volume to the complementary resources it provides. First, Rhonheimer will argue that "the action theory developed and thematized as practical wisdom in Aristotelian ethics" is not a "hermeneutic-dialectical type of ethics." In other words, it is not essentially or primarily a system of ethical norms determined through a dialectical engagement with the tradition of the many and of the elders. Rather, it is primarily "a theory of the rationality of *praxis* . . . and is ultimately therefore a theory of the practical reason." Second, he argues that Aristotle develops his theory of practical reason "on the basis of the Socratic-Platonic-Academic presupposition of the truth-attaining ability of the intellect," which guides action "unerringly and efficiently," presuming the agent is formed in moral virtue. Third, Rhonheimer concludes that "Thomas's doctrine of the natural knowledge of practical principles"—that is, Thomas's theory of the innate, intuitive knowledge of the first principles of natural law through synderesis—"leaves Aristotle's theory intact," while integrating "it into a larger context." This larger context includes advances regarding (i) the virtuous mean as established by the reason of the agent, and (ii) the theory of the will.

11. For this discussion of *Practical Reason and the Rationality of Praxis,* I rely primarily upon the conclusion of the German edition in an unpublished translation of that section by Gerald Malsbary. I offer more detailed remarks on the book here, as this complex work is available only in German and a complete translation is not yet in process.

It also includes advances regarding the "intentional" or goal-directed character (i) of appetition, (ii) of *praxis,* (iii) of choice, and (iv) of prudence. Furthermore, it includes an understanding of "practical principles," which are nothing other than the precepts of natural law, as *both* motive principles inclining the agent toward appetible goods—such as the inclination toward the good of nutrition—*and* as rational principles through which the acting person deliberately guides his action, such as the intuitive judgment that it is good now to eat lunch.

Fourth, for Thomas, the right reason that guides good actions and leads to the ultimate happiness of the agent pertains not merely—or primarily—to the philosophical discipline of "practical or moral science," but chiefly to the practical reason of the virtuous agent. Fifth, whereas Aristotle—in an attempt to distinguish his position from the Academics—opposes the Socratic-Platonic position regarding the immediate intuition of the practical good through his insistence on the need for moral virtue, Thomas offers a synthesis that upholds the Socratic-Platonic position on Aristotelian grounds. Thus, the virtuous man, who is able to attain moral truth through his practical reason, is himself the rule and measure for his actions. Sixth, Thomas's action theory is able to incorporate *both* the dialectical hermeneutic regarding the opinions of the best and wisest—including the application of these to life—*and* recourse to "the immediate self-experience of the acting subject." Therefore, in Rhonheimer's interpretation, Thomas allows for both practical/moral science, and for the recognition that the virtuous agent can grasp moral truth and thereby question the currently dominant *endoxa* (or approved opinions). This latter point becomes more important in an age when approved societal opinions favor not only the contraceptive practices that threaten the survival of European civilization, but also abortion, euthanasia, embryonic stem-cell research, cloning, and same-sex marriage.

Seventh, Rhonheimer notes that Thomas's development of the Socratic-Platonic insight about practical truth on Aristotelian grounds follows from his greater optimism than "the philosopher" regarding the possibilities of human nature, based upon the Christian doctrine of man's creation in the image of God. This recovery of Thomas's teaching about the truth-attaining power of the practical reason of the virtuous agent has great relevance for those seeking to read Thomistic ethics in light of Scripture, as encouraged by thinkers such as Servais Pinckaers and by *Veritatis Splendor.* For example, it allows the moral theologian to elucidate what it means to live in Christian freedom according to the Spirit and the "mind of Christ," as we see especially in the Pauline letters.

Eighth, in spite of Rhonheimer's emphasis on the truth-attaining capacity of the practical reason of the virtuous agent, he also insists that the "Aristotelian methodology of a dialectical/hermeneutic determination of the 'good life' remains fully relevant today." This dialectical/hermeneutic element is necessary in the effort to determine what is truly "best" and "wisest." It is also necessary "because the social life of man cannot be grounded on the intuitions of *single* acting subjects, but only on the *consensus* of what is taken for good in the context of the human *koinonia.*" Once again we see how moral philosophy requires a theological completion: given that moral conclusions drawn from human reason will differ, moral theology draws additionally upon both the communal experience of the Church and the witness of the saints, who are seen as exemplars of the heroic virtue that allows practical reason sufficient light to determine what is truly best and wisest.

Introduction to the Essays Included

The essays included here seek to provide a robust introduction to Martin Rhonheimer's contributions in fundamental ethics. To show how these essays reflect and complement the three major works described above, this section will introduce each piece, highlighting as appropriate some of its key features and its relation to his broader body of work.

The Intelligibility of Christian Morality as the True Humanism

The first essay, entitled "Is Christian Morality Reasonable? On the Difference between Secular and Christian Humanism," was originally published in 2001 and provides a fitting start for the volume. It helps us locate Rhonheimer's work in philosophical ethics in relation to several streams of thought, and especially to claims from both secularists and those inside the Church who employ consequentialist approaches and charge that traditional Christian morality is unreasonable, and even inhuman. In addition, this essay illustrates his approach to the relation between moral philosophy and theology and between faith and reason.

As we would expect, Rhonheimer argues for a profound continuity between unassisted practical reason (corresponding to natural law) and revealed Christian morality. As he puts it, "the basic moral requirements of Christian life are in principle fully intelligible and therefore accessible to reasonable argument and defense, but they simultaneously need in many cases the support of Christian faith to preserve fully their reasonableness." This fundamental continuity between reason and faith enables him to argue that Christian morality is not only more reasonable than secular theories of moral compromise (i.e., consequentialism), but also that it offers the most authentic, and indeed the true, humanism.

At least potentially, any interlocutor not completely given over to vice can agree about the goods that are perfective of the person, and about corresponding norms such as not harming others, rendering to others what they are due, telling the truth, and keeping one's promises. Without the support of Christian faith, however, Rhonheimer argues that such basic insights into moral truth will quite often either not be clearly perceived or dismissed as not practicable. For the agent who experiences a disjunction between what he intuitively recognizes as the good (the "ought") and what he judges himself able to do (the "can"), consequentialism provides a way to adjust the "ought" down to the "can," to reduce the original moral insight to an "ideal," and to set a lower moral standard corresponding to a character not sufficiently formed in virtue. It provides a mode of moral reasoning—a technique—to rationalize the gap between "ought" and "can," so that instead of ordering our practical reasoning to achieve the true good, we reason to achieve the most favorable consequences. This approach, however, requires that we contradict the moral principles that we grasp, at least partially, through natural reason.

Rhonheimer thinks that such compromise is an affront to the dignity of the person. Therefore, the human predicament requires liberation; moral philosophy requires completion by moral theology; Christian morality is properly understood as an integral part of a religion of salvation; and the true humanism is necessarily situated within the logic of redemption through the Cross of Christ.

Virtue Ethics over Consequentialism and Natural Law

The second essay is entitled "Norm-Ethics, Moral Rationality, and the Virtues: What's Wrong with Consequentialism," and it has appeared elsewhere in earlier forms. In it, Rhonheimer argues for the superiority of an ethic based on virtue over two alternatives: a natural law ethic that largely neglects virtue, such as the new natural law theory of Germain Grisez and John Finnis, and theories that fall under a broad notion of consequentialism or utilitarianism, such as those advocated by post-conciliar revisionists.

Rhonheimer argues that the fundamental strength of a virtue-based approach is that it addresses the realm of morality, properly speaking: the first-person perspective of "the acting person," the realm of "intentional actions" where the agent perceives the desirable and apparently good end, deliberates about possible means to achieve it, and then chooses either for or against what he judges to be good and true. A virtue-based approach is able to address this realm of intentional actions in several ways: because it takes into account the underlying inclinations of the person toward happiness, the good, and the true, and because it acknowledges how these appetites must be shaped by reason toward their perfection in the moral virtues. This provides the broader context in which to account for the various passions—such as love and fear—that influence the deliberation and choice of the moral agent. Moreover, Rhonheimer thinks a virtue-based ethic provides a broader context for understanding the place of moral norms, which have an important but limited role in the practical reasoning of the agent.

In dialogue with the work of Grisez and Finnis, Rhonheimer tries to make the case that their neglect of virtue leads to a diminished treatment of the "essence of morality" that he insists is found in the perspective of the acting person. Further, in response to a challenge by Finnis, Rhonheimer offers an explanation of how the virtues contribute to "the propositional content of moral norms," drawing upon his account of the "structures of rationality," which he treats more fully in *Practical Reason and the Rationality of Practice.*

In his engagement with post-conciliar revisionism, Rhonheimer notes the basic continuity between consequentialism, utilitarianism, and post-conciliar "proportionalism," and he offers a concise critique, along the lines of the more detailed treatment in *The Perspective of Morality.* The fundamental flaw with the theories of Catholic revisionists can be traced to their proximate roots in the manualist tradition of the seventeenth through the twentieth centuries: the consideration of actions through the third-person perspective of the confessor or speculative philosopher. This perspective allows a merely physical, external description of the act, and an inadequate, physical understanding of the object, according to which supposedly "human acts" are seen without reference to what is understood and freely chosen for the sake of an end, as mere events or natural processes that produce states of affairs. Because of this, such theories are unable to provide an accurate analysis of the distinctively "human acts" understood and chosen by the agent.

The "Moral Perspective" in Veritatis Splendor

The third essay is entitled "'Intrinsically Evil Acts' and the Moral Viewpoint: Clarifying a Central Teaching of *Veritatis Splendor,*" which was originally published in 1994, shortly after the 1993 encyclical. Here Rhonheimer argues that the central teaching of *Veritatis Splendor,* which insists that some kinds of human acts are intrinsically evil, can be properly understood only in light of "the distinctively moral viewpoint" of the "acting person," the standpoint of the person who grasps, through reason, the means to achieve a good end and freely chooses it.

Rhonheimer thinks progress in recent ethical debates requires various clarifications and developments at the level of meta-ethics. Because this is not the proper task of an encyclical, he offers his supporting contribution through a treatment of seven topics that will appear frequently throughout his broader corpus, including the "basic intention" of the proximate end, the need to understand the moral object as an object of practical reason, the moral relevance of the goods toward which individual potencies are ordered, the moral object, and the natural law. Because of the importance of his recovery of the proximate end, and his articulation of the "basic intention" of the proximate end, a few comments may be helpful.

Rhonheimer distinguishes the morally crucial sense of intention as "the basic intention" of—as *Veritatis Splendor* emphasizes—the *finis proximus* of the agent's will, an intentionality without which an act could not be considered as a human act, but would be merely a kind of event or process with some unintended result. This "basic intention" of the proximate end is the immediate intentionality implied in the performance of a particular "human act"—one that proceeds from both reason and will, and in virtue of which is an object of a choice. It explains why someone does what they do and defines a freely chosen behavior as a morally determinate "type," "kind," or "species" of human action. For example, taking an aspirin for the basic intention of *relieving my headache* makes the act to be one of therapy. Rhonheimer distinguishes this "basic intention" from the further intentions of the agent through which a determinate kind of action is oriented to further or additional ends. As we will see, this "basic intention" is not arbitrarily chosen but depends upon reason, which depends upon sensible objects: One cannot rationally claim to be intending an act of nutrition when swallowing stones.

Here I should note that this recovery of the proximate end includes an explicit rejection of the traditional interpretation of the distinction between the *finis operis* (end of the act) and the *finis operantis* (end of the actor), where the former is taken to be the "natural end" and the latter is taken to be the "further end" of the actor. With Servais Pinckaers and a growing number of scholars, Rhonheimer holds that this distinction is not operative in Thomas and is a later "development." Moreover, as this understanding of this distinction becomes widespread in the post-Tridentine speculative and casuist tradition, the decisive "proximate end" drops from the tradition, making it vulnerable to critique before the turbulence of the post-conciliar era, preparing the way for proportionalism and contributing to an ongoing stalemate in Thomistic ethics as this highly problematic distinction continues to be utilized by traditional/naturalistic Thomists.

Veritatis Splendor *on the Object of the Moral Act*

The fourth essay is entitled "Intentional Actions and the Meaning of Object: A Reply to Richard McCormick"; it was originally published in 1995 in response to a critique of the encyclical by the Jesuit moralist. In this highly influential essay, Rhonheimer provides a compelling and widely cited rebuttal of perhaps the leading advocate of the proportionalist moral methodology. He proceeds in five steps: (i) a clarification that the volitional component of the moral object is insisted upon by *Veritatis Splendor;* (ii) a distinction between such an "intentional" account of the moral object and the merely physical notion of the object in the post-Tridentine, casuist, and naturalistic tradition and at the root of the crisis of post-conciliar revisionism; (iii) an analysis and critique of McCormick's "expanded notion of the object," which expands beyond the physical object to include the further intention but overlooks the decisive intention of the proximate end; (iv) a discussion of how consideration of the "ends of the virtues" and "the structure of virtue" as part of the broader "structures of rationality" can help us to grasp the true intelligibility of human actions and to distinguish morally between behavior patterns that appear the same at the physical level; and (v) a rebuttal of the revisionist claim that the encyclical misrepresents their position.

I will limit myself to a few comments on the third section, where Rhonheimer examines and criticizes McCormick's "expanded notion of object," which includes not the basic intentionality that explains the proximate choosing of the external act but the further intention to realize the hoped-for benefits. He illustrates this through the example of Paul Touvier, a Frenchman who collaborated with the Nazis and was tried for shooting seven Jews, purportedly to save ninety-three. Touvier argued that his action should be understood not as deliberately killing (i.e., murdering) the former but as saving the latter. Rhonheimer correctly describes this action as deliberately killing/murdering (though under external coercion) seven in the hope of (realizing the consequence of) saving ninety-three. He shows that McCormick's expanded notion of the moral object, which is also evident in other revisionists such as Josef Fuchs and Peter Knauer, provides a framework for justifying actions in precisely this way. By ignoring the moral relevance of freely choosing the "basic intentional act" of murdering seven, and claiming that the ulterior end of hoped-for benefits determines the moral quality of the physical behavior, McCormick provides a theory that can justify almost any behavior as long as the agent is creative enough to hope for sufficient beneficial consequences. Therefore, this "expanded notion of the object" is completely unworkable as a moral theory, a form of consequentialism and therefore a mere technique for rationalizing behavior. It does not allow one to speak truthfully about what one deliberately chooses as a moral agent. Instead it makes morality depend upon one's preferences regarding what one wishes to consider the decisive goal of the act, and what reasons one considers valid in weighing the consequences.

Neglecting Reason in Favor of Nature?

The fifth contribution is entitled "Practical Reason and the 'Naturally Rational': On the Doctrine of the Natural Law as a Principle of Praxis in Thomas Aquinas," which has been translated from the German original for this collection. It contains Rhonheimer's response to the charge—issuing from what he judges to be a Kantian perspective—that he holds a naturalistic position, neglecting a supposed priority of reason over "nature." Because this is the opposite charge leveled against him by more "naturalistic" Thomists, who think he is Kantian, it provides an opportunity for Rhonheimer to argue that his position is clearly distinct from and superior to the Kantian alternative—and more authentically Thomistic than naturalistic forms of Thomism. I will offer introductory comments on what Rhonheimer will argue about (i) practical reason and its relation to nature, (ii) natural inclinations as *bona humana,* and the indirect normativity of pre-rational human nature.

First, the theoretical root of the debate concerns a proper understanding of practical reason and how it relates to what is often called "nature," meaning the pre-rational aspects of human nature—what Thomas sometimes calls "the nature we share with the animals." Rhonheimer argues against a Kantian reading of Aquinas that sees—at the beginning of the process of practical reason—something like "pure" or "autonomous" reason, which dominates and only "refers to" nature. Instead, he insists that, according to Aquinas, practical reason is embedded in the natural inclinations from the beginning. It begins with our grasping of what is "naturally rational," especially the first principles of natural law, and it is always the practical reason of an inherently unified body-person, with various inclinations toward human goods. In this perspective, the "first principle of practical reason" (i.e., good is to be done and pursued) is not merely rational but something within the unified body-person that "branches out" into the various intelligible inclinations or strivings of the person in pursuit of particular goods. These strivings correspond to the practical reasoning toward the various ends. Therefore, "human practical reason only exists in [pre-rational, bodily] nature, is always bound up with nature, and is conditioned by nature. It is not 'reason' that knows, but rather the *body-soul* unity, *as constituted in the person,* that knows by means of reason."

Second, regarding the indirect normativity of pre-rational human nature, because Rhonheimer follows the teaching of Thomas that practical reason is the proximate standard for moral actions and the eternal law is the ultimate standard, he holds that the natural inclinations provide a remote standard. This unified perspective follows from his understanding of the continuity between God's eternal law, the inclinations of our bodily nature, and our practical reason. Rhonheimer explicitly follows the teaching of Thomas that the *inclinatio naturalis* has a standard-giving function in relation to the *ratio naturalis,* and he thinks the natural inclinations are human goods *(bona humana)* by the fact of their belonging to human nature, but he specifies that they become *practical goods* only in the context of practical reasoning, rational judgments, and the choice that precedes the execution of the act. Rejecting a simplistic naturalism that would claim that the inclinations directly provide inviolable norms to guide actions, he therefore argues that the key question is the relationship between the proper end *(finis proprius)* of the natural inclinations and the *debitum,* that which ought to be done. He thinks the indirect normativity of nature is given a new form at the level of the person through the practical reason. Thus, his discussion of the sexual inclination, for example, leads harmoniously to a treatment of not just negative norms regarding sexual ethics, but the "truth of sexuality" and the human good of married love as a virtuous perfection of the human person.

The Moral Significance of Pre-Rational Human Nature

The sixth contribution is entitled "The Moral Significance of Pre-Rational Nature in Aquinas: A Reply to Jean Porter (and Stanley Hauerwas)." It was published in 2003 in response to these two leading English-language moralists who misunderstand Rhonheimer's account of the moral significance of the pre-rational aspects of human nature. It responds directly and primarily to a critical review of his book *Natural Law and Practical Reason* by Jean Porter, who charges that he neglects the moral significance of pre-rational human nature and cites against him Aquinas's discussion of "sin against nature." It also offers a brief response to the use made of Rhonheimer's work by Stanley Hauerwas, who cites it approvingly in his "thought experiment" on friendship with "gay Christians" in the context of an ethic of virtue, in which he notes that he is "more agnostic than Rhonheimer" about the extent to which the normativity of bodily nature can be known.

These interlocutors provide Rhonheimer the opportunity to clarify (i) that pre-rational nature is indeed part of the order of reason that determines the morality of human action, and (ii) that his theory in no way supports the claim that homosexual acts may be licit. So that this introduction may help clarify a widespread misunderstanding, and because of the contemporary importance of these interlocutors, I will offer more detailed remarks on Rhonheimer's interpretation of Thomas on the "sins against nature" and his reply to Hauerwas.

First, in light of an integral and personal Thomistic anthropology, Rhonheimer interprets Aquinas's account of the "sins against nature" as actions against the natural foundation that right practical reason presupposes. Second, he distinguishes "acting against nature" from "sinning against nature," pointing to actions such as wearing earplugs, shaving, cutting one's hair, trimming one's nails, donating a kidney, or chewing sugarless gum to demonstrate "precisely that there is an epistemological problem,[12] that the moral significance of the natural is not simply deducible from the sheer naturalness of the natural."

Third, Rhonheimer discusses how the "natural" (i.e., pre-rational nature)

12. Please see the essay itself, and *NLPR*, for the importance to Rhonheimer's thought of his distinction between the "ontological perspective," corresponding to what is typically called moral/practical science, and the "epistemological or cognitional perspective," corresponding to moral philosophy and practical reason in the strict and proper sense.

functions as a presupposition for reason, building upon an exposition of what Aquinas teaches in *ST* IIa-IIae, q.154, a.12, regarding "the sin against nature." The key texts from article 12 state (i) that "reason has to presuppose what nature has determined in order to arrange anything else as it sees fit" and (ii) "the transgression is only against that which has been determined according to right reason, but still presupposing the natural principles." These texts suggest that pre-rational nature does provide natural principles for reason and does determine some moral constraints, but these must be determined by reason. Therefore, the key question concerns how to determine that something "natural" is a presupposition for right practical reason and the moral order. Rhonheimer's answer is that we do so through practical reason, which corresponds directly to the formal, that is, rational, element of natural law. For example, he thinks the practical reason should grasp naturally both that the procreative meaning of the sexual inclination is a human good (note that this falls far short of claiming that everyone will naturally grasp the norm against contraception) and that chewing gum is not a violation of reason or nature. He argues that Thomas's point in this article is that the sin against nature is particularly grave because the order of reason is deprived of its natural principles and orientation toward the human good; however, he thinks that the moral relevance of this nature is grasped epistemologically at the level of reason and virtue, where the natural can be recognized as a human good. Consider once again the moral relevance of the bodily aspects of human sexuality. Although many will not recognize the full truth about human sexuality, this full truth is inherently intelligible, and it is manifest in our sexual inclination and our further orientation toward the human good of marriage, including procreation, mutual self-giving, friendship, and faithfulness. This full truth about human sexuality provides the context for a proper consideration of the moral significance of the pre-rational, bodily foundations of human sexuality.

Rhonheimer's response to Stanley Hauerwas seeks to clarify the relevance of "natural patterns," or the physical dimension of human acts, in the context of an intentional theory of action. He proceeds by distinguishing between actions that "regarding their natural or physical pattern, are open to many possible descriptions," and actions whose natural pattern does not offer this "intentional openness" and capacity to be described differently based upon different basic or immediate intentions. The former, for example, would include the bodily movement of "raising one's arm," which would be properly described as different human acts depending upon various basic intentions of proximate ends, such as to greet somebody, to signal the start of a competition, to swat a fly, and the like. The latter fall into two categories. The first involves natural patterns that are not capable of being informed by certain intentions; for example, the act of chewing sugarless gum cannot rationally be informed by the intention to nourish oneself. The second involves situations where intentionality with respect to some good is inseparable from a determinate natural pattern; for example, because the human person will intuitively grasp that sexual acts pertain to procreation, sexual acts cannot be separated from some basic intentionality with regard to this natural end. For example, the agent may engage in intercourse (i) precisely to procreate, (ii) while accepting that procreation may occur, (iii) while knowing and accepting that procreation is impossible, or (iv) in conjunction with a prior and properly contraceptive act—say inserting a diaphragm—that has deliberately rendered this act of intercourse infertile. Similarly, for Rhonheimer, acts of speech cannot be separated from a basic intentionality regarding communications. This is true because he sees "communication," as an aspect of justice, to provide the proper "ethical context" that is necessary to determine whether speech acts pertain to the virtue of truth-telling or the vice of lying.

Hauerwas mistakenly ascribes to Rhonheimer the view "that basic intentions are, in principle and always, formed independently from natural patterns." Rhonheimer objects that Hauerwas has improperly separated his understanding of intentional actions and the intentional structure of the object from his account of the natural law, and the meaning of pre-rational nature as a presupposition of the order of reason. He insists that the behavioral pattern of sexual intercourse is inappropriate matter, what Aquinas calls *materia indebita,* for incarnating personal friendship and love between persons of the same sex. It is "against nature" precisely in the sense that it is rationally inconsistent with the goal naturally inscribed in the sexual faculty, which provides the foundation for the order of reason and virtue regarding the use of that faculty. Human reason appropriately builds upon this natural foundation because it is the reason of a being formed by the substantial unity of body and spirit. With these clarifications, it is evident that Rhonheimer's approach results in a clear rejection of homosexual relations.

Natural Law as a Law of Practical Reason

In the seventh selection, "The Cognitive Structure of the Natural Law and the Truth of Subjectivity," Rhonheimer offers a detailed argument for an interpretation of Thomistic natural law—like all kinds of law—as something essentially and formally pertaining to the cognitive order of knowledge and not the ontological order of being. Therefore, it offers a more concise and more recent treatment of a central theme of his *Natural Law and Practical Reason.* Rhonheimer's emphasis on the cognitive structure of the natural law is an integral part of his overall program to make explicit what is often more implicit in the writings of Aquinas, namely the distinctively moral perspective of the acting person.

In the first of four parts, Rhonheimer mounts a serious challenge to the traditional interpretation of Thomistic natural law, which presupposes a dichotomy between "nature" and "reason" in which our bodily nature is seen to reveal the constraints imposed upon reason.[13] He argues instead that a proper understanding of natural law must emphasize the essential unity between nature and reason in the human agent whose nature is specified by reason. In the second part, he develops his argument that Aquinas and important witnesses from the Catholic tradition—including *Veritatis Splendor*—recognize the fundamentally cognitive character of the natural law and reject any dichotomy between "nature" and "reason." In the third, he argues for his cognitive interpretation of Thomistic natural law through a variety of texts, starting from those Fathers who provided a precedent for Thomas by transforming the Stoic interpretation of natural law through a shift from "nature" to "reason." In the fourth, he explains how such a cognitive understanding of the natural law, as "specifically something constituted in the natural judgments of the natural reason of each man," fits within the context of an ethics of virtue.

From the third part, let us note the central points of his interpretation of *ST* Ia-IIae, q. 94, a. 2, on the principles of the natural law. He emphasizes that (i) in its primary sense, natural law is not derived through speculative reason but is the work of practical reason; (ii) it is a practical and preceptive knowing of the human good that unfolds through the embedding of human reason in the dynamism of the natural inclinations;[14] and (iii) that practical reason *both* recognizes the goods and ends of the natural inclinations as constituting human good, *and* orders or integrates them into the whole of

13. I use quotes to indicate that Rhonheimer thinks traditional interpreters misunderstand both nature and reason by separating them. For him, to speak properly of human nature is to speak of a properly rational nature embedded in the strivings of somatic existence.

14. This is treated at length in *NLPR.*

the corporeal-spiritual being of the human person. He concludes with an account of how such a cognitive understanding of the natural law is properly located within an ethics of virtue.

The First-Person Perspective and the Object of the Human Act

The eighth contribution is "The Perspective of the Acting Person and the Nature of Practical Reason: The 'Object of the Human Act' in Thomistic Anthropology of Action." The Italian original was presented at a conference in 2003, and the English translation was originally published in September 2004. It provides a valuable synthesis and further clarification of various aspects of Rhonheimer's contemporary retrieval of Thomistic action theory, as initially developed in *Natural Law and Practical Reason* and treated further in *The Perspective of Morality.* Therefore, it is among the most rigorous and compelling treatments available on this difficult but crucial topic of moral philosophy and moral theology.

This lengthy essay is comprised of nine sections. The first defines the object of the moral act and indicates the importance of examining it more fully in "the perspective of the acting person." The second emphasizes that the object pertains to a human act and not a "thing" or merely physical description of an act. The third specifies how the external act is the object of the will, and the fourth clarifies how the object is something understood and ordered by reason. The fifth section explains that the object is necessarily oriented toward a goal and therefore has an "intentional structure," and the sixth addresses how it is dependent upon certain relevant circumstances—an "ethical context" pertaining to one of the cardinal virtues. In the seventh section, Rhonheimer illumines how the object pertains to what are called "objectively" or intrinsically evil acts. In the eighth he elucidates the way in which prerational nature can be said to provide a rule or measure for the object, and in the ninth section he offers a summary discussion of how such an account of the object reveals the intelligibility and coherence of a moral realism that addresses the perspective of the acting person. The sixth and seventh sections, which treat Rhonheimer's notions of the "ethical context" and of intrinsically evil acts, respectively, merit further discussion.

Rhonheimer's notion of the "ethical context" enables him to account for the morally relevant circumstances and to follow Thomas's principle of treating individual cases as pertaining to a particular moral virtue. Here Rhonheimer treats various acts involving the "enunciation of falsehood" and argues that, according to Aquinas, those acts that are "lies" in the proper sense are evil not simply because they go against the natural end of language to communicate truth. Rather, they are evil when and precisely because they are against the virtue of justice as exercised in communication (i.e., truthfulness). Analogous to his recognition that sexual acts necessarily include some intentionality with regard to procreation, Rhonheimer acknowledges the moral relevance of the natural nexus between language and truth-telling, but he specifies that the intrinsically evil act of lying—in its proper sense—occurs precisely in freely chosen acts of "communicative injustice." According to Rhonheimer's intentional description of actions, certain acts that have the material appearance of a lie (by enunciating false statements) should not be understood as lies in the proper and formal sense, because of their "ethical context." He offers the examples of "enunciating falsehood" within a party game, while testing a lie detector, or in deceiving the Gestapo in their search for Jews. He explains that these do not include the formal characteristic of lying—acting against truthfulness in communications—because the social significance of linguistic acts has been altered by the ethical context.

The seventh section addresses the challenging and disputed question of "intrinsically evil" acts, which he understands as a specific kind of "objectively evil" act. He insists that such intrinsically evil acts must be properly described as distinctively human acts (i) with reference to an object that includes a basic level of intentionality (the "intend directly" of *Veritatis Splendor*, no. 80) and (ii) with a specific ethical context. The notion of intrinsically evil acts also, however, implies something more. Many in the tradition would explain this "something more" to mean that such acts can be described simply as "external behaviors" or in their "physical materiality," but Rhonheimer would note that the category of intrinsically evil acts is much broader, while insisting that moral acts be described with reference to the volition that specifies them.

Aspects of Practical Reason, Metaphysics, and Ethics

The ninth article in this volume, "Practical Reason and the Truth of Subjectivity: The Self-Experience of the Moral Subject at the Roots of Metaphysics and Anthropology," was translated from the Italian for this collection. It complements several of the works discussed above, especially by providing a more detailed exposition of how Rhonheimer interprets the Thomistic tradition on the relationship between metaphysics and ethics. The first five sections are relatively short and summarize several of the themes that occur frequently in Rhonheimer's writing. The first addresses the place of moral truth in an ethical system that emphasizes the subjectivity of the acting person; for Rhonheimer, the objective dimension of moral action can be called "the truth of subjectivity," which concerns the ability of the virtuous agent to attain practical truth. The second section summarizes how the Aristotelian ethic of reason is ultimately an ethic of virtue, because the virtues reflect the broader structures of reasonableness within the architectonic ordering of the eternal law. The third discusses the "principles of practical reason," which are grounded in synderesis and allow each person to realize the objective truth of free human action. On this basis, the fourth section speaks briefly of the normative function of the "light of the natural reason," whereas the fifth discusses what Aquinas means when he calls the natural law "a work of the practical reason."

I will here consider only the third division of the sixth section, which articulates the parallelism and interaction between practical reason and speculative reason. Against a neo-Thomistic tendency, Rhonheimer insists that practical judgments are not deductions or applications from theoretical judgments. Instead, he holds that theoretical judgments have their place in practical reasoning through the minor premise of the practical syllogism, which Aquinas appropriates from Aristotle. This syllogism reveals the structure of practical reflection to be a series of judgments. For example, the *major premise,* which is necessarily practical and moves the subject to act, is of the type "it is good for me to do this or that." It does not express a speculative judgment of fact but a desire, such as "it is good for me to pursue a cure for this illness." The *minor premise,* which is a judgment of speculative reason, establishes a fact such as "this medicine has this or that property, and produces this or that effect." This leads to the *concluding judgment* of the syllogism, that "it is good for me to take this medicine," which leads to the action itself. The point is that this last and decisive practical judgment takes its departure from the major premise and does not *deduce* but *infers* from the minor premise to reach its conclusion. Therefore, although speculative judgments have a place within practical reasoning, they are not the starting point of this process, and the process is one of inference, not deduction. For this reason, he objects to the neo-Thomistic tendency to emphasize the dependence of practical reason on speculative reason in a way that implies that practical reasoning begins with a speculative judgment.

Critique of an Influential Work in Natural Law

The tenth essay is Rhonheimer's review of Jean Porter's book *Nature as Reason: A Thomistic Theory of the Natural Law,* which he was invited to write for the journal *Studies in Christian Ethics.* This contribution is particularly important as it illustrates the timeliness and efficacy of Rhonheimer's retrieval of Thomistic ethics in dialogue with a leading example of the emerging generation of revisionist Catholic moral theology, which eschews the proportionalism of the post-conciliar generation, appealing instead to the authority of Aquinas. Because of the constraints of a ten-thousand-word review, Rhonheimer focuses on a critical assessment of the work (resulting in a more polemic tone) and a further explication of his Thomistic alternative.[15] Although these three categories are interdependent, I will offer the following introductory remarks organized around his charges that her work is not Thomistic, that it is not adequately theological or Christian, and that it is instead relativistic.

Rhonheimer's argument that Porter's work is "far from Thomistic in any sense" includes the following: (i) She begins with a title—*Nature as Reason*—that obscures Thomas's "core doctrine" of natural law as the capacity of our natural reason to attain moral truth (i.e., *reason* as that which specifies human *nature*); (ii) because it thereby neglects a central implication of the doctrine of man as the image of God, the book departs dramatically from the Patristic and Scholastic traditions; (iii) instead of giving an exposition of this "core doctrine" about the fundamentally rational character of the natural law, Porter tries to de-legitimize it; (iv) her theory is not based upon a comprehensive or credible reading of Thomas's relevant texts; (v) the book does not reflect a recognition that a Thomistic ethic must be fundamentally an ethic of virtue, with natural law in a subordinate role; (vi) her theory neglects to provide a doctrine of "the principles of practical reason," which is an essential part of Thomistic natural law; and (vii) it does not include the ability to rule out certain kinds of acts as morally evil, which too is essential. For these reasons, Rhonheimer concludes that no theory with these deficiencies can call itself Thomistic in any meaningful sense.

Next, let us consider some of the ways Rhonheimer judges *Nature as Rea-*

15. Because of similar constraints, I will simply summarize Rhonheimer's critique and refer the reader to the published debate between the two authors.

son to fail in its stated goal of offering a theological and Christian account of natural law. First, as suggested above, he thinks the neglect of the truth-attaining power of natural reason reveals a defect in theological anthropology, failing to grasp the implications of man's creation in the image of God. Second, in neglecting the topic of sin—and related matters of moral evil and vice[16]—the book is unable to give a theological, Christian, or Thomistic explanation of why human reason sometimes fails to grasp the morally good and practically true. Third, because of the subordination of virtue to natural law, the book fails to take advantage of the openness of a virtue-oriented approach to a completion through the theological virtues of faith, hope, and charity. Fourth, it neglects the fact that, for Aquinas, the articles of the faith and the practices of the Catholic Church facilitate the attainment of practical truth in human action. Fifth, Porter's book addresses theological concerns within the context of Jacques Dupuis's theory of religious pluralism. Rhonheimer judges her employment of this theory for her moral pluralism to be decidedly inferior to the Christological perspective of an adequately Christian and theological ethic.

Because of its approach to pluralism, Rhonheimer argues that Porter's book advances a kind of moral relativism. He argues against her movement from the existence of cognitive disagreements about natural law to an argument for the existence of a plurality of natural law moralities, which are explained in terms of God's providential will to preserve moral insights through the existence of apparently conflicting traditions. This movement, from the existence of disagreement to pluralism, de-legitimizes the traditional understanding of universally valid norms of natural law. He sees her "fatal error" in identifying pre-rational nature and the principles/precepts of natural law as "morally underdetermined." Instead, Rhonheimer argues that they should be seen as "practically underdetermined," meaning that a practical judgment of prudence is additionally required to specify what the agent should do here and now. The need for this prudential judgment of what must be done, however, does not exclude the role of negative precepts regarding what the agent may never do. Along the lines of the above discussion of homosexual acts, Rhonheimer insists that such negative precepts of the natural law are an essential element of a Thomistic alternative to moral relativism.

This essay provides an especially fitting conclusion to this volume be-

16. Neither "sin," nor "moral evil," nor "vice" are found within the index or the table of contents.

cause it draws upon the earlier essays to respond to this leading revisionist alternative with solid textual evidence, rigor of argumentation, and an approach to natural law and action theory that reflects a close affinity to that encouraged by *Veritatis Splendor.*

I would be remiss if I did not express my gratitude to Gerald Malsbary for his expert translations of two essays for this volume, and to Damian X. Lenshek for his editorial assistance, creation of the bibliographies and creation of a preliminary index, and to Joseph T. Papa for his creation of the final index.

It is my hope that this introduction will assist and inspire readers to embark upon a careful study of these substantive essays from a major figure in the contemporary renewal in Thomistic moral philosophy, and that it will contribute to a renewal of moral theology in the spirit of *Veritatis Splendor.*

The Perspective of the Acting Person

1

Is Christian Morality Reasonable?

On the Difference between Secular and Christian Humanism

Christian Morality: Its Reasonableness and "Unreasonableness"

In his famous work "The Reasonableness of Christianity," published in 1695,[1] the British philosopher John Locke holds that in revealed Christian morality "as delivered in the Scriptures" there is nothing that cannot be grasped by human reason alone—unassisted by faith. He adds, however, that faith in revealed morality is still, and always will be, *psychologically* necessary for the large majority of people since they neither have the leisure nor the ability to apply themselves to the demanding task of philosophical inquiry.

Such a view sharply contrasts with both secular humanism and what I want to call Christian humanism. Secular humanism conceives itself as a kind of liberation from the constraints of Christian faith and clerical paternalism. In all its current forms, it would never allow one to assert that Christian faith is "psychologically necessary for the large majority of people" because of their lack of leisure and intellectual skill. Instead secular humanism, be it atheistic or not, contends that many of the typical demands of Christian morality, as, for example, taught by the Catholic Church, are utterly unrea-

1. The full title reads *The Reasonableness of Christianity, as deliver'd in the Scriptures* (London: Awnsham and John Churchill, 1695).

sonable, not demonstrable by rational means, and generally to be rejected as inhuman.

In turn, Christian humanism, as I understand it, implies that Christian morality is both profoundly reasonable *and* provokingly unreasonable. Such an affirmation might cause surprise, among other reasons because, though conceding that *some* contents of revealed morality are *beyond* or *above* reason, at least a Catholic will not easily admit any of the requirements of Christian morality to be properly *unreasonable.*

But this is what, paradoxically, seems to be the case. What I am going to argue is that for a Christian life there are specific moral requirements which could simultaneously be called both reasonable *and* unreasonable, without however being properly *beyond* or *above* reason.

Or, to put it in another way: the basic moral requirements of Christian life are in principle fully intelligible and therefore accessible to reasonable argument and defense, but they simultaneously need in many cases the support of Christian faith to preserve fully their reasonableness.

Without such support, so I will argue, these basic moral requirements appear to be unreasonable because they are obviously difficult to fulfill. They appear to overburden human beings, to be too demanding and unrealistic, and thus even oppressive. So their inherent reasonableness easily converts into the unreasonableness of an unattainable ideal, which is therefore unacceptable to most people. In my view, people in fact can fully accept these moral demands as practically achievable goals, but only on the ground of faith which engenders hope and becomes practical through charity. It is in precisely this context that these moral demands fully recover their reasonableness.[2]

I am not, of course, referring here to some strictly supernatural demands of Christian life, such as the reception of the sacraments, faithfulness and obedience to the Church's Magisterium, or even the willingness to suffer martyrdom. *Such* moral requirements are obviously only intelligible on the basis of faith in Christ, the Church, and the sacraments.

2. I would probably not go so far as to contend that, without the "announcement of Christ, Christian morality would be an incomprehensible puzzle"; see I. Carrasco de Paula, "El estudio y la enseñanza de la moral fundamental, hoy. Reflexiones en torno al quehacer teológico," *Scripta Theologica* 32, no. 3 (2000): 919. The "unreasonableness" of Christian morality I will be talking about, rather than complete "unintelligibility" (like a "puzzle"), is the unreasonableness of the *unattainable ideal* that, however, in itself and as a kind of *good,* is intelligible for everyone and, in this sense, "reasonable." Thus, there is a profound continuity between revealed Christian morality and unassisted practical reason or "natural law." This will be explained in more detail below.

Of course even these strictly supernatural features of Christian morality do not go undisputed nowadays, but the point is that they are contested mostly because of a deep crisis at a rather different and deeper level, which is precisely the one I'd wish to refer to: the level of the basic demands of natural law, as understood and taught by the Church. For instance—things like the indissolubility of marriage, the practice of responsible parenthood exclusively by means of periodic continence, the confining of sexual acts exclusively to marriage, the unconditional prohibition of the direct killing of innocent human beings (mainly abortion). And we must also include the moral requirements of justice and righteousness in, for example, business activity, politics, or scientific research and medical care, which will often demand heroic behavior on the part of a Christian.

The problem here is that what in principle looks intrinsically reasonable and human, such as the ideal of inseparable fidelity in marriage or the unconditional respect for human life, ends up appearing to unassisted human reason, at least in many cases, as unattainable in practice and therefore unreasonable and even inhuman. So—and this is my main point—Christian morality, to a large extent, throws light on the possibility of living a moral life which fully meets the intrinsic demands of human nature. This means that we can speak of a true *specific Christian humanism* which differs from the purely secular humanism of the non-believer. Thus, what initially appears unreasonable regains reasonableness through faith, hope, and charity. That is how faith in fact rescues reason and reason recovers all its power to make faith both human and effective. Rightly understood, reason therefore needs revelation to be capable of effectively working as moral reason and to maintain the "reasonableness of morality."[3] Let me now spell that out in some more detail. By doing this, I also hope to contribute to the well-known debate—though the subject has now become less topical—about the "specificity" or "distinctiveness" of Christian morality.[4]

3. Cf. J. Ratzinger, "Christliche Orientierung in der pluralistischen Demokratie? Über die Unverzichtbarkeit des Christentums in der modernen Gesellschaft," in H. Bürkle and N. Lobkowicz, eds., *Das Europäische Erbe und seine christliche Zukunft*, Veröffentlichungen der Hanns-Martin-Schleyer-Stiftung 16 (Cologne, 1985), 20–35, esp. 31f.; reprinted in Ratzinger, *Kirche, Ökumene und Politik. Neue Versuche zur Ekklesiologie* (Einsiedeln: Johannes Verlag, 1987), 183–97.

4. I refer to my earlier treatments of the subject: "Über die Existenz einer spezifisch christlichen Moral des Humanums," *Internationale katholische Zeitschrift 'Communio'* 23, no. 4 (1994): 360–72; *Natural Law and Practical Reason: A Thomist View of Moral Autonomy* (New York: Fordham University Press, 2000), 547–53; originally published in German as *Natur als Grundlage der Moral. Die personale Struktur des Naturgesetzes bei Thomas von Aquin: Eine Auseinandersetzung*

The Teaching of the Encyclical *Veritatis Splendor*

Catholic moral teaching holds that the basic requirements of morality are fundamentally accessible to human reason. Accordingly, *Veritatis Splendor* teaches that even though "[o]nly God can answer the question about the good, because he is the Good" he nevertheless "has already given an answer to this question: he did so *by creating man and ordering him* with wisdom and love to his final end, through the law which is inscribed in his heart (cf. Rom 2:15), the 'natural law'" (*VS* no. 12). Quoting Thomas Aquinas,[5] the encyclical then affirms that the natural law "is nothing other than the light of understanding infused in us by God, whereby we understand what must be done and what must be avoided. God gave this light and this law to man at creation" (ibid.).

This is not to say that Christian morality contains nothing more than what natural law demands, even though, in a sense that is also true. The above teaching of *Veritatis Splendor*, however, is related to the basic questions of "How do we, as humans, discern what is basically good and bad, right and wrong, and, accordingly, what does a life able to be ordered to God through supernatural charity consist in?"

Veritatis Splendor replies that the basic capability of a human act "*of being ordered to the good and to the ultimate end, which is God* . . . is grasped *by reason* [emphasis added] in the very being of man, considered in his integral truth, and therefore in his natural inclinations, his motivations and his finalities, which always have a spiritual dimension as well. It is precisely these which are the contents of the natural law. . . ." (*VS* no. 79, 2).

That is why the encyclical also approves the attempt "to find ever more

---

mit autonomer und teleologischer Ethik (Innsbruck-Vienna: Tyrolia-Verlag, 1987). A Spanish edition has been published as *Ley natural y razón práctica. Una visión tomista de la autonoia moral* (Pamplona: Ediciones Universidad de Navarra EUNSA, 2000), as well as a translation into Italian as *Legge naturale e ragion pratica. Una visione tomista dell'autonomia morale* (Rome: Armando, 2001). See further: "Moral cristiana y desarollo humano," in *La Misión del Laico en la Iglesia y en el Mundo.* VIII Simposio Internacional de Teología de la Universidad de Navarra, ed. A. Sarmiento, T. Rincón, J. M. Yanguas, and A. Quirós (Pamplona: Ediciones Universidad de Navarra EUNSA, 1987), 919–38 (this is an earlier, much shorter version of the above mentioned article in *Communio*). For some other related aspects see also my articles "Autonomia morale, libertà e verità secondo l'enciclica 'Veritatis Splendor,'" *Veritatis splendor. Genesi, elaborazione, significato,* ed. G. Russo, Seconda edizione aggiornata e ampliata (Rome: Edizioni Dehoniane, 1995), 193–215; "Morale cristiana e ragionevolezza morale: di che cosa è il compimento la legge del Vangelo?," *Gesù Cristo, legge vivente e personale della Santa Chiesa,* ed. G. Borgonovo (Casale Monferrato: Piemme, 1996), 147–68.

5. *In Duo Praecepta Caritatis et in Decem Legis Praecepta, Prologus,* in *Opuscula Theologica,* II, no. 1129 (Torino: Marietti, 1954).

consistent rational arguments in order to justify the requirements and to provide a foundation for the norms of the moral life." The reason for this optimistic encouragement is given in the very next sentence: "This kind of investigation is legitimate and necessary, since the moral order, as established by the natural law, is in principle accessible to human reason" (*VS* no. 74). This is so precisely because natural law *is* a "prescription of human reason": it is "human reason itself which commands us to do good and counsels us not to sin" (*VS* no. 44, quoting Leo XIII). Natural law is nothing other than "the light of natural reason" which enables us "to distinguish right from evil" (*VS* no. 42).

On the other hand, however, *Veritatis Splendor* clearly perceives the gap opening up between what reason, in principle, can justify as morally normative, and what may seem reasonable considering man's real possibilities. The encyclical insists that "[o]nly in the mystery of Christ's Redemption do we discover the 'concrete' possibilities of man." That is why it "would be a serious error to conclude . . . that the Church's teaching is essentially only an 'ideal' which must then be adapted, proportioned, graduated to the so-called concrete possibilities of man." The encyclical further asserts that the Church is talking of "man redeemed by Christ": "God's command is of course proportioned to man's capabilities; but to the capabilities of the man to whom the Holy Spirit has been given" (*VS* no. 103).

That means that only God's love "poured out into our hearts through the Holy Spirit who has been given to us" (Rom 5:5) can assure fulfilling what the natural law demands. Moreover, it implies that this is the only way that the full reasonableness of natural law can be preserved and the temptation resisted of making one's "own weakness the criterion of the truth about the good" (*VS* no. 104).

Two Levels of Moral Knowledge and the Ought/Can Dichotomy

What I have said so far, of course, raises several questions. But I shall now limit myself to tackling a problem which is one of moral knowledge (or epistemology). From what has been previously said, you might conclude that the problem of practicability or "feasibility" is simply a problem of execution and that, in order to fulfill what the moral law demands, one simply needs the help of grace, and that is all. But this is not the whole story.

First of all, and in a more fundamental way, we have here what amounts to a problem of moral knowledge (as I said—an epistemological problem). Humans are essentially reasonable beings. They act as free subjects, deliberately, willingly, and thus guided by reason and in a way we call "responsible." This is also true on the supernatural level, since grace does not suppress nature, but brings it—elevated—to its ultimate perfection. So the perfection brought about by faith, hope, and love necessarily involves a perfecting of moral knowledge as well. Conversely, the absence of these supernatural powers in the human soul will also have a bearing on the reach and the quality of moral knowledge.

You may now ask whether this is not to destroy the rightful autonomy of the created natural order. Is this not tantamount to declaring that human reason and will are incapable of perceiving and realizing the good which properly corresponds to human nature? You might even ask whether this does not amount to saying that supernatural grace is a necessary or essential complement to human nature, thus calling into question its supernatural and gratuitous character (grace is not "demanded" by nature). Such doubts in fact lead us to the core of this whole question.

Reason-guided moral perception has two dimensions which are closely connected and are never completely separate from each other. The first dimension is the capability of grasping human goods as such, and from there disclosing the corresponding "ought." This is properly the work of natural law.[6] The second dimension however is a judgment—also based on experience both personal and social—about the practical possibilities of realizing this good and carrying out the corresponding "ought." On this second level, the moral subject is confronted with experiences which conflict with the original insight into the human good and its proper intelligibility. So, on this second level, the good and the "ought" presented by natural law may now appear only as a more-or-less attainable ideal, rather than as a morally binding norm or, if formulated in a prohibitive way, as a moral absolute.

Consider, for example, the moral norm of indissolubility of marriage. Faithful marital love, meant to last for ever and not to be subject to the volatility of the human will and the changing circumstances of life, character, etc., is as a basic human good clearly intelligible to everybody—especially to children. But at the same time, on the level of the judgment about practicability, it may seem impossible and too hard in *all* cases and circumstances. People know very well that a society where all marriages are stable and faithful would be a much better society, with much happier people than in our present society. But they think that it is a fanciful idea and quite impossible to establish and uphold as a *moral norm.* There are of course really tragic

6. For details I refer to my previously cited *Natural Law and Practical Reason.*

cases where, from a purely human point of view, faithfulness to a spouse, abstaining from remarrying and from any kind of sexual relationship with another partner, simply doesn't seem to make sense anymore. In a situation like this an additional input of intelligibility, such as, for example, identification with Christ, is necessary in order to convert fidelity into a meaningful—and attainable—moral option.

In other words, to resume this point, the second dimension of moral insight—the judgment about the possibilities of realization or the "feasibility"—will necessarily influence the plausibility of the corresponding "ought," that is, it will influence the first level of moral insight. *For in itself, no moral "ought" can be grasped that reaches beyond the moral "can." And the "can" itself*—that is, what someone will admit or accept as being within his reach or power—*is deeply affected by any appearance of unreasonableness in the process of trying to achieve it.* Accordingly, persons who wish to act coherently on the grounds of a proper understanding of their moral obligations can find themselves faced with a chasm—an apparently unbridgeable gap—opening up between what they know to be the human good "as such" and what they judge to be achievable in practice and therefore reasonable.

Theoretically, of course, it is possible to cope with this predicament simply by declaring oneself incapable of doing all the good one feels obliged to do. Yet, such an attitude is not likely to lead to a rationally coherent and thus satisfying life-plan.[7] A much more plausible way of filling the gap between the "ought" and the "can" would be, therefore, *to simply adjust the "ought" to the "can,"* that is, to rationalize the experience of "not being able to achieve the human good," formulating in consequence a moderated and "revised down" or "diluted" version of this good and of the corresponding moral norm.

Yet, that does not at all suppress the intrinsic reasonableness of the origi-

7. I think this can turn out to be a rationally coherent way of life only for those who are willing to simultaneously accept sources of moral knowledge other than their own rational insight—e.g., some revealed moral norms received by faith. I refer here, among other cases, to the position taken by those who wish to follow the Church's teaching in everything. When they come to something they find difficult (e.g., not to adopt contraception or to refrain from abortion in a "hard case"), they try their best to obey the Magisterium. They do this because they are willing to accept, through *faith* rather than their *own reason*, the moral norms given to them by the Church. Notice that, however, in order to be a rationally consistent position, this presupposes one consider obedience to the Magisterium as something *reasonable* because one is convinced—again on the grounds of faith—that the authentic Magisterium of the Church, guided by the Holy Spirit, is really the voice of truth. Notice, moreover, that in order to live in such a way *consistently* and *faithfully*, these persons additionally should at least *try* to meet, through personal interior struggle, the moral demands they accept by faith. Otherwise they would fail to be rationally coherent.

nal insight into the human good. What it does is to downgrade it to an ideal that, when converted into a moral norm, will in its turn be perceived to be inhuman, and therefore to be unreasonable. But—except the case of culturally imposed prejudice, which is not what we are at present examining—also in the second case it will still be possible to *understand* the requirement of the "full" human good. But most probably one will not accept it as normative or as morally reasonable.

The Human Predicament and the Temptation to Consequentialism

As I have said, there are experiences in human life which tend to overturn and modify our genuine insight into the human good. They do that by inducing persons to rationalize the gap between the good and practicability. Let me now ask: which are these experiences?

You might expect me now to refer to original sin. In the present context, however, this would not be of much avail. The dogma of original sin only explains *why* man and the world, created by God, are found in so deplorable a condition. It thus throws light on the *origin* and the *punitive character* of the present predicament and hardship of mankind which we could never have known without the help of revelation. The dogma, however, does not help us to understand the predicament as such. On the grounds of quite obvious anthropological, psychological, historical, sociological, and other data known to everybody, it is no mystery at all. The *conditio humana* is a plain fact. Faith simply tells us where it comes from, that "from the beginning it was not so," and that of course does bear on our interpretation of man, of his moral possibilities and the sense of history.[8]

In the first place, therefore, we have to deal with something the dogma of original sin throws no light on at all, that is, the predicament as such. It is constituted by experiences of suffering injustice, disease, division between men, unfaithfulness, war and violence, being powerless in the face of evil and of material and spiritual misery, and also our own weakness. It also contains the experience of the senselessness of so many situations created by the actions of men (mine and those of my neighbors), as well as by circumstances that are beyond our control. If we interpret this *mysterium iniquitatis* against

8. I refer to the still outstanding treatment, from a Thomistic viewpoint, of this subject by M. J. Scheeben, *Die Mysterien des Christentums*, Gesammelte Schriften, vol. 2, ed. J. Höfer (Freiburg: Herder, 1951), 200–59, esp. 234ff.

the background of a history of the fall of mankind and of the redemption already at work at the core of history, we will draw conclusions about the moral "ought" quite different from those drawn by a non-believer.

In the course of the past centuries we have been given many specifically non-Christian answers to the riddles of human existence and the condition of the world. There are ideologies which promise inner-worldly salvation, and others which typically work by reductionism, asserting "that man is nothing other than," for example, "libido," or "matter," or "a result of the conditions of production," or an "outcome of selective advantage in the struggle for survival of the fittest," and so on. There are different kinds of humanism—the most coherent of which certainly are the openly atheistic ones—and there are different ways of answering the question: "What can we legitimately expect, what are we entitled to hope for?"

Furthermore, there is an even deeper self-contradiction that threatens human reason. In many cases, which sometimes seem almost unavoidable, doing good and abstaining from evil may be followed by very disadvantageous consequences. And conversely, the consequences of a misdeed often seem to be better than the consequences of refraining from such an action. And yet, for man's practical reason this is, so to speak, a "scandal." For it essentially belongs to the good—so we all are naturally inclined to think—that, at least in the long run, it should eventually lead to something good. But from a purely human point of view this is very often not the case. St. Paul did write to the Romans: "in everything God works for good with those who love him" (Rom 8:28), but that, of course, is only helpful to the believer.

Now, on a purely human level the question arises whether there is any point whatsoever in moral requirements which only seem to cause problems and disasters, without offering a prospect of happiness. Isn't it better and more human to have, instead, a kind of morality that allows us to seek, in any given situation, to optimize the outcome of our actions in terms of expected well-being and happiness? Let us not forget that the prospect of well-being and happiness is an essential feature of the good. They cannot reasonably be conceived as permanently separated. Otherwise one would be trying to reconcile the reasonableness of the good with a frustrated desire for happiness. And that, taking into account human nature, is impossible.

Moreover, considering humans as free and responsible beings, we would expect the exercise of responsibility and happiness to be somehow linked. But sometimes it seems that to be happy you just need to be lucky. It seems to depend more on chance than on one's efforts to be responsible in carrying out one's moral duties. So, good luck and bad luck seem to play a more decisive part than those achievements and decisions attributable to human persons and their free choices. Additionally, in quite a few cases, instead of leading to well-being, refraining from *doing* injustice will make you *suffer* injustice. Being moral does not seem to pay very well, and it certainly seems to pay much better when your moral standard is a consequentialist one.

The tempting attractiveness of consequentialism reveals precisely, and is a sign of, the predicament of the human condition and of moral reason functioning under its influence. Consequentialism is a sort of "technique" calling for continuous rationalization in order to overcome the gap between "ought" and "can" by adjusting the "ought" to "the best you can do." It teaches you that to know what is the right thing to do you just have to look at the possible outcome of this or that course of action, and then to choose the one which is likely to bring about the most desirable effects.

This shows again how reasonableness can be affected by simply modifying it according to concrete expectations regarding consequences and their evaluation, without, however, altering reason's original capacity of grasping the human good. I wish to emphasize that this alteration is brought about not on the first and fundamental level of moral understanding, characterized by the original grasp of human goods as practical aims, but on the second level where the judgments about practical realizability are made. Thus the reasonableness of the first level is not affected, but simply put aside or at least downgraded and thus relativized.

Christian Humanism as Salvation Morality

Consequentialism of course *is* a rational theory and it does express, although in a distorted way, a form of reasonableness. Consequentialism therefore can be rationally argued against and shown to be morally defective. Yet, it is not my present aim to do that.[9] With the previous remarks I only wanted

9. For a thorough critique of consequentialism I refer to my *Die Perspektive der Moral. Philosophische Grundlagen der Tugendethik* (Berlin: Akademie Verlag, 2001). Earlier versions of this book have been published in Italian as *La prospettiva della morale. Fondamenti dell'etica filosofica* (Rome: Armando, 1994) and in Spanish as *La perspeciva de la moral. Fundamentos de la ética filosófica* (Madrid: Rialp, 2000). See also chapter 4 of this book, originally published as Rhonheimer, "Intentional Actions and the Meaning of Object: A Reply to Richard McCormick," *The Thomist* 59, no. 2 (1995): 279–311; reprinted in *Veritatis Splendor and the Renewal of Moral Theology*, ed. J. A. Di Noia and R. Cessario (Princeton, N.J.: Scepter; Huntington, Ind.: Our Sunday Visitor; Chicago: Midwest Theological Forum, 1999), 241–68.

to indicate how the plausibility of consequentialist moral thinking properly springs from and is connected with the situation of man insofar as his moral reason is lacking the support it would have from the faith, and from the prospects and expectations which the faith generates.

To sum up what I have been saying so far: as long as the insight into the good, and thus into what is morally normative, is shaped or conditioned by the experience of one's own capabilities, as well as by one's "reasonable expectations" and related hopes, *then the understanding of the human good and its normative implications will necessarily differ between the faithful and the non-believer.*

This seems to be a serious problem which almost impedes rational communication between believers and non-believers. But that is not the case. In reality, what I have just said contains an opportunity. Notice that the basic requirements of Christian morality, which in fact are requirements of natural law, are not derived from revelation or faith. They genuinely spring from human reason. So there *is* a common platform for dialogue between the believer and the non-believer. And this platform is the platform of rational argument. At the same time, however, Christians and non-believers differ in their ability to accept fully what the human good demands.

Christian revelation essentially contains a message about our real capabilities and expectations. It provides a specific answer to the mysteries of the world and of mankind, as well as to the innermost desires of the human heart. The coordinates of that answer are the revelation of original sin, the fall, inherited guilt (not personal, but of humankind as such), redemption through God's becoming man in Christ, and the mediation of redemption through the Church.

Regarding the human good, salvation means liberation from the obvious incapability of meeting fully and truly all the requirements of being human—such as, for example, indissoluble fidelity in marriage or the heroic refraining from—legally—killing an innocent and defenseless human being in order to resolve a grave personal problem, or abstaining from unjust business practices when doing so gives rise to serious personal difficulties and professional disadvantages.

The real point about the integration of practical reason into the context of Christian faith is not just that grace comes in to help us fulfill what is required from a moral point of view. The question is not simply one of execution. The influence of faith goes much deeper. *It reaches to the root of mor-*

al understanding by affecting its second level, that is, the level of judgment about realization and human possibilities, and thereby fully restores the intelligibility of the human good.

This influence, however, and the corresponding "rescue of reason" take place on a higher level. It is the level of the Christian's being called to holiness and the logic of the participation in the Cross of Christ and his Resurrection. This is absolutely crucial for a correct understanding of Christian morality. The moral requirements—what the human good and its integral fulfillment demand—are thus brought into focus from the viewpoint proper to the history of salvation. Christian morality is essentially salvation-morality.[10] And it is precisely in this way that the inherent contradictions and inconsistencies of a purely secular humanism can be overcome. It leads to a specifically *Christian humanism* that we can also call a *Humanism of the Cross.* It is a *human morality* that is *specifically Christian.*[11] And it *is* a true humanism because it is a realistic way to restore to the human good its characteristic of being a promise of fulfillment and happiness. This of course is good news. And the Christian message *is* good news, it is *Evangelium.*

Christian Humanism and Virtue Ethics

From what has been said so far we can draw the conclusion that any purely secular or non-believing humanism will necessarily miss the truly "human." It will necessarily undervalue—from its point of view, "reasonably" undervalue—the real moral powers of man and fall short of his possibilities to fully strive at realizing what human reason grasps as its proper good: justice, faithfulness, benevolence, truthfulness, fortitude, temperance, chastity, etc.—that is, the whole range of the virtues.

We should never forget that the undervaluation of the human person's moral possibilities typically leads to justifying moral standards which increase rather than diminish the predicament of mankind. It also leads to

10. This is also the reason Christian faith can never be reduced to a kind of ethics, because a genuine *Christian* ethical discourse is always more than an ethical discourse: it implies truths, grounded in faith, about God, man, the world, and about the sense of history. That Christian morality—the "morality that springs from the encounter with Jesus Christ"—is essentially a "morality of salvation" has recently been emphasized also by Carrasco de Paula, "El estudio y la enseñanza de la moral," 922f.

11. Thus it overcomes the fallacious distinction between "salvation ethos" and "world ethos"; see for that my *Natural Law and Practical Reason,* 547ff. The dissociation between a worldly "ethical order" and an "order of salvation" was rejected by John Paul II, *Veritatis Splendor* (The Splendor of Truth, 1993), no. 37.

practical "solutions" and courses of action which normally make a victim of someone other than the acting person himself. By thus complicating matters further and entangling social relations—consider, for example, the social effects of broken families and divorced couples—this will in turn fatally increase the plausibility of any attempt at further underestimating man's possibilities and the plausibility, therefore, of a correlated secular humanism based on ideologies of "free choice" and unrestrained individualistic autonomy.

A Christian humanism, on the other hand, will be based on personal sacrifice, service, self-giving, and love—in the logic of following Christ and becoming progressively identified with him. If such a humanism is really Christian—unfortunately Christians do not always behave in a Christian way—it leads to solutions that, while demanding more from the acting person, are not carried out at the expense of third parties. They therefore tend to diminish the predicament of mankind and will definitely enrich both social relations and the acting person not only humanly but also supernaturally. Finally, by creating new and encouraging contexts of human experience, rooted in those values which typically spring from the practice of the virtues, this will also confirm and increase the intelligibility of the human good and therefore create and strengthen interpersonal bonds which, to a large extent, depend on a shared understanding of the good. So, we can argue and show that even considering its outcome, Christian morality turns out to be more reasonable than pure secular humanism.[12]

You might now perceive, arising from the depths of your soul, the accusation of "fundamentalism" or something similar. Yet, this charge, here, would be entirely unjustified. A fundamentalist is somebody who tries to integrally establish norms of Christian morality as a standard for coercive public order, for political institutions and law. This however is not what Christian morality demands. On the contrary, being dependent on revelation and faith—

12. This again shows the profound continuity of unassisted practical reason, as unfolded in natural law, with revealed Christian morality. This continuity, it seems to me, is rooted in practical reason as such, that is, in the fact that practical reason, as far as the human good is concerned, is intrinsically able to grasp this good, though not in its *full* intelligibility, which precisely stems from revealed Christian morality. In my view, to ground this continuity we therefore need not, as Carrasco de Paula ("El estudio y la enseñanza de la moral," 921) does, appeal to the theology of creation, even though the theological truth that the world and man have been originally created *in Christ*—which according to Carrasco explains the continuity between natural moral reason and revealed morality—may give some further *ontological* grounding to this continuity. Such a reference to creation theology, however, seems not to be needed from the standpoint of *practical reason,* which is the viewpoint of ethics, be it philosophical or theological.

remember that acceptance of the faith presupposes a free personal act—the reasonableness inherent in Christian morality cannot be the standard of coercive legislation valid for a multitude in a pluralistic society. Even in a society which is more or less homogeneously composed of Christians, standards of morality concerning free and responsible behavior and legally established and thus enforceable standards of behavior need not be identical. In my view, Christians should be opting for a political culture in which, within certain bounds, freedom and autonomy are conceived as essential moral goods to be protected by public institutions. The submission of the individual person to truth is not a task to be carried out politically or by legal means. But this rather complex topic is not one that I should be dealing with now.[13]

At any rate, in my view what Christians should aim at is not essentially to shape society through law and the imposition of coercive measures by political institutions, but to reform society from the inside through their behavior. This, of course, eventually will lead to change and improve many things on the level, for example, of legislation as well. Nevertheless, we should not narrow down the task of Christians to politics and organized action. The decisive part is the one carried out by "ordinary people" who are conscious that they are called to aim in their ordinary life at fully realizing the Christian vocation to sanctity, without fearing to be very often a "sign that is spoken against." With this, I come to my last point.

Christian Humanism: Reasonable and Ecclesiological

As we have seen, the basic moral requirements—the human good—contain an intrinsic reasonableness which, in principle, is independent of faith, and in that sense autonomous. Yet, only under the conditions of Christian faith is it possible to comply consistently with a morality which is in full agreement with the "human" and the "truth about man," because, so I have argued, only when integrated within the context of faith can these require-

13. See for this M. Rhonheimer, "Perché una filosofia politica? Elementi storici per una risposta," *Acta philosophica* 1, no. 2 (1992): 233–63; "Lo Stato costituzionale democratico e il bene comune," *Ripensare lo spazio politico: quale aristocrazia?* ed. E. Morandi and R. Panattoni, *Contratto—Rivista di filosofia tomista e contemporanea* 6 (1997), 57–122. Some general reflections about the distinction between the legal-political plane and the moral plane can be found in Rhonheimer, "Fundamental Rights, Moral Law, and the Legal Defense of Life in a Constitutional Democracy: A Constitutionalist Approach to the Encyclical *Evangelium Vitae*," *American Journal of Jurisprudence* 43 (1998): 135–83. An initial version, in Italian, of this article has been published in *Annales Theologici* 9 (1995): 271–334.

ments be defended and justified—precisely as *reasonable!* This is what restores full normative validity to what I have called the original moral knowledge, which is nothing other than the natural law.

The point I wanted to make here is that, by bringing together the human good, on one side, and the requirement of reasonableness, on the other, faith renders fully intelligible moral demands genuinely grounded in *reason.* Thus, I think faith to be a necessary condition of a person's being able both to reconcile the requirements of the human good with his striving for happiness, and therefore also to meet these moral requirements *consistently.*

As Christians we should never be afraid of reason. Reason is on our side, even though, to be given back all its strength, it must be permeated and enriched by the seemingly unreasonable foolishness of the Cross. And the Cross, apart from being a source of meaning and intelligibility, turns out to be the root of supernatural joy and spiritual regeneration.

John Henry Newman, at the end of his *Apologia pro Vita Sua,* pays homage to the truth-attaining capability of human reason. He points out how in fallen man reason is biased toward irreligiosity, and how this in fact, in his own words, leads it to "suicidal excesses" and to the "immense energy of the aggressive intellect."[14] Revelation, therefore, which is transmitted through the Church's Magisterium, precisely "supplies a need." Far from enfeebling human thought, it aims "to resist and control its extravagance."[15] So, Newman saw in the exercise of the infallible Magisterium something able to fully restore and permanently protect reason's truth-attaining capability. Correspondingly, we should be imbued with the conviction that the Church's moral teaching fundamentally reinforces the power of reason and moral understanding.

That is why, according to the encyclical *Veritatis Splendor,* we have "to find ever more consistent rational arguments in order to justify the requirements and to provide a foundation for the norms of the moral life" (*VS* no.74). We are entitled to be confident in the intelligibility of the human good and the capacity of man in general to understand what this good requires.

Yet that, of course, is only one part of the story. It still remains necessary to let this understanding be permeated and enriched by the prospects generated by faith. So, we have to urge Christians to assimilate what moral reason demands and apply it in living their faith. This implies two things. First,

14. J. H. Newman, *Apologia pro Vita Sua* (London: J. M. Dent; New York: E. P. Dutton, 1912), 221.

15. Ibid., 226.

to foster, in themselves and in others, *personal conversion*. That means acceptance of their own insufficiency, the need of grace, and the corresponding hope based on God's goodness and mercy. Second, from this conversion must spring the habitual disposition of Christian charity and fraternity, in the first place the disposition to forgive one's neighbor, over and over again, for any harm he might have done to us. Such a stable, and humble, attitude of personal conversion and of willingness to forgive others "seventy-seven times" is the basis on which a moral life has to be built up so as to prevent the distortion of reason by the hardening of one's heart.

Accordingly, also, the Church's mission can be described as twofold. First, it is precisely the commitment to illumine the human conscience regarding the truth of human existence *as fully human*. Second, it is to assist men and women—mainly through her sacramental power, which is the redeeming presence of Christ in this world—to struggle to meet the moral requirements that follow from this truth of human existence. By so doing, the Church helps them to become simultaneously light for others and leaven in the middle of society.

As to the first task, the Church has the primary responsibility for the formation of consciences. She does so while being fully aware of the fact that, although reasonable, her message will not be recognized by everyone as something reasonable, and will therefore be rejected by many. This not only because of what we have previously called the "unreasonableness" of overburdening people, but also on account of people's being entangled in the cobwebs they have spun with their own actions and which frequently weigh down their conscience with guilt and failure. This may lead to self-justification, resignation, or even desperation.

The more aggressively the Church's moral teaching is called unintelligible, the more we can suspect that the real problem is not its lack of intelligibility but rather the unwillingness of the critics to undergo personal conversion. That is why I wish to emphasize the second and very proper task of the Church in which she most resembles her divine founder: the invitation to conversion, accompanied by the offer and effective dispensation of divine forgiveness and "re-creation," mainly through the sacrament of penance. Only within the Church—in virtue of the Holy Spirit sent by the Father and the Son—are human lips able to offer divine forgiveness and mercy.

In so doing, the Church and her ministers precisely continue Christ's mission of rendering present among men the merciful love of the Divine Father. But that in turn has no sense without clearly—*importune, opportune*—teaching the integral truth about what is the good for man. It is not from the pulpit but in the confessional that the Church's ministers have to absolve.

But we are never to forget that only in the light of faith does the integral fulfillment of the human good as a moral norm regain its full reasonableness, and with that also its appeal as a meaningful prospect of happiness and fulfillment. This leads us to an attitude of understanding and tolerance, not of sin, but of the persons who feel unable to fully meet the requirements set forth in the Church's moral teaching. Without relativizing or unduly adjusting the "ought" to the "can" or graduating the moral norm, all pastoral work nevertheless has to try to gradually lead each person to fulfill all the good toward which their human nature, redeemed by Christ, aims.[16]

Christians therefore should always be acting, not with an inferiority complex, but with a confidence in the power of our faith to save human reason's truth-attaining capability. When the truth is announced to them, many people may seem not to understand, or be unwilling to accept it. But that does not mean that the Church and those faithful to its teachings have failed in their task of announcing the truth. Nor does it mean that those we have spoken to are not, in principle, able to grasp the truth of the teaching. Admittedly, improvements in ways of explaining are always possible, and most probably needed. But if and when people do accept difficult teachings, *it will be due to the changing dispositions of their hearts.* This change will make them capable of fully opening themselves to the intrinsic intelligibility of what natural law demands. This has never been achieved, in the first place, by arguments, but rather through prayer, through each Christian's personal struggle for holiness, and through the example of self-sacrificing and joyful service to our brothers and sisters.[17]

16. See John Paul II, *Familiaris Consortio* (The Role of the Christian Family in the Modern World, 1981), no. 34, 4, for the well-known distinction between the "law of gradualness" and "the gradualness of the law."

17. This essay was given as a talk at Boston College, Chestnut Hill, Mass., on April 10, 2000. It was given on the invitation of the Faculty of Theology, sponsored by the Jesuit Institute, and published in *Annales Theologici* 15, no. 2 (2001): 529–49. An earlier version of this paper was read during the conference Understanding the Faith, at Netherhall House, London, on April 16, 1997. For helpful comments, suggestions, and encouragement I am indebted to Stephen Reynolds and Arturo Blanco.

2

Norm-Ethics, Moral Rationality, and the Virtues

What's Wrong with Consequentialism?

The Quest for Truth and Moral Rationality

According to a conviction that I share with many others, morality is accessible to a rational discourse, and offering a clear understanding of this basis is essential for both Christian ethics and moral theology. I wish to add that this is properly the task of the philosopher, whose work is presupposed by the moral theologian, and integrated into his work.

Philosophical ethics has its proper methodology[1] and its own sources of intelligibility which are not in competition with the theologian's work; however, it will come to results which are not accessible to an exclusively theological method. Philosophy, even if it is understood as *ancilla theologiae,* has its own grounds and justification. So, given that human reason, to be fully reasonable and to attain truth in its integrity, needs the assistance of faith, one should not overlook that faith and theology, too, need reason's *proper* work and assistance. Otherwise, theology would risk becoming either a sort of "revelation-positivism" or a rationally uncontrolled discourse which would be anything but genuine scientific knowledge.

1. Cf. Martin Rhonheimer, *La prospettiva della morale. Fondamenti dell'etica filosofica* (Rome: Armando, 1994).

There existed formerly a tendency toward what I have labeled "revelation-positivism." It is, in the case of morals, the so-called "legalistic" position which gives to revealed moral standards the status of "moral rules" ("norms") and thus totally determines or even replaces the insight into the essence of morality. Therefore, it is not able to give evidence for the proposed "moral norms" in terms of human goods, actions, and choices to which they refer. Even the very term "moral norm" turned out to be unclear.

This tendency led to no problems as long as basic moral norms were not put into doubt, that is, as long as there existed a general social acceptance of these norms, so that dissenting from Christian ethics was equal to dissenting from generally accepted moral standards. Today, however, this is no longer the case. What formerly was dissent from moral standards is, in our day, generally accepted and lived. Today those who are really the dissenters are precisely the Church's Magisterium and those who follow it. The so-called "dissenting" or "revisionist" theologian is, in reality, the one who does what theologians in the past usually did: he identifies himself with the moral standards generally accepted and held as reasonable. He even asserts—and this is new—that the very generality of acceptance and practice of these standards forms part of their rationality. So, the moralist dissenting from the Church's teaching holds his position in the name of humanity, progress, and *rationality.* However, this is the question: which moral standards can claim for themselves to correspond to the rationality involved in every truth, including the truth of revealed morality?

The question of truth, however, which is the capital and fundamental question for the moral philosopher and the moral theologian, does not seem to be the question that concerns present-day moralists. They have, as they say, primarily "pastoral concerns." They want people to be well-off and happy. And they strive to convince people that Christianity, rightly understood, is something that indeed makes people well-off and happy. This desire of theirs is entirely legitimate. But by opposing pastoral concerns to the quest for truth, one makes a pivotal move: one implicitly maintains that the issue of happiness is not an issue of truth.

The Essential Moral Question

This, in any case, was not the classic view of moral philosophy. The Greek philosophers were convinced that the question about happiness was the question about what man *reasonably*—and that means: according to truth—may desire for its own sake and as his ultimate fulfillment. So "good action" *(eupraxia)* was intimately bound up with what Aristotle called "practical truth": the congruence of particular choices with right desire.

Having abandoned the quest for "truth," moral theory, with all its pastoral concerns, has instead found a new rationality: the one implied in every sort of proportionalism or consequentialism. This *is* rationality, but it is not, I would argue, the rationality of *moral* decision making. It rather belongs to what we may call the rationality of *poiesis,* that is, of *technical* decision making, of "making a better world."[2] The problem of the consequentialist talk about goods and evils[3] is exactly that, in order to determine whether an action is "right" or "wrong," they profess to speak about "goods" and "evils" only on a non-moral level. This, however, raises new problems: which is the better world, the one in which nobody suffers injustice or the one in which nobody commits injustice? This question, I think, can no longer be, for consequentialist moral thinking, a meaningful question. It is, however, the essential moral question, and means: by which kind of *actions* have we brought about certain states of affairs, independently from the degree of desirability they involve? For the consequentialist, this question is meaningless because he asserts that the evaluation of the moral rightness of an action depends precisely on the state of affairs it foreseeably brings about.[4]

The Rationality of the Virtues

The present turning of Catholic moral theology, or rather of the moral reasoning implied in it, toward kinds of consequentialism has to be seen, in my opinion, as the result of a traditional approach of looking at moral reasoning, an approach which falls short of doing justice to a *fundamental* understanding of human acting.[5] This tradition was, generally speaking, the tradition of the manuals, which were never able to provide a real understanding of what happens when a person is *acting.* So—leaving aside its unquestion-

2. For a criticism of confounding "action" with "technique" see Rüdiger Bubner, *Handlung, Sprache und Vernunft* (Frankfurt/M.: Suhrkamp, 1982), 74–90.

3. Editor's note: The author uses "evil" and "bad" interchangeably, to avoid monotony.

4. This statement seems to me to be valid also in the case of those adherents of so-called "teleological ethics," who affirm that the rightness of an action also depends on intrinsic properties of the action itself, for, in this case, these "intrinsic properties" are again described in relation to certain foreseen consequences of this action related to (non-moral) goods and bads.

5. See John Finnis, "Reason, Relativism and Christian Ethics," *Anthropotes* 9, no. 2 (December 1993): 211–30.

able utility in other regards—this tradition was not able to render intelligible the essence and the rationality proper to morality.

This rationality, I contend, is the rationality of virtues. I am aware of the fact that by saying this one will not easily escape the common misunderstanding that this is a mere rhetorical move, or even that it signifies not to have understood the question that normative ethics deals with. It is, moreover, the point on which I might disagree with John Finnis's approach. He holds that Aquinas's treatment of the virtues fails precisely to provide a basis for the formulation of the propositional contents of moral rationality.[6] This reproach is, however, quite close to saying that speaking about virtues has not a normative, but rather and exclusively a "parenetic" sense: that it exhorts and urges you to act justly without being able to give a clear, grounded articulation of what, in this or that circumstance, a just action is, that is to say, without resolving the problem about the "rightness" and "wrongness" of actions.

In contrast with this view I would like to argue that it is precisely the concept of virtue which, in a very fundamental sense, clarifies the question about what, in a moral perspective, it is (basically) right or (always) wrong to do.

In the tradition of the manuals, the virtues were reduced to a kind of habitual adherence and obedience to moral norms; instead of talking about virtues they talked much more about "conscience." A virtue was conceived as the internalization of moral norms or laws, which come from outside and impose themselves upon a person's conscience. To "make room" for human freedom, various so-called "moral systems" were elaborated.[7] In this same perspective today's consequentialism speaks about virtues: they are, as Bruno Schüller for example puts it, an attitude of being habitually determined to do the right thing.[8] However, *what* the right thing is, he says, must be made out by a decision-making theory like consequentialism.

The theory put forward by Germain Grisez and John Finnis[9] is, as I see it, a very powerful theory that justifies the main positions held by an alternative

6. John Finnis, *Fundamentals of Ethics* (Oxford: Clarendon Press; Washington, D.C.: Georgetown University Press, 1983).

7. For a historical account, cf. Servais Pinckaers, *Les sources de la morale chrétienne. Sa méthode, son contenu, son histoire* (Fribourg: Editions Universitaires de Fribourg, 1985), 258–82.

8. Bruno Schüller, *Die Begründung sittlicher Urteile: Typen ethischer Argumentation in der Moraltheologie,* 2nd ed. (1973; Düsseldorf: Patmos, 1980), 299.

9. See, e.g., Germain Grisez, Joseph Boyle, and John Finnis, "Practical Principles, Moral Truth, and Ultimate Ends," *American Journal of Jurisprudence* 32 (1987): 99–151.

view, which is the classical view of the virtues. But it remains in the logic of a moral theory which has its place in an "After-Virtue-age." Because this theory aims at rendering intelligible why proportionalism is false, it provides an anti-proportionalist decision-making theory, *but not* a *comprehensive* fundamental view about human *praxis.*

After these remarks I will now enter into a more analytic discourse. Obviously, I will not be able to provide an exposition of virtue ethics.[10] Rather, what I want to do is to examine its inner logic, exemplified by a concrete question: how can an ethics based on the concept of virtue settle the question about the fundamental "rightness" of human actions and, on the other hand, the so-called "intrinsic" wrongness of determinate kinds of acts, that is, of freely chosen behaviors?

It seems to me that this could shed some light on the encyclical *Veritatis Splendor.* Consequentialists (and proportionalists) unanimously assert that their views were misrepresented in *Veritatis Splendor.* Nobody affirms, so they contend, what the encyclical reproaches in consequentialist and proportionalist methodology. The point, however, is that *Veritatis Splendor* argues from a standpoint which is quite different from any form of proportionalist methodology. So, it could equally be the case that critics of this magisterial document did not really understand *why* their theories were so clearly rejected by *Veritatis Splendor.*

Dissociating "Morally Right" from "Morally Good"

It is commonly held among adherents of consequentialism and proportionalism that there is an important and basic conceptual difference between the "rightness" and the "goodness" of an action.[11] "Right-making-properties" refer to the normative question of which action is to be done in a given circumstance. The "good-making-properties," on the other hand, refer to the intentions, the attitudes, and inner disposition of the agent, to qualities of his will and his heart. So it is possible to do the right action with an evil will and the wrong action with a good will.

10. I tried to do this in my book *La prospettiva della morale* (quoted above). For my views about the formation of Aquinas's theory of practical reason in the context of Aristotelian virtue ethics, see M. Rhonheimer, *Praktische Vernunft und Vernünftigkeit der Praxis. Handlungstheorie bei Thomas von Aquin in ihrer Entstehung aus dem Problemkontext der aristotelischen Ethik* (Berlin: Akademie Verlag, 1994).

11. The distinction was introduced by W. D. Ross (who defended a "deontological" ethical position) in his 1930 book *The Right and the Good* (Oxford: Clarendon Press, 1965).

This, of course, is partly true.[12] But what defenders of this theory want to claim is that what an agent chooses to do is neither morally good nor evil; that it does not determine whether the acting subject is a good or an evil person, whether his heart is good or evil; what an agent decides to do can only be called "right" or "wrong," without determining whether the one who does it is a good or a bad person.

"Morally good" and "evil," they claim, refer only to properties of the willing, striving, choosing, or intending person; but they cannot be used as predicates for "actions" as such. This is because they hold that actions, as such, say nothing about the will of the person who performs them. As it will be further explained in the next section, according to this moral theory actions are not seen as objects of choice but rather as "realizations" of pre-moral goods and evils, to be judged as right and wrong according to the desirability of the state of affairs brought about by them.

According to consequentialists and proportionalists it would be therefore unreasonable to speak about actions which are, in all circumstances, morally evil. There may be, a consequentialist could theoretically admit, actions which are in all circumstances morally *wrong*—but this depends precisely on the circumstances which, then, would have to be unchangeable, a position that obviously is very difficult to defend.[13]

This view, I repeat, is a last elaboration of a moral theory centered in moral norms. The only difference is that moral norms are no longer considered as given, but rather as made according to a moral reasoning which could be precisely a proportionalist one.

So, the theory claims, the agent may work out what is the right thing to do. If he performs the corresponding action, he does the right thing; but this

12. See also the remarks by Peter Geach, "Good and Evil," *Analysis* 17 (1956): 33–42; republished in *Theories of Ethics,* ed. Philippa Foot (Oxford: Oxford University Press, 1967), 64–73, esp. 72.

13. It was explicitly rejected by Josef Fuchs, who also denied the possibility of formulating corresponding moral absolutes, i.e., universally valid prohibitive norms (referring to what he calls the inner-worldly realm); see his well-known article "The Absoluteness of Moral Terms," in *Readings in Moral Theology No. 1: Moral Norms and Catholic Tradition,* ed. Charles E. Curran and Richard McCormick (New York: Paulist Press, 1979), 94–137. "The reason is that an action cannot be judged morally at all, considered purely in itself, but only together with all the 'circumstances' and the 'intention' (124). Consequently, a behavioral norm, universally valid in the full sense, would presuppose that those who arrive at it could know or foresee *all the possible combinations* of the action concerned with circumstances and intentions, with (pre-moral) values and non-values *(bona and mala 'physica')*." Surprisingly, Fuchs fails in this place to distinguish between positive and negative (prohibitive) norms, a distinction that of course would make all the difference here.

does not yet mean that his action can be labeled "morally good." It will be so only on the basis of the intentions *with which* the agent does what he thinks to be the right thing to do. This, in a sense, is also true. But the problem arises as soon as one says that there is no describable action (or behavior) about which it may be said that the one who willingly performs it performs a morally evil action, and that only the further (evil) intentions *with which* an agent performs *any* action could determine its becoming an evil action.[14] So, the theory asserts, the right thing must be done "virtuously"; but the claims of virtues never can determine that which is the right thing to do or, more importantly, that which is the wrong thing to do, an action or behavior that must be abstained from in every case.

I would like to challenge this view by saying: what is right to do is precisely the action that is "morally good," and what must always be abstained from is "morally evil." This moral good or evil determines whether the acting subject in fact becomes, through his acts, a good or an evil person. So, my view claims that there are describable actions which may be called morally good and inducing moral goodness in the will of the agent, and which, *for this very reason,* are (at least basically, *in specie*) right; and, what is more important, there are describable actions which are, as such, morally evil, inducing moral evil in the will of the agent, and which, *for this very reason,* are morally wrong.[15]

The Basic Intentionality of Human Actions

This seems, at a first glance, to beg the question. But, in reality, it does not. In order to show this, I will first have to clarify some implications of any ethical theory that argues for a fundamental difference between the *rightness* and the *goodness* of an action.

Such ethical theories share two fundamental characteristics: first, they

14. Compare the revealing formulation in John Paul II, *Veritatis Splendor* (The Splendor of Truth, 1993), no. 79 (emphasis mine): "One must therefore reject the thesis, characteristic of teleological and proportionalist theories, which holds that it is impossible to qualify as *morally evil* according to its species—its "object"—*the deliberate choice* of certain kinds of behavior or specific acts, apart from a consideration of the intention for which the choice is made or the totality of the foreseeable consequences of that act for all persons concerned."

15. When I say "evil as such" I mean "intrinsically evil," which again means "evil independently from further intentions." For this I refer to chapter 3 of this book, originally published as Martin Rhonheimer, "'Intrinsically Evil Acts' and the Moral Viewpoint: Clarifying a Central Teaching of *Veritatis Splendor,*" *The Thomist* 58, no. 1 (1994): 1–39.

talk about human actions from the standpoint of an outside observer (the "third person"); and secondly, the actions to which moral norms and moral decision-procedures refer are considered by these theories not as intentional and properly human actions, but more like simple events or natural processes. Both characteristics also underlie the traditional (seventeenth to twentieth century) manualistic treatments. This may seem surprising; however, it only confirms that proportionalists and consequentialists in Catholic moral theology have simply drawn some consequences congruous with already existing "traditional" patterns. This, by the way, is what they themselves sometimes affirm.

Let me begin with the second point: the criticized theories do not treat actions as intentional actions. Of course, they say much about "intentions" and "intentionality," understood however as an element simply added to the action "as such," which, precisely "as such," is not understood as *intentional* action. So they fail to consider the intentionality necessarily *involved* in any choice of what one immediately does. Consequently, they speak instead about actions as events which produce more or less desirable states of affairs, where the criteria for the desirability of such outcomes are also the criteria for the rightness of an action which causes this outcome.

To this I would object that we might speak about earthquakes in a similar way: we consider it to be better (more desirable) that an earthquake kill only one person rather than a hundred. The outcome of the event in one case is better (or less evil) than in the other. But does that mean that in given circumstances (for example, in a case of hostage-taking) the "better" action would be to deliberately kill one person instead of permitting someone else—as a consequence of my abstaining from killing the one—from killing a hundred persons? If we consider the act of killing as a simple event with a definite outcome (a state of affairs), the "right" action would be, *ceteris paribus,* to kill the one, because it is, as such, a more desirable state of affairs that only one instead of one hundred persons are killed. This is the logic implied in consequentialist moral reasoning; it is not able, in my view, to distinguish between the "killing" effected by an earthquake and the (action) of killing performed by a human agent. This objection is not refuted by the fact that consequentialists will, in such a case, probably point to other foreseeable and undesirable consequences to try to show that the person blackmailed should not kill the one hostage; but this in no way alters the *logic* of their reasoning.

This does not mean that consequentialists do in fact propose and explicitly defend such an "eventistic" theory of action. I only want to suggest that the logic of decision making contained in their theory implicitly involves this view, in the sense that otherwise their claims would not be consistent.[16] This charge is supported by the fact that consequentialists contend that the concrete action performed by the agent does not determine the agent's *will.* Any determination of the will is precisely what I call (moral) goodness or evil. "Moral goodness" is nothing other than a quality of a free will. If, as consequentialists and proportionalists are necessarily compelled to assume, a person's *doing* or *acting* cannot, and actually does not, determine the will, then this doing or acting must be considered neither as *intentional* action, springing from a free will, nor as implying a *purpose* which shapes the very action as this *sort* of action (its "moral object"), nor as an action which may be blamed or praised, just as we cannot blame nature for killing persons by an earthquake, because nature is not an intentional agent.

That is why, I think, consequentialists are talking about human actions in the same way as we are accustomed to speak about birds building their nests: birds are gathering different materials by doing certain bodily movements, the outcome of which is a nest. So, on the grounds of observing what birds normally bring about when they perform these acts, we can correctly say the bird does this "for the sake of" building a nest. But does the bird perform the *action* of "building a nest"? It does not; to do this, it would have to *intend,* by gathering materials and performing certain bodily movements, to build a nest. What the bird lacks is precisely the *purpose* of building a nest, a purpose which as intentional content would shape the action and the will that chooses this action.

However, when a person kills another person, he not only tightens his finger around the trigger of a gun, shooting a projectile into the heart of another person, thus producing his death (this could also be done by a robot), but the killer *intends* the death of the other person, and it is precisely this purpose which shapes his action as a determinate *sort* of action: murder. This intentional content is what we call the *object* of a human act. So the action is right or wrong not simply on the grounds of considering whether the death of this person is, in given circumstances, the best or least bad outcome (it *could* indeed be the best for everybody), but on the grounds of considering whether intending the death of another person—which means choosing his

16. Cf. the excellent article by Anselm W. Müller, "Radical Subjectivity: Morality versus Utilitarianism," *Ratio* 19 (1977): 115–32.

death, setting one's will against the life of another person—is right or wrong. We judge it *wrong* precisely by judging that a will which intends this is an *evil* will.

Yet, a proportionalist such as Josef Fuchs will tell us that the action "as such" (for example, "killing as such") is nothing else than the "realization" of a "human evil" (a "pre-moral" evil), and this "may be morally good or morally bad; for killing as such, since it implies nothing about the intention of the agent, cannot, purely as such, constitute a human act."[17] This is erroneous simply because "killing as such" does not exist as a describable human *action;* "as such," "killing somebody" is not an act that could be chosen at all. To rationally choose it one should *at least want* (and therefore *choose and intend*) this somebody to be dead (for its own sake or to achieve a further goal).[18]

So we have to look at concrete performances of human acts *as* acts chosen by a will, *as* acts whose objective (basic intentional) content is precisely a determinate *purpose.*[19] This choice, however, is effected on the grounds of a practical judgment. This judgment cannot be interpreted in consequentialist terms; because the consequentialist interpretation of elective judgments omits exactly what is most typical and essential for these judgments: that it is not about the foreseen outcome of the action seen as an event producing consequences, but about the chosen action itself in which the agent's will determines itself to a particular end which precisely shapes the action as a specific *kind* of action. In this way, actions differing by their object (that is, their basic intentional content) are shaped.[20]

Virtues and the First-Person Viewpoint

Again, a consequentialist might object at this moment: "You are begging the question." Whether or not the chosen action determines the will as good or evil depends on its foreseen outcome, or more precisely, on the will to produce always the best possible state of affairs. What I seek by my own way

17. Fuchs, 119.

18. For a more detailed treatment of this question see again chapters 3, 4, and 8 of this book.

19. I refer to G. E. M. Anscombe, *Intention*, 2nd ed. (1957; Oxford: Basil Blackwell, 1963). For the concepts of "basic intentional content" and of "intentional basic action," see Rhonheimer, *La prospettiva della morale*, 39, 85ff., 239ff.

20. I have treated elsewhere some of the commonly discussed examples of corresponding intentional basic actions, as, e.g., lying, theft, murder (distinguished from killing in just war, killing in legitimate self-defense, execution in capital punishment), contraception, fornication, adultery, and masturbation. See the references in chapters 3, 4, and 8.

of reasoning is nothing other than to settle the *objective* meaning of my "action." This is done, he asserts, precisely by calculating its consequences. The object, so he asserts, is exactly the *result* of the consequentialist (or proportionalist) calculus.

With this, I come to the first characteristic of this theory, mentioned above: consequentialist and proportionalist theories are those that look at human actions from the observer's viewpoint, from a "view from nowhere," as Thomas Nagel has called it.[21] This means to speak about actions as performances of a "third person," but not as *my* actions. Actions are looked at as if they were processes enchaining causes and effects. That is why, normally, in a consequentialist view what Bernard Williams[22] called "negative responsibility" becomes central: the claim that I am just as responsible for what others do as for my own actions; so, the consequentialist would assert, I am also and equally responsible for the evil consequences of an act which another person foreseeably does as a result of my refraining from this act (for example, because I judge this act to be intrinsically evil). So it makes no difference, a consequentialist says, whether *I* do something or *another* person does it, as long as the foreseeable state of resulting affairs would be the same.

The classical tradition up to and including Aquinas, however, is the tradition of an ethic of the "first person."[23] This tradition was dominated by the question: What is the good thing for me to do? What is the good life for man to live? What really is the good which alone can be reasonably desired as ultimate and for its own sake? Which are the *subjective* conditions under which what *appears* to me as good is also *truly* good? How must my appetites be disposed so as to judge according to reason in every particular action?[24]

When Democritus pronounced that a person who commits injustice is unhappier than the person who suffers injustice,[25] he wanted to say that there is a difference between what *I* do and what *another* man does, even if in both cases injustice gets committed, and that precisely this difference can deter-

21. Thomas Nagel, *The View from Nowhere* (Oxford: Oxford University Press, 1986).

22. Bernard Williams, "A Critique of Utilitarianism," in J. J. C. Smart and Bernard Williams, *Utilitarianism: For & Against* (Cambridge: Cambridge University Press, 1973), 75–150.

23. This was well emphasized by John Finnis in his *Fundamentals of Ethics,* 114ff., and Giuseppe Abbà, *Felicità, vita buona e virtù. Saggio di filosofia morale* (Rome: LAS, 1989).

24. This, and not so much normative questions, is the central theme of Aristotle's ethic. That is one of my central arguments in my extensive research on Aquinas and Aristotle, *Praktische Vernunft und Vernünftigkeit der Praxis,* cited above (n. 10).

25. See Diels/Kranz, *Die Fragmente der Vorsokratiker* [The Fragments of the Presocratics] (Berlin, 1952), fragment B 45.

mine whether my life is a good or a bad one. The difference, of course, is not a difference concerning "the state of the world"; the difference is a difference *for me.* I can possibly, in a given situation, bring about the most desirable state of affairs; but only at the price of becoming myself a murderer. There remains the question: is such a "brave new world," brought about by *my becoming* a murderer, really a good one? Is the fact that the poor family with ten children does not lose their mother really a desirable "state of affairs" if she has, purportedly for the benefit of her family, aborted the child which foreseeably would have killed her? If we consider the act of abortion only as something akin to a natural event (abortion indeed often occurs naturally), it actually could be considered as better. The problem, however, is this: killing the child in the mother's womb was precisely not a natural event; the mother and I, her surgeon, *chose* it. And that is why the mother and I have changed into a different kind of person; neither I nor she is any longer the same person each of us was before choosing the abortion. The ten children now have a mother who is the murderer of the child whose coming-into-being would have foreseeably killed her. This, by the way, will not be without consequences for the relations between the mother and her children.

But the point I wish to make here is: the action the mother and the surgeon did was wrong, wrong in a moral sense, precisely *because* it was an *evil* action; it is morally evil to choose the death of another person for the sake of saving the life of oneself[26] or of a third person, or to bring about other desirable outcomes.

What, then, does "evil action" mean? It means an action which implies a will that is not upright; the action in question is *this sort* of action precisely because of the will which shapes its intentional content. Consequentialists willy-nilly are compelled to say, as we have seen, that "action" as such has nothing to do with "will."[27] But this is precisely their erroneous presuppo-

26. Aquinas says, in a famous passage of his *ST* II-II, q.64, a.7: "illicitum est quod homo intendat occidere hominem ut seipsum defendat." Here, "intendere" means the elective will referring to the concrete action ("occidere hominem"), while the defense of one's life is the *further* intention *with which* the concrete action is chosen. From the viewpoint of a consequentialist or a proportionalist, you could not distinguish the two cases, because the action "as such" would not be considered as intentional action but only (on the "physical" level) as "realization of a premoral evil" (here: death). Therefore, "proportionate reason" will determine whether "realizing the evil" is "right" or "wrong." Thus, the question of moral evil involved in the very *choice* of the action is eluded.

27. I already have referred above to Josef Fuchs and to how he denies that the concrete, particular action can be considered as possessing the characteristics of a "human act" (an act that

sition. In reality every human action—precisely if it really *is* what we call a "human action"—implies a will whose intentional content forms part of what we traditionally call the *object* of this act.[28] A human action springs from the rational appetite, and it determines this appetite as a good or an evil one. So it determines whether the person becomes a good or a bad person. The acting subject changes while acting. By choosing determinate actions, he or she shapes himself or herself. He or she becomes good or evil precisely by choosing this or that action. Let me specify: to become a good person, not only the choice involved in action but also the further intentions need to be good; to become an evil person, a single deficiency in the will is sufficient. *Bonum ex integra causa, malum ex quocumque defectu,* says the classical principle.

Virtues and Moral Norms

This leads us back to the virtues. For the so-called moral virtues are nothing other than perfections of sensual appetites or desires, and intentional drives—that is the rational appetite, which is called the "will" *(appetitus in ratione).* Virtue is not the faculty, nor even the perfect act of it; it is something between the faculty and the act: *habitus,* a stable inclination toward performing the faculty's proper act perfectly, which is according to reason. Human appetites are perfected by justice, fortitude, and temperance. But these virtues include their proper "structures of reasonableness." These are called the "end of the virtues"; those ends are identical with practical principles as established and pronounced by natural law.[29]

---

springs from deliberate will); only including *all* further intentions (which refer to bringing about an optimum of non-moral goods) can an action, he says, be considered as "human act." See also my discussion in "Menschliches Handeln und seine Moralität" ["Human Action and its Morality"], in Martin Rhonheimer, Andreas Laun, Tatjana Goritschewa, and Walter Mixa, *Ethos und Menschenbild* (St. Ottilien: EOS, 1989), 112, n. 42. Bruno Schüller affirms, in a similar way, that the determination of an acting person's will only takes place in regard to the "sittliche Forderung" ("moral exigency"), which, again, is the result of a consequentialist calculus of *all* foreseen consequences of a particular action; I refer to my book *Natur als Grundlage der Moral* (Innsbruck-Vienna: Tyrolia-Verlag, 1987), 292–309. The English translation is *Natural Law and Practical Reason: A Thomist View of Moral Autonomy,* trans. Gerald Malsbary, 1st English ed., Moral Philosophy and Moral Theology 1 (New York: Fordham University Press, 2000).

28. The importance of the first-person viewpoint to grasp what the meaning of the "object" of a human act is rightly emphasized in *Veritatis Splendor,* no. 78: "In order to be able to grasp the object of an act which specifies that act morally, it is therefore necessary to place oneself *in the perspective of the acting person.*"

29. For a thorough analysis see M. Rhonheimer, *Natural Law and Practical Reason,* and *La prospettiva della morale,* especially chapter 5, where I basically identify "practical principles," "natural law," and the "ends of virtues," calling them "structures of reasonableness."

But does this throw any light on the functioning of practical reason and its propositional contents? Does it help to make out the way in which we can settle and justify moral norms? It does, so I will argue, provided we understand that any moral norm refers to actions described as *intentional* actions. Norms are not always, or not basically, an expression of a previous weighing of pre-moral goods (and evils) on the grounds of proportionate reason. This is so, precisely because most *objects* of human actions are not the result of such a procedure of weighing goods or consequences either. For example, whether a person is innocent, or not, is not a question of weighing goods and evils resulting from his death. Neither is it a question of weighing goods, whether two persons are married, or not; nor is it a question of weighing goods whether what I appropriate against the owner's will something to which he actually has a right, or not.

Let me briefly say something about justice. The virtue of justice is, basically, a perfection of the acting person's will with regard to other persons, a perfection which consists in striving for the good of others with the same firmness as the natural striving for one's own good. The basic structure of justice is expressed in the Golden Rule. Justice presupposes the acknowledgment of other persons as "equal to me" and gives rise to a plurality of relations of one's will to other persons, corresponding to different areas of action. Justice is the basis of friendship, and is completed by it. Its rationale is generally expressed in the principle that one must render to each what one owes to him.

What we actually owe to a person is differentiated by different interpersonal relations. So, there exists contractual justice and the justice implied in keeping promises or in telling the truth. Whoever observes contracts, whoever is faithful to what he promised, and whoever is truthful relates, with his will, in a determinate kind of way to other concrete and particular persons (those with whom he has made a contract, or to whom he has promised something or affirmed something to be the case), independently of other consequences or further intentions.

Let's take, as example, promise-keeping. A rule-utilitarian would say: keeping promises is right, because it is beneficial to sustain a practice like promise-keeping for the good of society. So I should never break a promise. Rule-utilitarianism is norm-utilitarianism. Consequentialists and proportionalists are mostly norm-utilitarians. An act-utilitarian, on the other hand, would say that I have, in every case, to work out the consequences of holding or breaking a promise, or telling the truth; depending on these consequences, I can determine whether the one to whom I promised something has a *right* to have fulfilled his expectation that I will do what I promised. By looking at the consequences of each case, the applicability of a possible moral norm can be determined, or it may be determined that no norm applies.

In any case, this position presupposes a determinate description of the action "promising something to somebody." This description must necessarily be a merely physical one, to say for example: "To promise means to utter determinate words by which I produce in somebody else the mental state of being convinced that I will do x." A moral norm prescribing that promises should always be kept would express the *utility* of doing nothing that could weaken the reliability of such a practice among men. But then the "difficult cases" come about (quandaries, borderline cases), the discussions about possible exceptions, and finally the reproach, raised by act-utilitarians, of "rule worshipping."

In reality, the description of the action to which the norm was referred was an incomplete description. It included all but what "I promise you" means. The performance of a speech act by which A produces in B a mental state of being convinced that A will do x is not necessarily a promise. For example, "You can be sure that I will arrive tomorrow morning at nine o'clock": this *might* be a promise, but it can equally be a menace or a simple statement or a reassurance. What is peculiar to a promise is precisely that A confers on B the *right* of claiming that A will do x. The promissory act establishes, between A and B, a relation of *justice.* If what I promise turns out to be an unjust act, I will not be bound to keep my promise; I will even be obliged not to do x, because nobody has a right to claim that others perform unjust acts. By *this* exception to the simple *rule* "keep your promises," the practice of promise-keeping will not be weakened; on the contrary, it will be invigorated, because promise-keeping belongs to justice in interpersonal relations, thus fostering friendship between men. It is not guided by simple social benefit. But we can clearly see: whether I have to keep a promise does not depend on the whole set of foreseen circumstances; some of them may determine whether the act x, which is the subject of the promise, is a just act or not. But the basic question always will be the relation between A and B, and not the relation of A's acts to the "state of affairs" brought about by keeping the promise. The act of keeping a promise is intentionally shaped *independently* of the *overall* consequences of keeping it.

So, an ethics centered on virtues does justice to the fact that our actions are always shaped by commitments and specified relations to particular, concrete persons; our commitment is not, fundamentally, to fulfilling norms, or to constructing a better world, or to supporting socially useful practices.[30] Moral norms refer to intentional actions and express their rational and human contents. The "object" of an intentional action, however, is not what some proportionalists call an "expanded object,"[31] which would be formed as the *result* of previously weighing all circumstances and intentions, referred to consequences considered as morally relevant. So, contrary to the proportionalist, I think that killing an innocent person in order to save the life of ten others is an action of murder (object), chosen with the *further* intention of saving the lives of ten other innocent people, *and not* the action of "saving ten innocent lives" ("expanded object"), by simply "realizing" the (pre-moral) evil of killing ("putting to death") one innocent person (justifying this as "right" on the grounds of the proportionate reason of saving the life of ten persons and, thus, serving in an optimal way the value of "life").

On the other hand, "natural law" precisely is the rational ordering of intentional actions; it is not exactly the same as moral "norms." Norms are propositions, kinds of *speaking about* practical reasonableness by which the virtues are shaped and which precisely is the content of natural law. "Moral norms" belong to our moral language, but—unlike practical reason itself—they do not *constitute* moral contents; they are only propositional expressions of the moral content involved in intentional actions. Moral norms, therefore, relate to (1) practical knowledge and (2) virtues, as propositions generally relate to (1) intellectual judgment and (2) reality.

Therefore, an ethics centered on norms will necessarily lose its proper subject matter: the reality of the acting person and the practical reasoning that shapes the intentional content of human actions. In this way it will be understandable that "moral norms" concerning "right" and "wrong" refer to

30. This, it seems to me, is the reason why virtue ethics do not require a "personalistic complement." Modern personalism seems to be an attempt to overcome the one-sided views of modern rule-ethics. Ethics based on the concept of moral virtue are instrinsically "personalistic," but also probably more open to rational discourse than many forms of personalism.

31. See R. A. McCormick, "Some Early Reactions to *Veritatis Splendor*," *Theological Studies* 55 (1994): 501. See my more thorough critique of the notion of "expanded object" in chapter 4, originally published as "Intentional Actions and the Meaning of Object: A Reply to Richard McCormick," *The Thomist* 59, no. 2 (1995): 279–311; reprinted in *Veritatis Splendor and the Renewal of Moral Theology*, ed. J. A. Di Noia and R. Cessario (Princeton, N.J.: Scepter; Huntington, Ind.: Our Sunday Visitor; Chicago: Midwest Theological Forum, 1999), 241–68.

intentional actions, and not to mere physical events: moral norms (or rules) are not propositions about (physical) actions insofar as they produce certain mostly desirable results; instead they are propositional expressions of intentionality involved in particular types of action. Therefore the "right" and the "wrong" expressed in such norms is also the "good" and the "evil" for the acting person.[32]

Moreover, "moral norms" express, mostly in the form of absolute prohibitions, the very human identity of the acting subject as a subject related to himself (as a spiritual *and* as a bodily being), to other persons, and to God (for the virtue of religion, too, belongs to justice, as Aquinas says). Consequentialists and proportionalists will always have to refer to moral norms as relating to actions considered as "physical events" and as expressing a determinate, always provisional, result of weighing pre-moral goods and evils on the grounds of proportionate reasons. So, they are missing the point of morality, a point that is precisely and adequately expressed in the traditional concept of moral virtue. So-called "teleological ethics," I am convinced, undermines and perverts moral discourse to such an extent that it becomes incompatible with the intrinsic humanism of Christian ethics.

Of course, with this I do not mean that consequentialists or proportionalists would subscribe to an immoral principle such as "let's do evil so that good comes about" ("evil" here being *moral* evil). Neither will the proportionalist adhere to the principle that "a good end justifies a (morally) evil means." The problem of so-called "teleological" ethics precisely consists in ruling out, on the level of determining "right" and "wrong," the very possibility of committing such an immorality, and therefore the need of resisting the possible temptation. This is so because "evil," justified by proportionate reason, will, according to proportionalist methodology, always be considered

32. The fundamental identity of the good and the right has recently been challenged in an even more extreme and highly questionable way by J. F. Keenan, S.J., *Goodness and Rightness in Thomas Aquinas's "Summa Theologiae"* (Washington, D.C.: Georgetown University Press, 1992); see also J. F. Keenan, S.J., "Die erworbenen Tugenden als richtige (nicht gute) Lebensführung: Ein genauerer Ausdruck ethischer Beschreibung," *Ethische Theorie praktisch,* ed. F. Furger, Festschrift K. Demmer (Münster: Aschendorff, 1991), 19–35. Keenan's position is a coherent further development of the distinction between "goodness" and "rightness" of human actions that fully confirms my criticism: it leads to the result that the rightness of appetite, and therefore acquired moral virtue generally, has nothing to do yet with the goodness of a person. According to Keenan, such goodness of the person would be caused and consist exclusively in charity infused by grace. I abstain from further comments; but it seems to me a clear confirmation of how the distinction between "goodness" and "rightness"—in the way revisionist moral theology uses it—leads to the destruction of moral rationality on the level of human nature as such.

only as *pre-moral* evil. Thus, you can without any remorse "realize" what is only a pre-moral evil *provided there is in fact a reason proportionate so as to justify it,* that is, *provided the goal is a good one.* As a leading consequentialist has pointed out, the good goal not only *may* but necessarily *does* justify the realization of an evil, and even more: "The good goal is the only possible justification of causing a non-moral evil."[33] This kind of dealing with moral judgment and human agency is precisely what so worries critics of consequentialism and proportionalism.

Norm-centered ethics—as consequentialism, proportionalism, and all forms of utilitarianism are—actually tend to consider moral norms as socially accepted rules and standards, made by men through a historical and cultural process that is contingent and therefore also marks as contingent the norms it produces to regulate the life of societies in their different aspects. Such rules, of course, do exist; mainly as legal rules and social conventions. They are in many aspects contingent and man-made. But they are not the principal paradigm for what we properly call *moral* norms.

Moral norms are not, in their fundamental meaning, "rules" serving the regulation of human behavior and seeking to establish a well-ordered, peaceful, and prospering community of human beings. Moral norms are a linguistic expression of something much deeper, something rooted in what we call "human nature" or the "truth of man." Not only in their positive, but also in their negative or prohibitive form, they express the truth about human persons and about the basic relationships between them.

The world will be better and really human if we strive to live the virtues. The best world will always be the one that is brought about by virtuous actions, even if such a world will not be the one which, in terms of desirability, may be considered the best as such. But to produce the best world overall is not the task man has to fulfill. Suffering injustice is always better than committing it—even if by committing it there will be, as expected, fewer persons suffering it. In this sense Christian hope saves human reason from false expectations; because, in any case, every consequentialist calculus is, in practice, self-defeating since it undermines the intrinsic rationality of morality. Christian faith teaches us that the truly good world will come; it is not to be made by us, but will be given in the final restoration of all things. That does not mean that we should not care about a better world. But, in its most

33. Schüller, 77.

fundamental and basic sense, the "right action" is not the one which foreseeably makes the world better. Things are exactly the other way round: the most desirable state of the world will always be the one brought about by and compatible with morally right actions. For the morally right is that which involves rightness of the *will* and therefore purity of the heart. This precisely is the work of moral virtue.[34]

34. This paper was originally a response to John Finnis, "Reason, Relativism and Christian Ethics," at the John Paul II Institute's Conference on Reason, Revelation and Christian Ethics (Washington, D.C., March 20, 1990). An earlier version of it, with the title "'Ethics of Norms' and the Lost Virtues," appeared in *Anthropotes* 9 (1993): 231–43.

3

"Intrinsically Evil Acts" and the Moral Viewpoint

Clarifying a Central Teaching of Veritatis Splendor

Introduction: Choices, Their Objects, Further Intentions and Consequences

Many Catholic moral theologians have asserted during the last few years that to know what a person really *does* each time he or she is acting and, consequently, to qualify morally this concrete doing, one must take into account all the further goals for the sake of which this person chooses what he concretely does. Equally, so these theologians contend, a balance of all foreseen consequences should be established to make out whether a determinate behavior is the right or the wrong thing to choose. Therefore, according to this view it will always

> be impossible to qualify as morally evil according to its species—its "object"—the deliberate choice of certain kinds of behavior or specific acts, apart from a consideration of the intention for which the choice is made or the totality of the foreseeable consequences of that act for all persons concerned (*Veritatis Splendor* no. 79).

The encyclical *Veritatis Splendor* rejects this view of so-called "teleological" ethical theories[1] as incompatible with the existence of describable con-

1. The term "teleological" as a characterization of ethical theories became successful through C. D. Broad's essay "Some of the Main Problems of Ethics," *Philosophy* 21 (1946), reprinted in

crete actions which are "intrinsically evil," that is, which are evil "*always and per se,* in other words, on account of their very object, and quite apart from the ulterior intentions of the one acting and the circumstances" (*VS* no. 80). Consequently, this view finally is judged as incompatible with the existence of absolutely—without exception—binding prohibitive (or: negative) moral norms, that is: with so-called "moral absolutes."

The encyclical clearly distinguishes the object of a concrete choice, and the corresponding action, from *ulterior* intentions with which a choice is made. It seems to me that one of the central problems implied in thus distinguishing choices and their objects from further intentions may be formulated as follows: *What precisely* is qualified when an action or freely chosen behavior is qualified as "morally evil" *by virtue of its very "object"?* This point, I think, must be carefully elucidated if we want to talk reasonably about concrete actions, or choices of determinate behaviors, being morally evil by vir-

---

C. D. Broad, *Broad's Critical Essays in Moral Philosophy,* ed. D. R. Cheney (London: Allen & Unwin; New York: Humanities Press, 1971), 223–46. Broad simply identified any "teleological" argumentation with a consequentialist one: "One characteristic which tends to make an act right is that it will produce at least as good consequences as an alternative open to the agent in the circumstances. . . . We can sum this up by saying that the property of being *optimific* is a very important right-tending characteristic. I call it *teleological* because it refers to the goodness of the ends or consequences which the act brings about" (230). Broad, then, goes on to say that a "non-teleological" characteristic of an action would be, for example, the obligation, independent of considering consequences, to perform what one has promised. Already in 1930, however, Broad had distinguished "teleological" from "deontological" ethical theories; see C. D. Broad, *Five Types of Ethical Theory* (London: Routledge & Kegan Paul, 1930), 206ff. Many today call non-teleological ethics (in Broad's sense) "deontological"; cf. William K. Frankena, *Ethics* (Englewood Cliffs, N.J.: Prentice Hall, 1963). The term "teleological ethics" was thus "imported" by German moral theologians, mainly by Bruno Schüller; see his *Die Begründung sittlicher Urteile. Typen ethischer Argumentation in der Moraltheologie,* 2nd ed. (1973; Düsseldorf: Patmos, 1980), 282–98. According to Schüller, a normative ethic would be "teleological" if it affirms that "the moral character of *all* the actions and the omissions of man is *exclusively* determined by its consequences" (282). Therefore, he uses "teleological ethics" as synonymous with "consequentialism" (a term in fact created by G. E. M. Anscombe) and equivalent to "utilitarianism." Its counterpart would be "deontological ethics," which holds that there are *some* actions the moral rightness of which should *not* be judged exclusively on the basis of their consequences; see also Bruno Schüller, "Various Types of Grounding for Ethical Norms," in *Readings in Moral Theology No. 1: Moral Norms and Catholic Tradition,* ed. Charles E. Curran and Richard A. McCormick, SJ (New York: Paulist Press, 1979), 184–98. As it seems to me, however, these distinctions are not very clarifying; they rather seem to confuse judgments of prudence ("such and such is the right thing to do") with judgments of conscience ("I must do what I know to be the right thing, whatever the consequences"). Everyone must be a "deontologist" on *this* (second) level, if he does not want to deny that one must follow one's conscience (see for this some of my publications to which I refer further on). For supplementary terminological clarifications, see J. M. Finnis, *Fundamentals of Ethics* (Washington, D.C.: Georgetown University Press; Oxford: Clarendon Press, 1983), 81–86.

tue of their very object, that is, *independent* of further intentions. If we could not sustain the distinction between the "object" and "ulterior intentions" of a concrete choice, adherents of "consequentialism" or "proportionalism" could successfully deny being implicated in the encyclical's criticism of these positions.

In order to answer the above question, however, another very important assertion of the encyclical must not be overlooked. After having affirmed, in number 78, that "the morality of the human act depends primarily and fundamentally on the 'object' rationally chosen by the deliberate will," the text of the encyclical adds the following remark:

> In order to be able to grasp the object of an act which specifies that act morally, it is therefore necessary to place oneself *in the perspective of the acting person.*

And this is so, the encyclical continues, for the following reason (the emphasis is mine):

> The object of the act is in fact a *freely chosen* kind of behavior. . . . By the object of a given moral act, then, one cannot mean a process or an event of the merely physical order, to be assessed on the basis of its ability to bring about a given state of affairs in the outside world. Rather, that object is the proximate end of a deliberate decision which determines the act of willing on the part of the acting person (*VS* no. 78).

The above-quoted rejection (*VS* no. 79) which follows in the encyclical is in fact formulated in quite a sophisticated way (e.g., it refers both "object" and the predicate "morally evil" to "choice of behavior" and not simply to "behavior").[2] This sentence, repeated in number 82, remains the doctrinal core of the whole encyclical and one of the cornerstones of its argument. And it seems to me that no "teleological" ethical theory—be it "consequentialist" or "proportionalist"—can reasonably deny being affected, indeed, hit in the heart, by this rejection. For it is characteristic of all "teleological" ethical theories that they consider senseless any distinction between "objects" and "further intentions," as well as that they reject the possibility both of judging "wrong" a chosen action independently of all the foreseen consequences, and of speaking on this level as such about "moral evil."

During the following exposition I will, without referring much to the text

2. Compare this also with no. 1761 of the *Catechism of the Catholic Church* (Vatican City: Libreria Editrice Vaticana, 1994), quoted in John Paul II, *Veritatis Splendor* (The Splendor of Truth, 1993), no. 78: "There are certain specific kinds of behavior that are always wrong to choose, because choosing them involves a disorder of the will, that is, a moral evil."

of the encyclical, simply expose how—according to my views, which owe so much to the work of many others—the encyclical's teaching should be understood. I not only intend to follow Aquinas's ethical theory but also to render explicit some implicit presuppositions in the field of action theory that are necessary to render fully intelligible both Aquinas's account of "moral objects" as such and its pertinence for our present problem.[3]

I shall first clarify the term "object" as used in practical reasoning. I then clarify the basic perspective in which we have to consider our problem, the perspective of intentionality, showing how problematic it is when an ethical theory distinguishes "moral" from "non-moral" goods. This opens the way to speak properly about the "object" of a human act, which of course is fundamental for knowing *what* precisely is qualified when an action is qualified as "evil by virtue of its object". In the longest section, I will challenge the distinction between "right-making properties" and "good-making properties" of an action; I argue for a virtue-orientated rather than norm-based—or rule-based—ethics, showing why only the former is able really to explain why there are in fact some "intrinsically evil acts." Next, I shall show how intentionality explains the *rational* structure of what we call the "object" of a human act. Finally, I will add some remarks about how to integrate my analysis into the general frame of a natural law theory.

Objects of Actions as Objects of Practical Reason

According to Aquinas, every action intended by the will is a *"bonum apprehensum et ordinatum per rationem,"* a "good understood and ordered by reason."[4] Clearly human acts are specified by different objects; every potency has its own specific object which is its proper end. However, the human act is morally specified only by an "object insofar as it is related to the principle

3. See a more detailed account in the following of my books and articles: *Natur als Grundlage der Moral* (Innsbruck-Vienna: Tyrolia-Verlag, 1987); *La prospettiva della morale. Fondamenti dell'etica filosofica* (Rome: Armando Editore, 1994); "Menschliches Handeln und seine Moralität. Zur Begründung sittlicher Normen," in Martin Rhonheimer, Andreas Laun, Tatjana Goritschewa, and Walter Mixa, *Ethos und Menschenbild* (St. Ottilien: EOS Verlag, 1989), 45–114; "Zur Begründung sittlicher Normen aus der Natur" and "Ethik-Handeln-Sittlichkeit," *Der Mensch als Mitte und Massstab der Medizin,* ed. Johannes Bonelli (Vienna; New York: Springer-Verlag, 1992), 49–94, 137–74; finally, my investigations into Aquinas's interpretation and completion of Aristotle's action theory published under the title *Praktische Vernunft und Vernünftigkeit der Praxis* (Berlin: Akademie Verlag, 1994).

4. *ST* I-II, q.20 a.1 ad1. In *ST* I-II, q.18 a.10, Aquinas affirms that the object that specifies an action morally is a "forma a ratione concepta."

of human acts, that is reason."[5] One must, therefore, guard against identifying the object which provides the moral specification of an act with "things" or the natural ends of single potencies. As Germain Grisez has put it, "Human acts have their structure from intelligence. Just insofar as an action is considered according to its naturally given structure, it is to that extent not considered as a *human* act—i.e., as a moral act—but rather as a physiological process or as instinctive behavior. Action with a given structure and acts structured by intelligence differ as totally as nature differs from morality. Nature has an order which reason can consider but cannot make and cannot alter. Morality has an order which reason institutes by guiding the acts of the will."[6]

The object which provides the moral specification is always the object of a human act *just insofar as* it is an act of a *human* being. Without the act of practical reason which relates to any object in a specifically *moral* way, there is neither a human act nor a personal meaning of such acts. To speak of the "object of an action" is to speak of the content of an *intentional* action. That is to say, the morally relevant object of an action is the content of an act *insofar as* it is the object of an *intentio voluntatis* (whether this is on the level of the choice of concrete, particular actions, or on the level of intending *further* ends for the sake of which a concrete action is chosen as a means). With this we see that every object is equally the object of the practical reason which orders and regulates, the fundamental rule or measure of which is the natural law. Only in this way do both the various natural ends of human potencies and the *usus rerum exteriorum* become integrated into the personal *suppositum* in a cognitive-practical way. They thus become objectified in their intelligibility, which renders possible the recognition of their morally objective meaning.

Intentionality and So-called Non-Moral Goods

The *bona propria*, that is, the proper goods toward which the individual potencies are ordered as ends—considered in their ontic structure, independently of their being potencies of a human person, that is, considered on

5. "ab obiecto relato ad principium actuum humanorum, quod est ratio" (*ST* I-II, q.18 a.8). The "bonum virtutis" consists "ex quadam commensuratione actus ad circumstantias et finem, *quam ratio facit*" (*In II Sent.*, d.39, q.2 a.1).

6. Germain Grisez, "A New Formulation of a Natural-Law Argument against Contraception," *The Thomist* 30, no. 4 (1966): 343.

the level of their *"genus naturae"*—are not yet moral goods which are as such morally significant (they are not *bona debita* for the acting person as such).[7] But calling them "non-moral" goods seems to be equally erroneous. One simply cannot make moral judgments on the level of *"genus naturae."* However, to call these proper goods of potencies "non-moral goods" is actually a moral qualification since it is possible only from an ethical perspective. To be ethical, a perspective must take account of the acting subject's intentional relation to acts and ends. To affirm that the ends of natural inclinations are non-moral goods or non-moral values is to assert that they do not possess an inherent *"proportio ad rationem."* This would mean that they were exactly *as inclinations "indifferentes ex specie,"* in St. Thomas's language, or that these inclinations, acts, and ends are morally indifferent not only if we consider them "abstractly" in their *"genus naturae,"* but also if we conceive them as forming part of the human *suppositum*. Again, this would mean that only *further* circumstances or intentions of the acting subject *by which* he acts on these inclinations and performs the acts proper to them would have a moral qualification, while the inclinations themselves would not.

To look at natural inclinations and their ends in an abstract ontic way is, however, neither ethically nor anthropologically an adequate way of considering them. It simply can never lead to a morally qualifying judgment, and this is precisely what the assertion means which states that they are "indifferent" *("adiaphora")* or non-moral goods.[8] It is not the ends of these inclinations which are non-moral, but rather the abstract way of considering them which is non-moral. The problem springs from looking at natural inclinations simply as *natural* inclinations, inclinations of the *"genus naturae"* abstracted from the actual human person.[9]

7. The distinction between *("actus"* or *"finis") proprium* on the one side, and *debitum* on the other, goes back to *ST* I-II, q.91 a.2. See for this my *Natur als Grundlage der Moral*, 72ff.

8. Cf. *ST* I-II, q.18 a.8: Aquinas arrives at identifying an act as indifferent *"in specie"* by the assertion that the *act as such* has no proportion to the *"ordo rationis"*; considered in itself the choice of such an act is not yet meaningful for practical reason, "sicut levare festucam de terra, ire ad campum et huiusmodi." It is something quite different to consider an act, which by itself *does* possess such a "proportio ad rationem," *independently* of this relation to reason, that is, on its merely natural level (e.g., an act of eating or nutrition, an act of sexual copulation). In this case, this will be a biological, physiological, or psychological viewpoint that in no way allows a moral judgment. The qualification of an act as "indifferent," however, *is* precisely such a moral judgment.

9. Aquinas also sometimes uses the expression *"consideratio absoluta,"* that is, a consideration of acts detaching them from the wider context in which a moral qualification would be possible. Cf. *In IV Sent.*, d.16, q.3, a.1, qla.2 ad2: "aliqui actus ex suo genere sunt mali vel boni. . . . Hoc autem ex quo actus reperitur in tali genere, quamvis sit de substantia eius inquantum est ex

This means that inclinations, their proper acts, and ends are falsely looked at as "data," "facts," and "states of affairs," from the perspective of an outside observer, rather than as inclinations of an intellectually and thus willingly striving person. As such, every human being experiences his inclinations as *his* inclinations, as something that he willingly and intentionally *pursues*. This, precisely, is not recognizable from the viewpoint of an outside observer.

From the viewpoint of the external observer we also say that birds build nests because the outcome of a bird's gathering different materials and executing determinate bodily movement is in fact a nest. But do birds really build nests? That is, do they perform the *action* of "building a nest"? For this they should *intend*, in gathering materials, the goal of building a nest; they should gather materials, move, and work *for the sake of* building a nest. Moreover, they even should also intend the "why" of building the nest, for example, "to protect their offspring." With good reason we assume that they indeed are not doing this.[10] A human person, however, who strives for self-preservation or for the care of his offspring, and who performs corresponding actions, does not only "arrive at" preserving his life, etc.; rather, he also *intends* it *in* his actions. He does something *for the sake of* preserving himself and caring for his offspring, and this "for the sake of" is a content of his *will*. Self-preservation and care for offspring are, in this case, objects of an intending will, guided by reason. And as such, the corresponding goods (self-preservation, care for offspring) are much more than the resulting *states of affairs* of "self-preservation" or "protection of offspring." It rather is a practical principle which guided a freely chosen act and its intentional content, a content which determines as an intelligible good the agent's will.[11] These contents of intentionality (self-preservation, care for others, and similar things) are *already on the level of natural inclination* a "good" of a striving *human person* and, therefore, "good

---

genere moris, tamen est extra substantiam ipsius secundum quod consideratur ipsa substantia actus absolute: unde aliqui actus sunt idem in specie naturae qui differunt in specie moris; sicut fornicatio et actus matrimonialis." Both fornication and a matrimonial act are, as sexual acts considered in their *"genus naturae"* and in their corresponding physiological, biological, and in a sense also in their affective aspects, strictly identical acts. Nevertheless the human sexual act is not an *"actus indifferens"* if considered in its *"genus moris."*

10. This is not an argument against teleology in nature. In fact, just the opposite is the case. This teleology exists because we affirm both (1) that birds do not *intend* the goal of building a nest and (2) that they indeed do what they do *for the sake* of building a nest, so the "intention" is inherent in nature.

11. Compare again John Paul II, *Veritatis Splendor*, no. 78 (emphasis mine): "The object of the act of willing is in fact a freely chosen kind of behavior. To the extent that it is in conformity with the order of reason, *it is the cause of the goodness of the will; it perfects us morally.*"

for man" in the context of the person as a whole. It is precisely this which we call a "moral good." "Moral goods" are the contents of *acts of the will.* And the contents of acts of the will are precisely that which we call, from a moral viewpoint, their *objects.*

We can conclude that to call the ends pursued by natural inclinations "non-moral" goods signifies, in the final analysis, a moral qualification (or "disqualification") based on the *"genus naturae"* of these inclinations and their corresponding acts. This, however, is an illicit *transgressio in aliud genus* and, therefore, results in a conclusion easily recognizable as a sort of "naturalistic fallacy." The naturalistic fallacy is based on a failure to see that the *"genus naturae"* and the *"genus moris"* are not derivable one from the other.[12] The fallacy occurs when one adopts a morally qualifying predicate on the level of *"genus naturae."* But "moral indifference" actually *is* such a predicate. Equally, "morally right" is a morally qualifying predicate. It is a predicate which proportionalists adopt for actions on the basis of the resulting balance of nonmoral goods which can be foreseen.

In this context the Stoic doctrine of the *adiaphora* is sometimes invoked:[13] life, health, beauty, property, social status, honor, etc. are not, one says, goods which determine a person's being a *good* person. This depends exclusively on the goodness of the will. I would argue in the following way against this attempt to defend consequentialism by invoking this Stoic teaching: the Stoic doctrine intends only to differentiate the sphere of being from the sphere of acting. Indeed, whether somebody is a good or a wicked person does not depend on the state in which he happens to find himself or the state in which he happens to arrive *independently* of his willing as an acting subject. "Good" and "evil" as objects of practical reason and intentional striving, however, are not at all states of affairs, in which the acting subject happens to find himself. As soon as the agent relates *practically* to goods/bads as life, health, physical integrity, truth, property, it is no longer possible to call those goods or bads *adiaphora,* indifferent things or "extra-moral" goods; for the practical relation itself involves, with regard to them, one willingly taking a position on the basis of a judgment of practical reason; and it is precisely this which determines the

12. This reproach, which I have invoked against adherents of so-called "teleological ethics," is not, it seems to me, sufficiently refuted by W. Wolbert in his critique of my position; cf. Werner Wolbert, "Naturalismus in der Ethik. Zum Vorwurf des naturalistischen Fehlschlusses," *Theologie und Glaube* 79 (1989): 234–67, esp. 259ff.

13. Bruno Schüller, *Die Begründung sittlicher Urteile;* Werner Wolbert, *Ethische Argumentation und Paränese in 1 Kor 7* (Düsseldorf: Patmos, 1981).

quality of the *will* as a good or an evil will. So precisely insofar as a good is a *practical* good (or object of a free will orientated to action) it *cannot* be a non-moral good *because it is impossible that the will relates to "good" in a non-moral way* (not even to a piece of bread practically judged and chosen as "to be eaten here and now"). The Stoics only wanted to emphasize that moral goodness consists in an attitude of indifference with regard to any good other than virtue itself. So, they intended to render praxis itself indifferent as far as it relates to these goods called *adiaphora*. The important thing, the Stoics affirmed, is to be virtuous, which means to live in *apathia* with regard to indifferent goods. Consequentialists and proportionalists, however, are not Stoics. For they assert that precisely in the sphere of these "indifferent goods" man has to take responsibility for optimizing these goods (and minimizing the bads), and that this is the basic criterion of the "rightness" of an action. That means that they also consider the *practical* relation to single *adiaphora* as "morally indifferent" (while Stoics want to render insignificant this practical relation) and that only the action, which optimizes them, is morally right. This, however, is a thesis in the field of action theory which is profoundly problematic.

"Object" in the Perspective of Human Actions

This problematic consists in confusing the viewpoint of the "first person" (the agent's perspective) with the viewpoint of the "third person" (the observer's viewpoint). To a large extent, these two perspectives correspond to two quite different concepts of human action: the intentional and the causal-eventistic concept.[14] The latter looks at actions "from outside" and sees them as *events which cause determinate effects*. Events which cause effects, however, are not yet actions (it could, for example, be an earthquake). From such a perspective, "acting" can be *reconstructed*, as it were, only by interpreting the foreseen connection between act-event and its effect as being the reason for which a rational subject has performed this particular act. An action would be explained precisely when it was possible to indicate those *reasons* which the agent might have had for performing the action. The same applies to its moral qualification: the action itself and its effects are simply events or states of affairs (that is, non-moral realities). Only those reasons which an agent

14. Regarding the importance of the perspective of the "first person," see J. M. Finnis, *Fundamentals of Ethics*, 114ff.; Giuseppe Abbà, *Felicità, vita buona e virtù* (Rome: LAS, 1989); Angel Rodríguez Luño, *Etica* (Florence: Le Monnier, 1992), and my own *La prospettiva della morale.*

might have for causing through the action-event x the effect y (the state of affairs) are morally qualifiable; this, however, only as "morally right" or "morally wrong." This, I should add, is more a qualification of effects (of y) and their desirability than a qualification of the actions (of x) by which these effects are brought about.

For example, the action-event x brought about by A could consist in causing (in what way does not matter) the death of P. The caused state of affairs will be "death of P." Only the reasons for the desirability of P's death (in the context of a balance of other goods and bads) would determine whether "to do x" is right or wrong. Such a reason may be, for example, the foreseeable consequences of A's doing x for *all* concerned (i.e., also the effects of doing x with regard to the life of Q, R, S, . . . , Z as a consequence of A's doing x; e.g., in a case of hostage-taking and blackmail).

What here, however, is entirely put aside is precisely the acting person as a subject which *intends* something *in* doing x; the acting subject, therefore, which performs x *for the sake of* causing P's death (with the *purpose* of killing him). That is: what is put aside is the *choice* of "killing P" as a setting of A's will against the life of P. This also means: what is put aside is A's taking a position with regard to a specific *person* to which he owes, as to his fellowman, this and that. This act of choice can adequately be seen only by looking at human actions in the perspective of the first person: from such a viewpoint there are not only two states of affairs (an action-event and its resulting effect), but also the act of *intending* P's death. This intentionality (which here is a choice, the choice of an action) cannot be reduced to "causing the state of affairs of P's death." Otherwise there would be no difference between what an earthquake "does" and what an acting person does: the object and intentional content of "causing P's death" means to set one's will against the life of P (= against P in the dimension of what fundamentally is "good-for-him") and this positioning of one's will constitutes a specific relation between the acting person and P. The content of this "taking a position" shapes the agent's will and is, as such, the content of a free will, and is "good" or "evil" wholly *independently* of other (foreseeable) resulting states of affairs which might be brought about as a consequence of A's abstaining from killing P (as, for example, saving the lives of Q, R, S, . . . , Z).

From an observer's viewpoint there is, therefore, no difference between "causing P's death" and "killing P," that is, "doing something *for the sake of* causing P's death." From the observer's viewpoint we may say in the same way "John killed ten persons" and "the earthquake killed ten persons" (as we affirm "the bird built a nest"). What we cannot say in either case from this particular perspective is: besides the ten killed persons, there is also a *murderer.* In the case of the earthquake this would be simply nonsense; in the case of John, however, it *could* well be the case that he is, in fact, a murderer. But it will never be possible to justify such a differentiation from the observer's viewpoint (otherwise we should equally admit that an earthquake at least *could* be something like a murderer). In reality, however, "to kill P" is not simply "to cause P's being dead," but rather it is *to choose, to intend, to want* P's death (for the sake of *whatever* further end). Those practical goods which are objects of our actions (and here P's death is, for the agent, a "practical good," the content of his action) are never such objects simply in their natural, ontic value-quality as states of affairs, but rather as objects of an act of the will guided by reason. That is why objects of actions—precisely *because* of their being objects of a human action—are goods in a *moral* sense. As said before: *bonum apprehensum et ordinatum per rationem.*

Therefore, *practical* reason, which is embedded in appetite, and the corresponding moral reflection never relate to the *"bona propria"*—the particular goods of single natural inclinations—as mere state of affairs on the level of their *"genus naturae"*; as such they *cannot* be objects or contents of the natural inclination of a *human person* who relates to them appetitively, by will informed by reason. For whom is "self-preservation" ever simply something given, a good only to be "taken into account" or a mere state of affairs, no matter how desirable? For whom is it ever a "non-moral" good, that is, a good which does not concern him *as* a person striving for the fulfillment of his being? As it was said, the ontic-natural aspect of these goods or ends is a *posterior* abstraction which abstracts them from the context of practical self-experience; so, this purely natural aspect is a *reduction* of the proper intelligibility of these goods.

The goods of natural inclinations are never simply a set of given facts, and man is not simply the sum of various inclinations. They rather constitute the proper practical self-experience of persons as *a certain kind* of being. They form a whole, grasped by intelligence as "my" being. So, the practical self-experience of man as naturally striving for goods is precisely what constitutes the *identity* of a person as a *human* person: every inclination and its proper good are experienced as correlated to *my own* striving and not as something alien to me, as, for example, nature which surrounds me, the world in which

I am placed, my environment.[15] This "good-for-me" as object of a reason-guided will, as intelligible human good, is the content of true self-love which, through the Golden Rule (a rule of reason and as such a rule of the structural principle of justice based on acknowledgment of others as equal to me), leads to the command "Love your neighbor as you love yourself."

This kind of self-experience reflects the original ontological or anthropological integration of different natural parts of the human *suppositum.* On the basis of a metaphysic of the *suppositum,* such an experience is open for a deeper explanation. So it becomes obvious that each natural inclination by its very nature possesses, in the context of the person as a whole and precisely as an inclination *belonging* to a human person, a meaningfulness which from the beginning transcends the mere *"genus naturae."* This transcendence is destroyed or at least obscured by an abstract view which detaches these inclinations from their original context as inclinations of a human person. In a moral objectivation, the "natural meaning" of each natural inclination is precisely a *personal* meaning which must not be identified with its *"genus naturae."*

The proper work of natural reason—the acts of which are always acts of a person—consists in grasping the transcendence of particular goods, exactly on the basis of the fact that they are integrated into the whole of the human *suppositum:* as *intelligible goods.* As such an experienced intelligible whole of goods they form the "Self." In its natural act, which corresponds to a natural

15. This, it seems to me, is an often overlooked differentiation. An example is provided by Louis Janssens, "Ontic Evil and Moral Evil," *Louvain Studies* 4 (1972): 121 n. 34, and 135f. The bodily dimension of man is here conceived simply as "material part of the material world"; it is named "human" only insofar as this "material part of the material world" participates at the same time in the subjectivity of single human individuals. Therefore, Janssens considers the body, in a consequent way, as a "means to action," as an instrument of man's subjectivity for his being able to act in the sphere of the external world. With this, the properly "human" is restricted to a spiritually understood subjectivity (without taking into account that also the body *originally* forms part of man's subjectivity). This, however, is not a personalist view of man but a view that we could call a "personalistic spiritualism." The consequences of this view are, in the case of Janssens, absolutely clear; e.g., when he says that the exterior act *("actus exterior")* is an "exterior *event*" (120), which, in itself, does not possess a moral meaning because it does not yet participate in the subjectivity of man, i.e., before it is assumed by the spiritual "ego" as a "means to action." Therefore, bodily acts are, according to this view, a sort of "raw material," determined in their moral meaning exclusively by the spirit. This is obviously true as far as bodily acts need to be "operationally" integrated into the whole of the person. It is not true, however, as an anthropological thesis that reduces "moral meaning" to what proceeds from the spiritual part of the soul or even as a thesis that reduces "human person" to "spirit." Cf. also Martin Rhonheimer, "Contraception, Sexual Behavior, and Natural Law," *Linacre Quarterly* 56, no. 2 (1989): 20–57. Also published in *"Humanae Vitae": 20 anni dopo.* Atti del II Congresso Internazionale di Teologia Morale, Rome, November 9–12, 1988 (Milan: Edizioni Ares, 1989), 73–113.

inclination to virtue, that is, to a life guided by reason, reason comprehends these particular goods as *human* goods and, therefore, as fundamental practical goods of the person. These goods constitute our identity, the consciousness of *who we are* (I and the others) and fundamentally shape the will in respect of "the good for man."

A Fallacious Distinction: "Right Making Properties" versus "Good Making Properties"

Moral philosophers who defend—however divergent be their approaches—a consequentialist position (a "teleological ethic") usually are much concerned with emphasizing a fundamental difference between the "moral *rightness*" (or the "right-making properties") and the "moral *goodness*" (the "good-making properties") of an action.[16] The first, they say, concerns the question about the properties which render an action "right" or "wrong"; the second is related to those properties of an action insofar as it springs from a free *will.* By way of balancing goods and bads, only the question about the "rightness of types of actions" is meant to be resolved. And this, it is asserted, is the question which properly belongs to so-called "normative ethics." The question, however, about what makes the will of the acting subject a "good" will does not, according to their view, depend on whether an action is "right" or "wrong" but rather, for example, on whether one acts out of benevolence toward other persons, out of love of justice, with a will to fairness or to respecting the other's conscience, with a "Christian intentionality," etc.

Of course in a sense this is rather obvious. It is true in the sense that an involuntary, and thus not imputable, error about what one has to do—in this sense a wrong action—may not hinder the will of somebody who acts in this way from being a good will, even as it does the wrong thing, for example, a will which, in fact, intends justice even if it does not do the just thing. The corresponding action, then, would be at the same time "morally good" and "wrong." The widespread acceptance of this distinction seems to be caused, to a large extent, by the possibility of this state of affairs. It is, however, a case in which the agent in reality does not choose and thus willingly perform the

16. The distinction between the "goodness" and the "rightness" of an action was introduced by W. D. Ross, *The Right and the Good* (Oxford: Clarendon Press, 1930). The terms "right-making" and "good-making characteristics" ("wrong-making" and "bad-making characteristics") of an action was first used in 1946 by C. D. Broad, in his famous essay, quoted above, "Some of the Main Problems of Ethics."

action which he *thinks* he is choosing and performing. It is, therefore, an exceptional case which, for analytical purposes, must be set aside until *after* having determined what basically causes the goodness and the rightness of actions; precisely because of this, it cannot serve as a paradigm. To be able to justify a distinction between "right" and "good" we must start from the normal condition in which actions are chosen and performed, that is, from the condition that the agent chooses and thus willingly performs exactly the action which he *believes* he is choosing and performing.

Now, the predicates "right" and "wrong" are morally qualifying only insofar as we consider them as predicates for *human acts*. Certainly, a physician may perform an operation "rightly" (correctly, well, efficiently, competently, etc.); despite this, his way of acting may be qualified as "wrong" (e.g., if it is—in the first sense—a "well-done" abortion). The first type of qualification concerns the technical aspect of the physician's acting, the second concerns the *moral* rightness of the choice of this action. In *both* cases we may, instead of "right" or "wrong," also call the action, respectively, "good" or "evil." The designation derives from the *perspective* in which we consider the action: either we consider it from the technical perspective (the aspect of surgical techniques) or we consider it from a moral perspective (the aspect of its being the voluntary and deliberate action of a human person; this is the properly moral perspective). The second perspective includes the first (one cannot act in a morally right way without caring about one's technical competence). The distinction, however, between "*morally* right" and "*morally* good" seems to be off the point here. The only relevant distinction is the distinction between "*non-morally* (e.g., technically) right/wrong" and "*morally* right/wrong"; the second, however, is equal to (morally) "good" and (morally) "evil."

The position I am criticizing overlooks the fundamental difference between *praxis* and *poiesis.* taking its orientation from a "poietical" model of action.[17] It is indeed characteristic of technical actions that its (technical) "rightness" is distinguished from the goodness of the will of the person who performs a technical act. Aristotle, however, taught us that the goodness of a praxis (which is *eupraxia*) and the goodness of a moral agent (and this means his willful striving: *orexis*) is a specific kind of "rightness" *(orthotês):* the rightness of *prohairesis,* of the *choice* of an action. Indeed, we can say that there exist fundamental structures of the "rightness" of desire which reveal them-

17. See for this also Rüdiger Bubner, *Handlung, Sprache und Vernunft,* 2nd ed. (Frankfurt/M: Suhrkamp, 1982), 74–90.

selves precisely through the *"lex naturalis."* These structures determine—despite the legitimacy of a limited and well-defined balancing of goods—that certain actions are always *wrong,* precisely *because the desire or will involved in these kinds of actions cannot be "right." Yet a will which is not "right" is an evil will.* In this sense it is "wrong" to *choose* to kill a human person (that is: to set one's will against another man's life), whatever be the *further* intention or end for the sake of which this is chosen. To affirm that such a choice is "not right" (or "wrong") means precisely to affirm that this is a disorientated choice of the will, that this is a type of action which *as such* ("in itself") is *evil.* "As such" or "in itself" here signifies: independently of further intentions or foreseen consequences.[18] Such an action springing from a corresponding choice is evil, because it shapes the will, rendering it an evil will, a will directed against "the good for man" (here from the perspective of justice). This precisely is what we designate "not right" or "wrong" in a *moral* sense.[19]

Hence, the distinction between "right-making properties" and "good-making properties" is in principle questionable. We always have to describe actions and behaviors as objects of *choices* and, therefore, as *intentional* ac-

18. Of course it may be considered as "good" (desirable) that P finally dies (and we may even pray for it); in this sense we also say: "It was precisely the 'right' thing for him (and probably also for his relatives) that he finally died." With this, however, we do not qualify an action or the choice of an action, but a state of affairs and its desirability. The goodness, rightness, or desirability of such a state of affairs, however, cannot serve as a criterion for qualifying a possible *action* of mercy-killing. This is so because, in such an action, a will set against P's life is involved, with the *further* intention of bringing about a desirable state of affairs.

19. First, this affirmation, as is obvious, presupposes that killing as the execution of capital punishment (pronounced by the competent judicial authority), and taking into account the fact that the punished is really *guilty* according to the standards of penal law, cannot be described as a *choice* of the death of a person. Intentionally this action is (as *any* type of punishment is) "restoration of the order of justice," violated by the criminal and in danger of being disrupted without imposition of punishment. It is precisely *not,* however, the choice of the death of a person as resulting from weighing the good of a person's life against other goods, which by this person's death would be brought about. (Whether capital punishment can be considered as an *adequate, proportionate,* and in this sense, just kind of punishment *at all* is another question that still may be answered negatively; but in an objective-intentional sense it is "punishment" and therefore an act intentionally and objectively belonging to the virtue of justice, and not the choice that a person not be, whether as a means or as an end.) Cf. the excellent treatment of this question in John Finnis, *Fundamentals of Ethics,* 127ff.; and my own remarks in *Natur als Grundlage der Moral,* 371–74, and in *La prospettiva della morale* V, 3, d. Second, the above affirmation also implies the concept of non-intentional side-effects, e.g., in the case of self-defense that (physically) causes the aggressor's death. This means quite precisely that the aggressor's death was not *chosen for the sake* of defending one's life; cf. *ST* II-II, q.64 a.7: "illicitum est quod homo intendat occidere hominem ut seipsum defendat." Here, "intendere" means the elective will referring to the concrete action ("occidere hominem"), while the defense of one's life is the *further* intention *with which* the concrete action is chosen.

tions. From such a perspective, however, the goodness of the will is regarded as depending on the goodness of freely chosen, *wanted* actions which also includes the agent's willingly referring to the specific goal which constitutes the objective intentionality of this action (I will come back to this below). That is why acts of choice are always describable as forms of *rightness,* that is, of the rightness of desire or of the will. This enables us to indicate specific kinds of actions which are never to be chosen because they are not consistent with a good will, for example, the choice of killing a person, whatever be the further intention. On the other hand, it is indeed possible to choose what is morally right with an evil intention; or to choose to do the morally wrong thing with a good will. Moral philosophers and theologians have always known this in the past, and it has traditionally been considered in ethics.[20]

Certainly many decisions, probably even the great majority of them, are legitimately worked out on the basis of weighing goods and consequences. This is particularly true for decisions taken in a wider social context (e.g., social, economical, scientific, and research policy). But corresponding possibilities of action are, on the grounds of *moral reasons,* restricted. They are restricted by the condition that they be consistent with the fundamental "rightness of the will" on the level of concrete choices of actions. Here we encounter the kind of responsibilities which we are accustomed to expressing in so-called *absolute prohibitions.* On this level, the "right" and the "good" (or: the "wrong" and the "evil") basically are identical. Here, balancing goods and calculating possible consequences is *excluded.*[21]

It is one of the most important assertions of classical virtue ethics that there exist conditions for the fundamental rightness of actions which depend on basic structures of the "rightness of desire" and that it is therefore possible to describe particular types of actions, the *choice* of which always involves wrong desire. However, an ethic which understands itself—on the level of "normative ethics"—as providing a rational discourse for the purpose of justifying moral *norms* (or rules) will never be able to acknowledge this. "Norm-ethics" are "objectivistic" in the sense that they *may not,* on the lev-

20. Cf. Peter Geach, "Good and Evil," *Analysis* 17 (1956): 33–42; republished in *Theories of Ethics,* ed. Philippa Foot (Oxford: Oxford University Press, 1967), 64–73; see esp. 72.

21. This is why John Paul II, *Veritatis Splendor,* no. 77, rejects in a very specific and restricted way the method of balancing goods and evils: "The weighing of the goods and evils foreseeable as the consequence of an action is not an adequate method for determining whether the choice of that concrete kind of behaviour is 'according to its species,' or 'in itself,' morally good or bad, licit or illicit."

el of the concrete performance of actions, include in their reflection the acting subject and his willingly "taking a position" with regard to "good" and "evil" *in* choosing this or that particular action. Similarly they cannot pose the question about the "rightness of desire," or about the "truth of subjectivity," on the level of concrete choices of particular actions (*independently* of taking into account further intentions regarding the state of affairs or the weighing of consequences which foreseeably will be brought about by these actions or by refraining from them).

I concede it to be true, as has been argued,[22] that the traditional doctrine about the *"fontes moralitatis" as such* does not resolve problems of normative ethics; it rather presupposes these problems to be already resolved. For with respect to this approach, everything depends each time on what one considers to be the "object" of an action. Consequentialists will assert that to determine the object of a concrete action, one has to take into account its foreseeably resulting consequences for all concerned. In this sense, consequentialism does not deny the doctrine about the *"fontes moralitatis"*; it merely puts forward a specific solution about how to work out what the "object" of a particular action is.

Nevertheless this classical doctrine about "sources of morality" contains an undeniable assertion which, however, is implicitly denied by consequentialism. It is the assertion that, with regard to human action, it is possible each time to *distinguish* between (1) an "object" by which this action (and the agent's will) is already morally specified as "good," "evil," or "indifferent" *independently* of *further* intentions and (2) these further intentions. So the classical viewpoint holds that there are actions which are evil despite the best of intentions or despite the foreseen and intended outcomes precisely because the *choice* of this particular kind of action *through* which these laudable intentions are meant to be fulfilled must already be considered as morally evil. It will, however, never be possible to render intelligible this moral methodology on the grounds of an ethic which from the beginning is concerned with justifying "moral norms." This is so because in such an approach the *distinction* between "object" and *further* intentions necessarily drops out of view. The only thing which a norm-ethic can produce in the way of an action theory are the particular "occurrences" ("actions"), on the one hand, and the consequences brought about by them, on the other. If an agent *intends* the

22. Cf. Bruno Schüller, "Die Quellen der Moralität. Zur systematischen Ortung eines alten Lehrstückes der Moraltheologie," *Theologie und Philosophie* 59 (1984): 535–59.

best consequences, then it is these which come to be designated the "object" of his "act."

But this does not correspond to our ordinary experience as acting subjects and to the way we arrive at moral decisions; it rather has about it the air of casuistry. From the viewpoint of the acting subject we always encounter at least two intentionalities to be distinguished. If I break the promise of repaying somebody a determinate amount of money, causing by this his economic ruin because I, simultaneously, intend to prevent by this action the ruin of many others, I have *chosen* to break the promise given to my creditor *for the sake of* realizing an intention which is very laudable in itself. But here the object of choice ("breaking the promise") is not less intentionally "taking a position" than the further intention ("benefiting others"). The same applies to killing or lying with good further intentions.

Moral virtue is not only, as it is sometimes asserted, the will or the free determination to do "the right thing" each time. Were it like this, there would exist only one single moral virtue. Instead moral virtue is the habitual rightness of *appetite* (of sensual affections, passions, and of the will, the rational appetite) related to the various spheres of human praxis. An act which is *according* to virtue is an act which is suited to cause this habitual rightness of appetite which produces "the good person." To keep one's promise is indeed such an act according to moral virtue.

Certainly, we can describe the action "to promise" from the very beginning in an "eventistic" way, say, as a kind of uttering words (a "speech act") by which A causes in B the mental state of being certain that A will do x. One may for various reasons consider it very beneficial that in a society there exists a practice of this sort. So one will formulate a rule (or norm) according to which one is bound to abstain from any performance which could deprive others from being certain that, whenever A performs the speech act of "promising x," x will be brought about by A. The norm "never break promises" means precisely "always abstain from weakening the practice of promise-keeping." Even if one holds that the rightness of an action has to be determined exclusively on the basis of its foreseeable consequences, one must equally consider that the weakening of the practice of "promise-keeping" will be one of the consequences—probably the most weighty one—to be included in the balance. So, on the basis of such a rule-utilitarianism, one should insist that one is always obliged to keep promises. Or more precisely: one will not insist that promises have to be kept but rather that the *rule* or *norm* "keep your promises" has to be *observed.* This is an important difference (which will become clear immediately). The rule does not express the intrinsic morality of a type of action but rather *constitutes* the reasonableness of a certain behavior on the grounds of the utility of the rule under which this behavior is subsumed and which is to be maintained by this behavior (for the benefit of society, of course). It is obvious that there remains the possibility of conflict with other such rules ("conflicts of obligations"); consequently the rule cannot be valid "absolutely." As a result we have to work out which rule has to be followed in such a case: either on the basis of a "hyperrule," or by arguing in an act-utilitarian way. Utilitarian ethics thus tends to become a complicated attempt to resolve the problems of "norm-utilitarianism." Actually it becomes much more concerned with resolving the problems of utilitarian ethical theory than with resolving ethical problems.

It is quite clear that in all these cases an agent may very well do the "right" thing with an evil will, and sometimes the "wrong" thing with a good will (calculating or subsuming incorrectly or applying the wrong rule, though intending the overall benefit of society or of all concerned). Here, the discourse concerned with grounding norms and resolving cases of conflict of rules and obligations must be sharply distinguished from another discourse, the one concerned with the conditions of goodness and wickedness of appetite and will. This distinguishing does not, however, reflect the requirements and the structure of moral action but merely the requirements which arise from the particular characteristics of a "norm-ethic." As said before, with such arguments one does not resolve *ethical* problems, but at most, if at all, the intrinsic problems of a particular ethical theory.

In reality, as acting subjects, we neither observe nor follow norms or rules, nor do we work out our decisions each time exclusively on the basis of foreseeable consequences for all those affected by our actions. Instead, human action realizes itself in the context of definite "moral relationships," the relationships between concrete persons (fellow-men, friends, married persons, parents and children, superiors and subordinates, employer and employee, creditor and debtor, physician and patient, partners in a contract, persons who live in a particular community, etc.).[23] Here, it is always concerned with what we *owe*

23. This category of "moral relationship" and its importance for explaining responsibility in moral decision making was very well emphasized by Robert Spaemann, "Wer hat wofür Verantwortung? Zum Streit um deontologische oder teleologische Ethik," *Herder Korrespondenz* 36 (1982): 345–50 and 403–8. The subsequent criticisms by A. Elsässer, F. Purger, and P. Müller-

to others, with the question of right and of good will toward particular fellowmen, with the question of responsibilities toward concrete persons.

Let us consider again the example of promise-keeping. Above we have defined "to promise" ("eventistically") as an utterance by which A causes in B the mental state of being certain that A will do x. However, the bringing about of B's mental state of being convinced that A will do x is not necessarily a promise; it could also be a menace, an announcement, or a reassurance (what is really *meant* by a speech act like "You can be sure that tomorrow morning I'll come and see you"?). The above eventistic description of promising contains everything except the element which confers on this speech-act the quality of being a promise. This it will be only if A wants to *confer on B a right or* a *claim* on A's doing x. So B's certitude that A will do x is grounded in a relation of *justice* caused precisely by the promissory act. Exactly this relation between A and B (that is: B's having a claim or a right on A's doing x, and B's owing to A to do x)—a relation brought about by the speech-act "I promise you"—shows that a norm "keep your promises" is nothing else than a more particular or specific version of the principle of justice to render each one what one owes him. The promissory act indeed creates a relationship between persons in which this general rationale of justice now is valid.

It may happen that a situation changes in such a way that the doing of x (for whatever reason) subsequently turns out to be an unjust action; or even that doing x was unjust from the very beginning, that is, that A had promised B to do something unjust. Is it possible that B has a claim (a right) on A's committing an unjust act? Certainly not. The promise becomes in reality vain (or reveals itself as vain or immoral from the beginning). So the promise, in reality, is not "broken"; by not keeping it no injustice is committed; rather the very promissory act was unjust, and it now would be according to justice that A in a way indemnifies B, who has been deceived. In order to be able to judge whether a promise keeps binding the person who made it, the consequences of doing x must be considered (an action without *any* consequence is not an action at all). But these will always be the consequences in the sphere of the question whether B continues licitly to *claim* A's keeping the promise, that is: A's doing x. The question can never arise whether such an *existing* claim may be overridden in favor of other more important or more numerous goods

---

Goldkuhle (ibid., 509ff., 603ff., 606ff.) unfortunately do not enter into the fundamental question posed by Spaemann; Spaemann himself remarks upon this in his concluding reply (*Herder Korrespondenz* 37 [1983]: 79–84).

benefiting Q, R, S, . . . , Z (even if there may be cases in which the benefits for Q, R, S, . . . , Z precisely will determine whether B continues to have a claim on A's doing x). In any case, the relation between A and B established by making the promise, and the consequences relating to Q, R, S, . . . , Z, are two different things; one cannot say that we are, *on principle,* responsible for all the foreseen consequences of our actions or omissions. B's being deceived by a promise which may possibly not be kept certainly cannot be regarded as simply one among many consequences of not keeping the promise. So it *may* be possible that not keeping a promise is unjust with regard to B even if the state of affairs resulting from not keeping it were, as such, more desirable than the one brought about by keeping the promise. In this case, not keeping it would be morally *wrong* because the choice of an unjust action involves the wrongness of the will.

Anyhow, this view remains far too abstract. In reality things are resolved in other ways. In reality an agent who intends justice will try, for example, to achieve a delay in repaying the debt. Or he will find (or at least try to find) a way to prevent by other means the ruin of Q, R, S, . . . , Z. His refusal to commit an injustice against his creditor by breaking the promise will lead him to discover new lines of action, alternatives, and formerly unseen opportunities. To describe this we would need to tell a story. Virtuous actions are, in this sense, rendered intelligible only in a narrative context.[24] But the right thing to do will always be the action which is consistent with the rightness of appetite, with the rightness of our will's relation to concrete persons with whom we live together in defined relationships.

Many details should be added, and there is still much to be specified. But the fundamental difference between virtue ethics and norm-ethics consists in the fact that for the former the morally right is always determined, *as well* as rightness of appetite, with regard to the "good-for-man" on the level of concrete actions and in relation to particular persons, persons with whom the agent encounters himself living in morally qualified relationships (be they naturally given or relationships established by free acts, such as promises, contracts, etc.). That is why a virtue ethic can speak about actions which are "intrinsically," "always and per se," "on account of their very object" evil (cf. *VS* no. 80). A norm-ethic of utilitarian character, however, that in the last

24. This is one of the very valuable insights of Alasdair MacIntyre's *After Virtue,* 2nd ed. (1981; Notre Dame, Ind.: University of Notre Dame Press, 1984).

analysis is an argumentatively proceeding norm-ethic, cannot do justice to such qualified relationships. Consequently, it is compelled to detach the category of the "rightness of actions" from the category of the "goodness of the will." That is why it simply will not understand that the intentional relation of the will to "justice," i.e., the "just will," is at stake in every concrete choice of a particular action.[25]

Practical Objects: Intentionally Structured as "Forms Conceived by Reason"

So-called "teleological ethics" owes a large amount of its plausibility—as far as Catholic moral theology is concerned—not least to the fact that it was directed against a naturalistic (or "physicalist") misunderstanding of the *"moralitas ab obiecto."*[26] Yet, despite this justified aim, adherents to these "teleological" approaches do not seem to have recognized the real source of this misunderstanding, which consists in overlooking the fact that practical reason is embedded in the intentional process of human acting, being a part of it. That is why, I think, these new approaches remained themselves addicted to a surprising, even extreme, naturalism. Particular actions implicitly are considered by them as analogous to "events" and their outcomes as states of affairs. They implicitly presuppose, on the level of particular actions, a causal-eventistic concept of action (action as causing a state of affairs). I said "implicitly," because adherents of "teleological ethics" do not explicitly defend such a corresponding action theory (they actually deal very little with questions of action theory).[27] That is why they are compelled to reclaim the aspect of intentionality—the aspect of willingly taking a position with regard to "good" and "evil"—on the level of fundamental options and attitudes, on the level of *Gesinnung*. So, consequentialists fail to see that, independently of

25. This, it seems to me, explains why virtue ethics do not require a "personalistic complement." Recent personalism often seems to be an attempt to overcome the one-sided views of modern rule-ethics. Ethics based on the concept of moral virtue are intrinsically "personalistic," but they are also probably more open to rational discourse than many forms of actual personalism.

26. See, e.g., Franz Scholz, *Wege, Umwege und Auswege der Moraltheologie. Ein Plädoyer für begründete Ausnahmen* (Munich: Bonifatius, 1976), 16f.; Joseph Fuchs, "'Intrinsece malum.' Überlegungen zu einem umstrittenen Begriff," in *Sittliche Normen. Zum Problem ihrer allgemeinen und unwandelbaren Geltung,* ed. Walter Kerber (Düsseldorf: Patmos, 1982), 76f.; Peter Knauer, S.J., "The Hermeneutic Function of the Principle of Double Effect," in *Readings in Moral Theology No. 1,* 1–39.

27. A more recent attempt to do so by referring to Kant is not very satisfying, and it remains unclear to what extent the author may be called a representative of "teleological ethics." Cf. Ger-

further intentions required to optimize consequences or goods on the level of caused states of affairs, an action may already be qualifiable as *morally evil.* And this means: that a particular type of action, describable in behavioral terms, may be qualified as causing an *evil will* simply because it is *evil* to want (and, therefore, to choose) certain actions as practical objects (= as the "good to be done"). The problem is bypassed, even veiled, by describing chosen actions from the observer's viewpoint, thus leaving out of consideration precisely the act of choice. Probably the most famous example of such an argumentative reductionism is Caiaphas's advice to the Sanhedrin: "It is better for you that a single man dies for the people, than that the whole people perishes." As a judgment about a simple event or a state of affairs and its desirability this obviously is quite true. But it is well known that Jesus did not simply die but was killed.

Precisely because objects of our actions are intentional objects, that is, objects of acts of the will, they can only be "shaped" by reason; for the will is the appetite which follows the judgment of reason. As Aquinas emphasizes: "Species moralium actuum constituuntur ex formis, prout sunt a ratione conceptae."[28] This "form conceived by reason" is nothing other than the object of an action in its *"genus moris."*

This again is closely connected with the fact that every human action is an *intentional* action. And this is why it is something that does not simply "happen," but something *willingly pursued* and as such *formed* or shaped by reason. A concrete practical matter *("materia circa quam")*—the same applies to the "matter" of natural inclinations—is *as such,* considered in its pure "materiality," always *less* than the content or object of an action with respect to the natural inclination of a *human person.* If in greeting somebody or giving a starting signal, I raise my arm, then "raising my arm" (the matter of action) is *as such* something which can neither be chosen nor performed. The real content of an act of choice and of the describable behavior is exclusively the intentional, that is, human, action "greeting somebody" *or* "giving a starting signal." In this, however, the practical reason which judges the action as a practical good (something good to do here and now) is already involved. To know *what* a person is doing by raising his arm, one must know *why* (in the sense of "what for") he raises his arm. The "why" here is the formal aspect, the

hard Höver, *Sittlich handeln im Medium der Zeit. Ansätze zur handlungstheoretischen Neuorientierung der Moraltheologie* (Würzburg: Echter Verlag, 1988). This book, however, contains some valuable criticisms of positions defended by adherents of "teleological ethics."

28. *ST* I-II, q.18 a.10.

"forma rationis" which only renders understandable the event of the raising of an arm as a human *action.* This "why" (or "what for") confers on the action its *intentional identity* which is able to inform and shape the agent's will.[29]

In his *Philosophical Investigations,* Ludwig Wittgenstein asks, "What is left over if I subtract the fact that my arm goes up from the fact that I raise my arm?"[30] We might answer: what is left over is precisely the *purpose* or *intention* to greet somebody or to give a starting signal. That means that what remains is *"to want* to raise the arm *under the aspect of a specific description"* which is a description of the intentionality involved in the performance. To choose an action "under a description" again involves practical reason which judges "greeting somebody" or "giving a starting signal" as something which is "good" to do here and now. One might object: but you could just simply raise your arm. Well, I would answer, just try to do it! It is true that it might just "happen" (involuntarily, as a reflex, while sleeping); but this is not a human act. If, however, somebody wanted "simply" to raise his arm, he again would do more than simply "raise his arm." If we subtracted from his doing this action the fact that his arm goes up, we would have left over, for example, "wanting to show the author of this paper that he is wrong." What would be left over is a "why," the intentional content or the "form" of this act of "raising one's arm."

Therefore, "to greet somebody by raising one's arm" is properly the object of an action, which *in itself* possesses already an intentional structure. In precisely this structure, respectively the "whole" (the "matter" of the action + its "why" or "what for") is a *"forma a ratione concepta."* Things like "greeting" or affability or gratefulness or justice, that is, corresponding actions to these, do not "exist" in nature. Corresponding "natural forms" do not exist. These

29. Cf. for this G. E. M. Anscombe, *Intention,* 2nd ed. (1957; Oxford: Basil Blackwell, 1963), who conceives, in the course of her analysis, that the question "Why?" in a larger sense (any sort of motives, or also involuntary causes of actions) includes the "What for?" without being reduced to it. Insofar as we are concerned with properly human, voluntary actions, however, the "Why?" precisely is the "What for?" It properly concerns "intentions."

30. Ludwig Wittgenstein, *Philosophical Investigations,* no. 621, ed. G. E. M. Anscombe and R. Rhees, trans. G. E. M. Anscombe (Oxford: Basil Blackwell, 1958), 161e. Wittgenstein thinks that nothing is left over ("Are the kinesthetic sensations my willing?"). Wittgenstein refuses (see the next footnote) to differentiate conceptually, besides the physical fact, an act of willing. In any event, Wittgenstein here clearly confuses the observer's viewpoint ("the fact that my arm goes up") and the acting person's perspective ("I raise my arm"). Nobody ever can really *observe* "I raise my arm"; only "the fact that my arm goes up" is observable. "I raise my arm" can properly be described only as a *choice* by a willing subject. Everyone has personal interior experience of such choices as something different from "kinesthetic sensations."

acts are intentionalities *formed* by practical reason. That is why the *objective* content of human actions can be expressed each time only in an intentional description of the corresponding action. "What" we do is always a "why" we do something *on purpose.* It is a "material doing" *("materia circa quam")* chosen *under a description,* while it is the "description" which actually contains the intentional content of the action. That is why it seems to me correct when Elizabeth Anscombe writes: "We must always remember that an object is not what what is aimed at *is;* the description *under which* it is aimed at is that under which it is *called* the object."[31]

It is often overlooked (as, for example, by L. Janssens) that an object of the will necessarily is an action-matter *"apprehensum et ordinatum a ratione."* For this reason, it possesses by itself a moral specificity; it never can be wanted or chosen *as* a non-moral good or end.[32] Equally one overlooks that the "end" *("finis")* is not only an object of *further* intentions, but also that the particular choice of an action has its proper "end": the action as an object.

That is why, each time Aquinas speaks about *"finis,"* an author like L. Janssens reads *"finis operantis,"* overlooking thereby that the object of the exterior act of the will is in itself an end, but not this *further* end for the sake of which the action itself is chosen; instead it is the sort of end which Aquinas sometimes (very few times) calls the *"finis operis."*[33] This *"finis operis,"* however, is the *basic* intentional content of a concrete action (without which it would not be a human action at all), and therefore something like the "formal object" of an action.[34] Such basic contents are not events like "the raising of an arm," but rather "greeting somebody" or "giving a starting signal." They are neither "things" nor "qualified things" as, for example, a *res aliena;* but actions "under a description" as *"misapropriate a res aliena,"* that is "stealing." The arm

31. Anscombe, *Intention,* § 35, 66.

32. Here we may find probably Janssens's most decisive misjudgment. He assumed that the will is able to relate to "ontic" goods *as* ontic; so he asserts that it is possible to want "per se" an ontic evil on the level of its being only an ontic state of affairs, and that, as such, it can be the object of a choice that, then, would not be subject to moral qualification as a "good" or an "evil" choice. Only if the ontic evil is the end of the further intention with which a choice is performed—if it, therefore, were the proper *reason* of bringing such an evil about—could a corresponding will be called an evil will. Such an objectifying of ontic goods by the elective will, however, is simply impossible; it contradicts the very nature of the will which is "appetitus in ratione" or "intellectual appetite." The will receives its object *through reason.* Janssens's argument is simply naturalistic.

33. Cf. e.g., *In IV Sent.,* d.16, q.3, a.1, qla.2 ad3.

34. Regarding formal and material objects of actions, cf. Anthony Kenny, *Action, Emotion and Will,* 5th ed. (London: Routledge & Kegan, 1976), 187ff.

itself is not able to greet or to give a starting signal; and an action in which a "*res aliena*" is involved is not necessarily a theft (it may also be the action of seizing something stolen carried out by the police). Equally the so-called "*finis operis*" is an *agent's* goal; but it is the goal he pursues independently of the *further* goals he may pursue by choosing this concrete action. It is the goal which specifies the performed action as a determinate *type* of intentional action, the one which Aquinas usually calls the "*finis proximus*" of a human act, that is, its object.

The "species" of an action is precisely the species "*ab obiecto relato ad principium actuum humanorum, quod est ratio.*"[35] The "*finis operis*" is nothing other than the object of *choice* (the choice of the action), which by itself is an act of the will informed by reason.

The so-called "absolute prohibitions," that is, normative propositions which indicate that certain, describable actions may *never* be licitly chosen and willingly performed, therefore relate to actions described *intentionally.* It is impossible to do this independently of the content of the acts of choice which relate to such actions. So, for example (although this is not the case with such prohibited actions), a "norm" cannot refer simply to "raising one's arm" but to "greeting somebody by raising one's arm" or "giving a starting signal by a movement of one's arm." Only to actions described in such a way can a moral norm reasonably relate. The norm "never kill" receives, in this way, a clear structure.[36]

Natural Law: Fundamental Rule for the Goodness of Will

As Aquinas says in one of his most concise phrasings, "Natural law is nothing other than the light of the intellect given us by God by which we recognize what is to be done and what is to be avoided, a light and law which God has bestowed to man in creation."[37] Natural law is not simply an object of human reason, but, like all kinds of law, it consists precisely in judgments

35. *ST* I-II, q.18 a.6.

36. This is also true for the norm of never lying; see my *Natur als Grundlage der Moral,* 346ff.; 367ff. About both killing and lying, see also *La prospettiva della morale,* chap. 5, section 3d. About contraception, see my "Contraception, Sexual Behavior, and Natural Law."

37. *In Duo Praecepta Caritatis et in Decem Praecepta, Prologus:* "lex naturae . . . nihil aliud est nisi lumen intellectus insitum nobis a Deo, per quod cognoscimus quid agendum et quid vitandum. Hoc lumen et hanc legem dedit Deus homini in creatione." And further on: "lumen scilicet intellectus, per quod nota sunt nobis agenda."

of practical reason itself, it is a specific set of *"pro positiones universales rationis practicae ordinatae ad actiones,"* a set of "universal propositions of practical reason directed to actions."[38]

As I have shown elsewhere, there exists a parallelism between the constitution of objects of actions as moral objects on the one hand, and the constitution of the precepts of natural law on the other.[39] Both objects of human actions and precepts of natural law refer to an *"appetibile apprehensum et ordinatum per rationem."* Both the *praeceptum* of the natural law and the object of a concrete action (which is the object of choice, in itself "prescriptive") are *"aliquid a ratione constitutum"*[40] and spring from an *"ordinatio rationis."*[41] By natural law, this *objective*—that is, rationally ordered—meaning of natural inclinations is expressed *in universali.* And, therefore, natural law is properly the law by which particular judgments of practical reason are rectified.[42] So in two senses natural law is a "law of reason": it is a law *constituted* by reason (on the universal level), and a law *referred to* and *regulating* reason (on the level of particular judgments).

In this way the precepts of the natural law are recognizable as properly *practical principles* of the practical intellect determining concrete actions. This intellect possesses its perfection in prudence (practical wisdom). The questions dealt with here were not questions of "normative ethics"; I did not claim to ground specific moral norms. It concerned a question which first had to be clarified before one could even speak about the grounding of moral norms and normative ethics. I wanted to clarify *how,* from a properly *moral* perspective, we have to speak about moral norms and "normative ethics" and what "moral norms" even refer to. Briefly we now can say: "moral norms" are, in ethics and in the moral life, a quite specific way of *speaking* about intentional human actions and their practical principles. More precisely, norms are *normative propositions* (propositions in the mode of "ought," "may," "must not," etc.) about intentional actions *based on* practical principles.[43]

38. *ST* I-II, q.90 a.1 ad2.

39. See my *Natural Law and Practical Reason,* mainly part 2.

40. *ST* I-II, q.94 a.1.

41. Ibid., q.90 a.4.

42. "Lex naturalis est secundum quam ratio recta est" (*In II Sent.,* d.42, q.2, a.5). This would be the appropriate place to speak about the constitution of "prudential" (practical wisdom or "prudence") by the "fines virtutum," and about the twofold (intentional and elective) aspect of moral virtue; finally one must say something about the relation between "synderesis" and prudence. See for this *ST* II-II, q.47 a.6.

43. Regarding the relation of so-called "moral absolutes" to *intentional* actions, see also the

Theories like "teleological ethics" (consequentialism and proportionalism) sometimes present themselves as natural-law theories. They on principle rightly do so, because every natural law theory consists of a theory about practical reason and the structure of moral judgment performed by human reason. And teleological ethical theories, defending the cognitive "moral autonomy" of man, in fact *are* theories about what is meant by "to act according to reason."[44] However, we may now be able to give a critical evaluation of these theories. First, they do not properly have a conception about *principles* of practical reason. This can also be regarded as a consequence of their lack of action-analysis. "Teleological ethics" essentially and exclusively is a decision-making theory: it tries to explain how we work out decisions about what to do here and now. If adherents of this theory speak of *principles,* they do so only to establish some more general rules for the orientation of decision making. These rules or principles, however, do not have, according to this theory, a *proper* origin, that is, an origin different from the very logic of a particular decision-making process. So consequentialism and proportionalism do not really provide a natural-law theory. They provide a theory about reasonable action which basically fails to acknowledge what is most essential for natural law: the existence of real practical *principles* which are not derived from determinate forms of decision-making procedures, but are the real *moral measure* for the decision-making process.

Secondly, by measuring the moral "rightness" of single types of action exclusively on the basis of their foreseeable consequences related to non-moral goods and bads, this theory presupposes a concept of action which simply leaves out of consideration a basic aspect of human actions: the fact that the acting subject, that is, its *will,* takes a position with regard to good and evil already by *choosing* concrete actions which bring about such consequences. This taking a position relates to the agent's own person and to other persons (including God). So it seems that the theory does not acknowledge what actually follows from a more adequate analysis of human action: that *in the will* of the agent the properly moral qualities of "good" and "evil" may also appear *independently* of the whole of foreseeable consequences. Adherents of so-

excellent Marquette Lecture by William E. May, *Moral Absolutes: Catholic Tradition, Current Trends, and the Truth,* The Père Marquette Lecture in Theology 1989 (Milwaukee, Wis: Marquette University Press, 1989), esp. 40ff.

44. See Bruno Schüller, "Eine autonome Moral, was ist das?" *Theologische Revue* 78 (1982): 103–6. See for this my above-quoted article "Zur Begründung sittlicher Normen aus der Natur," esp. 67ff.

called "teleological ethics" consequently omit in principle an *intentional* description of those particular types of action which afterwards they qualify, on the basis of their decision-making procedure, as "right" or "wrong." To defend their theory, they are *compelled* to describe these actions as mere "events." Then at the same time they indicate the difficulties and aporias which logically derive from such a non-intentional concept of action, difficulties and aporias regarding the concept and the respective determination of the "object" of an action, so that, finally, they are able to offer their theory as the only reasonable solution for these problems, problems, however, created by their very approach rather than by the subject matter of ethics itself.[45] The solution offered by adherents of "teleological ethics" maintains that "action-events" brought about by acting subjects may be qualified as "right" or "wrong" according to whether they bring about the best overall consequences for all concerned, an optimum of goods or a minimum of bads.

I have argued, however, that even if the non-moral consequences of an action are optimal and mostly desirable, the action by which they have been brought about may nevertheless be an *evil* action. I would insist that everybody knows that this is possible. Whoever brings about "the best of all worlds" (the world with an optimum of non-moral goods or a minimum of non-moral bads) can, at the same time, be a murderer or a villain, and this not simply because he acted, say, to assure his own glory and, therefore, with a fundamentally evil intentionality, but precisely because we would judge as wicked the *actions* he performed. This obviously shows already that such a world would not be the best of all. The problem with consequentialist ethics is not that it does not share this conviction or that its adherents are inclined to plead for amorality, but that consequentialism is not able to *explain* what all of us know. The "secret" of consequentialism does not consist in denying this truth, just as it does not deny the truth of the proposition that a good intention cannot "sanctify" evil means. Instead the "secret" of these methodologies consists in making the *acting* subject disappear which, in its concrete choices of particular actions, takes a position with his will with regard to "good" and "evil." As a result, the verdict about the good intentions which

45. This approach, however, is not so different from traditional approaches that can be found in some classical manuals of moral theology. Some of them used to look at actions as physical processes or events, relating them afterward to the "norma moralitatis," an extrinsic rule determining whether it is licit or illicit to perform such and such an "action." What most classical manuals failed to do was precisely to render intelligible what a human action is and that its moral identity is *included* in it because it is included in the *intentional* structure of an action.

cannot "sanctify" evil means is simply rendered *irrelevant* and *pointless.* For if the "means" (that is: the concrete actions we choose and willingly perform) only can be "right" or "wrong," and this depending on their foreseeably resulting consequences in the field of non-moral goods and bads, then *by definition* there cannot exist such a thing as an "evil means." Instead there can be, at most, "wrong means," that is, means chosen on the basis of an error about which means would be the right one in order to achieve a determinate goal. To justify the concept of "intrinsically evil action," an intentional concept of action is required, and a corresponding concept of the intentional basic contents of concrete types of actions. This "intentional basic content" of an action is what we usually call its "moral object."[46]

We all understand a "good person" to be a person whose *will* is a good one, even if, to be good, such a will must often pay a high price: the price of accepting mostly undesirable consequences of its being a good will. But it is better to suffer injustice than to commit it.[47] This proposition precisely means quite specifically that it is *morally better* to abstain from an action the performance of which would be unjust, even if, as a consequence of refraining from it, a much greater injustice committed by others would foreseeably result, an injustice that, however, *I* will suffer. If we set aside the acting subject, the injustice *committed* by me and the injustice *suffered* by me (and committed by another person) appear just as two different states of affairs. The point (long ago expressed by Democritus) is that one cannot and *may* not compare these two consequences, nor may one weigh the action to be avoided against the undesirable consequences of refraining from this action. And this simply for the reason *that the action as such, considered in itself, is an unjust action.* This is precisely what a consequentialist ("teleological") ethic is unable to justify.

It can be seen that the natural law manifests itself as the totality of principles of practical reasonableness which not only moves us to act and to do the truly good but also compels us to refrain from committing injustice. Natural law is the proper "law" of a good will. It orients human persons, as *striving* subjects, to the "good-for-man," on the level of himself and of his fellowmen. It equally makes him refrain from evil, from "poisoning his soul." A life that maintains this orientation to the "good-for-man" in each and every sin-

46. For a full account of the concept of "intentional basic content" and "intentional basic action," see my *La prospettiva della morale.*

47. For the following I am indebted to A. W. Müller, "Radical Subjectivity: Morality versus Utilitarianism," *Ratio* 19 (1977): 115–32.

gle act of choice may rightly be called a "successful" life. A person who lives such a life therefore deserves praise and we consider him or her as a person who is on the way to sharing in true happiness, of participating in what the Greek philosophers called *eudaimonia.*

It will always remain difficult to disprove convincingly so-called teleological ethical theories (consequentialism, proportionalism) as long as one tries to do so in the logic proper to norm- or rule-ethics. The Church's teaching about "law"—"eternal," "natural," or "positive," "divine" or "human," "old" and "new"—was, in the past centuries, profoundly and not very happily influenced by the logic of norm- and rule-ethics. For different reasons, moral theologians emphasized the "observers' viewpoint." Unlike the classical and medieval tradition of moral theory, the modern tradition was not interested in exposing a comprehensive conception of the good life as part of the intellectual enterprise involved in coming to an understanding of man and of the sense of his existence. From the sixteenth century onward, moral theology, intensively permeated with casuistry, was rather concerned with judgments about whether particular acts were compatible, or not, with a conception of the good life already established by revealed positive law and the corresponding moral norms.

This concern, however, falls short of the genuine way we arrive at a proper understanding of the real requisites of morality. For this, also in a Christian context, a virtue-centered moral theory is needed, be it on the level of philosophical ethics or on that of moral theology.[48] So-called "teleological ethics" have not yet escaped from the logic of a legalistic approach; they only now try to "save" freedom from a supposed menace by law. By asserting in number 78 that "to be able to grasp the object of an act which specifies that act morally, it is therefore necessary to place oneself *in the perspective of the acting person,*" the encyclical *Veritatis Splendor* opens a new way directed to rediscovering the perspective proper to virtue ethics, which is the genuine perspective of morals.[49]

48. See an example of the latter in Romanus Cessario, O.P., *The Moral Virtues and Theological Ethics* (Notre Dame, Ind.: University of Notre Dame Press, 1991).

49. I thank Professor John M. Haas of Philadelphia for having carefully reviewed my English version of this paper, originally written in German.

4

Intentional Actions and the Meaning of Object

A Reply to Richard McCormick

In his article "Some Early Reactions to *Veritatis Splendor*,"[1] Richard McCormick discusses my article on *Veritatis Splendor* and its teaching about intrinsically evil acts.[2] He challenges my defense of the encyclical's views and poses some concrete questions for me. At the same time, McCormick complains once more about what he calls the encyclical's misrepresentation of the proportionalists' views, as well as about a general misunderstanding on the part of critics of what proportionalism, consequentialism, and their teleological approach are really about.

To begin with, I find it somewhat surprising that McCormick presents intentional understanding of human acts and their objects as something discovered by proportionalists. By this he obscures the fact that most critics of proportionalism, consequentialism, and so-called "teleological ethics" (I will not further distinguish these different labels) work with what is precisely an intentional conception of moral objects.[3] For example, my own position, sit-

1. *Theological Studies* 55 (1994): 481–506; see 500–502, 504.

2. Chapter 3 of this book, originally published as Martin Rhonheimer, "'Intrinsically Evil Acts' and the Moral Viewpoint: Clarifying a Central Teaching of *Veritatis Splendor*," *The Thomist* 58 (1994): 1–39.

3. There may be some exceptions, such as Russell Hittinger, "The Pope and the Theorists,"

uated in the context of virtue ethics,[4] is one in which an intentional conception of action plays a crucial role. McCormick seems to evade this level of argument, however, and in this way appears to beg the question about one of the central issues in the debate.

At the same time, it is not entirely surprising that McCormick had some difficulty in dealing with the central point of my argument (and of similar arguments),[5] because his methodology is so entangled in the categories of the strongly legalistic and casuistic manual tradition.[6] In my article, I explicitly dealt with the difficulty of understanding a virtue- and first-person-centered view from the perspective of the manual tradition:

> It will, however, never be possible to render intelligible this moral methodology on the grounds of an ethic which from the beginning is concerned with justifying "moral norms." This is so because in such an approach the *distinction* between "object" and *further* intentions necessarily drops out of view. The only things which a norm-ethic can produce in the way of an action theory are the particular "occurrences" ("actions"), on the one hand, and the consequences brought about by them, on the other. If an agent *intends* the best consequences, then it is these which come to be designated the "object" of his "act." (21–22)

McCormick's article thus confirms this assertion, since the author finally arrives at the conclusion that talking about "objects" and wrongness *ex obiecto*

Crisis 11 (December 1993): 31–36. G. E. M. Anscombe, one of the first and most incisive critics of consequentialism, attacked it on the grounds of an intentional concept of action, developed in her famous study *Intention*, 2nd ed. (1957; Oxford: Basil Blackwell, 1963). Cf. Anscombe, *Contraception and Chastity* (London: Catholic Truth Society, 1975).

4. See chapter 2 of this book. An early version of that essay appeared as Martin Rhonheimer, "'Ethics of Norms' and the Lost Virtues: Searching the Roots of the Crisis of Ethical Reasoning," *Anthropotes* 9, no. 2 (1993): 231–43; *La prospettiva della morale. Fondamenti dell'etica philosophica* (Rome: Armando, 1994); *Praktische Vernunft und Vernünftigkeit der Praxis. Handlungstheorie bei Thomas von Aquin in ihrer Entstehung aus dem Problemkontext der aristotelischen Ethik* (Berlin: Akademie Verlag, 1994). Contrary to the impression that McCormick gives in his article, I do not share the Grisez-Finnis theory about basic goods and practical reason, nor do I argue on its grounds, in spite of many important common views.

5. See William E. May, *Moral Absolutes: Catholic Tradition, Current Trends, and the Truth* (Milwaukee, Wis: Marquette University Press, 1989); John Finnis, *Moral Absolutes: Tradition, Revision, and Truth* (Washington, D.C.: The Catholic University of America Press, 1991); Alasdair MacIntyre, "How Can We Learn What *Veritatis Splendor* Has To Teach?" *The Thomist* 58 (1994): 171–95. See also Robert P. George and Hadley Arkes's contributions to "The Splendor of Truth: A Symposium," published in *First Things* 39 (January 1994) and rather unfairly criticized in McCormick's article.

6. This is also the case with Bruno Schüller and his disciples; see the recent paper by Werner Wolbert, "Die 'in sich schlechten' Handlungen und der Konsequentialismus," in *Moraltheologie im Abseits? Antwort auf die Enzyklika "Veritatis Splendor,"* ed. Dietmar Mieth (Freiburg: Herder, 1994), 88–109.

is not a helpful terminology and should be abandoned.[7] I shall return to this point.

The questions put to me by McCormick, and which I shall try to answer, deal with the following issues: 1) the meaning of "object" (which is, as he rightly states, the central point); 2) the closely related "question of intentionality"; and 3) what is according to McCormick "a key question" for my position: "Why in choosing to kill a person or deceive a person, does one necessarily 'take a position with his will with regard to "good" and "evil"'?"[8] Finally, I shall also have to say something about what McCormick falsely calls the encyclical's misrepresentation of proportionalism, because this is intimately connected with all the rest.

"Object" in *Veritatis Splendor:* Not Just a "Kind of Behavior"

Let me start by specifying some points about *Veritatis Splendor*'s teaching. In his presentation of the encyclical's understanding of the "object," McCormick says that according to the encyclical (and presumably also to me) an object simply is "a freely chosen kind of behavior." But it seems that he fails to grasp what the encyclical's text wants to stress in this passage. Its intention is not to tell the reader that objects are "kinds of behavior," but that objects are to be understood as something related to the acting person's *choices.* Therefore, the point made by the encyclical is about intention involved in choice of kinds of behavior and not about "kinds of behavior" as such.

The entire text (which I quoted at the very beginning of my article) runs as follows:

> In order to be able to grasp the object of an act which specifies that act morally, it is therefore necessary to place oneself *in the perspective of the acting person* (*VS* no. 78).

What *Veritatis Splendor* is saying is this: do not look at human acts "from outside"; do not focus only on what happens, what is the case, and on the state of affairs brought about by a behavioral performance; but rather put yourself in the perspective of the acting subject, for whom "actions" or "behaviors" are objects of choice, informed by reason, as immediate goals of the will. Thus the encyclical continues:

7. He had already drawn the same conclusion in his article "Document Begs Many Legitimate Moral Questions," *National Catholic Reporter,* October 15, 1993, 17.

8. McCormick, "Some Early Reactions to *Veritatis Splendor,*" 501.

The object of the act of willing is in fact a freely chosen kind of behavior. . . . By the object of a given moral act, then, one cannot mean a process or an event of the merely physical order, to be assessed on the basis of its ability to bring about a given state of affairs in the outside world. Rather, *that object is the proximate end of a deliberate decision which determines the act of willing on the part of the acting person.* (*VS* no. 78, emphasis added)

In his reading of this passage, McCormick's attention seems to be entirely conditioned by *his own* methodology—which adopts the standpoint of the observer, as is typical for norm-ethics and casuistry—and by the argumentative problems that logically arise in *this* perspective. Therefore he does not enter at all into the rather sophisticated argument set forth by the encyclical.

It is significant that immediately after this statement *Veritatis Splendor* quotes no. 1761 of the *Catechism of the Catholic Church* (which also focuses on choice). "There are certain specific kinds of behavior that are always wrong to choose, because choosing them involves a disorder of the will, that is, a moral evil." In no. 1755, the Catechism gives an example, fornication, to illustrate its teaching. Clearly, "fornication" is not simply a material behavioral pattern (this would be "sexual intercourse between male and female"). The encyclical's verdict about moral evil is not about *this* pattern, but about the *choice* of it, that is, *about a specific case of this choice,* called "fornication," that is describable in universal terms (as a "species " of human act), a description that applies to a multiplicity of particular acts independently of further circumstances or consequences. Notice that the description of an (observable) behavioral pattern as such and the description of the *choice* of this behavior may be two quite different things.[9]

Let me spell this out in more detail. When Jim chooses to have sexual intercourse with Jane, Jim actually not only chooses a behavioral pattern (to have intercourse with a female, or with Jane), because Jane either is or is not his wife. This is a circumstance relevant for practical reason that judges about the corresponding behavior as a practical good to be either pursued or avoided. It is a circumstance that, in this specific situation, is given and is thus prior to choice. It is not, however, inherent in the behavioral pattern as such; it is recognizable only by reason and it confers on the chosen behavior

9. The problem is that in common speech the choice and the corresponding act tend to be lumped together under a common designation derived from some characteristic behavioral aspects of the act. In reality, however, the two can never be equated one with the other. Here, as John Finnis has pointed out, "common speech . . . is not a safe guide" (*Moral Absolutes*, 72).

an inherent, though not simply naturally given, "form." The behavior could not be chosen at all *apart from this "form."*[10] Therefore, provided Jim and Jane are not married, Jim necessarily chooses, not just "intercourse with a female," but "fornication."[11]

Accordingly, the concrete behavior considered as an object of choice is much more than merely a material behavioral pattern. In choosing a concrete behavioral pattern, one necessarily chooses it "under a description," which is precisely the description of an intent formed by reason. Sexual intercourse, as a chosen kind of behavior, is the object of a judgment of reason of the following sort: "Having sexual intercourse with Jane, who is *not* my wife (or even is another's wife, etc.), is a good here and now to be pursued." This precisely indicates an intention that *defines* the act in question. If there were no intention—which is impossible—there would be no reason, nor would there be a perceived good to be pursued. There would exist nothing but an observable behavioral pattern, not a human act. Thus the chosen act is precisely what *Veritatis Splendor* calls the "proximate end of the [choosing] will." As such, *the very act includes an intention, formed by reason, without which it could not be described as a human act.* This intention (choice) of Jim to have intercourse with somebody who is not his spouse is perfectly describable and morally qualifiable *independently* of further intentions (e.g., the intention of doing it for the sake of obtaining some information necessary to save the lives of others).

The encyclical's understanding of the object of a human act explains the formulation in no. 79, which I quoted in the opening section of my article. This sentence, which contains the key formulation, is, however, mostly ignored by revisionists. The verdict here concerns "*choice* of certain kinds of behavior." In *VS* no. 80, "intrinsically evil" is referred to the object, and this again means: to kinds of behavior, insofar as they are objects of choice. What is called "intrinsically evil," therefore, is concrete choice, describable in behavioral terms, that cannot be reduced to simple "behavior," however, because every choice includes an intention of the will and a corresponding judgment of reason. That is also the reason why the encyclical speaks here

10. That is why (as I pointed out in sections 4 and 6 of my article) Aquinas calls objects "forms conceived by reason."

11. If Jim or Jane is (or both are) married, but not to each other, Jim and Jane choose what one calls "adultery." That is the classic example mentioned by Aquinas (*ST*, I-II, q.18 a.5 ad3); it illustrates well the difference between *genus naturae* and *genus moris.*

about *ulterior* intentions, and not about intention as such: because "object" and intention are not mutually exclusive terms. There is some intentionality required so that an object of a human act can be constituted.[12]

McCormick affirmed in his article that proportionalism makes precisely this point, imputing to *Veritatis Splendor,* and to critics of proportionalism generally, a different view, one rather easy for him to criticize. In this way he avoids the real issue and conceals the weakness of proportionalism and consequentialism. This weakness, however, is that a consequentialist refuses to speak about "actions" or about intention involved in the choice of concrete actions; he or she talks only about intentions as related to foreseeable consequences, thereby describing, and continuously redescribing, "actions" from the standpoint of a value-balancing observer; in this way he arrives at what he calls the "expanded notion of object." When McCormick says, "Intention tells us what is going on," he is perfectly right. But he neglects to ask: How are intentions shaped? Upon what do they depend? And, finally, what is, not intention and intentionality, but intentional *action?*

Intentionality and "Intentional Actions": The Implicit Physicalism of Proportionalism

Perhaps the reader of my article on *Veritatis Splendor* will remember the example of "arm raising," "greeting," and so on. It was a simple example—inspired by Wittgenstein and Anscombe—of showing how intentional actions are structured. I asserted:

12. If it is said that the "object is a *chosen* act, describable only by referring to an intention," one might wonder how one can then simultaneously affirm—as does *Veritatis Splendor,* along with traditional moral theology—that the goodness of the (choosing) will *depends* on the object. Someone might claim that we should be able to describe the object as something "given" and without *immediate* reference to an intention. The solution of this apparent puzzle, however, is easy: the object, its intentional element included, is *first* an object of reason, and in this sense it is prior to choice, insofar as choice is an act of the will shaped by reason. That is the point of Aquinas's teaching. See the following statements from the *Prima secundae:* "bonum per rationem repraesentatur voluntati ut obiectum; et in quantum cadit sub ordine rationis, pertinet ad genus moris, et causat bonitatem moralem in actu voluntatis" (q.19 a.1 ad3); "bonitas voluntatis dependet a ratione, eo modo quo dependet ab obiecto" (q.19 a.3); "actus exterior est obiectum voluntatis, in quantum proponitur voluntati a ratione ut quoddam bonum apprehensum et ordinatur per rationem" (q.20 a.1 ad1). Again, the object, like the "species," is a *forma a ratione concepta,* which includes the cognitive or rational element of intention, purpose. For more details, see Rhonheimer, *Natur als Grundlage der Moral: Eine Auseinandersetzung mit autonomer Moral und teleologischer Ethik* (Innsbruck-Vienna: Tyrolia-Verlag, 1987), 317ff., and also *Praktische Vernunft und Vernünftigkeit der Praxis.*

> The so-called "absolute prohibitions," that is, normative propositions which indicate that certain, describable actions may *never* be licitly chosen and willingly performed, therefore relate to actions described *intentionally*. It is impossible to do this independently of the content of the acts of choice which relate to such actions. (32)

I have always conceded that proportionalism and consequentialism in Catholic moral theology have aspired to overcome the limitations and flaws of a traditional physicalist understanding of the "moral object."[13] At the same time, however, I have contended that they have not succeeded because they have overlooked, and thus conserved, the basic error inherent in this tradition: to fail to understand human acts as embedded in an intentional process, that is, to fail to understand them from the perspective of the acting person.

This can be seen very well in the case of Josef Fuchs (one of McCormick's chief witnesses for the proportionalists' innocence). According to my judgment, Fuchs speaks about "intentions," but he does not seem to have a notion of what an intentional *action* is. He speaks only of (pre-moral) "physical acts" or behavioral patterns (realized, performed, etc.) to which he *adds* intentions (as a "pre-moral" element!). What Fuchs calls the "act" in itself or the "act as such" has no moral identity. Only the combination of the three pre-moral elements "act," "circumstances," and "intentions" becomes for him a moral whole.

The problem is that "physical act" plus "intention" (defined by some as "reason") will never result in an "intentional action." "Intentional action" is a concept belonging to action theory, not to moral casuistry. It is not part of a theory about how to combine "reasons" and "intentions" in order to justify an action normatively (that is, to know whether it is "allowed" and right or "illicit" and wrong). The concept of "intentional action" expresses the very nature of human acting. So one has to talk about the acting person and about what is going on in his or her will when he or she acts. The discourse will be about choice and about intention *involved* in human acts, that is, in chosen acts (or behaviors, to use the encyclical's term).

Let us have a look at Fuchs's well-known article "The Absoluteness of Moral Terms."[14] In this article, Fuchs argues that human acts are composed

13. See chapter 3, or Rhonheimer, "'Intrinsically Evil Acts' and the Moral Viewpoint," 27, and the Introduction to *Natur als Grundlage der Moral.*

14. *Gregorianum* 52 (1971); reprinted in *Readings in Moral Theology No. 1: Moral Norms and Catholic Tradition,* ed. Charles E. Curran and Richard McCormick (New York: Paulist Press, 1979), 94–137.

of three elements: the (physical) act; special circumstances; and the intention. He first points out correctly: "Morality, in the true (not transferred or analogous) sense, is expressible only by a human action, by an action which originates in the deliberate and free decision of a human person."[15] So a human action, Fuchs continues, must be performed "with the intention of the agent." He then adds the following example:

> One may not say, therefore, that killing as a realization of a human evil may be morally good or morally bad; for killing as such, since it implies nothing about the intention of the agent, cannot, purely as such, constitute a human act.[16]

The problem here is that "killing as such" is not an act, not even an "act as such," because "as such" it is not described as a *chosen* act, that is, as an act that is the object of choice. Of course, "killing" as behavioral pattern (putting another person to death) could also be the performance of a robot. Considered on this level, "killing" is nothing but a behavioral pattern defined by a specific outcome. But, we should ask, what is going on when John chooses to kill Harry (for whatever reason: either because John simply wants Harry to be dead; or because John wants his uncle Harry to be dead *for the sake of* getting an inheritance, or for the sake of revenge, or for the sake of marrying Harry's wife)?

The point is that "killing as such" is not conceivable as a describable action, as if this could be understood apart from intention. If John kills Harry, he already has, in *choosing* the killing, an intention: he wants Harry to be dead (this independently of whether he chooses "killing Harry" for its own sake or as a means to a further end). Fuchs, however, falling into the trap of dealing with acts as if they were pure events ("realizations of goods and evils"), continues:

> The conclusion in definitive terms is: 1) An action cannot be judged morally in its materiality (killing, wounding, going to the moon) without reference to the intention of the agent; without this, we are not dealing with a human action, and only with respect to a human action may one say in a true sense whether it is morally good or bad.[17]

From this it obviously follows that, *prima facie*, any "act" (in his sense of performing a behavioral pattern) can be justified, even if it brings about a (premoral) evil (e.g., "death"). This brings us to Fuchs's second criterion:

15. Josef Fuchs, "The Absoluteness of Moral Terms," in *Readings in Moral Theology No. 1*, 119.
16. Ibid.
17. Ibid., 120.

2) The evil (in a pre-moral sense) effected by a human agent must not be intended as such, and must be justified in terms of the totality of the action by appropriate reasons.[18]

Therefore, if I do not kill just for killing—without further reason besides the victim's death itself—then *any* killing *could* be, on principle, morally justified, provided there are "appropriate reasons." Or do I somehow grossly misunderstand Fuchs?

In this way, we are presented with an action analysis in which "acts" are simply physical events ("realizations of goods and evils" or of "lesser evils") to be given a moral character by intentions that justify these performances on the ground of "appropriate" (commensurate) reason. The acting subject focuses exclusively on the overall outcome of his or her doings, not on what he or she concretely does. The acting subject disappears as a subject that *chooses* and thus willingly performs concrete acts, acts that are not simply events causing consequences, but proximate ends of a choosing will.[19]

Fuchs sums up his argument by asserting:

A moral judgment is legitimately found only under a *simultaneous* consideration of the three elements (actions, circumstance, purpose), pre-moral in themselves; for the actualization of the three elements (taking money from another, who is very poor, to be able to give pleasure to a friend) is not a combination of three human actions that are morally judged on an individual basis, but a single human action.[20]

The example given by Fuchs, of course, is revealing and confirms what I reproach. The problem is that "taking money from another" is not a good description of a "chosen kind of behavior." A better description would be: "appropriating money, taking it from its legitimate owner, against his will." This is an intentional description of an action called "theft." It has its moral form independently of whether the acting person has this or another "purpose" (intention), and of whether the outraged person is poor or not. Provided he or she in fact is poor, then the theft may be more condemnable and called "mean." If the purpose is frivolous ("to give pleasure to a friend"), then the

18. Ibid.

19. Of course, I have never said that proportionalists *explicitly hold* such a causal-eventistic concept of action (since it is obviously absurd). Rather, my criticism was based on showing that they hold such a concept *implicitly*—because otherwise their position would not be coherent—and this demonstrates that their position is erroneous. Consequently I argued that they should pay more attention to action theory. See chapter 3, or Rhonheimer, "'Intrinsically Evil Acts' and the Moral Viewpoint," 27ff.

20. Fuchs, "The Absoluteness of Moral Terms," 121.

whole theft will be a frivolous action in addition. Such a theft, however, will not only be a frivolous one, but also, *by its very object,* an unjust one! If the purpose ("further intention") is laudable, the intention remains laudable, but not the action as such, which remains unjust, though it probably will be, despite its wrongness, more understandable. In any case, on the whole it will be an evil action, *malum ex quocumque defectu.* On the grounds of Fuchs's and McCormick's methodology, however, these kinds of differentiations are completely ruled out in favor of a uniform overall judgment about "rightness" or "wrongness" of the act.

To sum up, this methodology has three main characteristics. First, it confounds the intentionality involved in actions with the reasons one might have to judge certain outcomes as desirable. Proportionalism, of course, does not forget intention or intentionality, but it reduces "action" to "intending" and to "having appropriate reasons." What is lacking is an intentional concept of *action itself.* For proportionalists, action remains a purely physical event that realizes the state of affairs one has a "reason" to bring about. Splitting up human acts into "acts as such," on one side, and "reasons" and "intentions related to foreseeable consequences," on the other, proportionalists seem to assert that choice proceeds on a double track: one first chooses, on the grounds of appropriate reasons, the state of affairs to be brought about, and afterwards the physical "act as such" that will cause it (e.g., "killing as such") is chosen. The second choice—according to the theory—receives its moral species exclusively from the first ("as such," it has none); it has a purely instrumental relation to the first. That is precisely what I would call an "eventistic" and thus non-intentional notion of action.

The second characteristic derives from this: the "basic action," the concrete act or behavior immediately chosen and then referred to whatever end, is not conceived as an intentional action. This is a very important point, because I take the "object" of a moral act to be precisely the content of what I have called an "intentional basic action"[21] which itself can be distinguished from *further* intentions. This inability to isolate the *basic intentional content* of actions in relation to further intentions leads to the third feature of proportionalism, what McCormick calls the "expanded notion of object," an "object" that is to be understood as being already the *result* of a process

21. See Rhonheimer, *La prospettiva della morale,* 39, 85ff., 239ff. The term "basic action" was first introduced by A. C. Danto ("Basic Actions," *American Philosophical Quarterly* 2 [1965]: 141–48), but in quite another sense, i.e., not referring to *intentional* action.

of weighing and "commensurating" all foreseeable consequences. The "expanded object" thus contains the intentions that define what in a morally significant sense the acting person is doing (and so, *prima facie,* everything becomes morally possible, provided there is an appropriate reason). The expanded notion of object, however, in reality is equivalent to the abolition of the notion of object altogether, for the very notion of "object" necessarily implies a distinction between the *basic* intention that characterizes the object and *further* intentions.

McCormick's "Expanded Notion of Object"

The problem of the proportionalist "expanded notion of object" can be well illustrated with the case of Paul Touvier, a French Nazi collaborator in the Vichy regime, recently condemned, who was ordered to shoot seven Jews on June 28, 1944. On trial fifty years later, Touvier argued that both he and the chief commander of the militia of Lyon knew that Gestapo chief Werner Knab was planning to execute a hundred Jews in reprisal for the Resistance's killing of Philippe Henriot, the head of Vichy's propaganda organization. By convincing Knab to execute only thirty, and then in fact executing seven Jews, Touvier argued that they had in fact prevented the execution of one hundred desired by the Gestapo commander. The key point here is their argument that *what they did in reality (the morally relevant "object" of their doing) was not kill seven Jews, but save the lives of ninety-three of them.*

That is an argument based on an "expanded notion of object."[22] The corresponding reasoning that would, in proportionalist terms, justify such an action begins by affirming that "killing as such"—that is, "without reference to the intention of the agent"—is neither good nor evil, but only the "realization of a (pre-moral) human evil" that can be justified, provided one does not directly intend this evil as the goal of the action, and that there be a "commensurate reason." Taking into account "the whole of the action," circumstances and foreseeable consequences, Touvier came to the conclusion: if I do not kill the seven, then one hundred (these seven probably included) will be killed. Therefore, in killing the seven (which *as such* is beyond good and evil), I can save ninety-three Jews. Thus Touvier reasoned: the morally relevant "object" of my action—that is, *what I am really doing—has* to be called meritorious or at least responsible and justified as life-saving.

22. Or was it, mistakenly, not expanded enough?

Although a proportionalist can produce reasons why Touvier should have refrained from killing the seven Jews, this will be a consequentialist argument and will be accomplished by an even greater expansion of the object. For example, one could argue: "Acting in that manner could have foreseeably weakened consciousness of the criminal character of the Nazi regime, which would have cost the lives of even more Jews in the long run."

The problem here is not the *result* of the proportionalist reasoning, but rather its very *structure*. It is precisely the methodology of weighing the consequences, taking into account pre-moral "values"—in this case, lives of innocent human beings—so as to determine whether or not there is a "commensurate" reason for "realizing the pre-moral evil" of killing them. Why not simply admit that the intentional killing of innocent persons is immoral, unjust, criminal, that one is never allowed to do such a thing?

According to proportionalism, however, what one chooses are mainly the consequences of one's actions (actions therefore conceived as simple behavioral performances), but not the actions themselves. As Fuchs put it:

> The object of the ethical decision for an action is, therefore, not the basic (e.g., physical) act as such (in its ethical relevance, such as killing, speaking falsehood, taking property, sexual stimulation), but the entirety of the basic act, special circumstances, and the chosen or (more or less) foreseeable consequences.[23]

A problem here is that everything depends on your preferences—including the determination as to which reasons are commensurate and which are not. Yet is preference ever sufficient as a basis for moral judgment? Who would not prefer the killing of only seven, instead of a hundred innocent people? Who would not, to use McCormick's famous wording, prefer "to choose the lesser evil"?[24]

Of course, I prefer the lesser evil, too. I am happy when I learn that not one hundred but only seven innocents were killed, as I am happy to know that only seven instead of one hundred persons were killed in an air crash or

23. Josef Fuchs, "Das Problem Todsünde," *Stimmen der Zeit* 212 (February 1994): 83 (the English translation is that offered by McCormick in "Some Early Reaction to *Veritatis Splendor*," 500). In this 1994 article about *Veritatis Splendor*, Fuchs restates the same basic position he had presented in his article written more than twenty years earlier.

24. Cf. John Finnis, *Fundamentals of Ethics* (Washington, D.C.: Georgetown University Press, 1983), 93ff. For McCormick, choosing the lesser evil is simply a self-evident principle, "beyond debate: for the only alternative is that in conflict situations we should choose the greater evil, which is patently absurd" (*Doing Evil to Achieve Good*, ed. Richard McCormick and Paul Ramsey [Chicago: Loyola University Press, 1978], 38). This of course also means that we choose and therefore are responsible for the foreseen consequences of our omissions.

by an earthquake. But I will not *choose* and willingly perform an evil action because I think it to be less evil then another and because otherwise foreseeably somebody else would commit the greater evil (I shall try to prevent that, of course). The proportionalist will rebut: "Sorry, you did not understand me. I meant that choosing the lesser evil signifies that this action was precisely the *good* one." I then would reply: "So you really think that when choosing and freely performing an action, nothing else happens than what happens in an air crash or an earthquake? Are the evil results of certain actions somehow simply given, beyond both my power to change and my responsibility? Or are they rather intrinsically bound up with the action that I perform?"

On the grounds of this and similar examples, we can better understand why *Veritatis Splendor*, no. 77, pronounces a very important warning, a warning overlooked, it seems, by most proportionalists:

> The weighing of the goods and evils foreseeable as the consequence of an action is not an adequate method for determining whether the choice of that concrete kind of behavior is "according to its species," or "in itself," morally good or bad, licit or illicit.

Of course, in the light of the preceding example this statement is perfectly intelligible. The proportionalist "expanded notion of object," however, renders it meaningless because in proportionalist terms there simply *is no possible choice of a concrete kind of behavior* that could be called morally bad "by its species" or "in itself" *before* the foreseeable consequences have been weighed—consequences that change from case to case—and *before* a judgment about commensurate reasons has been reached. The problem here is with what are called intrinsically *wrong* or *evil* actions; in such cases already the very object should serve as an indication that one should not persist along this line of action. McCormick avoids facing this problem directly by employing examples like "one takes a vacation trip in order to commit adultery" to maintain that only in such cases can one discern "an intention in addition to the object," because "there are two distinguishable actions here, each with its own object."[25] This is then a simple means-end relation. In the example, the basic action is perfectly indifferent or even good, but not the end. Yet is not the situation radically different in the case, for example, of one who commits adultery in order to rescue an innocent person and save his life and one who kills seven Jews in order to save the lives of ninety-three? Are

25. McCormick, "Some Early Reactions to *Veritatis Splendor*," 498.

there not also "two distinguishable actions here, each with its own object"? McCormick's choice of examples serves to avoid the real issue.

Proportionalists thus describe and redescribe concrete chosen basic actions, without looking at what the acting person chooses on the level of action (or "means"); rather, they concentrate on what he or she chooses in the order of consequences and on the corresponding commensurate reasons, all of which finally constitute the "expanded object." As we have seen, however, the expanded notion of object is in reality not a notion of "object" at all, but precisely its abolition, because "object" means the basic intentional content of a human act, distinguishable from *further* intentions.[26]

To borrow an example from William May, it would be more truthful to say that Macbeth *killed* Duncan instead of saying that Macbeth *stabbed* Duncan and as a result Duncan died. Stabbing Duncan "as such" is not a sufficient description of a chosen kind of behavior or of an action. A description of the object must include, in Aquinas's terminology, both the *materia circa quam*,[27] "matter about which," and the "form" of the action: Macbeth stabbed Duncan for the sake of causing his death, or, because he wanted him dead (that was precisely his *reason* and his intention or purpose). We rightly call this kind of act an act of "killing." That is what he chose and what he did; that is the object of his action. In order to express our moral disapproval we also call it "murder." It would not make any sense to say: Macbeth chose stabbing Duncan with the *further* intention of causing his death, of killing him. You cannot describe "stabbing Duncan" as a reasonable, freely chosen action without indicating an intention.

This way of describing an act by the intention involved in it is not always truthful. Thus it is not truthful to say that Touvier "saved ninety-three Jews" instead of saying that "Touvier killed seven innocent Jews, and as a result ninety-three were saved." We cannot call this action an act of "life saving" merely because the foreseeable result (the sparing of the ninety-three) was a "commensurate reason" for shooting the seven, and thus "life itself" was "better served." We are not calculating with quantities of the "good of life," but relating to concrete *living persons*. To speak truthfully, Touvier killed seven innocent people (he shot at them with the intent of ending their lives), which is murder—with the *further* intention of preventing the killing of a hundred.

26. These, of course, are also "objects" of the will. See John Finnis, "Object and Intention in Moral Judgments According to Aquinas," *The Thomist* 55 (1991): 1–27.

27. *ST* I-II, q.18 a.2 ad2.

Thus it is not truthful to say that abortion, given that it means killing an innocent human being, is either an act of life saving when done for the sake of saving the mother's life or an act of saving family stability in certain difficult family situations. Nor can the manipulation and sacrifice of human embryos for the sake of health research (considered as a commensurate reason) be taken as simply an act of health care by virtue of its (expanded) object. The notion of expanded object does not work; or, better, it works for anything whatsoever. Again, everything depends on the preferences one has.[28]

McCormick conceals the problem by adopting examples that, in themselves, are precisely *not* examples of "expanded objects" (and that I would call intentional basic actions). Let us take the example of masturbation.[29] Of course, stimulation of the genital organs "as such" is not a kind of behavior that can be chosen or willingly performed by a human person; a basic reason, intent, or purpose is needed.[30] That is why the *Catechism of the Catholic Church* very correctly writes in no. 2352: "By *masturbation* is to be understood the deliberate stimulation of the genital organs in order to derive sexual pleasure." That seems very clear. If one chooses the same behavioral pattern (stimulating genital organs) in order to get semen for fertility analysis, then one simply chooses an action that is different by its object.

What happens, however, if one chooses to masturbate for the sake of psychological release? Is the action properly described by calling it "deliberate stimulation of the genital organs in order to have psychological release?" I think not. Rather, what one deliberately chooses is "the stimulation of the genital organs in order to derive sexual pleasure" (= object), and this with the *further* intention of getting psychological release. The key here is that the release obviously does not derive from stimulating genital organs "as such," but from the corresponding sexual pleasure. Thus what the intentional basic action (or its object) turns out to be is not simply a question of preference.

At the same time the behavioral pattern alone does not decide everything and is sometimes ambiguous. Consider the following situations. John, a col-

28. In the proportionalist schema, one simply calls "object" what one concludes to be morally relevant, "what one wanted to condemn as wrong *ex objecto*" (McCormick, "Some Early Reactions to *Veritatis Splendor,*" 504). In this way, one can simply keep expanding the object of one's action so as to justify one's preferences and reach the result corresponding to one's personal intuitions about what is morally relevant.

29. Cf. his example of organ transplantation, as distinguished from "killing for world peace" ("Some Early Reactions to *Veritatis Splendor,*" 504).

30. Likewise, one simply *cannot* choose to "remove a kidney from a living donor" purely "as such," without *any* reason that constitutes it as a human act.

lege student, for the sake of forgetting his girlfriend troubles drinks lots of whisky in order to induce a temporary loss of consciousness; in other words, he gets drunk. This is an act of intemperance, drunkenness. On the other hand, Fred, a soldier, for the sake of avoiding the pain of an emergency operation, drinks the same amount of whisky in order to induce a temporary loss of consciousness; in other words, he undergoes anesthesia. The behavioral pattern may be exactly identical,[31] but without indicating an intention (a "Why?"), it is impossible to describe properly *what* John and Fred are doing, that is, what, in a basic sense, they choose.[32] If you remove *any* intention or purpose whatsoever, there is no action. Thus in every case you arrive at a basic level, which is the level of intentional basic actions.[33]

There are also adherents of a non-intentional concept of object who fear that this consideration of intention opens the way to subjectivism.[34] Any behavioral pattern, they object, could serve for any object whatsoever: "by shifting intention to and fro, the agent constitutes out of whole cloth the moral properties of his act."[35] Moreover, their concern is "whether the *norm* of acts exists prior to human choice, or whether it only comes into being with our consideration of proportions, circumstances, and consequences."[36] And finally: is it possible to say that intention is so important; should we not hold "that the concrete nature of acts tells us whether an intention is morally good or bad"?[37]

These formulations are, however, somewhat misleading. First, the "nature of an act" necessarily *includes* an intention, because there *is* no human act without an intention formed by reason. And that is precisely why Aquinas calls the species of an act, which is determined by its object, a *forma a ratione concepta,* a "form conceived by reason";[38] likewise, he defines the good that is by nature specific to each virtue as a good formed *ex quadam commensuratione actus ad circumstantias et finem, quam ratio facit,* "from a certain

31. For an intentional notion of contraception, see Rhonheimer, "Contraception, Sexual Behavior, and Natural Law: Philosophical Foundation of the Norm of 'Humanae Vitae,'" *Linacre Quarterly* 56, no. 2 (1989): 20–57.

32. Cf. Anscombe, *Intention,* § 22.

33. The opposite is also possible, i.e., different or even contrary behavioral patterns, but the same intentional action, e.g., "the action of killing" and "the omission of a possible action of life saving." The objects of both choices are identical.

34. E.g., Russell Hittinger, "The Pope and the Theorists," *Crisis* 11, no. 11 (December 1993): 31–36.

35. Ibid., 34.

36. Ibid., 33–34.

37. Ibid., 34.

38. *ST* I-II, q.18 a.10.

commensuration of the act to circumstances and to the end, a commensuration produced by reason."[39] Such formulations seem to justify the position of Fuchs and McCormick, but only seemingly, however, because the underlying understanding of human action is different. What Aquinas and the tradition say is: One cannot simply "choose" a (physical) act and additionally *order* it to *any* intention formed by commensurate reasons that would justify the act. To deny this does not mean, however, that a human act could be described *without* referring to intention altogether.

Secondly, we have quite an extended power to organize our actions intentionally, and thus in a sense to constitute the moral properties of our acts. But there are what I would call *naturally given limits* to this. *Therefore,* (provided sound perception) I cannot shoot at a person's heart and truthfully say, "I love you," meaning that I am doing this with the intent of doing good to this person. What is crucial to recognize is that not every behavioral pattern fits for *any* intention. For example, I cannot shoot at a person and have the intention of healing his wound.

To have a human act one needs to have a basic intention; on this much we agree. But can one, as Hittinger fears, simply "shift intention to and fro"? Given a determined situation (which is precisely given and does not depend on the subject's will or preferences), it is not simply up to me to decide whether my shooting at a person's heart is or is not an action of punishment. And John, who drinks to forget his girlfriend troubles, simply *cannot* reasonably intend his act to be an act of anesthesia. Fred, on the other hand, who "does the same thing," *cannot* intend that what he does be an act of drunkenness. There are given contexts (shaped by circumstances and recognizable, as a morally significant contextual unity, only by practical reason) that, *in a basic sense,* decide what kind of intentions we reasonably *can* have if we choose a determined "kind of behavior," *independently* of *further* intentions.

From this it follows that even if there is no act (and no object) possible without an involved intention, *what* the intention reasonably can be does not depend on pure preferences, or decisions, or any other power of the subject. This is (in many cases, but not always) simply *given.*[40]

Thus Paul Touvier had no power to decide what would be his basic intention in killing seven innocent people. To describe his action properly,

39. *In II Sent.*, d.39, q.2 a.1. "Act" here means the physical or "material" part.

40. It belongs to the virtue of prudence to *understand* the contexts in which we act; see my *Natur als Grundlage der Moral,* 346ff., and *La prospettiva della morale,* 288ff.

one must include the purpose or the intention "wanting them to be dead" (even if he would *regret* it; that is only a motivational side-feature, but not the very intention of his acting). Touvier clearly *wanted* the seven to be killed; he chose their deaths for the sake of some greater benefit.[41]

If someone should wonder why "intention" should be included in the "object" or in the "intrinsic nature of an act," he also should wonder why generally things like "will," "intellect," "reason," etc., should be included in human nature. It seems rather obvious that the very "nature" of the acts of a spiritual being—moral acts—includes spiritual elements as "purposes" or "intentions" of the will, shaped by reason, and not only observable behavioral patterns. Is this not precisely the constant teaching of Aquinas?[42] Why should "realizing the evil of death" as such be taken as the adequate description of the object of a human act or express its "intrinsic nature," when exactly the same thing could be brought about by an earthquake or by a robot? Why should simple "solitary stimulation of genital organs as such" be the definition of the object and the intrinsic nature of a human act, when this contains absolutely no indication as to *why* one would do such a thing?

One can therefore describe concrete choices of kinds of behavior as wrong or evil independently of further intentions. Such descriptions, however, always *include* a basic intention, an intention that itself presupposes a given ethically relevant context without which no intention, formed by reason, could come into being. This has nothing to do with the "expanded notion of object." But it includes a certain complexity that is due to the plurality and multiplicity of virtues that in turn reflect human life and its richness in relations between persons, including the differences of ethically relevant practical contexts.

The Shaping of Intentional Basic Actions and the Virtues: Some "Manual Cases"

To explain accurately what I have just said at the end of the preceding section, I should explain how practical principles are generated in a moral

41. This is precisely what does not occur in the case of capital punishment (the argument applies also if one is for other reasons opposed to capital punishment), nor in that of legitimate self-defense, nor in that of killing in a just war (which must always have a defensive, anti-aggression character).

42. See *ST* I-II, q.1 a.3 ad3: "Fines morales accidunt rei naturali; et e converso ratio naturalis finis accidit morali."

theory based on the "ends of virtues."[43] While my approach grows out of a tradition rooted in classical virtue ethics, proportionalism is entirely situated in the context of the manualistic tradition.[44] In opposition to this classical tradition, proportionalism provides, on the basis of modern consequentialism, a relatively uniform theory of decision making, one that can be summed up in some very simple key principles: "What one does, considered *as such,* is not yet morally decisive; whatever one does, however, one ought never directly to intend pre-moral evil; rather, one should always act with a commensurate reason, so as to maximize benefit and/or to minimize harm or evil."

In order to justify his position, McCormick adduces a whole range of classical examples, self-defense, masturbation, lying, contraception, sterilization, theft.[45] Insofar as he deals with these problems as a proportionalist, however, he simply begs the question. By affirming that to describe a moral human action an intentional element is required, McCormick asserts what nearly all hold. There is more, however, to the proportionalist position. McCormick affirms that proportionalists "are saying that an action cannot be judged morally wrong simply by looking at the material happening, or at its object in a very narrow and restricted sense."[46] Yet by identifying the "object in a very narrow and restricted sense" with the "material happening," he has already accepted the physicalist fallacy.[47] So he is necessarily unable to understand how an intentional basic content can be formed. Like Fuchs, Knauer, et al., he will only look at material happenings (the act "as such") and then at *all* the intentions (among which those that will be morally decisive will be those for which one is able to adduce commensurate reasons).[48]

43. See my *La prospettiva della morale,* chapter 5.

44. In order to understand correctly the Catholic tradition of moral teaching, however, one must recover the classical standpoint of virtue ethics. From this standpoint, actions are not considered from the outside—as processes that cause, by combining (pre-moral) goods and evils, foreseeable states of affairs—but rather in terms of "my" intentional relating to good and evil in different ethical contexts (relations between persons, to community and communities, to myself and my body, to God, etc.), so that in choosing certain concrete acts or behaviors my will becomes an evil will, whatever the consequences. Only in this perspective can one understand the shaping of "intentional basic actions" (which correspond to different "moral species" of acts and "moral objects").

45. See also his article, "Killing the patient," *The Tablet,* October 30, 1993, 1410–11.

46. Ibid., 1411.

47. McCormick commits the same error, even more explicitly, in his article "Geburtenregelung als Testfall der Enzyklika," where he asserts that the "object in a narrower sense" is identical with the Thomistic *materia circa quam* (*Moraltheologie im Abseits?* ed. Mieth, 271–84). This is clearly false and shows a physicalist reading of the tradition.

48. We have already seen in the Touvier case that this methodology does not work; nor did it work in the case of masturbation or drunkenness. The problem with killing is that there are

What I maintain is that it is possible both not to be a proportionalist and simultaneously to assert that there is a difference in basic intentional content, that is, the object, in the case of the following actions:

•simple killing for any end whatsoever (an action against justice), even if the ulterior end is saving one's life (this is illicit murder).

•(legitimate) killing in self-defense (killing *praeter intentionem*).

•(carrying out of) capital punishment (an act of punishment, which *may* be regarded as unjust, but which is by its object different from simple killing for any further end whatsoever).

•killing of combatants in war, on the battlefield.

These are not actions to be defined differently only because of different "reasons" one might have for realizing them. Not only their intentional *content,* but also their very intentional *structure* is very different in each case. Since they represent different intentional basic actions, they also are different by their object. Take for example the difference between "self-defense" and "the choice of killing in order to save one's life." On the level of "reasons" regarding the *further* end, both cases are identical: the reason for acting is to save one's life. But if you look at the action not from outside, but from the acting person's perspective, you will notice that there is a different choice (and so there is a different object, too). In legitimate self-defense, what engenders my action is not a will or a choice for the aggressor's death. A sign of this is that I use only violence proportionate to stop his aggression. This may lead me to kill him *(praeter intentionem),* but the reason for my action is not wanting him to be dead (for the sake of saving my life); rather it is wanting to stop his aggression. Thus there is a difference of intention on the level of concrete chosen behavior, and that means, on the level of the object.[49]

Or, take "killing on a battlefield": am I a murderer or simply a soldier who is fighting against an aggressor? Provided the war is what one calls a

some apparent "exceptions," like capital punishment, killing in war, and killing the aggressor in self-defense.

49. This corresponds to the traditional distinction between "direct" and "indirect" killing, a distinction that reflects the easily misleading ambiguity of the word "killing." This is precisely what Aquinas very explicitly explains in the famous article 7 of *ST* II-II, q.64. What proportionalists never understand in their reading of this article is that Aquinas here not only maintains that actions are morally shaped by *id quod intenditur,* but also that the shaping of intentions depends *on what you are doing*—in this case, on the amount of violence you use to stop the aggression. In any case, however, he says: "illicitum est quod homo intendat occidere hominem ut seipsum defendat." It is not a question of "proportionate reason" but of intention involved in action.

just war (*ultima ratio—defense* against an aggression), it entirely depends on what is going on in my heart, that is, whether I want the enemy soldier to be dead, or simply to stop his aggression and to win the battle. Therefore, if as a soldier you do not want to be a murderer, you must care for wounded enemy soldiers. This shows that the object of your acting—the intention involved in your action—obviously was not wanting them to be dead, not even in the moment of battle, even if killing them in the moment was the foreseeable and necessary physical outcome of violence proportionate to stop their aggression.

With theft it is slightly different. Theft refers to property. Property is not a natural or physical entity, but a moral and legal one. Property is not simply "what I have in my hands," but "that to which I am entitled" or "that to which I have a right." Such entitlement and rights, in a given situation, do or do not exist (and this precisely does not depend on consequentialist reasoning). But situations may change: they are contingent. Unlike a person's life, property is not an unchangeable matter. It is a contingent matter, relativized by higher principles of justice. So there are situations of extreme necessity in which no one is reasonably entitled to say to the starving: "This is my property; you have no right to it." If the starving one takes what he needs to survive, it will simply not be the action we call "theft," meaning an action that is contrary to justice.

Therefore one has to analyze intentional contents as belonging to the structure of virtues. Admittedly, the traditional manuals were not very careful in this. Their methodology was rather legalistic, focusing on the external features of actions, referring them to positive law, and only secondarily applying some corrections to recuperate important intentional aspects.[50]

In any event, it seems clear that justice related to property and related to life are two quite different matters. Notice that my arguments adopted so far have nothing in common with a proportionalist reasoning. The question was not whether there was a commensurate reason to realize the pre-moral evil of appropriating another's property, so that the act would not be "theft" any-

50. Thus St. Alphonsus de Liguori treated natural law as if it were a positive legal codex, teaching that *epieikeia* could be applied to it; this meant, however, not negative precepts but those positive precepts that Aquinas describes as valid only "ut in pluribus" (as "deposita sunt reddenda"). Alphonsus's spirit is absolutely correct, but his methodology is of course misleading (he tries to argue within a legalistic framework). St. Alphonsus is today abused by authors who are nevertheless interested in maintaining the "legalistic" approach, so as to apply *epieikeia* even to *negative* precepts, without, however, noting the enormous difference. See Gunter Virt, "Epikie und sittliche Selbstbestimmung," in *Moraltheologie im Abseits?* ed. Mieth, 203–20.

more. Rather, the question was whether or not in a given practical context there existed a title of property (this certainly is not a question of commensurate reason or of utility). Once the question of rights is settled, however, these rights may not be overruled by consequentialist reasoning.[51]

If one applies the proportionalist methodology of decision making to these questions, one will never discern the differences, even though in certain more simply structured cases one will probably arrive at the same result. As a consequentialist, one arrives at this result by speaking only in terms of physical acts, foreseen consequences, and commensurate reasons, a level of discourse that will prove profoundly misleading in more serious questions, as illustrated by the Touvier case. Moreover, that is not how upright people really act and live. We act in given circumstances and personal relationships that form basic intentional contexts and corresponding intentional basic actions. Some of them are simply evil by their basic content. They divert the acting person from human good, and make the will and the heart evil.

The "Key Question" and the Encyclical on Proportionalism

At this point we finally arrive at what McCormick calls the "key question." Why, he asks me, in choosing to kill a person or deceive a person, does one necessarily "take a position with one's will with regard to 'good' and 'evil'"? While some elements of my answer are contained already in what I have explained in the foregoing sections, to answer the question systematically I would have to repeat all that I have said about the misleading distinction, fundamental for proportionalists, between "rightness" and "wrongness" of actions, on the one hand, and the "goodness" and "wickedness" of persons and their actions, on the other. I invite the reader to have a second glance at the original article. Let me add, however, the following.

Proportionalists say that an action is *right* if what one does is justified by commensurate reason. In this view, a person is a *good* person if he or she does not directly intend to realize a pre-moral evil, but intends to act so as to maximize goods or to minimize evils ("in the long run," Knauer would add), meaning to act responsibly by commensurate reasons.

I consider this to be simply erroneous. In my article I wrote:

It is one of the most important assertions of classical virtue ethics that there exist conditions for the fundamental rightness of actions which depend on basic structures of

51. See MacIntyre, "How Can We Learn What *Veritatis Splendor* Has to Teach?" 179–82.

the "rightness of desire" and that it is therefore possible to describe particular types of actions, the *choice* of which always involves wrong desire. (20)

With regard to proportionalist decision-making theories (and their characteristic as "rule-ethics") I then added that these theories *may not,* on the level of the concrete performance of actions, include in their reflection the acting subject and his willingly "taking a position" with regard to "good" and "evil" *in* choosing this or that particular action.

So, if I choose to kill P, I simply set my will against a fundamental right of P, which is moral evil; if I choose to have intercourse with Q, to whom I am not married, I act against the truth of sexuality, harming my own integrity (in the case of simple fornication), or, in the case of adultery, I moreover violate faithfulness due to the person to whom I am married. This implies disorder of my free will, and exactly this we commonly call an *evil will.* If I choose to utter falsehood to a person, given a practical context in which speech acts are meant to be acts of communicative justice (which is not the case in war situations, aggression, etc.), then I am lying to my fellow-man. This means setting my will against social ties due to this person, and this is disorder in my will, moral evil. The same, obviously, applies to theft. At the same time, the one who carries out a capital punishment does not do what he does because he wants the executed to be dead (this could be a further motive, but a condemnable one); he may even do it after having done everything to liberate him. This is an act of punishment, that is, of retributive justice.[52]

Following proportionalist methodology, one will not see, or not concede, the point because one omits focusing on what is going on in the acting and choosing person, precisely where moral evil comes about. Proportionalists are concerned with the reasons one might have to bring about certain states of affairs as the consequences of one's doings; and only this allows a judgment about "right" and "wrong." That is why consequentialists discuss for example the question of whether it could be right to execute the innocent, instead of simply asserting: to execute an innocent person for whatever reason is *evil by its object.* Thus precisely what proportionalists do not want to acknowledge is that, according to the encyclical's quotation of no. 1761 of the *Catechism of the Catholic Church,*

52. See Rhonheimer, *La prospettiva della morale,* 283; also, the helpful analysis by Agnes Heller, *Beyond Justice* (Oxford: Basil Blackwell, 1987), 156ff. I want to repeat that my argument does not yet settle the question whether capital punishment is a good or proportionate, and in this sense, just punishment; it only settles the *basic* objective meaning of the corresponding acts as actions of *punishment* or retributive justice.

> there are certain specific kinds of behavior that are always wrong to choose, *because choosing them involves a disorder of the will, that is, moral evil,*

and that, according to *Veritatis Splendor*'s key sentence in no. 79,

> one must therefore reject the thesis, characteristic of teleological and proportionalist theories, which holds that it is impossible *to qualify as morally evil* according to its species—its "object"—the deliberate *choice of certain kinds of behavior or specific acts,* apart from a consideration of the intention for which the choice is made or the totality of the foreseeable consequences of that act for all persons concerned.

Obviously, the encyclical goes right to the point, and McCormick's reaction, along with similar reactions, confirms that the Pope was right.

This relates to that for which McCormick most reproaches *Veritatis Splendor,* its "misrepresentation" of proportionalism,[53] namely, the encyclical's assertion in no. 76: "Such theories however are not faithful to the Church's teaching, when they believe they can justify, as morally good, deliberate choices of kinds of behavior contrary to the commandments of the divine and the natural law." McCormick repeatedly says that with this the encyclical gravely misrepresents the proportionalists' views, reproaching them falsely "that [the proportionalist position] attempts to justify *morally wrong actions* by a good intention."

This is simply not true. McCormick's complaint would be justified if the Pope held the same understanding of the nature of natural and divine law that is proper to revisionist moral theology. Unlike proportionalists, however, the encyclical holds that in natural and divine law there are included certain negative precepts that precisely refer *universally* to certain kinds of behavior that one never may choose. The encyclical does not reproach proportionalist theologians for wanting to justify by good intentions what is already determined to be morally wrong. The reproach is that proportionalism is a theory by which, in concrete cases, you can justify as morally right what the Church teaches to be universally, *semper et pro semper,* wrong. The Pope therefore reproaches proportionalism for denying that there are certain negative precepts that refer *universally* to certain kinds of behavior that one may never choose (killing the innocent, adultery, fornication, theft, contraception, abortion, lying, etc.).

In fact, what the encyclical rejects is the proportionalist notion of expanded object that allows one *in every concrete case* to "redescribe" concrete

53. McCormick, "Some Early Reactions to *Veritatis Splendor,*" 490ff., 497; "Killing the patient," 1411.

actions, reducing the commandments of law simply to forbid certain immoral *attitudes*, but not choices of determined and intentionally describable *behaviors* or *acts*.

Therefore *Veritatis Splendor* does not here affirm something about the *formal* structure of proportionalist moral judgment (imputing to proportionalists a theory that seeks to justify the principle "one may do good evil that good come about"); the reproach is a *material* one, that is, that proportionalism is a theory according to which such universal negative norms *cannot* exist, so that, according to this theory, one comes to declare to be morally right what natural and divine law, according to the Church's teaching, declares to be morally wrong and evil. Thus *Veritatis Splendor*'s assertion in no. 76 does not characterize proportionalism as a theory, but it characterizes the *result* of this theory, its *material* implications, as leading to moral judgments explicitly contrary to what the Church teaches as morally wrong and evil.

As evidence for this judgment, I refer again to the example of Fuchs, who wrote in 1971: "What value do our norms have with respect to the morality of the action as such, prior, that is, to the consideration of the circumstances and intention? We answer: They cannot be moral norms, unless circumstances and intention are taken into account."[54] Some pages later, referring to norms related to actions that "could never be objectively justified," he concludes:

> Viewed theoretically, there seems to be no possibility of norms of this kind for human action in the inner-worldly realm. The reason is that an action cannot be judged morally at all, considered purely in itself, but only together with all the "circumstances" and the "intention." Consequently, a behavioral norm, universally valid in the full sense, would presuppose that those who arrive at it could know or foresee *all the possible combinations* of the action concerned with circumstances and intentions, with (pre-moral) values and non-values (*bona* and *mala 'physica'*).[55]

Of course, Fuchs—like others—neglects to distinguish here between negative (prohibitive) and affirmative norms, which would make all the difference. And so, in a recent paper, he even speculates that in a future, yet unknown time, the command "you shall not commit adultery" could change and no longer be valid without exceptions; there could be imaginable "rare exceptions, on the grounds of highly important reasons and with mutual consent."[56]

54. Fuchs, "The Absolutness of Moral Terms," 121.

55. Ibid., 124.

56. Josef Fuchs, "Die sittliche Handlung: das instrinsece malum," *Moraltheologie im Abseits?* ed. Mieth, 183. Of course, for Fuchs this should not be called "adultery" any more; one would have to devise another name for it.

Similarly, it is not surprising that with regard to "murder, adultery, stealing, genocide, torture, prostitution, slavery, etc." McCormick cites with approval the argument of Lisa Sowle Cahill: "These phrases, Cahill correctly notes, do not define acts in the abstract, 'but acts (like intercourse or homicide) *together with the conditions or circumstances* in which they become immoral.'"[57] In their view, precisely because these "conditions or circumstances" can be discerned only in each particular case, the general norm indicating a *species* or *kind* of behavior tells us nothing definitive about whether the act is right or wrong, but merely provides us with a *name* for something of which we disapprove. Yet McCormick misses the point when he complains that Robert P. George "misrepresents proportionalists as maintaining that rape, murder, and adultery could be justified by a proportionate reason,"[58] for what the critics of proportionalism are arguing is that the acts that proportionalists would not designate as "adultery" or "murder" because of the "conditions or circumstances" are in fact precisely acts of "adultery" or "murder," regardless of the new names given to such acts by the proportionalists. McCormick's complaint simply begs the question.

The notion of "expanded object" requires that any universally formulated norm be open to exception because of a "commensurate reason" that redescribes the act in question. Proportionalism thus teaches that *precisely on the grounds of intention,* determined behaviors that are held by the Church's teaching to be *semper et pro semper* immoral, evil, and wrong according to divine and natural law may be become "right," *here and now*—when the "expanded object" is taken into consideration.[59] The trick is precisely to affirm this by a theory that is immune against the reproach, "you are trying to justify evil means by good intentions," since the very theory eliminates even the *possibility* of doing such a thing, for it argues that only evil intentions render an act evil and that a well-intentioned act is necessarily good. And that is why this theory is not only erroneous, but moreover dangerously confusing moral reasoning. Proportionalism is a methodology by which one in fact always can *with good conscience* act according to the principle "let us do evil

57. McCormick, "Some Early Reactions to *Veritatis Splendor,*" 492; the quotation is from Cahill's article, "Accent on the Masculine," *The Tablet,* December 11, 1993, 1618–19.

58. McCormick, "Some Early Reactions to *Veritatis Splendor,*" 487.

59. This is clearly seen in John Paul II, *Veritatis Splendor* (The Splendor of Truth, 1993), no. 56, where the encyclical points out that according to the methodology that it rejects "a certain concrete existential consideration . . . could legitimately be the basis of certain *exceptions to the general rule* and thus permit one to do in practice and in good conscience what is qualified as intrinsically evil by the moral law."

so that good come about," because the methodology gives one the conviction that, provided good comes foreseeably about, what you did was not evil at all, but just the morally right thing, so that the ominous principle does not apply in your case. Whoever nevertheless reproaches you for trying to justify, on the grounds of "good reasons," what in reality is morally evil, will be "misrepresenting" your position.

McCormick said that the reason for what he sees as my error was probably that I had "taken one general description of consequentialism and applied it indiscriminately to all recent revisionist analyses." I do not think this is the case. But even if it were true, McCormick's position is still included in what I criticized in my article. And I also think that his position is one of those reasonably rejected by *Veritatis Splendor.*

5

Practical Reason and the "Naturally Rational"

On the Doctrine of the Natural Law as a Principle of Praxis in Thomas Aquinas

Lex naturalis: A Doctrine of the Principles of Practical Reason

The debate on the interpretation of the Thomistic doctrine of the *lex naturalis* that has been going on for the last thirty years has been driven by two things: first, a renewed interest in the specifically philosophical ethics of St. Thomas, and second, the attempt by moral theologians to make the idea of a "natural law" fruitful for understanding the autonomy of the human person as a moral subject. Despite a wide palette of interpretations, a few basic insights have become crystallized, and are approved almost without exception today by anyone familiar with the field.[1] The most important of these basic insights would probably be that the doctrine of the *lex naturalis* is not a doctrine about nature, or about a natural order imparted beforehand to human moral insight and only awaiting human realization, but rather a doctrine of the practical reason of the moral subject and the principles of this reasoning—in other words, a philosophical-ethical doctrine of principles.

1. Editor's note: This comment refers mainly to German-language scholarship on natural law and Aquinas.

Secondly, it may today be accepted in general that practical reason has an independence vis-à-vis theoretical reason, and that practical judgments cannot be derived from theoretical ones, but possess instead their own unassailable starting point. This means that there is a certain parallelism between the theoretical and practical. A third point, in consequence of these two, and here again there is wide consensus, is that the subject matter of ethics cannot be derived from that of metaphysics. Metaphysics—and its corresponding philosophical anthropology—is rather a subsequent illumination and deeper explication of independent, self-experienced practical reasoning by the subject of action.[2]

While the neo-Thomistic conception of the "natural moral law" seems to be obsolescent in current research, nevertheless in today's reading of Thomas, the "autonomistic"[3] interpretation of the doctrine of natural law that was supposed to have superseded the neo-Thomistic meaning has been increasingly recognized as inadequate. This "autonomistic" position conceived the *lex naturalis* simply as the natural tendency of the practical reason to formulate ever new moral norms in a creative manner, and finally as the obligation to act according to reason, and treated the natural inclinations of the human person merely as "raw material" for the shaping function of reason.[4] In recent years, the exponents of this concept have presented their position

2. Fundamental for this new orientation are: W. Kluxen, *Philosophische Ethik bei Thomas von Aquin* (Hamburg: Meiner, 1980); G. Grisez, "The First Principle of Practical Reasoning: A Commentary on the *Summa Theologiae,* 1–2, Question 94, article 2," *Natural Law Forum* 10 (1965): 168–201, a slightly abridged version of which is in A. Kenny, ed., *Aquinas: A Collection of Critical Essays* (Garden City, N.Y.: Anchor Books, 1969); J. Finnis, *Natural Law and Natural Rights* (Oxford: Clarendon, 1980). The most prominent opponent of the thesis of a parallelism of theoretical and practical reasoning is R. McInerny: cf. for example "The Principles of Natural Law," *American Journal of Jurisprudence* 25 (1980): 1–15; *Ethica Thomistica: The Moral Philosophy of Thomas Aquinas* (Washington, D.C.: The Catholic University of America Press, 1982); and *Aquinas on Human Action: A Theory of Practice* (Washington, D.C.: The Catholic University of America Press, 1992), esp. 184ff. In the same perspective, cf. R. Hittinger, *A Critique of the New Natural Law Theory* (Notre Dame, Ind.: University of Notre Dame Press, 1987).

3. Editor's note: By using the term "autonomistic" instead of "autonomous," Rhonheimer wants to distinguish that it is not the "position" of these theologians that is "autonomous." Rather, they understand man to be autonomous. Therefore, by "autonomistic" Rhonheimer means to indicate "autonomism" in the sense of an ideology.

4. F. Böckle, *Das Naturrecht im Disput* (Düsseldorf: Patmos-Verlag, 1966); Böckle, "Natürliches Gesetz als göttliches Gesetz in der Moraltheologie," in F. Böckle and E.-W. Böckenförde, eds., *Naturrecht in der Kritik* (Mainz: Matthias Grünewald, 1973), 165–88; Böckle, *Fundamentalmoral* (Munich: Kösel, 1977); K.-W. Merks, *Theologische Grundlegung der sittlichen Autonomie. Strukturmomente eines "autonomen" Normbegründungsverständnisses im lex-Traktat der Summa Theologiae des Thomas von Aquin* (Düsseldorf: Patmos-Verlag, 1978).

in substantially modified form,[5] and the view itself has been categorized as extreme.[6] And not very long after this they have been taken to task not only for introducing "a serious historical distortion, or even a mutilation of the Thomistic project," but also for revealing "a deficient understanding of the problem from a systematic perspective."[7] Now this at least establishes in a way what I already attempted to demonstrate years ago, namely that this interpretation, although it represented a serious attempt, nevertheless was not capable of answering the demand for a scientifically respectable interpretation of Thomas, and was not in a position to grasp adequately the moral autonomy of the human person as a finite, spiritually and corporeally constituted, created being.[8]

Now, the account of the Thomistic doctrine of the *lex naturalis* as presented in *Natural Law and Practical Reason* has been further developed in subsequent studies which take account of the genesis of Thomas's action-theory and interpretation of the practical reason within the problematic of Aristotelian ethics.[9] Along with much agreement, this interpretation has also met with

5. Cf. F. Böckle, "Was bedeutet 'Natur' in der Moraltheologie?" in F. Böckle, ed., *Der umstrittene Naturbegriff. Person—Natur—Sexualität in der kirchlichen Morallehre* (Düsseldorf: Patmos-Verlag, 1987), 45–68; and K.-W. Merks, "Naturrecht als Personrecht. Überlegungen zu einer Relektüre der Naturrechtslehre des Thomas von Aquin," in M. Heimbach-Steins, ed., *Naturrecht im ethischen Diskurs,* Schriften des Instituts für Christliche Sozialwissenschaften 21 (Münster: Aschendorff, 1990), 28–46, esp. 39f. In any event, it is not completely clear whether these modifications really affect the fundamental structure of the interpretation.

6. E. Schockenhoff, *Naturrecht und Menschenwürde. Universalethik in einer geschichtlichen Welt* (Mainz: Matthias-Grünewald-Verlag, 1996), 150. [Editor's note: Schockenhoff's book has been published in English as *Natural Law and Human Dignity: Universal Ethics in an Historical World* (Washington, D.C.: The Catholic University of America Press, 2003). In the English version, the criticism of Rhonheimer's position has been substantially modified (see esp. 140ff.).]

7. F. J. Bormann, *Natur als Horizont sittlicher Praxis. Zur handlungstheoretischen Interpretation der Lehre vom natürlichen Sittengesetz bei Thomas von Aquin,* Münchner philosophische Studien, Neue Folge, Band 14 (Stuttgart/Berlin/Cologne: Verlag W. Kohlhammer, 1999), 223.

8. M. Rhonheimer, *Natural Law and Practical Reason: A Thomist View of Moral Autonomy* (New York: Fordham University Press, 2000). As noted above, this is an English translation of *Natur als Grundlage der Moral* (Innsbruck-Vienna: Tyrolia-Verlag, 1987). A similar conclusion was reached at the same time by R. Bruch, "Das sittliche Gesetz als Gottes- und Menschenwerk bei Thomas von Aquin," *Zeitschrift für Katholische Theologie* 109 (1987): 294–311.

9. Martin Rhonheimer, *Praktische Vernunft und Vernünftigkeit der Praxis. Handlungstheorie bei Thomas von Aquin in ihrer Entstehung aus dem Problemkontext der aristotelischen Ethik* (Berlin: Akademie Verlag, 1994); Rhonheimer, *La prospettiva della morale. Fondamenti dell'etica filosofica* (Rome: Armando Editore, 1994); this last book has also appeared in a slightly expanded and updated edition in Spanish translation: *La perspectiva de la moral* (Madrid: Rialp, 2000). [Editor's note: There is also a substantially enlarged and updated edition in German: *Die Perspektive der Moral. Philosophische Grundlagen der Tugendethik* (Berlin: Akademie Verlag, 2001). As previously noted, an English translation is forthcoming from The Catholic University of America Press.]

disagreement, and this latter has come not only from neo-Thomists[10] but also from those who, in their concern with natural law doctrine, have the same interest in developing a doctrine of practical principles. The objection—and in fact it bears on a central issue—is twofold. On the one hand, such critics say that, according to the interpretation developed in *Natural Law and Practical Reason,* the relationship of the practical reason to the *inclinationes naturales* is viewed merely as an affirmation by the reason of the naturally given appetitive goals, such that the shaping and ordering function of the reason is overlooked and its difference from the theoretical reason obliterated. Such neglect of the function of the reason as creating order in all that is natural would bring us at last to assume an identity between the material appetitive goals of nature and what is recognized as good by the reason, encouraging us to derive concrete practical guidance from these natural strivings.[11] On the other hand, and in close connection with this, it has been objected that *Natural Law and Practical Reason* and its further development, *Praktische Vernunft und Vernünftigkeit der Praxis,* plead for a conception of practical reason according to which—through a neglect of the gradations of moral judgment and the contingency of concrete experience—the concrete judgments of prudence would be derived from the principles of the *lex naturalis* in an infallible manner and without any recourse to experience.[12]

These are the two chief points of controversy. The present paper will concentrate on the first of the two objections.[13] But first it will be necessary to

10. A brief review of the reception of *Natur als Grundlage der Moral* can be found in the Postscript to the English translation of *Natur als Grundlage der Moral:* Rhonheimer, *Natural Law and Practical Reason,* 555–92.

11. G. Wieland, "Secundum naturam vivere. Über das Verhältnis von Natur und Sittlichkeit," in B. Fraling, ed., *Natur im ethischen Argument,* Studien zur theologischen Ethik 31 (Freiburg: Herder, 1990), 13–31, esp. 21–26; L. Honnefelder, "Natur als Handlungsprinzip. Die Relevance der Natur für die Ethik," in L. Honnefelder, ed., *Natur als Gegenstand der Wissenschaften* (Freiburg/Munich: K. Alber, 1992), 151–90, esp. 179 n. 92; Schockenhoff, *Naturrecht und Menschenwürde,* 150, 154, and 168, and *Compte Rendu* of Martin Rhonheimer, "Praktische Vernunft und Vernünftigkeit der Praxis," *Studia Moralia* 34 (1996): 133–47; Bormann, *Natur als Horizont sittlicher Praxis,* 223–27. [Translator's note: Most often "appetitive goals," and less often "sought-for goals," "goals of striving," etc., are used here to capture the German *Strebensziele,* which uses the Germanic root common to English "strive" and German *streben* to convey the technical Scholastic term *appetitio,* or "seeking."]

12. Schockenhoff so indicates in *Naturrecht und Menschenwürde,* 153ff., and in the same author's *Compte Rendu,* 138ff. [Editor's note: This objection by Schockenhoff has been omitted in the 2003 English version of his book, published subsequent to Rhonheimer's response (as noted in the next footnote).]

13. For a detailed response to the second objection, see my "Praktische Prinzipien, Naturgesetz und konkrete Handlungsurteile in tugendethischer Perspektive. Zur Diskussion über praktische Vernunft und lex naturalis bei Thomas von Aquin," *Studia Moralia* 39 (2001): 113–58.

sketch out briefly the contested position. This will make it easier to clarify some of the misunderstandings that have emerged in the course of the debate.

Lex naturalis: A Principle of Praxis Orientated to the "Naturally Rational"

For the position developed in my earlier works it was necessary to show that Thomas Aquinas understood the *lex naturalis* as a principle of action.[14] What this means is that the natural law is those first principles of human action which constitute the subject of actions as an acting subject, and of course, from the outset and necessarily, in the horizon of what is naturally good for man. Precisely because the *lex naturalis* is a principle of action, it is likewise a principle of moral action and thereby a moral principle. It constitutes man, at one and the same time, as both acting and moral subject. The doctrine of the natural law is more precisely not a doctrine about "nature" but rather about the (practical) reason insofar as it is a natural reason, that is, insofar as it has the "naturally good" as its object. The doctrine of the *lex naturalis* is therefore a doctrine about the practical reason insofar as it is nature and therefore what Aquinas (following Aristotle) calls the *intellectus principiorum,* "the intellect of principles."[15]

A theory of the practical reason cannot be exhausted in the doctrine of the *lex naturalis;* this is because the latter involves merely the function of a doctrine of practical principles. Practical reason is oriented toward action, and action takes place in the realm of the particular and the contingent, of what "can be otherwise." Practical principles are starting points, a foundation, a basis of justification. Nothing goes on without this foundation, everything is related to it, but in itself it is insufficient and underdetermined for practical purposes.[16] Nothing concretely practical can be immediately and necessarily derived from it, even though there are boundaries of the "morally possible" and corresponding negative normative statements, since it can be quite convincingly shown in some areas of activity that a certain concretely describable action contradicts the principle or cannot be justified by the principle. Thanks to this underdetermination of general practical principles,

14. According to R. Schönberger, this was a "new thesis" of Thomas's interpretation; cf. his review of *Praktische Vernunft und Vernünftigkeit der Praxis* in *Zeitschrift für philosophische Forschung* 49 (1995): 631.

15. Translator's note: This renders the German "Prinzipienvernunft."

16. See Rhonheimer, *Natural Law and Practical Reason,* 274, 279f., 525f.

when it comes to concrete guidance for actions, the practical reason needs prudence, a practical judgment that is directed to concrete action. Only reasoning that is directed to concrete action is practical in a full and conclusive way.[17] Nevertheless, prudence is not possible without the intentional guidance of principles, which ultimately contain nothing other than the goals of the moral virtues. This intentional guidance by principles secures the morality of the means. Prudence is not craftiness. For example, the prudent person is not only the one who seeks justice, but the one who does what is just, here and now. Concrete action can be "just" and thus "morally right," only insofar as it is action guided by the principle and runs in its course, and in this way concretizes and fulfills the principle. This is precisely how the "practical truth" of concrete action, understood in the Aristotelian sense, is constituted: through its agreement with "right appetition."[18] However, this means that quite various actions, but still not just *any* actions—can pertain to the same right end,[19] and that ethics can therefore only be a "science in outline."[20]

To grasp the *lex naturalis* as a principle of praxis—and that means understanding it as that fundamental, cognitive, and appetitively-moving orientation toward the good, through which the human being is constituted as an acting subject—is to place oneself from the outset in the perspective of the first person. Whoever speaks about the *lex naturalis* in St. Thomas's interpretation does not speak in fact about moral norms or the normative grounding of the rectitude of actions, but rather about the body-and-soul unity of the human person as a subject of actions and about the origin of the person's reason-guided striving,[21] through which this person can be understood as a subject that moves himself toward the good for man. If the *lex naturalis* is understood in this sense, it becomes clear that its content is in fact not commandments, duties, or demands of the ought, but rather the "good for man," as it comes into the view of the natural reason, partly with natural spontaneity and partly through the discursive unfolding of the first principles. Only in reflection, then, is the good as "command" or "norm" objectified, and appropriate normative statements formulated.[22] The *lex naturalis* as such is never-

17. Rhonheimer, *Practische Vernunft und Vernünftigkeit der Praxis,* 565ff.

18. This was the central theme of *Praktische Vernunft und Vernünftigkeit der Praxis.*

19. See Rhonheimer, *Natural Law and Practical Reason,* 322–23.

20. See Rhonheimer, *La prospettiva della morale,* 295ff., 299.

21. Translator's note: *vernünftgeleitete Streben,* or "reason-led appetition"; see n. 11 above.

22. Cf. Rhonheimer, *Natural Law and Practical Reason,* 58ff., 257ff.; *Praktische Vernunft und Vernünftigkeit der Praxis,* 545ff.

theless just the practical reason itself that moves a person to the good, on the level of its general principles. It does not in the first place want to *say* something about "good" and "evil," but rather does what originally belongs to the practical reason to do: *move* a person toward the good. This is how it constitutes the human being as at once an acting and moral subject.

Not all interpreters of Thomas understand the *lex naturalis* in this sense as a "principle of praxis"—not even those who support the autonomy of the practical reason. Most of the misunderstandings (and particularly the criticism that the idea which I present is supposed to support a simply deductive "derivation" of the concrete guidance of actions from the natural goals of appetition, making possible a corresponding "infallible" rectitude of judgments in the particular actions of the prudent person), are based, most likely, on treating the theme of the *lex naturalis* primarily from the point of view of the typical problems of normative ethics.[23] So the question in the foreground is, how concretely and conclusively can the practical principles, understood as commands of the *lex naturalis*, provide norms for concrete action? In *Natural Law and Practical Reason*, but even more in subsequent works on the theme, my attempt has been to move from this perspective to that of action-theory and to grasp the practical principles in the sense of the *lex naturalis* as the goals of the moral virtues. In this way concrete behavior is recognizable as a realization, or non-realization, of a goal. This has nothing to do with the question of the derivation of judgments for concrete actions from general norms, nor with maintaining an infallibility of the prudent person in determining what is "right" in every instance. What is meant is not a factual rectitude, but rather the moral "being-right" or "being-good" of action, on the basis of its "practical truth," that is, its coincidence with the goal of virtue.[24] Now it is part of the Aristotelian concept of the "prudent" man or

23. This seems to me to be notorious in the works of E. Schockenhoff and F. J. Bormann, despite their many quite positive points. [Editor's note: In the English edition of his book *Naturrecht und Menschenwürde* (published subsequent to the appearance of the original German version of the present chapter), Schockenhoff has abandoned this line of criticism, having, as it seems, recognized it as a misunderstanding of Rhonheimer's position; see his *Natural Law and Human Dignity*, 140, n. 19.]

24. In this perspective, however, also "actions that are evil in themselves [*intrinsice malae*]" can be defined as missing the goal of the virtue, but this is by no means the main task of ethics. The widespread and typical "derivation anxiety" goes along with an equally widespread bias toward emphasizing the existence of "exceptions" (for example, in the prohibition of killing). In *Natural Law and Practical Reason* the attempt was made to criticize the dominant normative ethics perspective from the viewpoint of classical virtue ethics (which in any case should not be seen as the opposite of normative ethics, as contemporary Anglo-Saxon "virtue ethics" sees it-

spoudaios—he is a paradigmatic ideal—that he never errs in this way, but in carrying out the affective certainty of his reason always hits the truth.[25] Prudence in the Aristotelian sense (φρόνησις) is "a reliable habit of rational action in things which can be good or evil for human beings."[26] The concrete actions of the prudent, however else they may come about, are in this sense "right," that they realize "justice," "temperance," "courage," "discretion," "generosity," and so forth in the concrete and particular, and thereby lead to the goal of the corresponding virtue and human fulfillment.

It appears then that there are two extreme positions, both of which fall short of the idea of the *lex naturalis* and push normative discourse too far to the fore. First, there is the traditional conception, represented by a few neo-Thomistic currents, according to which the natural law is equated with "natural lawfulness" and an "order of nature," which human action is then obliged to realize. Practical reason here appears as a kind of "organ" for "reading off" moral-normative guidance from nature. It does not seem necessary to concern ourselves further with this position in the present context. The other extreme position is one which goes so far in denying this first conception that it places the reason in a completely different position against nature, and whether this be in the above-mentioned extreme "autonomistic" variant (F. Böckle), or whether it be in weaker forms (W. Korff, L. Honnefelder, G. Wieland), all such interpretations display an essential likeness despite differences of detail. They do accept the doctrine of the *lex naturalis* as a doctrine of the practical reason, but nevertheless they do not take the next step of understanding this reason as that which constitutes man in a fundamental way as an acting subject that moves himself toward the good; thereby they are not capable of explaining how the orientation of man toward what is naturally good for him comes into existence through the practical reason, or how the "naturally rational," which alone has the character of a principle, is

self; it is rather a case of reversing the priority of point of view). Cf. also M. Rhonheimer, "Intrinsically Evil Acts and the Moral Viewpoint: Clarifying a Central Teaching of *Veritatis Splendor*," in chap. 3 of this book or *The Thomist* 58, no. 1 (1994): 1–39; "Intentional Actions and the Meaning of Object: A Reply to Richard McCormick," in chap. 4 of this book or *The Thomist* 59, no. 2 (1995): 279–311; "'Ethics of Norms' and the Lost Virtues: Searching the Roots of the Crisis of Ethical Reasoning," *Anthropotes* 9 (1993): 231–43. On the difference between classical and contemporary Anglo-Saxon virtue ethics, see the important remarks by J. Annas, *The Morality of Happiness* (Oxford: Oxford University Press, 1993), 439ff. On the same topic see also J. Schuster, *Moralisches Können. Studien zur Tugendethik* (Würzburg: Echter, 1997).

25. Cf. Aristotle, *Ethica Nicomachea* III, 4, 1113a15–1113b2.

26. Aristotle, *Ethica Nicomachea* VI, 5, 1140b4–6.

constituted.[27] The real "normative discourse" is thereby largely detached from its link to "nature," and this shows, to say the least, that it becomes difficult, in the framework of such a conception, to recognize the relevance of a virtue-ethical approach to normative ethics.[28]

In a certain way, this second position is extreme because it is ultimately incapable of understanding the practical reason as nature, nor the first principles of practical reason as (substantial) goals of the moral virtues, which Thomas says, in fact, are "determined by nature."[29] This point of view can think of "rationality" as being "nature" and "natural" to man only in a *formal* sense—the indwelling compulsion of human nature to act according to the reason but not as an act of reasoning as related to a good of specific *content.* "Nature" as naturally given, material content, as the "good" and "goal," according to this interpretation, is always opposed to the "reason" and stands over against it. The relationship between practical reason and naturally-striven-for goals is thought of in this context as bipolar, and in effect, if not deliberately, comes very close to a certain dualism. Indeed, insofar as this interpretation contains a doctrine of the practical reason, it is not about the *lex naturalis* at all, but rather only about the reason as a criterion of moral configuration, standing in front of everything natural. On the other hand, to the extent that this interpretation does speak about "nature," it ceases to be a doctrine of practical reason. The category of the "naturally rational" is foreign to it. Reason as reason remains contentless and formal, and it has the tendency not even to recognize a *lex naturalis* in the strict sense, but only a "natural inclination" (nature) on the one side and a shaping reason that comes forth to formulate moral norms, on the other.

To understand the *lex naturalis* as a principle of praxis means to see in it the fundamental orientation of the human person toward the good, operating within the context of the natural inclinations, without which praxis would not

27. The treatment by E. Schockenhoff, *Naturrecht und Menschenwürde,* perhaps comes the closest to this conception, above all because it rightly recognizes the moving character of the first principle of practical reason (cf. 170). In Bormann's *Natur als Horizont sittlicher Praxis* can be found an action-theoretical understanding of the *lex naturalis* in the context of the "natural will," which likewise approaches the idea of a *lex naturalis* as principle of action. Certainly C. Schörer's *Praktische Vernunft bei Thomas von Aquin* (Stuttgart/Berlin/Cologne: W. Kohlhammer, 1995) points in a similar direction. On closer inspection, however, the question arises as to whether these authors have really thought the initial idea through to its conclusion.

28. This holds as well for the Thomistic natural law theory put forward by J. Finnis and G. Grisez. On this question see also Schuster, *Moralisches Können.*

29. Cf. Aquinas, *In Ethic.* VI., lect. 2.

even be possible. The principles of the practical reason, commands of the natural law, and goals of the moral virtues all come to the same thing.[30] For it is precisely the practical reason of body-soul constituted human persons which already guides the human being toward the good through the most general and highest judgments, thereby laying the foundation for the phenomenon of moral obligation. The last-mentioned is originally nothing other than attractive power of what appears as good, emerging before the reason in the judgment, "this is good." This is why, according to Thomas, the *lex naturalis* has its power to oblige only from the practical judgment of the natural reason, insofar as this determines to do or avoid this or that.[31] The reason needs no recourse to the fact that the *lex naturalis* is a participation in the eternal divine law. In the actual field of operations of the natural law, the eternal law does not itself possess any behavioral guiding function, but is simply a supplementary interpretation, a speculative referencing to its creational foundation.[32] In any event, the insight into this creation/theological and metaphysical context allows, among other things, some explanation why revelation of the natural law is also possible, which can then become immediately directive of action in the supernatural order as positive "divine law."[33]

On the basis of this summary presentation, I have tried to place in correct context the following attempt to turn aside the accusation that I have mistaken the relationship between reason and natural inclination. This context is that of a virtue ethics in the Aristotelian tradition, which in Thomas's hands was expanded into a doctrine of principles in the form of the doctrine of the *lex naturalis*.

30. On this point see especially Rhonheimer, *La prospettiva della morale*.

31. Cf. *ST* I-II, q.104 a.1; on which see Rhonheimer, *Praktische Vernunft und Vernünftigkeit der Praxis*, 532; cf. also *La prospettiva della morale*, 260ff.

32. Bormann, *Natur als Horizont sittlicher Praxis*, 200ff., makes an effort to show that I hold the opposite position. Bormann's account is based on an erroneous and careless reading of *Natur als Grundlage der Moral* and *Praktische Vernunft und Vernünftigketi der Praxis*. Bormann understands all statements about the creational-metaphysical significance of the doctrine of the participation of the *lex naturalis* in the eternal law (brought up as proof for the impossibility of the "autonomistic" interpretation of Thomas) as statements about the basis for the obligatory nature of the commands of the natural law. What is intended as a statement at the reflective level in the realm of "philosophical ethics" is understood by Bormann as a statement about the practical reason of the acting subject himself, and this reaches its peak in his reproach that I put myself "in direct opposition to the standpoint of Aquinas" (200) and that I run the risk of "tossing out the decisive results of W. Kluxen's scientific analyses" (201). A similar reproach with a different justification already appeared in F. Ricken's, article "Naturrecht I," in *Theologische Realenzyklopädie*, vol. 24 (Berlin/New York: W. de Gruyter, 1994), 144f. Further treatment of this will have to await another opportunity.

33. Cf. Kluxen, *Philosophische Ethik bei Thomas von Aquin*, 237.

Practical Reason and Natural Inclinations

A Problematic Thesis: "The Two-Stage Operation of the Practical Reason"

Along with L. Honnefelder,[34] G. Wieland represents above all the position that the "structure of the practical reason in general" is to be understood as normative for nature: "In order for nature to become meaningful for the context of actions at all, man must be in a condition to relate to nature, and that means he must be thought of as already rational and free. In the first principle of practical reason Thomas formulates the foundation of all morality, which must be presupposed when someone stands in relation to nature for a practical purpose."[35] Wieland takes issue with the interpretation presented in *Natural Law and Practical Reason,* because it mistakenly conceives, according to him, the relationship between "natural inclinations" and "practical reason"; it allows the naturalness of the *inclinatio naturalis* to become a rule for the reason, instead of acknowledging the contrary, namely that "in the beginning" reason is there and not nature.[36]

In maintaining this, Wieland is following, to my knowledge, the thesis formulated by L. Honnefelder of a "two-stage operation of the practical reason" in Thomas.[37] First of all, according to Honnefelder's thesis, the subject constitutes itself, under the most universal practical difference between "good" and "evil," as rational and free, in order afterwards to relate itself in this reflected and even rational manner to the natural inclinations and corresponding appetitive goals that are found in its nature. "This two-stage opera-

34. L. Honnefelder, "Praktische Vernunft und Gewissen," in A. Hertz, W. Korff, T. Rendtorff, and H. Ringeling, *Handbuch der Christlichen Ethik,* vol. 3 (Freiburg/Basel/Vienna: Herder, 1982), 19–43, esp. 24; "Die Begründbarkeit des Ethischen und die Einheit der Menschheit," in G. W. Hunold and W. Korff, eds., *Die Welt für morgen. Ethische Herausforderungen im Anspruch der Zukunft* (Munich: Kösel, 1986), 315–27, esp. 320; "Wahrheit und Sittlichkeit. Zur Bedeutung der Wahrheit in der Ethik," in E. Coreth, ed., *Wahrheit und Einheit in der Vielheit* (Düsseldorf: Patmos-Verlag, 1987), 147–69, esp. 156; "Die ethische Rationalität des mittelalterlichen Naturrechts. Max Webers und Ernst Troeltschs Deutung des mittelalterlichen Naturrechts und die Bedeutung der Lehre vom natürlichen Gesetz bei Thomas von Aquin," in W. Schluchter, ed., *Max Webers Sicht des okzidentalen Christentums* (Frankfurt am Main: Suhrkamp, 1988), 254–275; "Absolute Forderungen in der Ethik. Im welchem Sinn ist eine sittliche Verpflichtung absolut?" in W. Kerber, ed., *Das absolute in der Ethik* (Munich: Kindt Verlag, 1991), 13–33. Cf. also Honnefelder, "Natur als Handlungsprinzip," 176.

35. Wieland, "Secundum naturam vivere," 25.

36. On this objection see *Natural Law and Practical Reason,* Postscript, 564f.

37. Honnefelder, "Praktische Vernünft und Gewissen," 23ff.; "Natur als Handlungsprinzip," 175; "Die Begründbarkeit des Ethischen und die Einheit der Menschheit," 320ff.; "Wahrheit und Sittlichkeit," 156ff.; "Absolute Forderungen in der Ethik," 25ff.

tion"—says Honnefelder—"puts Thomas in the position of meeting the difficulty that is persistent in Aristotle, of having to choose between treating the goal of action as a mere prolongation of the appetitive goal (and thus founding its obligatoriness in a naturalistic way), or of seeing it anchored in the current ethos (and thus accepting its obligatoriness as an immediate, unquestionable position)."[38]

Honnefelder's sense of a two-stage operation of the practical reason implies further that in the first principle of the practical reason "to do good and avoid evil," a first difference comes to expression, which places action under a most universal and underivable formal rule. This rule then obliges the subject to act according to reason—with justification—instead of simply following causes, that is, the drives of the natural inclinations. In this way the first principle of the practical reason provides "the *form,* which all statements must have which are going to lead to action, just as the principle of contradiction provides the form which all statements must follow that are going to say anything. Secondly, it makes sure that knowledge of the current good also *obliges* the will and action of the knower. In regard to content it says nothing but the requirement to follow the reason."[39]

Honnefelder appears to conceive of the highest principle of the practical reason as a "statement" that "says" something, a binding expression, in fact.[40] But when we consider it closely, neither the highest principle of the practical reason nor all consequent principles can be called "sentences" or "normative statements"; they only become such in the mode of reflection of reason upon its own practical act.[41] The principles of the practical reason (= precepts of the natural law) are those first practical judgments, which through being embedded in the appetitive dynamism of the natural inclinations have a fundamentally practical/moving character, and as such, independently of linguistic formulation, they first of all constitute the subject as an acting subject through its orientation toward the naturally known good.[42] Secondly, it

38. Honnefelder, "Absolute Forderungen in der Ethik," 25.

39. Honnefelder, "Natur als Handlungsprinzip," 176.

40. Cf. also Honnefelder, "Die ethische Rationalität des mittelalterlichen Naturrechts," 259.

41. Cf. Rhonheimer, *Natural Law and Practical Reason,* 59, where the expression "normative statement" is introduced.

42. This is why, in the case of "laws," Thomas speaks of them in I-II, q.90 a.2 ad2 as *propositiones universales rationis practicae ordinatae ad actiones* (universal propositions of the practical reason ordered to actions). *Propositio* is intended to mean not only a "statement" but a *judgment* of the reason; cf. I-II, q.94 a.1, "lex naturalis est aliquid per rationem constitutum; sicut etiam propositio est quoddam opus rationis" (the natural law is something constituted through the reason, just as a proposition is a certain work of the reason).

scarcely seems possible that the highest practical principle only provides the "form of moral judgment" in the sense of a mere constitution of the subject as such which, in its action and its own relationship with its natural inclinations, must in each case inquire into justifications. To be sure, nothing further concerning what is "good" for man can be derived from the first principle of the practical reason *bonum est prosequendum et faciendum, malum vitandum.* But it becomes normatively effective and then "says" something with content insofar as, on the basis of this principle, the appetitive goals, being offered to the reason by the natural inclinations and put into order by the reason, are grasped as "things-to-be-carried-out-in-action" *(opere prosequenda).*[43] Now here—and this is a third point—is where Honnefelder's "two-stage operation" breaks down: man does not constitute himself as a practical/rational subject beforehand and independently of the relationship of the practical reason with the appetitive goals of the natural inclinations, but right *in* the grasp of the *bona* as revealed by the natural inclinations, a grasp that in any event is always a rational grasp. This holds in an analogous fashion for rational understanding in general: the speculative intellect does not grasp the first principle of the theoretical reason (the principle of non-contradiction) prior to all knowledge of what exists, but rather in and through its knowledge of being: "that something exists" is foundational and implicit in such knowledge, and in fact makes possible all knowledge whatsoever.[44]

On closer inspection it becomes clear that Honnefelder is restructuring in a questionable way the parallelism between theoretical and practical reason which Thomas presents in I-II, 94, 2. First, Thomas uses the expression *apprehensio simpliciter,* "cognition in general"—for grasping "something" as such—the first object of which is "what exists." Now, nothing indicates that what Thomas says here about *apprehensio simpliciter* does not also hold for practical reason—even if the practical reason goes beyond it in some way.[45]

43. On both these points cf. Rhonheimer, *Natural Law and Practical Reason.*

44. Rejection of the "two-stage operation" thesis by no means implies, however, the denial of a multi-level nature of the practical reason in another respect, as (1) a difference of several levels of principles (the first, most general, and highest principles on the one hand, and the action-specific principles, the *propria principia,* on the other), and (2) the difference between the level of principles in general and the concrete, action-directed judgment applied to the particular. Honnefelder's "two-stage operation" of the practical reason concerns only the relation between practical reason and natural inclination, that is, the view that the reason is constituted as practical, previous to any approach to a natural inclination or corresponding appetitive goal and the goods formulated through it.

45. Thomas's commentary on the Aristotelian treatise *De Anima* supports this: *In De Anima,* Book III, lect. 15, no. 820 (Marietti), where we read: "[intellectus] speculativus speculatur

But more importantly, Honnefelder appears to look at the parallelism in the following way:[46]

Theoretical Reason	*Practical Reason*
1) difference of direction: true/false ("yes"/ "no")	1) difference of good/evil
2) implied in this, the first principle of theoretical reason: the principle of non-contradiction	2) implied in this, the first principle of practical reason: good is to be done, evil is to be avoided

As it seems to me, we can detect here a first imprecision in the assumption that, according to Thomas, the highest difference of the theoretical as well as the practical reason is of a logical nature (in the former epistemological, in the latter praxeological).[47] But the *Prima secundae* speaks a different language, and not only on this point:

We note that Thomas in fact says nothing about the difference "true and false" on the side of *apprehensio simpliciter;* instead he speaks of the *ratio entis et non entis;* "the principle of non-contradiction," he says, "is founded on this dichotomy." The concern here is not merely with the form of theoretical judgments, but about the constitution of intellective apprehension in general through the reality of what is, to which what does not exist stands in absolute ontological opposition, so that as a consequence, both being and its opposite cannot at the same time (in the same respect) be both affirmed or denied.

In an analogous way, Honnefelder's questionable reading carries over into the side of the practical reason. The foundation of the first principle of practical reason for Thomas is not, as Honnefelder maintains, the difference between good and evil as the "form" of practical judgments, but rather the *ra-*

veritatem, non propter aliquid aliud, sed propter seipsum tantum; practicus autem speculatur veritatem propter operationem" (the speculative intellect does not consider truth for the sake of something else, but for its own sake only; the practical intellect however considers truth for the sake of action). Practical understanding is also a faculty for truth-cognition. Cf. also *De Veritate,* 22, 10, ad4: "obiectum intellectus practici non est bonum, verum relatum ad opus" (the object of the practical intellect is not the good, but the true, related to an action). Of importance here as well is Aquinas, *ST* I, q.79 a.11: "intellectus per extensionem fit practicus" (the intellect becomes practical by way of extension); cf. Rhonheimer, *Natural Law and Practical Reason,* 24ff.

46. Cf. Honnefelder, "Natur als Handlungsprinzip," 176; "Praktische Vernunft und Gewissen," 24.

47. In "Die ethische Rationalität des mittelalterlichen Naturrechts," 259, Honnefelder slightly departs from this schema by identifying the difference "good/evil" with a "yes/no" practical response.

Theoretical Reason ("apprehension simpliciter")	*Practical Reason ("apprehensio rationis practicae, quae ordinatur ad opus")*
1) ". . . illud quod primo cadit in apprehensione est ens." (→"ratio entis et non entis")	1) ". . . bonum est primum quod cadit in apprehensione practicae rationis" (= In De Anima III: "primum apprehensum a ratione practica est appetibile") (→"ratio boni: bonum est quod omnia appetunt")
2) ". . . primum principium indemonstrabile est quod non est simul affirmare et negare,quod fundatur supra rationem entis et non entis."	2) ". . . primum principium in ratione practica est quod fundatur supra rationem boni . . . (. . .) . . hoc est ergo primum praeceptum legis, quod bonum est faciendum et prosequendum, et malum vitandum."
3) ". . . . et super hoc principium omnia alia fundantur."	3) "Et super hoc fundantur omnia alia praecepta legis naturae: ut scilicet omnia illa facienda vel vitanda pertineant ad praecepta legis naturae, quae ratio practica naturaliter apprehendit esse bona."

tio boni—the "aspect of the good"—which, in the words of Aristotle, consists in the fact that "the good is what all things seek." The *ratio boni* is the aspect of the "sought for," "striven after," or the "seekable"—the *appetibile*—through which being, or reality, is objectified as a "good" in the horizon of that which seeks. The point of departure here is the correlation between "good" and "seeking," and this is what the first principle of practical reason brings into the open: "good is to be sought, evil is to be avoided." The real difference in praxis which is expressed here is not the difference between "good" and "evil" (this is not objectified as a constitutive difference until later, by reflection), but rather the difference between *prosecutio* and *fuga,* between *pursuing* and *fleeing, doing* and *avoiding*[48] (cf. the second table, right hand side, 2). This gives us the following parallelism:

This refinement of distinctions may look like mere hairsplitting. But its relevance to the issue is great. The most important result is as follows: the first principle of practical reason is not a judgment that one should at each opportunity use reasoning, but rather the actual moving principle of rational beings which in fact constitutes one as an acting and moral subject. This does not come about by the first principle of practical reason first ordering

48. *Prosecutio* and *fuga* are consequently referred to in *Natural Law and Practical Reason,* 32, as the "practical copula" as parallel to the "theoretical copula" *est* and *non est.*

Theroretical Reason	*Practical Reason*
ens—non ens	*bonum—malum*
affirmatio—negatio	*prosecutio—fuga*

us in general, as it were, to pursue good and avoid evil, and then in a second step extending this general seeking to the various goods that correspond to the natural inclinations. Instead, the first principle of practical reason is already operative in the practical understanding of these goods. This is analogous to the principle of the law of non-contradiction: this is not recognized beforehand, in order, on its basis, to then grasp further reality; rather, it demonstrates its foundational presence and effectiveness in every single act of knowledge directed toward being.[49] The first principle is not a first act of knowing, to be followed by other acts of knowing, but is rather first in the sense of being fundamental and always implied in any every single practical act of knowing. In this sense, the first principle of practical reason as foundational for practical knowing in general, is only operative in the grasping of single *bona humana*. Honnefelder seems to have taken I-II, 94, 2 as too much a logical "schedule of events," and not as the analysis of the structure of the cognitively guided foundation of praxis.[50]

What comes to the forefront here is that in Thomas's view, the constitution of the acting subject we have referred to is not to be understood as the constitution of a being in a purely "formal" and contentless fashion, but rather as a subject that operates "rationally" with "justifications," as a subject that from the beginning—that is, naturally—finds himself ordered to that good

49. Cf. Rhonheimer, *Natural Law and Practical Reason*, 73: "It is important to note that the first principle, '*bonum est prosequendum . . .*' (or, to be exact, the judgment of the *prosecutio boni* as such) cannot arise or become known in isolation from any further content. It is not otherwise with the theoretical knowledge of being, where the contradiction of 'being' *(ens)* and 'not-being' *(non ens)* does not arise as such in its pure formality. It is always experienced in concrete being, and it is in this fundamental characteristic of being (in its concrete state) that the principle of contradiction *reveals itself* as the first principle of the knowledge of being. It must likewise be emphasized that the first principle of the practical reason always reveals itself only in the materially determined areas of the *prosecutio;* it appears as somehow compartmentalized into distinct areas that are naturally present to the natural reason as it makes its evaluations. And because it is 'the ordering and moving principle' *(principium ordinans et motivum),* it is here that it develops its efficacy as the foundation of actions."

50. To be sure, Honnefelder is not saying that something can be concluded from the highest principle (cf. Honnefelder, "Die ethische Rationalität des mittelalterlichen Naturrechts," 260f.). He does, however, understand it as a *pre-disposed* way of approach to the single natural inclinations, and this is why he uses the expression "two-stage."

which his natural inclinations reveal to him. And this is exactly that from which Honnefelder would like to distance himself, because he finds it too "naturalistic." It seems scarcely possible, however, to call upon Thomas in support of such a position.

The Constitution of Practical Reason: The Role of the Naturally Sought-For

In a valuable paraphrase of *De Anima* III, where Aristotle is investigating the principles of the movement of living beings, Thomas expresses in new words the compactly formulated thought of the *Summa Theologiae,* thereby bringing into the open the Aristotlelian background of his conception (see above, Table II, right side, 1). This is what we find: the reason is constituted as practical through the apprehension *(apprehensio)* of what is striven-for, that is, of a good: *primum consideratum ab intellectu practico est appetibile.*[51] Here, in the good as the correlate of a seeking, lies the point of departure for the practical reason, which is independent with respect to theoretical judgments and in this sense—in the underiveability of practical judgments from theoretical judgments—is autonomous. Nevertheless we are concerned with the same reason which grasps reality, but here however the reality of a naturally pre-given and goal-directed seeking. The reason becomes practical through this kind of *apprehensio,* it moves toward doing: *propter hoc dicitur intellectus practicus movere, quia scilicet eius principium, quod est appetibile, movet.*[52] The *prosecutio* follows, which in its conclusion manifests itself as an action under the difference of good and evil. And once again it becomes clear: practical reason possesses its own and in this sense autonomous point of departure; practical judgments are not derivations from or "prolongations" of theoretical judgments, which means, again, that ethics is not simply to be deduced from metaphysical premises. It acquires its principles in its own way by reflection on praxis that illumines praxis. But holding to this autonomy of the practical reason does not negate the relationship of practical reason to reality or truth, nor does it exclude the possibility of subsequent, mutual illumination through the philosophical and metaphysical considerations of anthropology and ethics.[53]

51. *In De Anima,* Book III, lect. 15, no. 821 (Marietti).

52. Ibid. Cf. also Rhonheimer, *Natural Law and Practical Reason,* 24f., and *Praktische Vernunft und Vernünftigkeit der Praxis,* 507–15.

53. On the complex relationships among ethics, anthropology, and metaphysics, see *Natural Law and Practical Reason,* 15–42.

Now, this does not mean that we have arrived at a naturalistic position. Such is supposed to happen when the practical good is reduced to the natural characteristics of things. The good to which a natural inclination is directed is nevertheless no natural characteristic of something, but rather the correlate of a "seeking." Now again, the relationship to such a seeking would be naturalistic if the seeking in its natural givenness were already considered ethically normative. But this is not what Thomas holds: he is speaking about a rationally guided seeking which reaches for goals that have been grasped as good by the reason and, correspondingly, have become ordered within the horizon of rationality. In contrast to Honnefelder's stark opposition between "following causes" and "acting with reasons,"[54] we need to recall that what is known as good—the judgment by the reason that "this is good"—operates as a cause for reason-guided seeking (the free will) precisely because it is a reason. Honnefelder himself writes that for man "to act according to reasons" means "only that what he recognizes as good, he also recognizes as doable, and vice versa."[55] But precisely for this reason it is not in the least necessary to understand the constitution of the subject as a rational being that acts according to reason *prior* to the relationship to the sought-after goals of the natural inclinations. Instead, the question arises—and it is the question about practical principles in the sense of natural law—whether the practical reason recognizes something as by nature "good": the question of the "naturally rational." Such would be a primary, non-circumventable reason for acting, as well as a cause that would bring about such action.[56]

All of this has really nothing to do with naturalism. A naturalistic position would maintain that the sexual drive is normative *as nature*, its repression in certain situations as unnatural and hence immoral. An ethical position like the one I maintain, which argues for parental responsibility for temporary abstinence from sexual acts and for unconditional marital fidel-

54. Cf. Honnefelder, "Praktische Vernunft und Gewissen," 37: "Only an action that is determined by reason, that does not result from a cause but follows reasoning, is an action that happens in freedom." See also, "Natur als Handlungsprinzip," 176: The human being is different from animals because "he determines himself in his action though his reasoning, that he does not simply follow causes, but acts by reasoning."

55. Honnefelder, "Natur als Handlungsprinzip," 176.

56. This is not "cause" in the sense of a necessity from which one could not freely withdraw oneself. This is because what the will necessarily seeks as good, since it has been judged as such by the reason, can also be not-willed on a higher level, since will, like reason, can reflect upon its own act (Thomas Aquinas, *De Malo*, q.6, a.unicus; cf. Rhonheimer, *La prospettiva della morale*, 152ff.). Cf. also below, section four. This does not change the fact that intentions are also causes of actions.

ity (and also abstinence at times when the natural inclination might be directed toward another potential sexual partner), could not rightly, it seems to me, be suspected of naturalism. Likewise, according to my interpretation of Thomas, even the natural inclination to self-preservation would not already be a moral norm. As a good sought-for by reason, self-preservation is rather to be brought into harmony with the demands of justice, but can also be set aside or relativized by love for another person. Even the natural inclination of man to live in a community with others is not to be explained naturalistically, but only on the horizon of rationality. It is really the task of reason to set into order, but it can only do that once it has already recognized something as good and consequently as meaningful.[57] The rational pursuit of a natural inclination means—this was one of the principal themes of *Natural Law and Practical Reason*—the integration of every one of these inclinations and their goals into a unified whole of all natural human strivings, and thus their hierarchizing, relativizing, and mutual interrelationship. Only in this way are the various sought-for goals constituted—through the reason—as the goals of moral virtues. For its part, philosophical ethics has the job of reconstructing this process through argumentation.[58]

The Relationship between Reason and Natural Inclination: Knowledge of Principles and Concrete Experience

The question that now presents itself concerns the relationship between reason and natural inclination. The term "natural inclination" is admittedly ambiguous. Is the "natural" inclination to be understood as something in a

57. This is why the statement of Wieland cited in the beginning of this paper seems questionable: "For nature to become significant at all for the context of human action, man must be in a position to behave toward nature, as if he were already thought of as rational and free" ("Secundum naturam vivere," 25). Of course, without rationality there would be no such thing as "human action" or morality at all. The expression is nevertheless, in a certain, not-trivial respect, somehow not sensible, which is seen when we put materially appetitive goals and their corresponding goods in the place of "nature." Then the statement would mean, say, that "in order for 'life' ('nourishment,' 'sexuality,' etc.) to become significant at all for the context of human action, man must be in a position to behave toward life, nourishment, sexuality, etc., as if he were already thought of as rational and free." Now this sentence, so long as it is not taken in the trivial sense I mentioned, appears to be false, since "life" is meaningful even for non-rational beings. In fact it is the other way around: "In order for a human being to relate freely and with reason to life, nourishment, sexuality, these things must already be thought significant for human action." This significance precisely is *given* through the naturalness of the fundamental human strivings. This givenness, taken up by the reason and ordered into its perspective, is, once again, a condition for the possibility of a *lex naturalis*.

58. Cf., e.g., Rhonheimer, *La prospettiva della morale*, 242f. (on the origin of the principle of "justice").

natural, merely spontaneous, state, or rather at the level when it has already been grasped by the reason as a "good of the reason" *(bonum rationis)?* To put it more precisely, the question is, "How are we to think about the relation between reason and nature, so that there is a kind of cooperation between the two, and 'inclination' can be understood in the second, and thus morally relevant sense?" G. Wieland maintains that, in *Natural Law and Practical Reason,* my view was that the relationship between reason and nature was a reciprocal one, that is to say a kind of interacting identity.[59] E. Schockenhoff also sees this "identity" in my account.[60] Schockenhoff himself advocates, by contrast, a formal "complementarity" of practical reason and natural inclinations,[61] or a "bipolarity" of reason and nature.[62]

It is curious that the above-mentioned interpretations of Thomas not only leave largely out of account the fact that Thomas himself describes the relationship between reason and natural inclination as one of form and matter (in the metaphysical sense), but they also appear to overlook how the key to understanding the relationship as presented in *Natural Law and Practical Reason* is to be found precisely here.[63] Seen in this way, "reason" and "natural inclination" are no more "identical" than "body" and "soul" (where there can be no question of "reciprocity"). And formulas like "bipolarity" or "complementarity" likewise prove inadequate to the form/matter schema, either by reifying the relationship and making it dualistic, or by losing themselves in the indefinite, using picturesque images that end up leaving the reason/nature relationship still vague and open-ended.[64]

The question whether reason and natural inclination are "complementary" or "identical" does not really help us with the form/matter schema.

59. Wieland, "Secundum naturam vivere," 25.

60. Schockenhoff, *Naturrecht und Menschenwürde,* 154. Bormann, *Natur als Horizont sittlicher Praxis,* 226, follows Schockenhoff on this. [Editor's note: In the English edition of his book, Schockenhoff has abandoned this line of criticism, recognizing that Rhonheimer (as he will explain in the next paragraph) rather sees the relation between natural inclination and reason as one of "matter" and "form" (yet, still without completely agreeing with him). See *Natural Law and Human Dignity,* 141ff.]

61. Bormann, *Natur als Horizont sittlicher Praxis,* 226.

62. See his *Compte rendu* of M. Rhonheimer, *Praktische Vernunft und Vernünftigkeit der Praxis,* 146. Likewise, see Bormann, *Natur als Horizont sittlicher Praxis,* 230.

63. It also enables one to see the connection of this doctrine with the doctrine on the constitution of objects of action and of the kinds of actions as *formae a ratione conceptae;* see Rhonheimer, *Natural Law and Practical Reason,* 87ff., 410ff. On the *bonum rationis,* which is an important concept in this context, see Rhonheimer, *Praktische Vernunft und Vernünftigkeit der Praxis,* 124ff.

64. Cf. Schockenhoff, *Naturrecht und Menschenwürde,* 172f.; Bormann, *Natur als Horizont sittlicher Praxis,* 236.

For instance, are the soul and body of the human being "complementary" or "identical"? Let's say they are complementary: does the soul give the body something that the body doesn't already have, or does the body give the soul something that it doesn't have? Certainly everyone would agree with this in a sense. But in the existential unity of the soul and body we nevertheless find a single entity that does not seem to possess within itself several "parts" non-identical with each other but still complementary. Consequently, the relationship would seem to be an identity, but still it is an identity in which the two components—or better, co-principles—by being united become something new or undergo change, and especially the matter, or the body.

The relationship between reason and natural inclination can be thought of analogously, if not exactly the same way. The natural inclination that has been objectified by the reason and pursued at its horizon, is still *natural* inclination: the "form" of the reason is certainly something more than the mere naturalness of the inclination, but at the same time, would not be considered as something non-identical with the inclination, once the inclination becomes known under that form. At the same time, the inclination that has been formed and informed by the reason is thus more than the merely natural inclination.[65] "Self-preservation," as an inclination of a rational human person who can stand in a relationship to others by attending to them and loving them, is something other than it is at the level of natural, spontaneous seeking, without ceasing to be identical with such seeking. "Sexuality" as a loving gift of self to another person, in a true bond between man and woman and in the service of life, is something other than mere natural sex drive—and yet it still *is* this natural drive, but it is such on the level of the anthropological "truth of sexuality."[66] This is precisely why sexuality is not only a natural inclination, but also a responsibility that needs to be shaped. Sexuality is by no means naturally determined from the outset to monogamy;[67] it becomes this only in the context of what is the good for reason, which can view the sexual partner as a person and object of love.

Nevertheless E. Schockenhoff views my position as a naturalistic one,

65. In his latest exposition of the theme, Merks, *Naturrecht als Personrecht,* says in a similar fashion that "knowledge of 'good' and 'evil,' the judgment about 'good' or 'evil,' do not come partly from the reason, partly from the inclinations, but rather have been integrated as a whole through the reason" (39).

66. Cf. Rhonheimer, *La prospettiva della morale,* 246ff., and Rhonheimer, *Sexualität und Verantwortung. Empfängnisverhütung als ethisches Problem* (Vienna, 1995).

67. This is confirmed—in their own way—by the proponents of evolutionary psychology; cf. R. Wright, *The Moral Animal: Why We Are the Way We Are* (London: Vintage, 1995).

which conceives of the *lex naturalis* "as pure self-explication of the natural reason,"[68] and which the order-making function of the reason is limited "to a mere knowledge of these natural appetitive goals through the reason."[69] This viewpoint results from a significantly reduced reception of the Thomistic doctrine of the discursive unfolding of the *lex naturalis* through the process of *inventio* as presented at some length in *Natural Law and Practical Reason,*[70] where it is clarified that "in the discursive process, as in all knowing, man must depend on experience, and first of all on sense experience, which he is able to comprehend in its intelligible content with the light of natural reason. This process of *inventio* Thomas also calls 'the path of experience' (*via experimenti;* II-II, 47, 15); it needs sense experience and deliberation, and finally—on the 'path of judgment' *(in via iudicii)*—comes to an end by a *resolutio* into the first principles."[71] The process of discursive *inventio* is a process of the explication of principles through the mediation of experience that is at first external to the reason, and in this way amounts to a "concretizing" of the highest principles which are increasingly illuminated in the very process of *inventio,* as still needs to be shown.

In *Natural Law and Practical Reason* can be found a presentation—running to many pages—of the Thomistic doctrine of the inventive/discursive explication of the first principles of the *lex naturalis* through the *ratio naturalis,* and the point is central to the interpretation of Thomas developed in that book. However, this appears not to be known to the critics of my interpretation, or even been acknowledged by them in any way.[72]

68. Schockenhoff, *Compte rendu* of M. Rhonheimer, *Praktische Vernunft und Vernünftigkeit der Praxis,* 143.

69. Schockenhoff, *Naturrecht und Menschenwürde,* 168.

70. Rhonheimer, 267–87.

71. Ibid., 286. E. Schockenhoff remarks in *Naturrecht und Menschenwürde,* 153 [Editor's note: These remarks are omitted in Schockenhoff's English edition], that in *Praktische Vernunft und Vernünftigkeit der Praxis* I mention at only one place (553) that one can arrive at precepts derived from the natural law only by way of discursive mediation and experience. In claiming this, he appears to have overlooked the reference to *Natur als Grundlage der Moral* 216–39 (*Natural Law and Practical Reason,* 267–87) where the same reference to Thomas can be found.

72. Unfortunately this also holds true for the work considered as a *magnum opus* on the theme by Bormann, *Natur als Horizont sittlicher Praxis,* where to my knowledge no evidence can be found of the author's awareness of the meaning of the *inventio* doctrine, which is shown also in his comments on the relevant statements from *Natur als Grundlage der Moral,* which he treats mistakenly and without regard for context. The discursive *inventio* of the *ratio naturalis* is ignored by C. Schröer, *Praktische Vernunft bei Thomas von Aquin,* Münchener philosophische Studien. Neue Folge 10 (Stuttgart; Berlin [etc.]: W. Kohlhammer, 1995). Ricken, in his article "Naturrecht" (n. 32 above) I, 145, appears, by contrast, to have taken my exposition of the theme

There could be several reasons for this. One reason may be that, not rarely, "discursive reason" is identified with the reason that arises from judgment of concrete actions, and therefore those passages where I speak of the discursive discovery of principles are mistakenly taken as referring to statements about the concrete level of action.[73] But on the other hand, it also appears that many interpreters confuse the *inventio* doctrine with the *adinventio* mentioned in I-II, 91, 3 but only in the context of the treatise on human law. In fact, some scholars of Thomas have recourse to this over and over again, in order to characterize as a process of "discovery" the relationship between a natural appetitive goal and its rational transformation all the way to the formulation of secondary precepts of the natural law.[74] Through such confusion, the *inventio* doctrine as presented in *Natural Law and Practical Reason* appears as an awkward, shrunken, "deductivist" version of Thomas's teaching on the practical reason. But the concept of *adinventio* for Thomas pertains exclusively to the *lex humana:* it cannot be applied to the *lex naturalis* itself. For the exegesis of Thomas, the reference to I-II, 91, 3 in this context is not permissible.[75] Equally mistaken in this context is reference to I-II, 95, 2 and the concretizing of the *lex naturalis* mentioned there which takes place *per modum determinationis,* which Thomas contrasts with a derivation *per modum conclusionis* (as in the sciences, where further true statements are

as an opportunity to blame me for maintaining that man could "understand the eternal law within himself" so that it could be understood as immediately directive of action. I cannot really understand this reproach, since the *inventio* doctrine explains how the *lex naturalis* is unfolded in the natural reason of man, and how the eternal law becomes known to man through this very unfolding of the natural law (cf. I-II, 19, 4, ad3: "licet lex aeterna sit nobis ignota secundum quod est in mente divina; innotescit tamen nobis aliqualiter vel per rationem naturalem, quae ab ea derivatur ut propria eius imago; vel per aliqualem revelationem superadditam." (Although the eternal law be unknown to us the way it is in the divine mind; nevertheless it becomes known to us in a certain way through the natural reason, which is derived from it as its very own image; or through some additional kind of revelation.) The *inventio* doctrine is no less than an analysis of how the natural reason knows as an *imago* of the *mens divina.*

73. This is the case with Bormann, *Natur als Horizont sittlicher Praxis,* 263.

74. I-II, q.93 a.3: "particulares dispositiones adinventae secundum rationem humanam" and "cognitio . . . per industriam rationis inventa" ('particular dispositions discovered in addition according to human reason' and 'discovered through the effort of human reason'). Cf. also ibid., q.94 a.3, where Thomas says that "many things are done according to virtue, to which nature itself provides no inclination," "sed per rationis inquisitionem ea homines adinvenerunt, quasi utilia ad bene vivendum." (But people have discovered these things additionally through the investigation of reason, as if useful for the good life.)

75. The reference is used, however, by Schockenhoff, *Naturrecht und Menschenwürde,* 179, who calls on Kluxen and Honnefelder for support. [Editor's note: See English edition of *Natural Law and Human Dignity,* 171 n. 83.] Kluxen, *Philosophische Ethik bei Thomas von Aquin,* 235, points out expressly that *adinventio* only holds for determinations of the *lex humana.*

concluded from first principles).[76] The determinative *modus,* Thomas says, is more like an action to be carried out. With this second *modus,* Thomas characterizes the relationship between the *lex naturalis* and positive human law, but only positive human law. The *modus conclusionis* is doubtless also the mode through which the secondary precepts of the natural law are concluded from the first and highest principles, by discursive *ratio* of course.[77] It would be a misunderstanding of the entire Thomistic moral theory to believe that this implies a purely deductive reasoning that does *not* have recourse to experience. Although the *lex naturalis* does not take its origin from theoretical knowledge, but instead from a specific, practical process of knowing, it nevertheless still involves a process of knowing reality and knowing truth. This could not be maintained in the same way for the *determinatio* of concrete human laws—the *adinventio* of the *utilia ad bene vivendum* ("the added discovery of what is useful for human life").[78]

Just as important as the doctrine of the discursive *inventio* of the natural reason in this connection (and which remains, for the most part, just as neglected) is the Thomistic teaching on the *praestitutio finis* through prudence.[79] Thomas says, namely, that prudence, which is specifically at our disposal for the determination of concrete actions, "in a certain sense" also *sets the goal* for moral virtues.[80] Prudence—bound up as it always is with experience—guides moral virtues not only in the choice of actions that lead to the goal, but also in establishing the goal itself. The reason for this is that specific actions are in fact the goal of each virtue, and thereby the arrival in every case at the means appropriate for each realm of action. In order for this goal of virtue to be reached—acting according to reason—prudence is needed. The general appetitive goal of virtue is not enough for the knowledge and

76. Cf. for example Honnefelder, "Absolute Forderungen in der Ethik," 27.

77. This could also be ascertained by Schröer's view, *Praktische Vernunft bei Thomas von Aquin,* 200, that "the load-bearing concept of the whole project" of Thomas's moral theory is "the application of the Aristotelian theory of justification in the *Posterior Analytics* to the realm of action."

78. To be sure, this is not meant to say that such an "added discovery" is valid only for human law-making. It is also a peculiarity of prudence as directed to concrete action, which must realize the good in each case in a flexible and creative manner; cf. the remarks in *Natural Law and Practical Reason,* 545. Still, however, this does not hold for the cognitive development of the principles of action in the sense of the *lex naturalis.*

79. Cf. Rhonheimer, *Praktische Vernunft und Vernünftigkeit der Praxis,* 362ff., 583ff.

80. See Aquinas, *In Sent.* II, 33, 2, 3, "Quodammodo praestituit finem virtutibus moralibus" (In a certain way, it sets out beforehand a goal for the moral virtues). Cf. *Praktische Vernunft und Vernünftigkeit der Praxis,* 362ff., 583ff.

choice of that to which such appetition is aiming: concrete, rational, action. This means that action-specific principles—the *principia propria* of the *lex naturalis*—become fully unfolded only by way of the mediation of a reason that is bound to a concrete ethos, and directed to the determination of concrete actions—and it is only by such reasoning that those principles are really able to direct action.[81]

As already stated, practical principles, or the *lex naturalis,* are discovered through experience in particular cases. This has to be so because in the human world there are no general things but only concrete, particular things, persons, relationships, actions, etc. General truths about reality are always the content of a knowledge after the fact, in the light of which the concrete particulars can again be more deeply grasped, that is, as pertaining to a universal: concrete actions as particulars to be put into practice "here and now" can be understood as a concretizing of the "good life," of what is "good for man." Concrete ways of acting become intelligible as the way to the good that is the goal of human striving and virtues—the good which itself, in turn, provides the content for the practical principles. And looking at it in another way, certain ways of action are intelligible by being contradictory to moral commands and goods.[82]

Even the very first principles, including theoretical ones such as "that the part is contained in the whole," which can, in a way, form themselves naturally and spontaneously, need the initial grasp of a particular in which the principle is understood (even the good that is objectified as a striven-for goal of a natural inclination will at first always be the experience of a particular good). In any event, this is why a certain inner cognitive connection comes into be-

81. A certain "priority of prudence" cannot be denied (cf. D. M. Nelson, *The Priority of Prudence: Virtue and Natural Law in Thomas Aquinas and the Implications for Modern Ethics* [University Park: Pennsylvania State University Press, 1992]), although the *lex naturalis* as action-guiding practical reasoning-with-principles cannot be reduced to a mere "explanatory function rather than the function of providing specific moral information" (100). P. M. Hall, *Narrative and the Natural Law: An Interpretation of Thomistic Ethics* (London/Notre Dame, Ind.: University of Notre Dame Press, 1994), is critical of Nelson and M. C. Nussbaum, and sees the relationship between prudence and natural law correctly, in my view. See also D. Westberg, *Right Practical Reason: Aristotle, Action, and Prudence in Aquinas* (Oxford: Clarendon Press, 1994). It must of course be conceded to Nelson that the *lex naturalis* does not have the cognitive function of determining what is to be concretely done (145); but Nelson misses the foundational importance of the *lex naturalis* as a principle of praxis in general and as the principle of a praxis directed to what is good for man. To this extent the natural law has a moving function as well as a "significant epistemic function," both of which Nelson appears to overlook.

82. See also Schröer, *Praktische Vernunft bei Thomas Aquin,* 202.

ing between the discovered universal, or the principle, and the particular.[83] In reconstruction after the fact, the one can be presented as a conclusion from the other, such as the prohibition to kill as a conclusion from the universal principle of justice, "give to each what is due," without this meaning that the specific or particular can be derived immediately and without experience from the universal. We are concerned here not with a deductive, but rather a reflective process, a constantly deepening reflection by the practical reason on one's own action and judgment which—to employ an image—operates not so much in a linear-deductive, as in a circular or spiraling-inventive way.

Consequently, in their basic structure, practical principles or the *lex naturalis* are by no means opposed to prudence. Knowledge of a universal relevant for praxis is inconceivable without a reasoning applied to particulars, whose perfection is the virtue of prudence, and which determines the principles specifically through a process enriched by experience. Now to say this is not to argue in a circular fashion: what is being described does not contradict the fact that principles are principles, that is, logically prior to what is determined on their basis. This is because the forming of principles and their interaction with the situational experience possess the character of a process with a narrative kind of structure.[84] The human being develops as a moral subject in time. He or she is not simply already that way or born that way. There is no doubt that fundamental principles, especially those of justice—and here in particular justice in matters of communication and ownership—form themselves very rapidly and definitely in children. On the other hand, it often requires long and varied experience in complex situations before someone can adequately understand the content of practical principles. For these principles carry out the task of ordering concrete actions toward fundamental goals, the basic structure of good built into our natural inclinations. They should bring about practical truth in action, that is, the agreement of action with the right striving. This requires not only general knowledge of principles, but also prudence and experience. Here again, social context, the help and formation provided by parental models and authority figures are of de-

83. See R. Elm, *Klugheit und Erfahrung bei Aristoteles* (Paderborn: F. Schöningh, 1996), 279, on the fact that even with Aristotle the distance between the universal and the particular of praxis is not infinite, and that the two do not belong to different worlds: the universal is not established independently of its particular instances, and every case is related to the universal and realizes it.

84. Cf. Hall, *Narrative and the Natural Law.*

cisive importance for adequate cognitive development. The concrete *ethos* to which the subject is bound will also be decisive for certain concretizings of what is morally obligatory,[85] but can also be questioned in the light of practical principles and be recognized as needing correction. The concrete *ethos* as well as emotional misguidance of the reason can hinder the process of the inventive knowledge of principles, for "it is the characteristic of vice, to destroy principle."[86] And this is also why, Thomas emphasizes, "not all have the same righteousness." This is not only because, now and then, a concrete situation brings it about that the application of a principle of justice would cause injustice (as when someone refuses to return a borrowed weapon to a friend who has suddenly become insane), but also because vicious individual and social customs, or pathological natural dispositions can damage moral judgment.[87] In fact—and this is rightly brought out by Honnefelder, who follows Kluxen[88]—the *lex naturalis* cannot be capable of guiding action without its own further evolution into an *ethos* (to which would pertain human/positive legal systems and culture in all its dimensions). But even so the *lex naturalis* is necessarily something more than a mere "structure of principles open to design" (on the level of the *principia communia*), which then is fulfilled and perfected "through the positive human laws as well as the positive law of God as the determinations of this structure that happened in history."[89] The

85. Cf. Rhonheimer, "Menschliches Handeln und seine Moralität. Zur Begründung sittlicher Normen," in M. Rhonheimer, A. Laun, T. Goritschewa, and W. Mixa, *Ethos und Menschenbild. Zur Überwindung der Krise der Moral,* Sinn und Sendung 2 (St. Ottilien: EOS Verlag, 1989), 45–114, esp. 60.

86. Aristotle, *Ethica Nicomachea,* VI, 5; 1140b20.

87. This is essentially the content of *ST* I-II, q.94 a.4, and the fundamental statement there, "non eadem est rectitudo apud omnes" (not all have the same righteousness). This is often cited in support of the view that, according to Thomas, the "certainty" of practical knowledge decreases with an increase in concreteness. This idea is strange, because such a "law of decreasing certainty" is indeed valid for theoretical reason, which can say nothing of more certainty for the individual, and consequently does not have it as an object. For the practical reason, everything is reversed: the closer a judgment is to an action, so much the nearer is the practical reason to its goal, and thus the knowledge of what to do is more certain. If it were the other way around, a choice of action could never be made. I grant that the possibilities of erring increase, but that is trivial, because it also applies to theoretical knowledge. The further the process of knowing goes, the more errors can crop up (with the increasing concreteness of practical judgments, however, obscurities are often removed and the certainty of the one who knows is increased). It is even the case that universal and necessary (epistemic) expressions are not able to grasp what is required for concrete action. In this sense, from the perspective of the universal principle, the concrete is "uncertain," i.e., not predictable by the principle nor derivable from it.

88. Kluxen, "Menschliche Natur und Ethos," *Münchener Theologische Zeitschrift* 23 (1972): 1–17; Kluxen, *Ethik des Ethos* (Munich: K. Alber, 1974).

89. Cf. Honnefelder, "Die ethische Rationalität des mittelalterlichen Naturrechts," 267.

lex naturalis contains, at least in the Thomistic understanding of the reason, fundamentally accessible action-specific principles of a material kind, which not only are capable of being the standard of legitimization for an *ethos,* but are also substantial enough to establish the outline of a specific moral ideal, which corresponds in turn to a specific view of the human being and a corresponding anthropological truth.[90]

Freedom and the Reflective Distancing of Reason from Nature

We can now return to the "two-stage operation of the practical reason" proposed by Honnefelder. It should be acknowledged that this thesis articulates an important concern: that of securing the freedom of the acting subject vis-à-vis the natural drives, the possibility of distancing oneself from "nature" as something merely given, and the ability to approach this nature and behave as a free being toward it, which is really what makes "morality" possible at all. In fact, this must be possible, because otherwise practical reason would be a mere extension of natural drives. Whether Aristotle ever considered this problem, and if he did how fully he dealt with it, is a question that can be postponed for the moment.[91] The problem can be solved with Thomistic means, without needing any recourse to concepts of autonomy that oppose rationality to nature. But Honnefelder and Wieland appear to have looked for the solution in the wrong place. In reality, the solution is to be found in the Thomistic doctrine of the reflexivity of reason as a spiritual capacity: reason itself can judge its own acts, and take up a position with regard to those acts, even the ones it carries out spontaneously as "natural reason." Precisely here arises the phenomenon of conscience, which Honnefelder characterizes as "the self-reference of action-guiding reason."[92] Now, he is right to say that in a certain sense the subject constitutes itself as a moral subject just through this self-reference of the action-guiding reason. Nevertheless, we must also realize that this rational self-reference, in which the human person in a certain way

90. For this reason it is also possible—and theologically relevant—that the "positive Law of God" is not simply "the completion and fulfillment" of the natural law, as it appears to be in Honnefelder's account ("Die ethische Rationalität des mittlelalterlichen Naturrechts," 267), but also, as in the case of the Decalogue, its revelation. That this possibility also contradicts the "autonomistic" interpretation of a "creative reason" should have been obvious: where nothing had been provided beforehand, and everything is supposed to be formed creatively by man, there would be nothing for God to reveal (except in the sense of a threatening restriction of human freedom).

91. For a full treatment cf. Rhonheimer, *Praktische Vernunft und Vernünftigkeit der Praxis,* 211–18.

92. Honnefelder, "Praktische Vernunft und Gewissen," 26.

understands himself as a subject that is at once both self-determining and responsible for his action,[93] would not, according to Thomistic logic, even be possible without the previous constitution of the subject as practical through the striving of the "naturally rational." Human reason thought of as prior to all relationship to nature cannot bring about the "reflexivity" of the reason or the self-reference of the action-guiding reason. This relationship to nature, and self-reference of the reason that follows from it in reflection, belong inseparably together and mutually condition one another.

This is how the possibility opens up (for the reason and thereby for the acting subject) of being distanced from nature: no longer only to "be" one's own nature but to "have" it as well. In any case it does this—and this reveals its difference from Honnefelder's idea in its real meaning—not as a contentless reason that declares the principle of practical reason as such—but as reason that as practical reason is already present, embedded in the appetitive dynamism toward what is naturally good for the human being. It can distance itself from this, and that even holds for the most fundamental of all strivings, the desire for happiness. It is possible to will to not be happy, to renounce a natural and necessary desire to be happy. But because of its necessity, it is not possible for a human being to want something *instead* of happiness. For whatever someone wishes instead, he does so because he hopes to find happiness in doing it. On the other hand, one can distance oneself from "self-preservation," and seek something instead of it, for example one's own physical death. In any case—and this is the point—you cannot will this *rationally;* the reason does not participate, but distances itself precisely to the extent to which it distances itself from the "naturally rational," as if from itself. That it can actually do this is a proof of the freedom and autonomy of the subject, which in this case lose their meaning as rationally guided realities.[94] Now this makes it apparent that normative-ethical discourse already begins at the level of the "naturally rational," and this is so, first, because there does exist something that is naturally rational, and second, because the reason itself has the capability to question this naturally-and-rationally-known-something through reflecting on it again *from a different perspective,* and not with a view to its rationality, but with a view to its desirability. Ethical discourse would not be possible without this kind of reflection.

The concept of an "empty" reason preceding "nature," which declares a

93. Ibid., 28.

94. Cf. my exposition of this in *La prospettiva della morale,* 152ff.

pure imperative to act rationally with justifications, and in this most general and "formal" sense commands to do good and avoid evil, without there being a good for this reason to look at, is not only not to be found in Thomas, but is simply inconceivable. The originality of the Thomistic solution consists in understanding practical reason as autonomous and independent, as constituting the subject as an acting subject, but at the same time as a principle of movement that orders toward the good: in one stroke, as it were, man is conceived of as constituting both acting subject and moral subject. For Thomas there is no such thing as "reason in itself." C. Schroer[95] has seen this quite rightly: every thinking (or knowing) is always already a thinking-of-something, and he rightly has understood Thomas's dictum that in order to think of himself as a thinking being, he must have "thought of something before."[96] The experience of the acting subject as a knowing, practically thinking, and judging subject is not previous to knowledge of the good, but can only be conceived of as a subsequent reflection upon the act of the practical reason; in such reflection the reason has already—from the perspective of reason—recognized the goods contained in the natural inclinations as *bona prosequenda* (goods to be pursued), or as opposed to the good as *mala vitanda* (evils to be avoided).

The attempt by Honnefelder and Wieland to establish human freedom and autonomistic subjectivity against "nature" appears then—at least as regards Thomas—as misplaced. Both authors, in my opinion, commit the same error of confusing the original act of the practical reason, in which this reason is established as practical, with the level of reflection *upon* this act—to have interpreted the former as if it were the latter.[97] This error results from neglecting what I have attempted to demonstrate as fundamental for understanding the natural law, that is, the difference between the "preceptive-practical" and "descriptive-reflective" levels.[98] The difference of reason from "nature" and the

95. Schröer, *Praktische Vernunft bei Thomas von Aquin*, 49.

96. Aquinas, *De Veritate*, q.10 a.8: "Nullus autem percipit se intelligere nisi ex hoc quod aliquid intelligit, *quia prius est intelligere aliquid quam intelligere se intelligere*." ("Nobody perceives that he understands except from the fact that he understands something, *because to understand something is prior to understanding that one understands*.")

97. In another passage ("Praktische Vernunft und Gewissen," 23), Honnefelder points out that this structure of practical rationality, or the highest practical principle, can only be known in "reflective analysis." Cf. also Honnefelder, "Die ethische Rationalität des mittelalterlichen Naturrechts," 259. If I am not mistaken, by "reflective analysis" Honnefelder means merely the philosophical-ethical analysis of practical reason, and not the freedom-constituting, action-guiding reflection of the practical reason on its own act.

98. Cf. my *Natural Law and Practical Reason*, 58ff.

grasp of the "structure of practical reason as a whole" is not the primordial thing, but only emerges in reflection upon the natural act of the practical reason.[99] This reflective examination and the possibility of self-distancing that comes along with it assumes this primordial grasp of the "naturally rational" and can be carried out only on its horizon.

In Honnefelder's view, however, there is 1) the "highest rule," the first principle of the practical reason as "the most general principle of moral knowing"; 2) the "natural inclinations," which "provide the goals in rough outline, in which human existence comes to its fulfillment"; and finally, 3) prudence, "for the acquisition of concrete rules of action," practical judgment as the concrete judgment that guides action.[100] The question remains, Where does the *lex naturalis* "fit in" here, as a naturally known "universal of the practical reason"? There seems to be, at the least, a lack of explanation: how do the "natural inclinations"—natural givens as they are—ever become a (morally relevant) "goal" of a natural entity, or a (normative) principle for the "fulfillment" of human existence, thereby the principle and goal of moral virtue? Honnefelder's account appears to bracket questions that are decisive for every doctrine of the *lex naturalis:* what is the "naturally *rational,*" and what is "naturally good for man"? And this means setting aside as irrelevant other questions as well, questions such as, which principles are materially significant as providing normative orientation for prudential judgment, and thereby formulate the "naturally rational"? According to Honnefelder, "practical rationality" is thus to be found in a way relevant to actual content only as concrete norm-setting on the level of prudence. The *lex naturalis* however, one would think, rather emerges as a kind of norm-setting that is prior to prudence, and establishes and justifies it.[101]

Interpretations that do not want to recognize a "naturally rational" will

99. For this see W. Kluxen, "Anmerkungen zur thomistischen Naturrechtslehre," in D. Schwab, D. Giesen, J. Listl, and H.-W. Stratz, eds., *Staat, Kirche, Wissenschaft in einer pluralistischen Gesellschaft.* Festschrift Paul Mikat (Berlin: Duncker & Humblot, 1989), 119–28; 124: "What is immediately objectified in the practical reason is not 'nature' but rather the 'good'—and this of course as the human good, as related to the fulfillment of existential capacity, and as in the multitude of fundamental 'human goods,' which corresponds to the 'structured order of the natural inclinations.' This is how we can speak of nature as the 'foundation' of morality; but it [i.e., nature] is this as practically known, and as rationally guiding" (124).

100. Honnefelder, *Die ethische Rationalität des mittelalterlichen Naturrechts,* 264.

101. Similar problems can be found in W. Korff, "Der Rückgriff auf die Natur. Eine Rekonstruktion der thomanischen Lehre vom natürlichen Gesetz," *Phil. Jahrbuch* 94 (1987): 285–98, esp. 289. Schröer is critical of Korff's treatment: *Praktische Vernunft bei Thomas von Aquin,* 129 n. 179.

oppose the view that natural inclination, as an intelligible inclination, is already taken up by the reason into the order proper to reason. It thereby comes to itself as the "nature" (of man) and to the practical rational principle, thus to the principle of prudence as well, and the subsequent discourse about norms. This should not mean that such principles, for example that of self-preservation, are immediately action-guiding; rather, that—in any ethics at least that ties morality to rationality—the question about the possibility of boundaries of the morally possible that are not subject to whim comes up for debate.[102] If "nature" is to be understood as an ethically relevant boundary-concept, it must be more than a "natural given," insofar as it is a "necessary condition for the rectitude of the field of normativity."[103] In fact it is that only in the perspective of reason, which here operates as a standard, but only insofar as it encounters what it regulates as something given.[104]

Unity has certainly been achieved on one point—and this is in contrast to the naturalistic position—that in fact reason does not simply grasp the natural, convert it into its own logic, and confirm it in the mode of the "ought," or, to use Kluxen's words, immediately subject it to the moral differentiation of good/evil.[105] The objectivization of every originally non-spiritual natural inclination through the reason gives it, simply as a practical good, a new "form" on the level of a personality with its own spiritual formation. In the dimension of the practical—and that means always as objects of the will—the natural inclinations cannot otherwise emerge as objects of the reason on the horizon of the self-experience of the subject. And they do this already as intelligible, that is, as grasped by the reason and as goods judged on the horizon of rationality as the "good of the reason."[106] The first principle of practi-

102. Here, too, however, arguments are needed. Specific behavior, or prohibitions of behavior, cannot be immediately derived on the basis of the guidance of the naturally appetitive goals. The now widespread opinion that the argument against "artificial" contraception that I suggested does precisely this has probably contributed to the prejudice that has been the origin of a series of other misunderstandings. Cf., e.g., Schockenhoff, *Naturrecht und Menschenwürde,* 173f. (*Natural Law and Human Dignity,* 165). It has apparently escaped these critics that my argument is founded on, and explicitly maintains, a differentiated action-theory analysis, that—in contrast, say, to the argument of G. Grisez—nothing can be derived about the morality of concrete acts of "artificial" contraception on the basis of the naturally appetitive goals; cf. above all Rhonheimer, *Sexualität und Verantwortung* (e.g., 48f., 73ff., 126ff.).

103. Wieland, "Secundum naturam vivere," 25.

104. This is the meaning of the formula I have often used but which Wieland rejects: that the reason effects an ordering not *of* but *in* the natural inclinations.

105. Kluxen, "Menschliche Natur und Ethos," 15.

106. A more detailed account of this is found in Rhonheimer, *La prospettiva della morale,* chap. 5, 1, 239–48. As J. Finnis convincingly argues in *Natural Law and Natural Rights,* 88f., 100ff.,

cal reason subdivides itself into intelligible, but still materially differentiated "strivings" or appetitions, which correspond at the same time to the first and foundational principles of the practical reason and which give practical realization to this principle through a plurality of areas of action.[107] The primacy of reason over mere nature is true, but trivial, since (human) action can only occur through reason and freedom anyway. On the other hand, it would be less true, and anthropologically dualistic besides, to say this, and take it to mean that "nature" only acquires significance for praxis through reason's application to it.[108] For the reason—as practical—would simply reach into nothingness without the nature that we are. Reason becomes practical through the good that nature presents to it, and the good is in itself "significant for praxis." Without nature, then, reason would possess even as reason neither practical nor moral significance and could never be point of departure for what—at least since Aristotle—we have been calling "praxis": the self-movement of rational living things toward what is known as good and thus toward what perfects their own being.

To understand the *lex naturalis* in this sense as the principle of praxis opens up the possibility of integrating it as a doctrine of the principles of practical reason into a virtue ethics of an Aristotelian type.[109] A virtue- and prudence-ethics program of classical form is not opposed to a doctrine of

"practical rationality" is itself a human good. Wieland, "Secundum naturam vivere," 24, also emphasizes the difference between the anthropological/ontological constitution of the *bonum humanum* and the practical constitution thereof.

107. This plurality and differentiation of contents form the theme of I-II, q.94 a.2. This was recognized in a later article by F. Böckle, "Was bedeutet 'Natur' in der Moraltheologie?" 54–58. Merks, *Naturrecht als Personrecht,* 39f., on the other hand, is still of the opinion that this article (of Thomas) is concerned above all with the unity of the various commands through their gounding in reason. That is certainly not correct, since this unity through rational grounding, which is actually the starting point of the Thomistic conception of the natural law, could lead to a view rejected by Thomas, that really only one commandment pertains to the natural law, the command to act according to reason. Thomas only wants to show here that, corresponding to the plurality of natural inclinations, there is also a multiplicity in the "naturally rational," and a corresponding multitude of natural law commands.

108. Cf. the sentence quoted from Wieland, "Secundum naturam vivere," 25, at the beginning of this paper.

109. This thesis, as developed in *Praktische Vernunft und Vernünftigkeit der Praxis,* was intended as a kind of supplement, or realization, of one possible extension of Aristotelian ethics (cf. the exposition on the double meaning of the concept "Aristotelian ethics," 6ff.). This is not the *historical* thesis that Thomas filled up an actual lacuna in Aristotelian ethics with his doctrine of principles. This misunderstanding can be found in the important book by D. J. M. Bradley, *Aquinas on the Twofold Human Good: Reason and Human Happiness in Aquinas' Moral Science* (Washington, D.C.: The Catholic University of America Press, 1997), 250ff.

material principles of the practical reason in the sense of the "naturally rational,"[110] nor does it contradict the necessity of normative-ethical discourse. The latter acquires another value, through its recourse to a virtue-ethics program. In the first place, such discourse is now no longer the real, foundational theme of ethics. Secondly, one will understand what a norm is through the concept of virtue, instead of (in the reverse direction) understanding virtue as an internalized norm or as the habitual fulfillment of a norm. To grasp the phenomenon of "moral norm" by way of the concept of moral virtue means explaining it through the concept of "intentional action."[111]

All the elements of a virtue ethics, that is both eudaimonistic and grounded in action-theory, can be found in Thomas. Virtue ethics is here understood not in the modern Anglo-Saxon sense of a non-cognitive approach to ethics, but rather in the classical sense[112] of an ethics that sees the very paradigm of rationality in the virtuous person, and sees, in the judgments of the same, judgments that always reach what is truly good. Thomas Aquinas succeeded in placing the Aristotelian type of classical ethics into the broader context of a doctrine of principles, which he developed by way of fitting it into the context of an (ultimately, scripture-based) doctrine of law, as a doctrine of natural law. This is essentially a doctrine of the principles of the practical reason of the acting subject, through which the treatise on happiness as the final end, the theory of human actions and the doctrine of virtue that follows it—especially the doctrine of prudence—all contain their ultimate foundation and justification.[113]

110. Classical virtue ethics enquires precisely into the conditions of the rationality of praxis. On this see Annas, *The Morality of Happiness,* e.g., 66ff., 84ff.

111. See Rhonheimer, *La prospettiva della morale,* for a systematic explication of this notion.

112. On the difference between these two see the important remarks of Annas, *The Morality of Happiness,* 439ff. See also Schuster, *Moralisches Können.*

113. This essay originally published as "Praktische Vernunft und das, 'von Natur aus Vernünftige.' Zur Lehre von der Lex naturalis als Prinzip der Praxis bei Thomas von Aquin," *Theologie und Philosophie* 75 (2000): 493–522. Translated by Gerald Malsbary.

6

The Moral Significance of Pre-Rational Nature in Aquinas

A Reply to Jean Porter (and Stanley Hauerwas)

In her review[1] of my *Natural Law and Practical Reason: A Thomist View of Moral Autonomy* (hereafter referred to as *NLPR*), Jean Porter declines to offer a judgment about my "theory of natural law as a moral theory." She doubts, however, that it is a valid reading of Aquinas. The difficulty, she says, lies in my account "of the relation between pre-rational nature and moral reason." According to my view, which understands natural law as a law of practical reason, "pre-rational aspects of human nature, much less nature as manifested in non-rational creation, cannot have any direct moral significance. Humans share some natural inclinations with other animals, but even these inclinations are morally significant only insofar as practical reason grasps them as orientated toward distinctively human goods."[2]

This, Porter objects, is not what Aquinas really teaches. He "explicitly says that the inclinations we share with non-rational creatures are to be interpreted in the light of their expressions among those creatures" (Porter refers to

1. Jean Porter, *Theological Studies* 62, no. 4 (December 2001): 851–53. I am very grateful to William F. Murphy Jr. for many helpful suggestions regarding the first draft of this chapter.
2. Ibid., 852.

ST I, q. 60, a. 5).[3] Moreover, Porter invokes against me a passage from Aquinas's treatment of sexual sin as a "sin against nature," where St. Thomas literally says that "the principles of reason are those which are according to nature, for reason, presupposing what is determined by nature, disposes other matters in accordance with what is appropriate to these" (II-II, q. 154, a.12). This, as Porter emphasizes, indicates "that Aquinas is here speaking of nature as expressed in pre- and non-rational aspects of creation, since he goes on to say that the sin against nature 'violates against nature, that which is determined by nature concerning the use of the sexual act' (ibid.), and this is particularly serious, because 'just as the order of right reason is from the human person, so the order of nature is from God himself' (ST II-II, q. 154, a. 12, ad 1)." "In other writings"—Porter continues—"Aquinas explicitly says that the sin against nature is contrary to the nature we share with other animals in contrast to sins that are contrary to our nature as rational creatures" (Porter refers to *Ad Romanos* 1, lect. 8; *Summa contra Gentiles* 3, chap. 122, and *De malo,* q. 15 a. 3).

"Reason" and "Nature": A Complex Relationship

Porter rightly highlights my insistence on the fact "that Aquinas holds that the order and intelligibility inherent in natural processes must be grasped by reason in order to be morally significant." She however objects: "But this does not mean that the scope of morality is limited to an ordering generated by reason itself (albeit, reason operating through inclinations toward intelligible goods), as R. claims. Such an interpretation is difficult to reconcile with Aquinas's repeated appeals to the moral significance of pre-rational nature, appeals that are not simply offered as illustrative or supporting considerations, but are central to his moral argument."[4]

Now, "that the order and intelligibility inherent in natural processes must be grasped by reason in order to be morally significant" seems to be a relatively trivial point. Porter refers to it, but it is important to notice that this is not all that I say about the relationship between "reason" and "nature." My argument, as will be seen in the following, is more complex. But first I would like to restate my basic intention: it consisted in trying to show—based on textual evidence—that Aquinas's ethical theory is not simply naturalistic (or "biologistic," "physicalist"), that is, that he never claimed the natural to

3. I must admit that I do not really understand the relevance of this article to the present purpose.

4. Porter, review of *Natural Law and Practical Reason,* 853.

have moral significance *just because of its mere naturalness.* Yet, this view is not tantamount to asserting (as Porter, however, makes me to assert) "that the scope of morality is limited to an ordering generated by reason itself." I agree with Porter that the relation between "nature" and "reason" is somewhat more complex. However, as Porter seems to have failed to see, the subject of *NLPR* consists in trying to unfold just this complexity in a way consistent with both Aquinas's affirmation of the moral significance of natural inclinations/patterns/ends, and his insistence that the moral order formally and thus essentially is an order of *reason.*[5]

The charge, then, brought by Porter against my interpretation seems to be clear: she charges me with unilaterally reducing Aquinas's account of the "moral order"—as an "order of reason"—to an account of principles and other judgments of reason. She, therefore, thinks that my interpretation of Thomistic natural law as being essentially an ordering of reason *(ordinatio rationis)* has failed. Surprisingly, with this Porter seems to concord with quite a few criticisms of my views coming from the quarters of those Thomists who think me guilty of having distorted Aquinas's moral theory by denying not only the dependence of natural law on "nature," but also the dependence of practical reason on theoretical reason, as well as the dependence of ethics on metaphysics.[6]

5. In her book *Natural and Divine Law: Reclaiming the Tradition for Christian Ethics* (Ottawa: Novalis; Grand Rapids, Mich.: Eerdmans Publishing Company, 1999), 85–98, Porter extensively discusses the relationship between nature and reason as it was conceived in Scholastic natural law theory. She rightly emphasizes that for the medieval thinkers there was never a sharp contrast between "nature" and "reason" as it is typical for modern thinking. In Scholastic natural law theories, instead, reason itself appears as something natural. Moreover, Porter notices that "Aquinas is noteworthy among the Scholastics for his readiness to appeal explicitly to aspects of pre-rational nature in support of moral conclusions" (94). Unfortunately, Porter does not seem to go deeper into the analysis of Aquinas's account of the structure of natural law and the relationship between nature and reason. She rightly says, however, "No Scholastic would interpret reason in such a way as to drive a wedge between the pre-rational aspects of our nature and rationality. . . . [T]hey always presuppose an essential continuity between what is natural and what is rational" (93). In particular, Porter asserts that for the Scholastics, "the pre-rational components of human nature have their own intelligible structures, in virtue of which they provide starting points and parameters for the exercise of practical reason." Most surprisingly, and correctly, she then attributes such a view to my reading of Aquinas: a note added to this sentence refers to the original German edition of *NLPR,* asserting that "Martin Rhonheimer makes this point with respect to Aquinas in particular. . . . In general, I found his discussion of Aquinas's account of our knowledge of the natural law to be illuminating, although I did not agree with him in every particular." She refers to the German edition of *NLPR,* 63–84. In her review of the English edition of the book she now seems to be more critical.

6. Of course, these are not Porter's concerns. If I do not misunderstand her, she is fascinated by Aquinas's "naturalism" because this allows her to relativize "nature" in at least two respects.

The most surprising feature of Porter's criticism, however, is that in her review she completely failed to mention that in *NLPR* I have actually dealt at length with this problem, through an extensive discussion of Aquinas's account of "sins against nature."[7] Even more surprisingly, she seems to overlook that precisely this section of my book contains an analysis of II-II, q. 154, a. 12 about luxuriousness, which Porter, considering it a decisive piece of evidence, invokes against me. In this section of *NLPR*, I try to explain Aquinas's concept of "sin against nature" in a way consistent with my understanding of natural law as a law of practical reason. Of course, this interpretation may be criticized as unsound. Yet, having ignored it, Porter has yet to offer any argument against it.

Moreover, when she—as it has been already mentioned above—acknowledges that in my view "Aquinas holds that the order and intelligibility inherent in natural processes must be grasped by reason in order to be morally significant," I do not think she really understands what this means in the context of my view of natural law. It certainly *does not* mean that "pre-rational aspects of human nature, much less nature as manifested in non-rational creation, cannot have any direct moral significance." I have never affirmed anything of the sort and have labored to say exactly the opposite. My explicit view is that pre-rational aspects of human nature actually *can* have such a significance—and that according to Aquinas they do have such significance—but that this can be understood only by analyzing them as being an integral component of the substantial human unity of body and spirit. As we will see, understood in this context, pre-rational aspects of human nature are "presuppositions" of the

---

There seems to be first a theological relativization, because human nature is "nature wounded by sin," from which follows that "morality deserves to be respected and cherished, not as an ultimate value, to be sure, but as a genuine penultimate human good" (*Natural and Divine Law,* 101). In some sense, according to Porter "morality" is (albeit being an expression of the "fundamental goodness of the human person considered as creature of God") not a "perspicuous expression of the divine will. It is essentially a mundane reality, and as such it is both flawed and limited" (308). Porter seems to give much more attention to the fallen character of human nature than to the healing and transformative effects of grace. The second relativization is due to the evolution of human nature (she discusses these aspects of evolutionary theory on pages 102ff.). In Porter's eyes, a moral theory and a corresponding interpretation of natural law grounded not on "nature" (relativized by the fact of original sin and of evolution), but rather on the intrinsic and naturally given *reasonableness* of the precepts of natural law, must lead to moral norms that will probably seem to be too "absolute" and inflexible. This becomes clearer in chapter 4 of her book ("Marriage and Sexual Ethics").

7. See the section of *NLPR* with the title "Beyond naturalism and dualism: the problem of the so-called 'sin against nature' *('peccatum contra naturam')*," 94–107. (In the original German edition this corresponds to pages 98–113; Porter never refers to it in her *Natural and Divine Law.*)

moral order which, however, by its very nature is an order of reason.[8] Porter is of course correct to say that, according to my view, "humans share some natural inclinations with other animals, but even these inclinations are morally significant only insofar as practical reason grasps them as orientated toward distinctively human goods." Yet, the point of my treatment of the question, entirely silenced in Porter's review, is to show that this is exactly what Aquinas says in II-II, q. 154, a. 2. As a matter of fact, in *NLPR* this article, which Porter paradoxically invokes against me as if I had ignored it, works in reality as the main support of my argument.

A Crucial Distinction: The Ontological and Epistemological Points of View

But before stepping further into this problem, it will be useful to point out that throughout my treatment of natural law I operate with a crucial distinction: the distinction between the ontological (or metaphysical, anthropological) and the epistemological (or methodological) viewpoints. Although this distinction is made clear in the opening section of the book, pp. 3–57, it is apparently overlooked by not a few critics.[9] From an ontological/metaphysical viewpoint, one typically deals with questions like whether "moral good" is based on "nature"; whether natural patterns/inclinations/goals are morally significant or not; whether the "moral order" is in some way based on an "order of nature"; and so on. In other words, this first viewpoint considers how the moral order is grounded in the order of being; it tries to understand human nature as the source of moral requirements. The second point of view, however, is proper to moral epistemology; it refers to how moral good and its order is originally and practically *known*. Thus it considers how practical reason is structured and how it works. My central thesis in *NLPR* was that the moral order, although rooted in the order of being, is not simply knowable through a theoretical/metaphysical knowledge of "being." Moral epistemology has its own logic, which is not the same as the one typical for metaphysics and theoretical knowledge in general. This means: even if practical reason is grounded in nature at the pre-rational level (which is the object of the theoretical intellect) and the practical intellect—as a faculty—is nothing but

8. See for this the subsection titled "The 'Praesuppositio': An Essential Perspective," 106ff.

9. For a fair and comprehensive but nevertheless critical account of my view that does not overlook this distinction, see instead William F. Murphy Jr., "Martin Rhonheimer's *Natural Law and Practical Reason*," *Sapientia* 56, no. 210 (2001): 517–48, esp. 519ff.

an "extension" of the theoretical intellect, this does not mean that also practical *judgments* are mere "extensions" from, and "applications" of, theoretical judgments about human nature.[10] It is one thing to recognize the foundation of the moral order in nature (open to metaphysical analysis), and to recognize the foundation of practical judgments in the same intellectual faculty which also originates theoretical knowledge (note that this also means that practical reason leads to *knowledge* and *truth,* though of a special kind). It is quite another thing to hold that practical *judgments* derive from theoretical judgments about human nature, as "applications" of theoretical knowledge to action.

Against such a way of seeing things, I argue that human practical reason is itself an essential part of this "human nature" in which the moral order is embedded and from which it springs. The "moral order," as rooted in human nature, is not as such an object for the intellect to be "known" and subsequently to be "applied" or "followed"; it is not in this sense originally contained in nature (albeit the moral order unfolds *according* to nature). That the moral order is just the order of nature was asserted by Stoicism, which identified the eternal law with the cosmic order. For the Christian tradition, the image of God is not to be found in the cosmic order—it only contains the *vestigia Dei*—but exclusively in the spiritual human soul. Only through its cognitive acts, the eternal law, as far as it concerns human action, comes to be an existing reality in the created world. This is why, according to the Christian tradition, the moral order is not primarily contained in the order of nature as such, but in divine providence and, thus, in the eternal law; in a secondarily and derived—participated—way, it is found in human natural reason, which is properly "the image of the Divine mind."[11] Therefore, the moral order should be understood as an element of the participation in the eternal law at every level of human existence, including the activity of practical reasoning, which orders human acts. So, the naturally cognitive dynamics of the practical intellect—that is, the judgments of natural reason and their propositional contents—are themselves constitutive of human na-

10. Cf. *ST* I, q.79 a.11. See for this Rhonheimer, *NLPR,* 24ff.

11. Cf. *ST,* I-II, q.19 a.4 ad3: "licet lex aeterna sit nobis ignota secundum quod est in mente divina; innotescit tamen nobis aliqualiter vel per rationem naturalem, quae ab ea derivatur ut propria eius imago; vel per aliqualem rationem superadditam." This was well understood by J. Hirschberger, "Naturrecht oder Vernunftrecht bei Thomas von Aquin?," in *Gegenwart und Tradition. Strukturen des Denkens (Festschrift für Bernhard Lakebrink),* ed. C. Fabro (Freiburg i. Br.: Rombach, 1969), 53–74, esp. 69ff.

ture from which springs what we call the "moral order." Through these judgments we participate freely in divine providence and actualize our human nature by recognizing and pursuing the good and by growing in virtue.[12] So, only through the cognitive acts of understanding the natural, "human nature" in its dimension of being the foundation of the moral order becomes manifest. The judgments of the practical intellect are "constitutive" precisely in the sense that through them the eternal law is properly known and nature is rightly interpreted in its moral dimension. The eternal law and the moral order established by it are not, so to say, inscribed in nature and then read off from it by the human intellect. Human practical reason is itself an active participation of the eternal law which unfolds and becomes effective through its judgments about good and evil. Congruently, the practical intellect does not start its work by "extending" theoretical knowledge to the sphere of human action. Instead, it has its own starting point, as is explicitly and famously stated in I-II, q. 94, a. 2.[13]

This is why—and here we approach the core of the argument—the first notions of morality *originally* appear in the spontaneous moral experience, based in the practical intellect, of each acting subject. These first notions are, most fundamentally, the basic moral difference of "good" and "evil": through the first principle of practical reason "good is to be done and pursued, evil is to be avoided," which is the first precept of natural law, the whole range of human actions is put under the moral dichotomy of "good" and "evil." Subsequently, the same applies to the fundamental human goods grasped by natural reason in the different natural inclinations, that is, they also originally appear in the spontaneous moral experience of each acting subject. It equally applies to the basic notions of justice, in particular the notions of *debitum* (the due) and *iustum,* both of which imply basic equality as expressed in the Golden Rule. Through the first principles of practical reason, which are

12. In her book *Natural and Divine Law,* 27f., Porter mentions me as representing a "natural law ethic." It seems to me important to emphasize that to develop a theory of natural law and to confer on natural law an important role in ethical theory, as in fact I try to do, does not mean that such a theory is a "natural law ethic." Natural law, in my view, is only an element of what I understand as (classical) *virtue* ethic: the moral task and the good for human persons is not "to fulfill the precepts of natural law," but to become and to live as virtuous persons. This, however, is not possible without natural law, which is the guide to moral virtue. See chapter 2 and my "'Ethics of Norms' and the Lost Virtues: Searching the Roots of the Crisis of Ethical Reasoning," *Anthropotes* 9, no. 2 (1993): 231–43, and mainly my book *Die Perspektive der Moral. Philosophische Grundlagen der Tugendethik* (Berlin: Akademie Verlag, 2001).

13. Cf. chapter 5 of this book, or *NLPR,* 8ff.

precepts of natural law, the human subject is constituted simultaneously as a *practical* and as a *moral* subject: as a *practical* subject, because, from its very beginning, practical reason is embedded in the dynamics of appetite and of volitional striving so that practical judgments are *imperative* acts (they have the character of what Aquinas calls *imperium*) and therefore *move* the subject to act; as a *moral* subject, because all practical principles fall under the "moral dichotomy" of good and evil: every human act falls on one side of the dichotomy. There is no human act which is not either good or evil in a moral sense; this means that there is no human act through which we do not either become (morally) better or worse human beings (more or less just, more or less temperate, generous, faithful etc.). Thus, insofar as we are practical beings, we are also moral beings ("moral" not in the sense of "morally good" or "virtuous," but in the sense of "subsuming our actions and behavior under moral categories" corresponding to the principles of the natural law).

Only in the light of practical principles, which embody the basic notions of morality and, therefore, form the founding guidelines for moral virtue, human nature manifests itself as an object of theoretical knowledge. In this way, an understanding of the "human nature" has become available for theoretical reflection leading to a speculative account of what *naturally* constitutes the human person. Notice that this theoretical reflection is subsequent to already cognitively *possessing* the principles by the work of practical reason. The point I want to make, and which seems to me of the utmost importance, is that in order to be able to give an adequate speculative account of "human nature" we have already to understand ourselves as practical and moral subjects (in the above-mentioned sense). No "human nature" could be theoretically known as the fundament of a "moral order" if we did not interpret nature from the beginning in moral categories which, however, originally and primarily stem from the natural principles of practical reason, that is, from natural law. First we are moral subjects, and only afterwards we are able to theoretically understand human nature, to recognize its place as foundation and guide toward moral perfection, and to elaborate a sound metaphysical anthropology based upon it.

For the same reasons, without this original moral experience no experience of the human good, of freedom, or of moral responsibility would be possible. The acting person does not read off the human good, or the moral values of freedom and moral responsibility and other basic moral truths from nature, but experiences them as a practical and moral agent. If this were not the case, "morality" and "freedom" would not even be a theme for the theoretical intellect or for metaphysics. Nor would "friendship" or any kind of moral virtue be a possible theme because these things are not found in nature unless "nature" is interpreted in the light of the original moral experience unfolded by the practical intellect. To avoid misinterpreting the point I want to make, it is absolutely crucial to understand that we are talking here about a kind of moral experience that is *natural* to human knowers.[14] This is a cognitive experience of the *natural* principles of practical reason (which is "natural law"), of *natural* reason and of a kind of *natural* knowledge of the truth about the human good, and exactly in this sense it is genuine knowledge of nature and of truth. Equally, the moral categories of perfection, virtue, and freedom, which spring from, and are included in, such experience, are really *natural,* in the sense that they are properly a part of nature. They are natural categories, belonging to human nature, which is essentially rational and, therefore, to be fully manifest to ourselves, needs the cognitive unfolding of the practical intellect. The nature of brute animals can be adequately interpreted by mere observation, because the good of their nature is achieved by natural instinct. So, as Aristotle remarks, through observation of what generally is the case, we can have knowledge of nature and its ends.[15] This is not so in the case of human beings. The good of human persons cannot in this sense be read off from "natural regularities" because this good is the object of reason which is a principle of freedom. Humans often, in some regards sometimes even regularly, behave in ways which are opposed to the good of their nature. To know what, in a moral sense, is natural to them, we therefore previously need a conception of the moral good and of virtue; this conception is acquired through natural law.

So, epistemologically speaking, the principles of practical reason, and the cognitive dynamics by which they are generated as described in I-II, q. 94, a. 2, are themselves a constitutive part of that rational dimension of specifically human nature from which springs the moral order. This, by the way, is the reason why natural law is really and authentically, as Aquinas says, "a participation of the eternal law in the rational creature" (I-II, q. 91, a. 2). At a closer look, this definition includes much more than is commonly understood, including the implication that the moral order, proper to human nature, is

14. Furthermore, if I am not wrong, John Finnis wants to make the same point.
15. See Aristotle, *Physics* II, 8.

originally known (i.e., epistemologically speaking) through the practical judgments of human natural reason. So, in the order of knowing, knowledge of the moral order, as far as the basic human goods are concerned—natural law—is prior to the theoretical-metaphysical knowledge of human nature.

To summarize: if we had not already experienced human good, freedom, and responsibility in ourselves, we could never "find" them in nature conceived as a simple object of the theoretical intellect! Or, to put it differently: we can originally "find" the human good and our being free and responsible beings "in nature" only through our basic moral knowledge as it unfolds in the natural law.[16] Consequently, without this human self-understanding, originally accessible only—but simultaneously to everybody—through natural law, no subsequent and anthropologically correct interpretation of human nature could be given. What we "see in front of us"—and not reflecting on inner experience of our practical understanding of the human good—are only bodies and mammals of a determinate species, not human persons. The unfolding of natural law in us is by itself a constitutive, non-derivable, and unrenounceable part of our understanding of human nature and of others as *human persons*, that is, as bodily beings informed by a spiritual soul and, therefore, free and responsible agents. Therefore, a metaphysical-anthropological understanding of human nature *presupposes*, as an essential part of our inner self-experience as persons, the proper work of the practical intellect and the existence of natural law in each of us by which we know of ourselves as moral agents.[17]

Let us return to Porter's charge that in my view "pre-rational aspects of human nature . . . cannot have any direct moral significance." Viewed in light of my crucial distinction between the ontological and the epistemological,

16. This, I think, is what derives from taking seriously *ST* I-II, q.94 a.2. Of course, the process of acquiring the principles of natural law has itself a narrative structure and evolves not independently from educational processes and experiences, as well as specific traditions, in determinate communal contexts in which a human person lives. These contexts and communal experiences, however, can also distort the unfolding of moral knowledge through natural law. In light of the danger of an exaggerated communitarianism, we must uphold the basic rationality of the moral good. I have analyzed this in more detail in my *Die Perspektive der Moral*, 253–63.

17. See for this *NLPR*, 22–42. Notice that traditions, education, or socialization in a determinate community would never be capable of transforming us into moral agents if such external influences were not assimilated and understood in moral terms, which, however, is only possible because what constitutes us as moral agents is already "in us": It is our intellectual faculty that, in its practical judgments, discloses and commands the morally good. Without being able to thus grasp the basic moral notions, we could not even understand the moral meaning and implications of revealed moral precepts, such as those of the Decalogue, as directed toward our exercise of responsible freedom and achievement of moral perfection.

which Porter has apparently overlooked, this charge must be judged ambiguous at best. Does such a statement refer to the ontological or to the epistemological thesis? Does it express that "pre-rational aspects of human nature" are *ontologically* irrelevant for the moral order, that is, that the moral order does not *ontologically* presuppose pre-rational aspects of human nature? Or does it refer to a thesis in moral epistemology, that is, that *knowledge of "moral significance"* does not derive directly from the *knowledge of the naturalness* of something, for example, pre-rational aspects of human nature? Because she has overlooked the distinction that is crucial to my interpretation, Porter gives the impression that I mean the first. But this is mistaken; I mean the second. And even if Aquinas does not explicitly treat the question in these terms, I try to show that his theory of natural law and way of dealing with the question imply exactly the interpretation that I offer.[18] I try to show this in order to demonstrate the error of blaming Aquinas for "biologism" and naturalism, as many moral theologians did after the Second Vatican Council in an attempt to justify a new sexual morality. However, I think that even for a "Thomist" it is licit not only to repeat what Aquinas said, but also to try to resolve problems not explicitly addressed by him, though using the very means and categories offered by his moral philosophy. There *is,* of course a problem, which I have never denied. On the contrary, it was one of the main reasons for writing *NLPR* and a major part of its subject matter. This problem is that Aquinas asserts *both* the formally and thus essentially *rational* character of the moral order and the natural law,[19] *and* that there are things which are directly morally significant, although they are not established by reason but determined by nature. These two poles have to be put together, in a single, comprehensive view. Thus, "moral significance of pre-rational nature" must be understood in the broader context of a moral theory that also affirms that "by the law of God, these things are alone prohibited, which are against reason."[20]

Were such a comprehensive view not possible, then Aquinas's moral theory would be marred by a fundamental inconsistency. Thus, Porter's critique, which challenges my proposal by simply invoking some of the problematic

18. This, I think, is why referring to passages such as *In Ad Rom.* 1 lect. 8, *Contra Gentiles* 3, 122, and *De Malo,* q.15 a.3 does not settle the question. I will come back to this below.

19. See, e.g., *ST* I-II, q.94 a.2: "all inclinations of whatever part of the human nature, that is, the concupiscible and irascible part, belong to the natural law *insofar they are regulated by reason.*"

20. Aquinas, *Summa contra Gentiles* III, 126.

texts—without mentioning my discussion of them and without proposing an alternative solution—does not seem to be very helpful.

"Sins against Nature": The Substantial Union of Body and Spirit

In the following section, I will try to briefly summarize the argument contained in the section of *NLPR* that Porter failed to notice. According to that argument, the problem consists in an apparent inconsistency of terminology in Aquinas. He often declares that sins are "against nature" exactly to the extent that they are "against reason." Every sin, therefore, seems to be a violation of the natural order only insofar as it is a violation of the order of reason (which is the order of the natural law). In spite of that, "in certain contexts Thomas speaks of a 'sin against nature' *(peccatum contra naturam).* But given the ordering role of the reason, such a thing could not exist if we wanted to speak precisely. We seem to be faced with inconsistent terminology."[21] I subsequently mention Aquinas's distinction between the "two natures" of the human being: the *natura rationalis* and the *natura animalis.* Only in considering nature "as distinct from reason and as what is common to the other *animalia,* then one would understand the *peccatum contra naturam* in a more limited sense," as Aquinas says in I-II, q. 94, a. 3, ad 2.

Therefore one has to show that it is impossible to consider human beings as having "two natures" (which is only a traditional way of talking about different parts, belonging by nature to the whole of the human person). There is, of course, substantial unity of all bodily and spiritual aspects of this being. The human person is the substantial unity of body and spirit. That means that *ontologically* the "natural" or "pre-rational" is a part of the human person and as such—from an ontological viewpoint—directly and profoundly morally significant.[22] This is referred by Jean Porter in a substantially correct way. When she however says that, according to me, "pre-rational aspects of human nature, much less nature as manifested in non-rational creation, cannot have any direct moral significance," she is clearly mistaken, insofar as this refers to the *ontological structure* of the human person. Under this aspect, I precisely say the opposite, emphasizing that we have to avoid a spiritualistic or dualistic anthropology, which I have argued is characteristic of Karl Rahner and many of his disciples. In particular, *NLPR* asserts:

21. Rhonheimer, *NLPR,* 94.
22. Ibid., 95ff.

By "spiritualism" is meant an anthropology and ethics in which bodiliness and sensuality are granted no constitutive moral significance in the context of human actions; instead, through the dualistic antithesis of "person" and "nature," *all* human acts are viewed as *originally* spiritual phenomena. Such phenomena are only subsequently allowed to "express" or "incarnate" bodiliness and sensuality on a plane that is itself "subhuman" or "subpersonal," and indifferent toward such acts; this plane of "expressive behavior" is a "material" field for the soul, and lacks any proper moral significance; upon this field its shaping force can be "disposed."[23]

By thus opposing "an anthropology and ethics in which bodiliness and sensuality are granted no constitutive moral significance in the context of human actions," I oppose precisely the thesis which Porter in her review imputes to me when she declares that, in my view, "pre-rational aspects of human nature, much less nature as manifested in non-rational creation, cannot have any direct moral significance."[24]

The truth, then, is that by rejecting dualistic and spiritualistic forms of anthropology, I as a matter of fact explicitly reject the view attributed to me by Porter *as an ontological or anthropological affirmation,* and in this sense the rejection is a cornerstone of my argument. (As an epistemological statement I do not properly reject it, but hold that it must be formulated in a way that is able to show the *epistemological* character of the affirmation.) I contrast with the above-mentioned dualistic or spiritualistic view what I call the "personal and integral anthropology and ethics of St. Thomas." In such an anthropology, the ultimate significance, moral specification, and order springs, it is true, from the spiritual (and therefore rational) "part" of man. "At the same time, however, it is recognized that bodiliness and sensation are the *foundation* for all spiritual acts."[25]

The moral problem of "sins against nature" must be analyzed in the context of such an integral and personal anthropology. Sins against nature are offenses not simply against the ordering part of the soul (reason), but against what this ordering task naturally *presupposes;* it is not directed against the order established by reason *in* the natural inclinations and thus against the due act of these inclinations, but it is a manipulation and perversion of the prop-

23. Ibid., 102f.

24. Porter's mention of "nature as manifested in non-rational creation" seems to me in this context to be beside the point. We have to clearly distinguish, as *NLPR* does and Porter does not seem to do, the "nature" that *we are* (mainly our own bodiliness), from the "nature" that *we are not,* which is the nature that surrounds us, in which we live, or with which we are dealing.

25. Rhonheimer, *NLPR,* 102.

er natural goal of some of these inclinations itself, and consequently—considering the dependence of practical reason and intellect altogether on the naturally given—a basic disorientation of practical reason.[26]

The Epistemological Dimension: Distinguishing "Acting" from "Sinning" against Nature

At this point, however, the question arises why acting in this way—that is, manipulating and "perverting" the natural goal of a natural inclination—is morally wrong and a sin. Or formulated in a different way: how do we *know* that something "naturally given" is morally significant in the sense that its proper natural meaning must be respected as an integral part of its moral meaning? At this point it is necessary to avoid making what I called the mistake of "moralizing the natural order."[27] This means: one has to avoid falsely identifying *agere contra naturam* ("*acting* against nature") with *peccare contra naturam* ("*sinning* against nature"). Shaving and cutting one's hair or nails is acting "against nature." But, hopefully, no one will call this a sin. Neither is swimming immoral just because such an act is not natural for human beings. More dramatically, cutting off a kidney or some other paired organ from one's body in order to donate it to some other person in need seems quite obviously a case of "acting against nature." But generally this is considered to be not only a morally good, but even a recommended act (albeit many moral theologians in the twentieth century have condemned it as self-mutilation, that is, as perversely acting "against nature." This demonstrates precisely that there *is* an epistemological problem, that the "moral significance" of the "natural" is not simply deducible from the sheer naturalness of the natural.) Or else, to take Germain Grisez's example,[28] to masticate sugarless chewing gum means using a natural faculty besides or even against its natural purpose. It is obvious that gum-chewing is not for this reason immoral. Similarly, taking a contraceptive pill in order to protect oneself from foreseeable rape does not seem to be a sin, even if one thereby seriously interferes with natural patterns

26. Ibid., 103.

27. Ibid., 105.

28. See *The Way of the Lord Jesus*, vol. 1, *Christian Moral Principles* (Chicago: Franciscan Herald Press, 1983), 105. Another fine example for an act "against nature" that seems to be perfectly licit, comes from G. E. M. Anscombe's *Contraception and Chastity* (London: Catholic Truth Society, 1975): Installing "a substitute for lung-breathing by some reversible operation (with a view to underwater exploration, say)."

and naturally given bodily processes and even if, on this purely natural level, there is no external difference from a contraceptive act performed with the intent of having sex without the risk of getting children. The latter, however, *is* considered to be sinful behavior.[29]

Therefore, showing that someone has *acted* against nature is not sufficient for asserting that he or she has also *sinned* against nature. Only by crudely "moralizing the natural order" could one affirm the opposite and identify "agere" and "peccare," "acting" and "sinning" against nature. In this case, one would assert that "the fact that something is *a natura*" is "reason enough for something to be beyond the power of human control,"[30] that is, its naturalness should be respected in its morally normative character just because it is "natural"; so, for example, one should never intentionally use the masticating power of one's jaws, frustrating thereby their natural function of facilitating the eating process in order of nutrition. "No chewing of gum!" then, would be a strictly moral command, based on nature.

Yet, the correct argument, as exposed in *NLPR*, goes exactly the other way round:

> If someone argues, therefore, that "interference" into the natural order represents a moral evil, this is not maintained because of the inviolability of this order in itself, but rather because it is known that some moral evil is involved, and because of the reasons why it is evil. In other words, it is due to a recognition that certain natural things have moral significance, and that between them and the *ordo rationis* there is an intimate and indissoluble connection.[31]

Since, as has been noticed above, Aquinas emphatically asserts that "by the law of God, these things are alone prohibited, which are against reason" (*Summa contra Gentiles*, III, 126),[32] *NLPR* asserts that "it must be shown in the logic of Thomistic ethics how, and to what extent, *contra naturam agere* contradicts the *reason;* since only in that case is it recognized as a '*peccatum*

29. For contraception, see in more detail, M. Rhonheimer, "Contraception, Sexual Behavior, and Natural Law: Philosophical Foundation of the Norm of 'Humanae Vitae,'" *Linacre Quarterly* 56, no. 2 (1989): 20–57; [Editor's note: an extended account of this essay is presented in M. Rhonheimer, *Etica della procreazione: Contrazzezione, Fecondazione artificiale, Aborto* (Milan/Rome: PUL-Mursia, 2000), 15–109]. See also "L'uso preventivo di anticoncezionali in caso di minaccia di stupro: un'eccezione?" in *Etica della procreazione,* 110–25.

30. Rhonheimer, *NLPR,* 105.

31. Ibid.

32. Quoted in ibid., 106. (In *NLPR* it is falsely quoted as chap. 125, which is my mistake, contained already in the German original.)

contra naturam' and expressly stated by Thomas to be in contradiction with the will of God."[33] "Contra naturam *agere*" is known as "contra naturam *peccare*" exactly insofar as it turns out to be a violation of the moral order, conceived as the order of reason.

The Natural as a "Presupposition" for Reason

Exactly at this point II-II, q. 154, a. 12 becomes relevant. In the following, I shall quote the passage as it is quoted and translated in *NLPR*, p. 107 (also with the original emphases):[34]

> In every class of things the corruption of the principle of the class is the worst, for everything else depends upon it. Now the principles of reason are those things that are according to nature [*secundum naturam*]. *For reason has to presuppose what nature has determined in order to arrange anything else as it sees fit.*[35] This appears in theoretical matters as well as in the reasoning concerned with actions. And thus, just as in speculative reasoning, that error is most serious and shameful that has to do with things of which the knowledge is naturally given to man, so in matters of action, to do that which is against the things that have been determined by nature is most grievous and shameful. Therefore, because in the vices that are against nature man transgresses that which is according to nature in the area of sexual behavior [*circa usum venereum*], in this kind of actions, this is the most serious sin. . . . With the other forms of lust, the transgression is only against that which has been determined according to right reason, but *still presupposing the natural principles.*

In my view, the most important aspect of this text in the present context is that Aquinas deals here with the question of how nature or the "naturally given" bears upon moral knowledge. Aquinas's assertion that *"reason has to presuppose what nature has determined in order to arrange anything else as it sees fit"* (or in Porter's translation: "reason, presupposing what is determined by nature, disposes other matters in accordance with what is appropriate to these") clearly indicates the viewpoint of moral epistemology. The ontologically "natural" is a moral principle not insofar it is just natural, *but insofar as it is a principle for reason.* Of course, I do not want to suggest that Aquinas reflected in the present context of the *Secunda secundae,* and perhaps in gen-

33. Ibid.

34. I only omit the article "the" before "reason," which seems to me somewhat unusual.

35. This is the sentence Porter quoted against me, in a somewhat different translation: "The principles of reason are those which are according to nature, for reason, presupposing what is determined by nature, disposes other matters in accordance with what is appropriate to these."

eral, much about this differentiation between the ontological/anthropological and epistemological aspect of the question. The distinction is nevertheless used and thus implicitly present, and in the first part of *NLPR* I tried to explain why this is so and how it can be shown.

Yet, the question that arises at this point, but which already has been answered by Aquinas elsewhere (in the *Prima secundae,* so that in the treatment of "sins against nature" of the *Secunda secundae* it can be presupposed) is the following: how do we *know* in a specific context of human action (e.g., sexuality, speech, human life, property. . . .) that something "natural" is a *presuppositio* for practical reason and therefore for the moral order? This question, not to be dealt with by Aquinas at this place, has been answered in the context of the theory of human acts, of the virtues and of natural law of the *Prima secundae.* The answer is that we—that is, every single acting person, independently of being a student or a scholar of ethical theory—know this through natural law which is the *ordinatio rationis* that directs our natural inclinations to their due end and good. In the context of one's self-experience of the substantial union of body and mind, which in turn presupposes the self-experience of the first principles of natural law in one's own practical reason and the reflection thereupon, the ontological naturalness of the procreative function and meaning of the sexual inclination is naturally understood as a human good (which ultimately turns out to be, as John Finnis calls it, the "good of marriage"). It is not difficult to recognize that the masticating capacity of one's jaws, on the other hand, is not. In the former, the naturalness of the procreative meaning of sexuality will be acknowledged as a "natural principle" for practical reason and for human action; that is, it will be recognized as "nature" which right reason *presupposes* in order to "arrange anything else as it sees fit" (see the quotation above).

In II-II, q. 154, a. 12 the doctrine of the natural principles of reason is simply referred to, but not argued for. It simply is not the subject matter of the article to address why the procreative function of sexuality is a good and therefore, why in this case nature is directly morally significant; it is concerned, rather, with showing why sins against nature are the *gravest* of all the sins of lust.[36] The argument is *not* that this is the case because nature is acted against, but because—by so acting against nature—the order of reason is de-

36. This, as the title indicates, is the subject matter of the article: "Utrum vitium contra naturam sit maximum peccatum inter species luxuriae."

prived of some of its natural principles, without which practical reason loses its orientation toward the human good that is originally disclosed by natural law.[37] This is why Aquinas affirms that "to do that which is against the things that have been determined by nature is most grievous and shameful. . . . because in the vices that are against nature man transgresses that which is according to nature in the area of sexual behavior, in this kind of actions, this is the most serious sin. . . ." The plausibility of this interpretation follows from its adherence to the basic hermeneutical principle that the article should be read in light of the declared purpose of the text, here announced in the title of the article.

Thus, the very point of my argument is one of moral epistemology. *Ontologically,* the moral order builds upon nature *(agere sequitur esse).* The moral order is not only a rational order, but a rational order established *in* natural drives/tendencies/inclinations, so that it also depends on the very naturalness of these drives.[38] The naturalness of these inclinations, drives, and tendencies, however, is morally relevant only insofar as, and because, they are presuppositions for the order of reason, and thus for the order of virtue. For, in Thomistic terms, moral acts are equal to human acts and these proceed from reason—that is, deliberated will—so that the moral order, which is the order of the virtues, is essentially an order of reason. To make out the moral significance of naturalness or pre-rational nature, one therefore has to show its connection with this order of reason, its character of being a *presuppositio* of the moral order, that is, of being a natural principle for practical reason and its acts of understanding the basic human goods and the variety of moral virtues.[39]

37. I think it is useful to remind that by "natural law" is meant, in a Thomistic context and in *NLPR,* a cognitive power of the human person, that is, practical reason insofar as it commands to do and pursue the good, and to avoid evil, through grasping the basic human goods in one's natural inclinations; in a second and derived sense, natural law is also the whole of the basic contents of these acts of practical reason, the precepts formulated as propositions.

38. This was one of my main points against Franz Böckle's attempt to understand Thomistic natural law as "creative reason," overlooking the embedding of human reason in nature. You will find this extensively treated in *NLPR.* In a more moderate, but in my view nevertheless mistaken way, and influenced by Kantian principles, Ludger Honnefelder and Georg Wieland have tried to conceive Thomistic natural law as originating in reason, understood as a cognitive power that, in the beginning, works in a "distant" way from nature, formulating principles of "pure reason." Consequently, they have blamed my view of being too "naturalistic" (what also, in a way, proves that Jean Porter must have overlooked something). For my reply to Honnefelder and Wieland, see chapter 5 of this collection, originally published as "Praktische Vernunft und das 'von Natur aus Vernünftige': Zur Lehre von der Lex naturalis als Prinzip der Praxis bei Thomas von Aquin," *Theologie und Philosophie* 75 (2000): 493–522.

39. In a first review of the original German edition of *NLPR* (*Natur als Grundlage der Moral. Die personale Struktur des Naturgesetzes bei Thomas von Aquin: Eine Auseinandersetzung mit au-*

This may seem to be a trivial point. Notwithstanding, it is important and fundamental (what is basic is mostly trivial). It was important to make this point, considering the charge of "naturalism" laid on Aquinas by some critics or the attempt to interpret him—mostly for "tactical" reasons—as an advocate of "creative reason," as did the adherents of so-called "autonomous morals."[40] Yet, I am fully aware of the fact—as Aquinas was in his commentary on the sixth book of Aristotle's *Nicomachean Ethics*[41]—that there is kind of a circle. Considering, however, that we are arguing on the level of *principles,* this is not a vicious circle. There is no *petitio principii* because principles cannot and need not be demonstrated. I therefore do not intend to *demonstrate* or otherwise "prove" the moral significance of the naturalness (for example, the procreative meaning) of sexuality. I only say that epistemologically—in the order of knowing—its moral significance, clearly affirmed by Aquinas, *does not derive from its naturalness as such.* This moral significance rather springs from its being rationally understood as a human good and, therefore, as a constitutive part of the order of reason, that is, of the moral order which is nothing other than the order of the virtues. Yet, for sexuality to have a procreative meaning does not mean that this meaning is *established* by the ordering act of the reason—this would be rather absurd—but that it has the character of being a (natural) *presupposition* of such ordering acts of practical reason. The ultimate *ontological* justification of this is the anthropology of the substantial union of body and spirit, as is extensively argued for in *NLPR.* But as a human good, it primarily appears through natural law, which belongs to practical reason.

In *NLPR* I have extensively tried to analyze how the knowledge of natural moral significance truly and properly originates in natural law. The first principles of natural law are "constituted" in the naturally performed act of "apprehension" of the proper ends of natural inclinations as human goods by

---

tonomer und teleologischer Ethik [Innsbruck-Vienna: Tyrolia-Verlag, 1987]), published in *Theological Studies* 49, no. 2 (June 1988): 358–59, G. Simon Harak has rightly pointed out the importance, in my reading of Aquinas, of the relationship between natural law and moral virtue. He has also, I think, correctly understood the real meaning of my "anti-naturalism."

40. With "naturalism" I do not mean in this context the affirmation of the intrinsic goodness and intelligibility of the (created) "natural order," such as to give rise to moral requirements independently from divine mandate or sheer convention (see Porter, *Natural and Divine Law,* 98). This naturalism is typical not only for Aquinas but also for Scholastic philosophy and theology as a whole. By "naturalism" is meant in the present context the immediate derivation of moral norms from natural structures, givens, etc., as I have already explained. Moral theologians call this form of "naturalism" also "biologism" or "physicalism."

41. *In Ethic.* VI, lect. 2.

practical reason.[42] In the act of understanding these natural ends and goods of the inclinations as *human goods,* the naturally given *proper* goods and ends *(bonum et finis proprius)* of natural inclinations are ordered by reason to their *due* good and end *(bonum et finis debitus).*[43] So, in the case of sexuality, the proper and natural end and good is the union of male and female that has a procreative function (this is simply natural and, according to Aquinas, also common to other animals). But this natural good of the sexual inclination is not yet the whole truth about the very natural inclination insofar as it is the inclination of a *human person.* Human sexuality is more. To be understood in its full truth, the naturally determined pattern of sexuality needs to be understood as part of the order of what is characteristic for human persons: mutual self-giving, friendship, and faithfulness. These, together with the natural procreative meaning of sexuality, form a higher and complex spiritual-bodily unity of value and human good, which we call "marriage."

So, it seems clear that there "is an *ordo naturalis* that the natural law presupposes, and without this order both the natural law and the order of reason and virtue lose their foundation."[44] Notice that this "natural order" which the order of reason presupposes corresponds to the passive participation in the eternal law. It corresponds to a "being measured-ness" which, in its turn, is the presupposition of all measuring and ordering acts of practical reason by which the order of reason, as the moral order, is established.

42. If I talk about the principles (or precepts) of natural law as being "constituted" by reason, I obviously do not mean that they are "creatively invented" or "arbitrarily established" by the human intellect, but that they are properly *known* and in this sense cognitively constituted as a judgment or "proposition." This is what Aquinas explicitly asserts, using exactly this terminology, in his treatise on natural law. He does not only say that the natural law is "something constituted" by reason ("aliquid per rationem constitutum"), but he even declares that it is "a work of reason" ("opus rationis"). See *ST* I-II, q.94 a.1: "Dictum est enim supra quod lex naturalis est aliquid per rationem constitutum; sicut etiam propositio est quoddam opus rationis." The point is that the precepts of natural law are *propositions,* that is, *judgments* that are properly the work of the intellect. (You cannot find propositions in nature: they are emanated by the intellectual faculty of the human person.) This is why the natural law, as any law, is constituted by reason. (Notice, however, that we are always talking about *cognitive* acts that contain truth and therefore do not "create" anything. The truth, however, is to be found in the proposition or judgment; insofar as the judgments of practical reason are *true,* they also form part of the eternal law and are a real participation of it.) The above-mentioned "dictum est enim supra" refers to *ST* I-II, q.90 a.1 ad2, where we read: "in operibus rationis est considerare ipsum actum rationis, qui est intelligere et ratiocinari, *et aliquid per huius actum constitutum.* . . . ideo est invenire aliquid in ratione practica quod ita se habeat ad operationes, sicut se habet propositio in ratione speculativa ad conclusiones. Et huiusmodi propositiones universales rationis practicae ordinatae ad actiones, habent rationem legis." This is extensively treated in *NLPR,* 58–80.

43. See the classical text *ST* I-II, q.91 a.2, and my analysis of this passage in *NLPR,* 67.

44. Rhonheimer, *NLPR,* 109.

Moreover, the other texts invoked by Jean Porter against my view of natural law—namely *Ad Romanos* I, 8, *Contra Gentiles* 3, 129, and *De malo* q. 15 a. 3—do not support her criticism. I argue that these texts need to be interpreted in the light of the whole of Aquinas's moral theory. Yet, understood in this way, they turn out to contain only Aquinas's contention that the natural pattern of sexuality (its procreative meaning) is a constitutive part of the moral good as it is determined by nature. But by alleging that, the sheer "naturalness" of the pattern is not asserted to be the *reason* why they are morally significant in so direct a way. Notice that in order to show this moral significance, each of these three texts seems to offer a slightly different "reason." One would think that, in reality, the reason would be rather unimportant. The truth is that it is not the reason at all. The real reason, as we will see, is that "the conjunction of male and female" and the procreative dimension naturally inscribed in this conjunction is a human good (what is known through natural law). So, in the lectures on the Epistle to the Romans, Aquinas refers to the "generic" nature of man which is its "animal" nature: by intentionally frustrating the generative function of the sexual act, Aquinas asserts, man acts "against the nature of man insofar as he is an animal." In the *Contra Gentiles* passage, on the other hand, Aquinas refers to the fact that the emission of the semen is necessary for the propagation of the human species and that this is the proper good and end of such emission. Therefore every emission of the semen from which *per se* this end cannot be achieved—as when it happens outside the coital act between male and female—is a sin "against nature" (here, however, nothing is said about "animal nature"). In the *De malo* passage, finally, Aquinas simply states that an act of lust from which "no procreation can follow" is against nature.

Now, these three descriptions of the sin against nature, of course, in no way contradict each other. On the contrary, they all fit very well together. But none of these three descriptions of natural patterns, functions, and goals really gives the basic reason why thus *acting* against nature involves also a *sin* against nature, that is, a moral evil. Put in another way, none of these descriptions serves as an *argument* for the moral significance of the described natural act. The real reason that founds such moral significance is instead a normative premise implicit in the description, a premise that might seem trivial, even so trivial that it is entirely overlooked, but is nevertheless absolutely basic and necessary for contending that something "natural" is morally significant. As I have already noted, it is, in the present case, the premise that "the conjunction of male and female" and the procreative dimension naturally inscribed in this conjunction, is a *human good.* This precisely is primarily and originally grasped and affirmed by natural law, that is, by practical reason as Aquinas describes it in I-II, q. 94, a. 2 (if the function of natural law were not to *originally* grasp the human goods as goods to be pursued, what else *then* would be the function and relevance of the natural law?) And this is why from an epistemological point of view the natural patterns/functions/goals belong to the order of reason, which is the moral order.[45] So, what initially seemed to be the *argument* for moral significance turns out to be only the *description* of what has already previously been understood as morally significant by practical reason—insofar it is natural law—and can now, in this context, be identified, in the very sense of II-II, q. 154, a. 12, as a natural "*presupposition*" or "natural principle" of the order of reason, a presupposition against which to act means to sin "against nature."[46]

Allow me just one additional remark: Jean Porter quotes—and she seems to think it to be important—the response to the first objection of II-II, 154, a. 12, where Aquinas says that "while the order of right reason is from man, the order of nature comes from God. Therefore, by sinning against nature, where the very order of nature is violated, one does injustice to God himself." Well, I do not think that this is quite relevant in our context. The point of this answer is that, here, Aquinas only gives an additional answer to the question whether "sinning against nature" is more grave a sin than the other sins of lust, like adultery or rape, which involve offense against one's neighbor and therefore violate the order of justice and charity. Aquinas holds that "sins against nature" are worse because they destroy in a particular way our com-

45. Porter rightly says "to describe an action from the moral point of view *is* to form a moral evaluation of the action" (J. Porter, "The Moral Act in Veritatis Splendor and in Aquinas's Summa Theologiae," in *Veritatis Splendor: American Responses,* ed. Michael E. Allsopp and John J. O'Keefe [Kansas City: Sheed & Ward, 1995], 281). She, however, seems to overlook that there are also naturally given moral evaluations, given precisely by the precepts of natural law.

46. I do not hold, however, that this statement is sufficient to prove the sinfulness of contraceptive sexual behavior. Contrary to Grisez and Finnis, I do not believe that the moral disorder of contraception is rooted in a contralife will. My above statement properly applies to acts of sodomy and masturbation. To show that contraception is immoral, and in a way against nature, we need an additional argument, which I have developed in my article "Contraception, Sexual Behavior, and Natural Law" (see n. 29 above). This article has been published in German in a much enlarged version as *Sexualität und Verantwortung: Empfängnisverhütung als ethisches Problem* (Vienna: IMABE, 1995); it is also published in an Italian translation in my *Etica della procreazione* (n. 29 above), 15–109. There you will also find my critique of the Grisez-Finnis argument against contraception.

munity with God, because the "order of nature comes from God." I am not sure about how compelling and morally relevant this argument really is (and, considering the *corpus* of the article in question, it is not the main argument for asserting the special graveness of "sins against nature"). But it certainly is not meant as an argument to show why "*acting* against nature" implies a "*sin* against nature." It is only an argument for determining an order of gravity of sins (which is the declared scope of the article), not the reason why it is understood as a sin altogether (the latter, however, was what we were discussing). A *sin* it is, because it destroys a principle of the order of reason and, thereby destroys this order itself.[47]

Reason, Objects, and Intentionality: Hauerwas on the Relevance of "Natural Patterns"

I hope that with the preceding account of my reading of Aquinas I have succeeded in shedding some light on the fact that the concept of "sins against nature," as used in II-II, q. 154, a. 11 and 12, is an integral part of this reading. Equally it should now be clearer why this reading of Aquinas does in no way overlook the direct moral significance of pre-rational aspects of human nature. On the other hand, in *NLPR* and more explicitly in publications subsequent to it, I have strongly argued in favor of an intentional understanding not only of human acts, but also of the *object* of the human act. For some critics, this seems to be incompatible with acknowledging a natural "substructure" of human acts. Moreover, according to this criticism such an intentional understanding of the object undermines the possibility of there being "intrinsically evil acts" and opens the door to continuously, and fatally, redefining and redescribing human actions, contrary to a sound moral realism, clearly defended by Aquinas.

Yet, this fear is unreasonable, because the assertion that the object of a human act can only be adequately described by including into its description a

47. In the preceding article of *ST* II-II, q.154, "vitium contra naturam" is defined as being opposed not only to "right reason" but also "to the very natural order of the sexual act *as it is proper to the human species*" ("repugant ipsi ordini naturali venerei actus *qui convenit humanae speciei:* quod dicitur vitium contra naturam"). The decisive point does not seem to be the fact that a sin against nature opposes what has its origin in divine creation, but rather that it is opposed to what is fundamental to mankind as such, i.e., to the human *species.* This, again, shows that it is not the mere "naturalness" of nature that makes acting against nature a *sin* or a *vice* against nature, but its moral significance, the feature of being a principle of the order of reason—that is, of moral virtue, and therefore of being a human good.

basic intention (or: intentionality) does in no way imply that, in each particular case, the object of the performed action is just what the acting person, say, "freely chooses to be his intention." Of course, there actually *do exist* many actions which, regarding their natural or physical pattern, are open to many possible descriptions. So, I can, for example, perform a bodily movement as "raising my arm" in order (1) to greet somebody, or (2) to give a starting signal in a competition, or (3) to try to hit an aggressor to stop him. There you have, depending on the basic intention with which the arm is raised, three different human acts, which are different by their very object. "Raising one's arm" *for itself* and *as such* is no human act at all, but simply a bodily movement which, as such, cannot be performed as a human act. As a human act, it must be chosen, and choice involves an act of the reason-guided will, and that implies a goal pursued as the good of the action in question. This goal/intent/proposal is precisely not "the raising of the arm," but "greeting," "giving a start signal," "stopping an aggression," and so on. Thus, these are, on the level of what I have called the "intentional basic action," the (intentional) descriptions of the objects corresponding to three different human acts.[48]

However, in contrast to acts like "raising one's arm," there are *some* acts for which the natural pattern does not offer this "intentional openness" and the capability of being redescribed as a human act. There are two possibilities. The first is that a determinate natural pattern is not capable of being informed by certain intentions. For example, you can't redescribe the act of masticating rubber as an act of nutrition and self-preservation. Rubber is not, to use Thomistic terminology, *materia debita* for being a means of nutrition. No intention of self-preservation will render an act of "masticating rubber" into a nutritive act, simply because by its very nature rubber does

48. Without such a theory of intentional basic actions, one arrives at asserting the possibility of redescription of human acts in a rather arbitrary way. Thus, according to Porter ("The Moral Act in Veritatis Splendor," 285), "someone who does not accept the traditional arguments for capital punishment might well insist that an act of execution *is* a form of murder." This, as it seems to me, is wrong. Provided that we do not accept the traditional argument for capital punishment, even then an act of execution, legally performed in the way it was traditionally justified, can never be considered to be an act of *murder,* but only one of "unjust" or "illegitimate" *punishment.* To execute a legitimately convicted criminal is in no case to "murder" him, but perhaps to punish him in an unjust, disproportionate, illegitimate, or inhuman way. The reason is that there is a (intentional) basic action that is not just "killing" (so that "murder" would be "unjust killing," including the execution of capital punishment). Instead of "killing" (understood as a private action), in this case the intentional basic action is rather "punishing," that is, the compensation for and restoration of violated justice by public authority. In the above case, then, you might call the executioner (or legislator) somebody who is in grave error about what kinds of punishment are morally legitimate or just, but you will certainly not be allowed to call him an assassin!

not serve this purpose. It is *materia indebita.* ("Masticating rubber" might be intentionally an act of nutrition only due to someone's highly improbable, invincible ignorance.) The intention of performing an act of nutrition and self-preservation thus includes some natural "presuppositions." On the other hand, masticating bread, for example, can be performed and described as a "human act" (and therefore a moral act) only insofar as the physical process is in some form deliberately chosen, wanted, finalized to the good of self-preservation. Neither the bread nor the physical process of masticating it are properly the "object" of the moral act "nutrition" and "self-preservation"; only the basic intention of doing so forms that object (an intention, however, which *for being shaped as such an intention* needs the natural pattern of "eating bread"). So it is possible to assert both the shaping of objects by (basic) intentions, and the dependence of objects and of *some* basic intentions from natural patterns.

Not all intentions are what traditionally is called the "finis operantis." This notion specifies what we might call the remote or additional intention, namely a goal to which an action, already morally specified by its object, is additionally ordered by the agent. For example, someone might choose and perform the act of "greeting somebody" (object) in order to get a favor from him (additional goal or intention). Also the object itself (e.g., "greeting someone") includes an intention, a "basic intention," without which no human act whatsoever is conceivable and therefore no "moral object" of a human act can possibly be described.[49] *Some* of such basic intentions are inescapably bound to natural patterns inherent in the action. Talking of "intention" does not necessarily mean talking about the freedom of doing what one does with such or such an "intention" as the agent happens to decide (as in the case of "raising one's arm").

This leads us to the second possibility. It is the one in which intentionality directly, and necessarily, depends on a determinate natural pattern. The most obvious cases are sexuality and speech: sexual acts, by their naturally procreative meaning, involve an inherent intentionality. The procreative meaning equally includes and ultimately shapes other meanings of sexuality, mainly the significance of loving union of two persons engaging in sexu-

49. I understand my conception of the "moral object" as very close to Aquinas, but as simultaneously departing from not a few subsequently formed traditions of this understanding in the course of the moral theology of the manuals. For my understanding of the moral object in Aquinas, I am much indebted to Theo G. Belmans, *Le sens objectif de l'agir humain* (Vatican City: Libreria Editrice Vaticana, 1980).

al intercourse. Through the procreative dimension of the sexual inclination, corresponding love is shaped as a *specific kind* of love: love which serves the transmission of human life. Analogously, speech has an intrinsically communicative meaning. Speech acts which therefore violate communicative justice are performed with an intentionality that contradicts the very natural purpose of speech.[50] Having sex or speaking is not, like "raising one's arm," an intentionally and thus morally undetermined bodily behavior. You cannot, on the most basic level of the "object," engage in sexual acts or speak just for this or that purpose. Whoever engages in sexual intercourse necessarily *intends* an act of a generative *kind* (even if he tries to render it infertile by contraceptive devices). What he does and chooses is already by its very nature meaningful. And whoever speaks engages in communication of some sort, even if by his words he tries to deceive. So, his intention is to perform what by nature is a communicative act, even if he misuses speech for other purposes like deceiving (which is only possible because speech is by its very nature a means of communication and therefore oriented toward telling the truth). Inversely, by "raising one's arm," nothing is decided yet about *what* one is doing; this depends on the choice by which one raises one's arm and only this choice shapes the very (moral) object of the act.[51]

Amazingly, Stanley Hauerwas,[52] praising my understanding of intentional actions and of the concept of "intrinsically evil acts," connected with the former, has ascribed to me the opposite view, that is, the view that basic intentions are, in principle and always, formed independently from "natural patterns." Hauerwas's enthusiastic espousing of my views—in the way he un-

50. Please notice that this is not the whole argument against lying. Things are somewhat more complicated. The intrinsic evilness of lying must be seen in relation to the ethical context of communicative justice. See for this *NLPR*, 452–58, 475ff. I think I have considerably improved my account of lying in my *La prospettiva della morale. Fondamenti dell'etica filosofica* (Rome: Armando, 2006); Spanish *La perspectiva de la moral. Fundamentos de la ética filosófica* (Madrid: Rialp, 2000); German edition, *Die Perspektive der Moral. Philosophische Grundlagen der Tugendethik* (Berlin: Akademie Verlag, 2001). [Editor's note: An English translation is in preparation from The Catholic University of America Press.]

51. This does not exclude that it is possible that certain acts by their very nature are intentionally determined. For example, a physical act, willingly performed by a private person, that by its very nature causes the death of a human being, can, *per accidens,* be reduced to being nothing but the "materia" of another intention, as for example "self-defense" or "life saving." This is the case when the proper effect of the action is realized only *praeter intentionem.* This is possible in very special cases to be identified and described carefully. I think one of these cases was the classical one of "craniotomy," but I cannot go further into this issue here.

52. "Gay Friendship: A Thought Experiment in Catholic Moral Theology," in his *Sanctify Them in the Truth* (Nashville, Tenn.: Abingdon, 1998), 105–21.

derstands them—might have confirmed against my reading of St. Thomas some of those who see my understanding of natural law and human acts as dangerously "subjectivist" and at odds with sound moral realism. To prove that they were right, I fear that they will now perhaps refer not only to Hauerwas's misreading of my conception of the intentional structure of moral objects, but also to Jean Porter's charge that I have distorted Aquinas's teaching on the moral significance of pre-rational nature.

In his defense of "gay friendship" as not being an "intrinsically evil act," Hauerwas in fact asserts that I have "come as close as anyone" he knows "to getting the issue right"[53] (the issue of "intrinsically evil acts"). He rightly refers to my main point that actions can be properly described only as *intentional* actions and further, that the intrinsic evilness of what is called an "intrinsically evil act" does not simply refer to something simply "given" independently of one's intentions. He then goes on to say:

> For "intrinsic evil" makes it sound like certain actions are "out there," abstracted from agents, and they are to be evaluated either by their intrinsic nature or in terms of the consequences they produce. But that is exactly what Rhonheimer is suggesting cannot be done if we are to rightly understand *Veritatis* [*Splendor*]. That certain actions are evil makes sense only in a view of the moral life as a life shaped by the virtues in which human actions are understood from the perspective of the first person.[54]

Of course, Hauerwas makes here an important point and I fully agree with it. Unfortunately, however, he espouses my understanding of intentional actions and of the intentional structure of the object of human acts *independently* of my understanding of natural law and the meaning of "nature" as a presupposition of the order of reason. Intentionality and virtue, of course, build upon this basis.

This is why Hauerwas in his intent of describing bodily (sexual) love only referring to the intention of friendship, excluding natural sexual patterns, does not seem to me to be entitled to refer to my views. Hauerwas is right in saying, "Rhonheimer shows that the same behavioral pattern alone cannot decide

53. Ibid., 111. Hauerwas refers to my articles "'Intrinsically Evil Acts' and the Moral Viewpoint: Clarifying a Central Teaching of *Veritatis Splendor*," *The Thomist* 58, no. 1 (1994): 1–39; and "Intentional Actions and the Meaning of Object: A Reply to Richard McCormick," *The Thomist* 59, no. 2 (1995): 279–311. Both articles are reprinted in this book as chapters 3 and 4, respectively, and in J. A. Di Noia and Romanus Cessario, eds., *Veritatis Splendor and the Renewal of Moral Theology* (Princeton, N.J.: Scepter Publishers; Huntington, Ind.: Our Sunday Visitor; Chicago: Midwest Theological Forum, 1999), 161–193, 241–268.

54. Ibid.

everything."[55] This, of course, applies perfectly to the above example of "raising one's arm." In a different sense, it also applies to the classical distinction between "copulating" (natural pattern) as an act of adultery or a marital act;[56] or of "killing" (as a physical event) and the distinction of "murder," "revenge" or "executing capital punishment."[57] But asserting "that the same behavioral pattern alone cannot decide everything" does not mean that a behavioral pattern may not, at least in some cases, decide *something,* that is, something decisive for the forming of basic intentionalities. It does not mean either that there cannot exist certain behavioral patterns which are unable to incarnate determinate intentions (that is, that they are *materia indebita* for these intentions).[58] So it is perfectly possible to argue that sexual intercourse is *materia indebita* for incarnating personal friendship and love of persons of the same sex. Such a kind of sexual act is "against nature" in the sense analyzed above: it frustrates the goal naturally inscribed in the sexual faculty which is grasped, by natural reason, as a fundamental human good and therefore as an integral part of the order of reason and virtue.

To conclude: one of the central features of the view of natural law put forward in *NLPR*, and of my reading of Aquinas altogether, was to try to overcome the fateful dichotomy between "nature" and "reason." Human reason generally, and practical reason in particular, are part of that very "nature" we consider as morally significant and normative when we are talking about "human nature." Misunderstandings of my views like those of Porter or Hauerwas (or others I deal with in the Postscript of *NLPR*), normally stem from overlooking what might be called *ratio ut natura,* "reason as nature." It is true that *ordinarily* "reason" and "nature" designate opposed principles: what springs from reason is precisely not what is natural. The natural is what is determined to a single and definite goal; the reasonable instead is open to a variety of conceptions of the good.[59] Human reason, however, is the reason of

55. Ibid., 114.

56. See *ST* I-II, q.18 a.5 ad3.

57. See ibid., q.1 a.3 ad3. For Aquinas's treatment of "killing" see my essay "Sins Against IIa IIae, qq.59–78)," in *The Ethics of Aquinas,* ed. Stephen J. Pope (Washington, D.C.: Georgetown University Press, 2002), 287–303.

58. See for this again chapter 10, or William F. Murphy Jr., "Martin Rhonheimer's *Natural Law and Practical Reason,*" 541ff., and especially footnote 47 where Murphy correctly says: "Thus, Rhonheimer holds with Thomas that there are naturally given limits to the intentions that correspond to a given behavioral pattern" (and refers to "Intentional Actions and the Meaning of Object").

59. Cf. *ST* I-II, q.17 a.1 ad2.

a being formed by the substantial unity of body and spirit. Therefore, reason must also possess a natural dimension. It is embedded in the whole of human naturalness and, therefore, is both dependent on this naturalness, and shapes it according to the dimensions of good and truth, which is accessible to the person only through the intellectual powers of the soul.

Thus, the "nature" we call "human nature" cannot be understood besides and independently of the ordering acts of practical reason which naturally orientate human freedom toward what is "the good for mankind." These acts are practical judgments, "constituting" what Aquinas calls "propositions," which because of their being embedded in the appetitive and volitional dynamics of the human person have an imperative or prescriptive force.[60] Practical judgments *move* human subjects to do and pursue, or to avoid, what they present as good or evil. The first judgments of practical reason, which possess the character of naturally known principles, are the precepts of natural law. They are not properly "derived" from a human nature previously understood by the theoretical intellect, but they rather are a constitutive part of the very human nature that subsequently must be metaphysically understood and is a subject matter of moral theory. Therefore, an essential and original part of my interpretation is that natural law, in its most proper sense as an ordering act of the practical reason, is not a moral code derived from other kinds of knowledge (i.e., of pre-rational nature or of metaphysics) but is rooted in the first-person moral experience of practical reasoning in pursuit of human goods. However, to argue that this epistemological understanding is at least implicit in the work of St. Thomas should not be understood to undermine metaphysical reflection on the natural law, or to argue that pre-rational human nature does not have moral significance.

60. The precepts or principles of natural law are not properly the "acts" of practical reason (knowing, understanding, reasoning), but rather what by such acts is, in Aquinas's terminology, "constituted," that is, the judgments or propositions. See again the above-quoted text (footnote 37) from *ST* I-II, q.90 a.1 ad2. As Cajetan, however, has perspicaciously observed in his commentary to *ST* I-II, q.58 a.5, Comm. VIII, we are generally used to speak, in a somewhat deceitful way, of practical judgments "in actu signato," that is, in a reflective way, while originally they should be understood in "actu exercito" (see for this *NLPR*, 147, n. 3). Thus, the first principle of practical reason, "good is to be done and pursued, evil to be avoided," is, as a practical principle, not "asserted" in this way, but rather in the form of an imperative: "do this," "avoid this." It still *is*, however, a judgment. The "copula" of such judgments, however, is not the "is" / "is not" copula, but rather the volitional response to (understood) good and evil; i.e., what Aquinas calls pursuit *(prosecutio)* and fleeing *(fuga)*. In reflection *(in actu signato)* we will express this linguistically as "is to be done," "is to be avoided." About the "practical copula" see my article "Praktische Vernunft und das 'von Natur aus Vernünftige,'" 504f. (presented here in English as chapter 5), and *NLPR*, 32.

7

The Cognitive Structure of the Natural Law and the Truth of Subjectivity

A "Dualistic Fallacy": The Essentially Cognitive Character of the Natural Law

A Historical Reminiscence: The "Nature-Reason" Dichotomy

In a book bearing the title *Lex naturae,* which was published almost half a century ago and became before Vatican Council II an obligatory work of reference, moral theologian Josef Fuchs presented a systematic exposition of the formulations of the Magisterium of the Church on the natural moral law.[1] He thought that he had found "two series" of formulations. The first series referred to the "ontological foundation" of the natural law, the "nature of things": these formulations identified the natural law with the "corporeal-spiritual nature of man" and thus understood it as nature, which was normative for human action. On the basis of this first approach, the natural law was regarded as a normative order placed within the order of things. On the other hand, the second series of formulations was said to refer to what Fuchs called "the noetic aspect of the natural law, its being written into the heart, its natural ability to be recognized by man."[2]

1. Josef Fuchs, *Natural Law: A Theological Investigation,* trans. H. Reckter and J. Dowling (New York: Sheed and Ward, 1965), from the original German edition (Dusseldorf: Patmos Verlag, 1955). For more details see Martin Rhonheimer, *Natural Law and Practical Reason: A Thomist View of Moral Autonomy* (New York: Fordham University Press, 2000), 8ff.

2. Fuchs, 6–9.

With this schematization, Fuchs echoed an approach that was widespread in the neo-Scholastic theology and philosophy of the period, which without doubt also influenced the language of not a few documents of the Magisterium. According to this approach, the "natural law" is an order of nature that is knowable by man, and, once known, imposes itself immediately as a norm of moral action.[3] This schema, in essential terms, is dualistic because it is based upon a dichotomy between "nature" and "natural order" (the objective aspect) on the one hand, and "reason" and "moral knowledge" (the subjective aspect) on the other: the natural law is situated in the sphere of nature; it is the function of reason to read the moral order placed in nature and to follow this order in free action. Only in this sense can one affirm that the natural law "is written in the heart of man": it is an objective, normative natural order that is subjectively known and applied to action. But an observation must be made here: according to this notion what is "written in the heart of man" is not so much the natural law in its objective being as it is the subjective knowledge of this law. The natural law itself is said to be a kind of code of moral norms, found in nature as an "object" of knowledge—though, as "law," independent of this last.

This notion is based upon what I would like to call a "dualistic fallacy." In my judgment, it is difficult to match this way of speaking about the natural law with the long tradition of the doctrine on *lex naturalis,* of which St. Thomas was not only a privileged witness but also perhaps the most lucid and original continuator. For this tradition, the natural law was never simply a "natural order," the object of the knowledge of the subject which only through this knowledge would become something "written in the heart" of man. Indeed, this tradition understood the natural law as a special form of moral knowledge (i.e., as natural knowledge of good and evil), and thus affirmed the essentially cognitive character of the natural law. According to this tradition, the natural law is "written in the heart of man" not only because it is "something known" but specifically because the very intellectual opening of the human subject to moral good constitutes a "law" for human acts. Since this opening takes place in a natural way it can really be called a

3. Cf. ibid.: "In these [texts concerned with the ontological aspect] the being, the very essence or nature of man as composed of body and spirit appears as a norm of moral behavior and of law. . . . [R]eason reads the natural law in the nature of all things and particularly in the nature of man." Fuchs's assertion that this schema expresses in a completely general way the opinion of traditional moral theology is certainly not correct. Cf. Rhonheimer, *Natural Law and Practical Reason,* 9ff.

natural law. Thus St. Ambrose, almost a thousand years before St. Thomas Aquinas, when paraphrasing the famous passage from the letter of St. Paul to the Romans (2:14ff.), spoke about the natural law, which for him was like the "word of God" written into our hearts, in the following terms: "for this reason the ideas of good and evil have sprung up in us, whereby we understand by nature that what is evil must be avoided, and equally by nature we know that there has been prescribed for us what is good."[4] The natural law is this practical, and thus preceptive, natural knowledge of moral good and evil.[5]

Understood in these terms, the natural law shows that it is located specifically on the side of the subject and, as a result, that it is really "subjective." Its objectivity—and thus the objectivity of the moral norms based upon it—consists in the fact that in this natural knowledge of human good the truth of subjectivity is expressed. As we will see in a more detailed way later on in this paper, the natural law is, in fact, the intrinsic principle of truth of practical reason.

It is certainly the case that for the purposes of daily communication and pastoral language expressing oneself in the terms of this dualist schema can in many cases be sufficient and even useful. This schema can also be enough to defend the existence of a natural right—that is to say, the idea that underlying and prior to any positive legal norm there exists an objective normative order of good and right. Finally, it expresses the idea that for subjectivity—for the moral knowledge of the acting subject—there exists an objective rule of truth that is not to be identified with what the subject in fact believes to be true and good. In this last sense, the natural law, indeed, is that moral norm that establishes the truth of subjectivity, defending it from affirming as really good that which is good only in appearance.

However, the dualistic schema does not fail seriously to lead astray the analysis of the natural law and the whole of the ethical-normative discourse

4. St. Ambrose, *De Paradiso,* 8, 39: "opiniones queaedam nobis boni et mali pullulaverunt, dum id quod malum est naturaliter intellegimus esse vitandum et id quod bonum est naturaliter nobis intellegimus esse praeceptum" (in *Sancti Ambrosii Episcopi Mediolanensis Opera* [*Tutte le Opere di Sant'Ambrogio,* ed. bilingua], 2/I, ed. Carolus Schenkl, introduction, translation, notes, and indexes by P. Siniscalco [Milan: Biblioteca Ambrosiana; Rome: Città Nuova Editrice, 1984], 98–99). Cf. also A. Trapé, "L'universalità e l'immutabilità delle norme morali e l'oggettività del giudizio morale secondo i Padri latini, in particolare secondo Sant'Agostino," in *Universalité et permanence des lois morales,* ed. S. Pinckaers and C. J. Pinto de Oliveira (Fribourg: Éditions Universitaires; Paris: Éditions du Cerf, 1986), 90–101.

5. Cf. also St. Augustine, who speaks in his *De libero arbitrio,* I, 6, 15, 48, of "illa lex quae summa ratio nominatur, cui semper obtemperandum est et per quam mali miseram, boni beatam vitam merentur."

based upon it, to the point of rendering such a discourse unintelligible and not very convincing in rational terms. The counterposing of objective "nature" (the "natural order") on the one side, and subjective "reason" ("moral knowledge") on the other, favors a "physicalist" understanding of the natural law. In a physicalist notion of the natural law, this "law" is identified with the merely natural structures and ends upon which a moral normativity is conferred in an immediate way.

An Alternative: The Essential Anthropological Unity of "Nature" and "Reason"

This dualistic fallacy obfuscates the fact that reason, as a cognitive faculty, and thus the very subjectivity of the moral agent, is a part of what we call the "nature of man." It is precisely the intellectual acts, of which reason is the discursive part, that open the human subject to an understanding of the human good according to the truth of his "being a person" (i.e., a corporeal-spiritual unity). This is a good that reveals itself to be a "good of the person" only in the face of intellectual cognition. This good, therefore, is not a simple "object" which is said to be face to face with the knowing subject as a simple "natural given fact." It is also a part of the same knowing subject because in the cognitive acts it is manifested, and in a certain sense constituted, through its intelligibility.

We are here face to face with an anthropological and metaphysical fact that, through the employment of the right approach of moral philosophy, seems to me to be of decisive importance: the "nature of man" is not conceivable without the intellectual part and the corresponding acts of the intellect and of reason. As I have argued in detailed fashion elsewhere,[6] action always certainly follows and expresses, according to St. Thomas Aquinas, the being of every thing *(agere sequitur esse)*, but at the same time this means that the being of things, that is to say their essence or nature, of which acts are a consequence, in itself is unknown to us. We know it by knowing the specific faculties of each nature. The faculties are known by their acts, but we know the acts by their objects.[7] The object of human freedom—which lies in reason and the will as *appetitus in ratione*—is specifically good in the multiple forms

6. M. Rhonheimer, *La prospettiva della morale: Fondamenti dell'etica filosofica* (Rome: Armando, 1994), 159ff.

7. Thomas Aquinas, *De Veritate* q.10 a.1: "Quia vero rerum essentiae sunt nobis ignotae, virtutes autem earum innotescunt nobis per actus."

of its self-expression. For this reason, to know the nature of man we must first know, however paradoxical this may seem, the specifically human good. This applies, in principle, also to non-rational animals—however, in this case we can know their good through an observation of their behavior (i.e., certain typical regularities and normalities).

In the case of man, who acts on the basis of freedom, that which takes place regularly and with "normality" is not a criterion by which to determine his good. Human persons act on the basis of reason and thus with freedom, since reason is "open to many things" and can have "various notions of good"—false ones as well as true.[8] Thus the ethical question is raised. Ethics is not a philosophy of nature; it does not describe regular, and thus natural, behavior.[9] The human nature that we are looking for as a foundation for human action, and of which moral good is the adequate expression, can be found by us only to the extent to which we already know the human good. Knowledge of human nature is not the point of departure for ethics, and even less for the practical reason of each acting subject: it is, rather, its result. We must already know the human good to interpret "nature" rightly and thereby reach the concept of human nature, which is full of normative meaning. This human good we know, indeed, through the natural law, which therefore must be understood as a cognitive principle—as a form, that is to say, of moral knowledge.

We can now state clearly, therefore, that the human good is not simply an object "given" to intellectual acts. The very nature of the intellect—emanating as it does from the spiritual soul which is a substantial form and thus the life principle of its corporeality—means that what is really good for man is, in a certain sense, constituted and formulated only in the intellectual acts themselves.

The human and moral good is essentially a *bonum rationis:* a good of reason, for reason, and formulated by reason.[10] Only within the horizon of this good, as it appears before the intellectual acts of the soul, does "human nature" reveal itself in its normative significance. As a result, and even if at first sight this may seem paradoxical, knowledge of the human good precedes the

8. *ST* I-II, q.17 a.1 ad2: "Ex hoc enim voluntas libere potest ad diversa ferri, quia ratio potest habere diversas conceptiones boni."

9. Cf. Aristotle, *Physics,* II, 8.

10. For a broader exposition of the notion of *bonum rationis* see M. Rhonheimer, *Praktische Vernunft und Vernünftigkeit der Praxis: Handlungstheorie bei Thomas von Aquin in ihrer Entstehung aus dem Problemkontext der aristotelischen Ethik* (Berlin: Akademie Verlag, 1994), 124ff.

right understanding of human nature. This cannot reveal its normative character before all that is natural in man has been interpreted in the light of that good that is the object of the acts of the intellect—and (as we will see later) not of the speculative intellect but of the practical intellect, from which the natural law emanates.

As a consequence, it does not seem adequate in moral philosophy, and even less in an analysis of the "natural law," to depict human reason as the faculty "that knows" in the face of a nature that is "that which is known." This schema simplifies things, just as certain neo-Scholastic theories have simplified the analysis of the natural law, obscuring its real nature.[11] We need once again to discover human reason specifically because it is also "nature"; the reason, that is to say, that naturally knows the good to be done and the evil to be avoided.

The Approach of St. Thomas Aquinas: Beyond the Dualistic Fallacy

A Long-Forgotten Text

It is symptomatic that Fuchs in his above-mentioned book did not take suitably into account a text of the Magisterium on the natural law that is, to my knowledge, the only one in which the notion of the natural law appears as the subject of papal teaching, and not simply in order to expound on a particular subject of morality. I am referring here to the brief and summarizing exposition on the natural law that is presented, within the much wider context of the teaching on human freedom and the moral law, in the encyclical *Libertas Praestantissimum* of Leo XIII.[12] Fuchs quotes this text only in an incomplete fashion, without ascribing particular importance to it, and, it appears, without grasping its deep meaning. In fact, the text could not be associated with either of the two "series" of texts that make up Fuchs's schema. But it is also fitting to mention that this text had never been taken up in any subsequent document of the Magisterium! It was not until the encyclical *Veritatis Splendor* of John Paul II, published in 1993, that it was quoted once again (and

11. In my judgment, the incorrect approach of so-called autonomous morality has its roots precisely in this dualistic fallacy and the consequent "physicalist" understanding of the natural law, "liberation" from which is sought by turning terms upside down, by declaring that reason is "autonomous" in relation to nature, but in a way that does not go beyond but instead continues, in opposite terms, the traditional dualism. I have engaged in a broad analysis of this in my *Natural Law and Practical Reason.*

12. Cf. Rhonheimer, *Natural Law and Practical Reason*, 11ff.

suitably emphasized) in a document of the Magisterium, together, as we will see, with another key text by St. Thomas Aquinas on the natural law.

In fact, according to the doctrine of St. Thomas, which was admirably summarized in the encyclical of Leo XIII, the concept of the natural law did not form a part of the rather simplistic alternative mentioned above. For St. Thomas, the natural law is placed at one and the same time on the side of the knowing subject and on that of the objectivity of the truth of "nature." According to this conception, the natural law is first and foremost the natural way by which man knows the human good in a practical and imperative way according to truth, a knowing that, for its part, renders manifest that moral order that we usually call the "natural order."

The Natural Law: A "Praescriptio Rationis"

The text of Leo XIII, taken up in *Veritatis Splendor* (no. 44), fundamentally contains three assertions. The first places us in a decisive way within the right approach. This text affirms first of all that the natural law "is written and engraved in the heart of each and every man, since it is none other than human reason itself which commands us to do good and counsels us not to sin." These words provide a formal or essential definition of what the natural law is: it is not "human nature" or "an order of nature"; nor is it a norm encountered in the nature of things. It is something "written and engraved in the heart of each and every man." It is "human reason itself" because it commands us to do good and forbids us to sin. The natural law, therefore, is specifically practical reason, and, in more precise terms, the set of determined judgments of practical reason—those judgments, that is to say, that naturally make us do good and flee from evil. For this reason, in the next sentence, the text of Leo XIII calls the natural law a *praescriptio rationis,* a "prescription of reason," a term that is near, if not identical, to the terminology of St. Thomas, for whom the natural law, like every law, is an *ordinatio rationis.*[13]

Because of this, the natural law possesses in a precise sense the character of a "law." It is not a law in the sense of the physical or natural laws of modern science. This way of speaking about the "natural laws" as natural regularities, orientations, and structures, knowable to man and then applicable at a practical level, is already a derived and improper use of the term "law," which, although it also has roots in Stoic thought, arose with modern science. When Kepler spoke about the *"leges celeritatis et tarditatis"* of the earth,

13. *ST* I-II, q.90 a.1 ad3.

and Newton formulated his *"leges motus,"* they were certainly not speaking about a rational principle that orders acts, but rather of structures and regularities that are, indeed, nature. Inasmuch as these "laws" are nature, they are certainly an effect of the ordering reason of the Creator, but considered in themselves they remain a natural structure that is simply an object of speculative knowledge.[14]

It would be an anachronism to interpret texts such as those of St. Thomas Aquinas on the natural law within the approach of the modern natural sciences.[15] When St. Thomas speaks about a "law," he speaks about it in a legal-political sense, by analogy with human laws, with the divine law, and with the eternal law that is the ordering reason of God. In this sense, "law" is an *ordinatio rationis,* or rational prescription, that is to say an imperative act of reason that directs, in a given sphere, human acts to their end, which is always a certain good.[16] "Nature" as nature does not have the character of being law. "Law" is always *aliquid pertinens ad rationem:*[17] laws can be established by the eternal reason of God, by the reason of a human legislator, but also naturally by the natural reason of every individual man precisely because this last knows in a natural and prescriptive—that is to say, practical—way the good to be done and the evil to be avoided, thereby ordering his action to the due end. For this reason, for St. Thomas the first principle of practical reason and the first precept of the natural law are exactly the same: *bonum est faciendum et prosequendum et malum vitandum.*[18]

14. It is true that Aquinas calls a "law" not only that which regulates but also that which is regulated by certain laws, such as the inclinations that come from some laws. This, however, is not called law "essentialiter, sed quasi participative." In its own sense, that is to say in the sense of that which regulates, "lex est in ratione sola" (*ST* I-II, q.90 a.1 ad1).

15. Thus, for example, Johannes Messner wanted to assimilate the concept of "natural law" in the moral field to that to be found in the natural sciences (J. Messner, *Das Naturrecht* [Innsbruck-Vienna: Tyrolia-Verlag, 1966], 55). In his unfavorable critical review of my *Natural Law and Practical Reason* (German original: *Natur als Grundlage der Moral*), A. F. Utz refers explicitly to the position of Messner, calling it the authentic position of Aquinas: "Naturgesetz ist bei Thomas zunächst ein Gesetz im naturwissenschaftlichen Sinn, d.h. ein Gesetz des Seins" (A. F. Utz, "Wonach richtet sich das Gewissen?, Die neue Ordnung," *Heft* 2 [1988]: 155). Utz's criticism, however, is based upon a very serious misunderstanding; see the "Postscriptum" to *Natural Law and Practical Reason* (560f.).

16. Thus is explained how the *definitio legis,* which contains all the essential elements in a real sense, is that of civil law. See *ST* I-II, q.90 a.4: "definitio legis, quae nihil est aliud quam quaedam rationis ordinatio ad bonum commune, ab eo qui curam communitatis habet, promulgata." For the practical-political origins of the notion of law in Aquinas see W. Kluxen, *Philosophische Ethik bei Thomas von Aquin* (Hamburg: Felix Meiner, 1964), 230ff.

17. *ST* I-II, q.90 a.1.

18. Ibid., q.94 a.2. We will come back to this principle later.

The formally rational and cognitive character of the natural law is confirmed by a text of St. Thomas that is twice quoted in *Veritatis Splendor* (nos. 12 and 40). It affirms that the natural law is "nothing other than the light of understanding infused in us by God, whereby we understand what must be done and what must be avoided."[19] Without doubt, this formulation expresses in a more categorical and a clearer way the rational and cognitive character of the natural law. Like every law, the natural law is, as St. Thomas would later say in *Summa Theologiae,* "something constituted by reason" *(aliquid a ratione constitutum)*[20] and a "work of reason" *(opus rationis).*[21] The natural law, in fact, proceeds from the light of understanding that God gave to man at the moment of his creation. The natural law is a set of cognitive acts that make us perceive in an imperative, that is to say practical, way the good to be performed and the evil to be avoided. This law is called the natural law precisely "because the reason which promulgates it is proper to human nature," in the same way that the intellect that has been given to man by the Creator is a part of human nature. It is a law that man through his intellectual acts establishes, formulates, or promulgates naturally.[22]

The Natural Law: "The Participation of the Eternal Law in the Rational Creature"

We now come to the second assertion of the text by Leo XIII that is quoted in *Veritatis Splendor:* "But this prescription of human reason could not have the force of law unless it were the voice and the interpreter of some higher reason to which our spirit and our freedom must be subject." Paraphrasing Leo's text, *Veritatis Splendor* then continues: "Indeed, the force of law consists in its authority to impose duties, to confer rights and sanction certain behaviour." *Veritatis Splendor* then goes on by quoting Leo: "Now all of this, clearly, could not exist in man if, as his own supreme legislator, he gave himself the rule of his own actions."

This second assertion says that these prescriptive acts of human reason

19. Thomas Aquinas, *In Duo Praecepta Caritatis et in Decem Legis Praecepta Expositio,* prologus I: "lex naturae . . . nihil aliud est nisi lumen intellectus insitum nobis a Deo, per quod cognoscimus quid agendum et quid vitandum. Hoc lumen et hanc legem dedit Deus homini in creatione."

20. *ST* I-II, q.94 a.1.

21. Ibid.

22. Ibid., q.90 a.4 ad1: "promulgatio legis naturae est ex hoc ipso quod Deus eam mentibus hominum inseruit naturaliter cognoscendam."

really have the character and the force of a law: they impose duties and confer rights, as well as sanctioning certain behavior. Reason can have such authority only because it is the voice of a higher authority on which it depends and to which it is subject. This statement is important not only because it affirms the subjection of human reason to the reason of its Creator, but also because it refers human reason, in the establishing of its normativity, not so much to "nature" or to a "natural order" as to divine reason! This last is the eternal law which is the *ratio* of divine wisdom by which it guides all acts and movements,[23] thereby ordering things to their due end.[24] The providence of God is manifested in a natural way in the natural law: God teaches man his own true good in an imperative way, that is to say, in the form of law, through man's own cognitive acts.

With this we come to the third assertion of the text by Leo XIII, an assertion that exactly confirms the perspective that has just been outlined: "It follows that the natural law is itself the eternal law, implanted in beings endowed with reason, and inclining them towards their right action and end; it is none other than the eternal reason of the Creator and the Ruler of the universe." Human reason, therefore, because it is the natural law, refers back not to nature but to God. It is important not to misunderstand this statement. The idea is not that to know good human reason needs to be instructed by God in the sense of receiving a revelation that is added to what human reason is able to know. The text that has been quoted asserts precisely the opposite. The natural law is the eternal law itself: the eternal law of God manifests itself in the natural law and specifically through it achieves its goal of directing human action to its due end. The eternal law is thus known to the extent to which the natural law is explained and becomes effective, that is to say, through the natural reason of man. In other words: the natural law is really a participation of eternal law; it is its possession in a cognitive and active way.

"Participated Theonomy": The Normative Task of Human Reason

Therefore, practical reason, because it is natural law and proceeds on the basis of the natural law, is really the authoritative guide for action, imposes duties, and formulates rights. Man possesses real autonomy precisely because his autonomy is "participated theonomy": participation and self-possession

23. Ibid., q.93 a.1: "lex aeterna nihil aliud est quam ratio divinae sapientiae, secundum quod est directiva omnium actuum et motionum."

24. Ibid.: "ratio divinae sapientiae moventis omnia ad debitum finem, obtinet rationem legis."

of the eternal law.[25] This is expressed by St. Thomas Aquinas in various famous formulations such as "the natural law is none other than the participation of the eternal law in the rational creature,"[26] or that by his reason man "shares in divine providence, providing for himself and for others,"[27] and that the eternal law, leaving aside an additional revelation, which is always possible, is revealed specifically through the natural law, that is to say through the "natural reason," which "derives its own image" from the eternal law.[28] In the logic of the argument of St. Thomas all these texts, and in particular the most famous one according to which the natural law is the participation of the eternal law in the rational creature, do not aim in the least to affirm the theonomic character of the natural law, but seek, rather, to establish the normative character of human reason, since this last is none other than an "impress of the divine light within us," by which we can discern good from evil, which is precisely what the natural law does.[29]

These clarifications are important because the reference to the eternal law, that is to say, the affirmation of the subjection of prescriptive acts of human reason (which are called "natural law") to a higher wisdom, does not relativize in any way the preceptive task of the practical reason of the human person, nor does it make us think that to know the human good one needs every time an explicit reference to God. Indeed, commanding and moving belongs to the nature of practical reason. Practical reason is the beginning of practice and moves the agent to follow or to avoid what he believes good or bad. This is not to be understood as if human reason were only directed to knowing relations of adequacy in an indicative but not yet imperative way, requiring (in order to become preceptive and properly practical) to have recourse to knowledge of God as the author of this order of good, and thus as legislator (this was in the early seventeenth century the opinion of Francis-

25. Cf. John Paul II, *Veritatis Splendor* (The Splendor of Truth, 1993), no. 41. On this subject see the excellent article by J. De Finance, "Autonomie et théonomie," in M. Zalba, ed., *L'agire Morale,* Atti del Congresso Internazionale (Rome-Naples, April 17–24, 1974): *Tommaso d'Aquino nel suo settimo centenario,* vol. 5 (Naples: Edizioni Domenicane Italiane, 1974), 239–60. I took full advantage of this article in *Natural Law and Practical Reason,* 319ff.

26. *ST* I-II, q.91 a.2: "lex naturalis nihil aliud est quam participatio legis aeternae in rationali creatura."

27. Ibid.: "fit providentiae particeps, sibi ipsi et aliis providens."

28. Ibid., q.19 a.4 ad3: "licet lex aeterna sit nobis ignota secundum quod est in mente divina; innotescit tamen nobis aliqualiter vel per rationem naturalem, quae ab ea derivatur ut propria eius imago; vel per aliqualem revelationem superadditam."

29. Ibid., q.91 a.2: "quasi lumen rationis naturalis, quo discernimus quid sit bonum et malum, quod pertinet ad naturalem legem, nihil aliud sit quam impressio divini luminis in nobis."

co Suárez).[30] Human nature is already in itself constituted in such a way that reason, because moved by the will and inserted into the appetitive dynamism of the natural inclinations, really moves to practice and to good.

Explicit knowledge of the participatory character of this intellectual motion toward known good—knowledge, that is to say, of the subjection of man's reason to the reason of his Creator—is not necessary to explain the existence of an awareness of a real and specific obligatory character of known good. This is due to the fact that because "good" is something "true"—otherwise it would not be intelligible—the true and the good mutually include each other. The judgments of practical reason have as their object good as regards acting from the aspect of its truth. Like the speculative intellect, the practical intellect knows truth.[31] Known good, therefore, is a "practical truth."[32] Truth, however, imposes itself on the conscience because of its own "being true." Thus, the known good of reason obliges the knowing subject in the same way in which known truth requires assent. Furthermore, the judgment of practical reason has the character of a dictate which includes in itself the *vis obligandi.*[33]

Explicit cognition of the participated nature of the natural law and the moral order established by it does not therefore constitute the practical and imperative value of human reason, but enriches it in a way that is known as practical truth derived from a transcendent higher source, that which in certain circumstances and extreme situations can also supply the decisive motive for an effective subjection to the dictates of the natural law. In addition, explicit awareness of the "participative subjection" of human reason to divine reason prepares the moral experience to take part in an experience that is also specifically religious, an experience that is eliminated by the mistaken affirmation of absolute autonomy on the part of man.

30. Cf. M. Bastit, *Naissance de la loi moderne: La pensée de la loi de saint Thomas à Suarez* (Paris: P.U.F., 1990), 338ff.

31. *ST* I-II, q.79 a.11 ad2: "verum et bonum se invicem includunt: nam verum est quoddam bonum, alioquin non esset appetibile; et bonum est quoddam verum, alioquin non esset intelligibile . . . obiectum intellectus practici est bonum ordinabile ad opus, sub ratione veri. Intellectus enim practicus veritatem cognoscit, sicut et speculativus; sed veritatem cognitam ordinat ad opus."

32. For the concept of "practical truth" in this context, see M. Rhonheimer, "Praktische Prinzipien, Naturgesetz und konkrete Handlungsurteile in tugendethischer Perspektive: Zur Diskussion über praktische Vernunft und 'lex naturalis' bei Thomas von Aquin," *Studia Moralia* 39 (2001): 113–58.

33. Cf. *ST* I-II, q.104 a.1: "praeceptorum ciuscumque legis quaedam habent vim obligandi ex ipso dictamine rationis, quia naturalis ratio dictat hoc esse debitum fieri vel vitari. Et huiusmodi praecepta dicuntur moralia: eo quod a ratione dicuntur mores umani." Cf. for this question Rhonheimer, *Praktische Vernunft und Vernünftigkeit der Praxis,* 531ff.

As a result, the knowing of the participated character adds the "*ratio legis*" in the real sense of the term, being subordinated and subjected to a higher law, the law of God. Even if the natural law, as the work of practical reason, possesses in a real sense the character of a "law," the *ratio legis* is not made explicit or concomitantly reflected at the moment when these practical judgments of the natural law are carried out. The fundamental moral experience of man is not that of following a "law," but the experience of the truth of good, and, in more precise terms, in the light of the first practical principle, the experience of *bonum faciendum,* of "the good to be done." However, in knowing explicitly the participated character of these practical judgments, man is able to understand that his autonomy is expressive of a theonomy: he will understand the good known by him not only as a "good to be done" but also as the will of God.[34] St. Thomas Aquinas, in fact, on this aspect of the natural law, says rather little. As a good Aristotelian,[35] he emphasizes, rather, the other aspect, that is to say the prescriptive and driving nature of practical reason, which it is thus capable of specifically actuating as "natural law." In this sense, St. Thomas does not hesitate to affirm that reason, which is the principle of morality, in man relates to his proper good just as the prince and the judge relate to the good of the state.[36]

The Natural Law as the *Ordinatio* of Practical Reason: The Approach of St. Thomas Aquinas

Human Reason in the Context of the Natural Inclinations

Having arrived at this point,[37] and to save the idea that the natural law and the "natural order to be known and applied" are the same, one could

34. In this sense, but only in this sense, the natural law can be understood as the "principium exterior" of human acts (cf. *ST* I-II, q.90, prologue.): because the natural law is participation of the eternal law it "comes from without," but because it is the natural law, one is dealing, rather, with an intrinsic principle of action. One should also take into consideration the biblical context of the moral theology of St. Thomas, who wanted to insert Aristotelian practical reason into a theological context that was deeply characterized by the biblical tradition of law.

35. For the profoundly Aristotelian structure of Aquinas's moral philosophy see K. L. Flannery, *Acts Amid Precepts: The Aristotelian Logical Structure of Thomas Aquinas's Moral Theory* (Washington, D.C.: The Catholic University of America Press, 2001); and my *Praktische Vernunft und Vernünftigkeit der Praxis.*

36. *ST* I-II, q.104 a.1 ad3: "ratio, quae est principium moralium, se habet in homine respectu eorum quae ad ipsum pertinent, sicut princeps vel iudex in civitate."

37. For further clarifications I take the liberty of referring the reader to my above-cited works *(Natural Law and Practical Reason; La prospettiva della morale; Praktische Vernunft und*

make the objection that God in fact reveals himself "in nature" and that reason is participation of the eternal law of God precisely to the extent to which it knows and makes its own an order that is inserted into nature. Indeed, such a notion of the natural law and its relationship to the eternal law is well known, historically. This is the Stoic notion, which influenced the tradition of natural law that came down to us through Roman law. The idea, typical of Stoa, that the eternal law is to be identified with the cosmic order and that it is therefore decipherable through a knowledge of nature, of which man is a part, opens the way to a notion of law and natural right that in the Western tradition has been very important.

This historical tradition certainly contains a part of the truth. However, a majority of the Fathers of the Church, who were themselves influenced by Stoicism, placed emphasis on the rational, intellectual, and cognitive character of the natural law, and thereby introduced a significant transformation into their reception of Stoic philosophy.[38] The Fathers perceived nature as the creation of a God and coming from an eternal law that are transcendent and thus not to be identified with the natural order. For the Stoics, human *ratio* is not the participation and image of a transcendent *ratio,* but a *logos* that is inherent in nature itself. The human *ratio* thus becomes a kind of reflection of what nature already contains in terms of inclinations and ends; man, in *oikeiosis,* rationally assimilates this natural order.[39] It is thus that one explains the famous formulations of Cicero which, read within a post-Stoic and even Christian context, appear rather ambiguous or at least insufficient: law is said to be "highest reason, inherent in nature which commands us as to what must be done and forbids the contrary."[40] It seems no less ambiguous and in-

Vernünftigkeit der Praxis), in which I examine this whole subject in detail. In addition, clarifications and additions can be found in the Spanish edition of *La prospettiva della morale* (*La perspectiva de la moral: Fundamentos de la ética filosófica* [Madrid: Rialp, 2000]) and even more in the German edition (*Die Perspektive der Moral: Philosophische Grundlagen der Tugendethik* [Berlin: Akademie Verlag, 2001]). Finally, and to avoid any misunderstanding, readers may find it useful to consult my article "Praktische Vernunft und das 'von Natur aus Vernünftige': Zur Lehre von der Lex naturalis als Prinzip der Praxis bei Thomas von Aquin," *Theologie und Philosophie* 75 (2000): 493–522.

38. Some aspects are addressed by M. Spanneut, "Les normes morales du stoïcisme chez les Pères de l'Église," in *Universalité et permanence des lois morales,* 114–35.

39. On the doctrine of *oikeiosis* cf. M. Forschner, *Die stoische Ethik: Über den Zusammenhang von Natur-, Sprach- und Moralphilosphie im altstoischen System* (Stuttgart: Klett-Cotta, 1981), 142ff.

40. Cicero, *De Legibus,* I, 6, 18: "lex est ratio summa, insita in natura, quae iubet ea quae facienda sunt, prohibetque contraria."

sufficient to speak about an "unwritten but naturally given law . . . which we grasp, take and tear from nature,"[41] and finally (to cite Cicero's most famous formulation) to call the natural law simply "right reason, in agreement with nature."[42]

For the Fathers of the Church, the *imago* of this God in the world is neither nature nor the cosmic order: the image of the Creator is present solely in the spiritual soul of man, in particular in his intellect and thus in his acts of practical reason. Practical reason does not simply reflect "nature"; rather, in being an active participation of the divine intellect, human reason in its turn illuminates nature, rendering it fully intelligible. This is how one explains the statements on the natural law such as the one cited above of St. Ambrose, which agrees perfectly with the Thomistic notion of the natural law because it emphasizes its cognitive character: "we understand by nature that what is evil must be avoided, and equally by nature we know that there has been prescribed for us what is good." It seems evident that the author of these words conceives of the natural law first and foremost as a form of moral knowledge: namely, the practical and natural knowledge of good and evil, which, for St. Ambrose, is "the word of God" within us. We do not find the divine logos either in nature or on "tablets of stone," but "imprinted in our hearts, because of the living Spirit of God. Thus the judgment of our conscience constitutes a law to itself."[43]

Nature as a "given natural order" and in this sense an "object" for reason belongs to the concept of the natural law in yet another fashion: once it has been established that the natural law is the natural way of achieving practical knowledge of the human good, we are directed to the question of how such natural practical knowledge of good can be acquired. In order to understand this, it should be kept in mind that man, although he has an intellectual faculty, is not his intellect. Analogously, not even the acts of the intellect or reason (both theoretical and practical) are carried out by intellectual power alone. *Actus sunt suppositi:* acts are not of the individual faculties but of the concrete subject in the totality of his being. It is not reason that knows

41. Cicero, *Pro Milone,* IV, 10: "non scripta, sed nata lex . . . rerum ex natura ipsa adripuimus, hausimus, expressimus" (in M. Tulli, *Ciceronis Orationes,* ed. A. C. Clark, e. typ. [Oxford: Clarendon Press, 1964]).

42. Cicero, *De re publica* III, 22, 33: "recta ratio naturae congruens."

43. St. Ambrose, *De Paradiso* 8, 39: "Dei autem praeceptum non quasi in tabulis lapideis atramento legimus inscriptum, sed cordibus nostris tenemus impressum spiritu dei vivi. Ergo opinio nostra sibi legem facit" (ed. Schenkel, 98).

but the person in the globality of his corporeal-spiritual being who knows through his reason. Man is a set of tendencies and vital, sensual, and intellectual/volitional inclinations. The "person" is all of this.

It is certainly the case that man is a "person" thanks to his spirituality, but the "human person" is all that is formed by the spirit and body in a unity of substance. Man is not an embodied spirit since he does not belong to the order of spirits. Man belongs to the order of animals, and before anything else he is an animal.[44] The human person is essentially a living body, animated, however, by a spiritual soul that allows this living body, this animal, to carry out not only spiritual acts but also all the other acts of his animal character in a way that is impregnated with the life of the spirit and thus under the guidance of reason: the unity of substance of corporeity/animal character and of spirituality transforms the meaning and the contents of man's corporeity and animal character themselves. Inversely, however, they also confer on the spiritual being of man its specifically human and earthly character—that is, the character of a spiritual existence that never takes place at the margin of the same natural corporeity and animal character of man and his natural environment (the world), but specifically through it. This applies to all the acts both of the speculative intellect, which without a body are not possible for us, and of the practical intellect, which without the natural inclinations could not be practical and move toward action.

At this point, however, the question poses itself: how can we understand these natural functions and inclinations, in particular those that arise from the corporeal and animal being of man? Undoubtedly, these tendencies and inclinations—we may think for example of the inclination to conserve oneself or the sexual inclination—are obviously practical, that is to say they push the agent to pursue their good and their own end and thus move toward action. Every natural inclination possesses *a natura* its own good and end *(bonum et finis proprium)*. However, at the level of their mere naturalness, does following the tendency to conserve oneself or the sexual inclination also mean following the good and end due to man? How can we know what is not only specific to these inclinations according to their particular nature but also due to the person, that is to say, at the moment of following these inclinations, good for man as man?[45]

44. For an excellent approach to the question, cf. D. Braine, *The Human Person: Animal and Spirit* (Notre Dame, Ind.: University of Notre Dame Press, 1992).

45. The important and significant distinction between "actus et finis proprius" and "actus et

It is at this point that there begins in a real sense the analysis of the internal structure and of the "functioning" of the natural law. This analysis, in fact, will explain how the natural law forms a part of the order of nature, expresses it, and in a certain sense constitutes it. However, this natural order, to repeat the point once again, is not an entity that man as a knowing and acting agent finds himself, so to speak, in front of. It is a natural order of which the same natural cognitive acts—the natural acts of practical reason—form a part. Thus one discovers a reason that is also specifically nature (a kind of "*ratio ut natura*"). It is for this reason that the natural law can really be called "inside man" and that one can say that it is "engraved in his soul."

But how can one say that the natural law, understood as practical reason which naturally moves toward good, constitutes the moral order? Precisely because the *lumen rationis naturalis* so much spoken about by St. Thomas Aquinas is created *ad imaginem* by divine reason.[46] Specifically, because the natural law is a real participation of the eternal law—and this, in the particular case of the rational creature, in an active way—the natural law can be considered properly as constituted by natural reason, just as the entire order of good is at its origins constituted by divine reason, which is the eternal law.[47] This participation displays itself not only in subjection to the eternal law, but also by its participation in the specific ordering function of the eternal law that constitutes the moral order, even if human reason, as only participated and created cognitive light, does this not by creating any truth at all but by knowing it and thereby finding it in its own being, essentially constituted by the natural inclinations as well.[48]

finis debitus" (or "conveniens"), often ignored by the interpreters, is found in *ST* I-II, q.91 a.2, or in *IV Sent.*, d.33, q.1 a.1. I sought to bring out this distinction in a suitable way in my *Natural Law and Practical Reason,* 67, 75; cf. also G. Abbà, *Felicità, vita buona e virtù. Saggio di filosofia morale* (Rome: LAS, 1989), 183.

46. *ST* I-II, q.19 a.4 ad3. The commentary of Aquinas on the Gospel according to St. John is very interesting, the principal texts of which are brought together in *Natural Law and Practical Reason,* 264ff.

47. Therefore, as has already been observed, Aquinas does not hesitate to call the *lex naturalis* in *ST* I-II, q.94 a.1: "aliquid per rationem constitutum: sicut etiam propositio est quoddam opus rationis."

48. The natural inclinations, too, in their natural being, are participations of the eternal law but in a merely passive manner, as something that is regulated by the eternal law but not as that which regulates, as in the case of man (cf. *ST* I-II, q.91 a.2), or rather, to employ another terminology, *per modum principii motivi,* and not in an active way, that is, *per modum cognitionis* (*ST* I-II, q.93 a.6). The question is addressed with great clarity in G. Abbà, *Lex et virtus. Studi sull'evoluzione della dottrina morale di San Tommaso d'Aquino* (Rome: LAS, 1983), 260f.

To Re-read Summa Theologiae *I-II, q. 94 a. 2*

The *locus classicus* where St. Thomas Aquinas expounds the genesis and the cognitive structure of the natural law is the famous article 2 of question 94 of the *Prima secundae.* Here St. Thomas affirms three things:

(1) The natural law is the work of practical reason, which has its own starting point and does not derive its principles from speculative reason.

(2) The natural law is a practical and preceptive knowing of the human good which unfolds on the basis of the embedding of human reason in the dynamism of the natural inclinations.

(3) Grasped by practical reason, the goods and ends of the natural inclinations are understood and affirmed as constituting human good; at the same time, however, these inclinations with their goods and ends are regulated and ordered by reason, that is to say integrated into the whole of the corporeal-spiritual being of the human person, and thereby also transformed. Only as such do they belong to the natural law and are the natural law.

I will now explain these three points in greater detail, keeping closely to the text of *ST* I-II, q. 92, a. 2 as I do so.

1. *The natural law is the work of practical reason, which has its own starting point and does not derive its principles from speculative reason.*[49]

As St. Thomas expounds in detail, the precepts of the natural law have a relationship to practical reason that mirrors the relationship of the demonstrative principles to speculative (or theoretical) reason. The precepts of the natural law are, therefore, principles—practical principles—and thus are not derived from other forms of knowledge. The practical principles or precepts of the natural law are not applications of forms of speculative knowledge of human nature. Rather, they are acts in which the natural order of human good at its origins manifests itself rationally, that is to say as an *ordo rationis.* The practical principles, having their own point of departure, which is not derived, are thus immediately intuited (otherwise they would not be principles, as St. Thomas

49. For a better understanding of this point I am much indebted to G. Grisez, "The First Principle of Practical Reason: A Commentary on the Summa Theologiae, 1–2, Question 94, Article 2," *Natural Law Forum* 10 (1965): 168–201; an abbreviated (but not authorized and not fully satisfactory) version can be found in A. Kenny, ed., *Aquinas: A Collection of Critical Essays* (London and Melbourne: Macmillan, 1969), 340–82.

affirms). Just as the speculative intellect has its starting point in the experience of being and in the evidence of the absolute contrary nature of a being and a non-being, and in this way comes to formulate its first principle (viz., the principle of non-contradiction), so also, not in a consecutive or derived way but in parallel fashion, practical reason begins from a primary experience, irreducible to other experiences—namely, the experience of "good" as a correlate and formal content of our tendencies *(bonum est quod omnia appetunt).*[50]

From this point of departure there springs, in an immediate and indemonstrable way, the first principle of practical reason, which is also the first precept of the natural law: *bonum est faciendum et prosequendum, et malum vitandum.* Just as the principle of non-contradiction is not a principle apart, from which would be deduced other forms of knowledge, but rather a founding principle that is implicit in every other form of knowledge of being, so also from the first principle of practical reason nothing more concrete can be derived. It is, rather, the foundation, which is implicitly always present, of every further form of practical knowledge of both a universal and a particular kind. This principle confers on the judgments of practical reason the operative dynamic of the *prosecutio* or of the *fuga.* These last are what we can call the "practical copula," which is not that of theoretical affirmation and negation ("is"/"is not"), but a specifically practical kind of affirmation/negation, which, in fact, moves: it makes good be done and evil be avoided.

The first principle of practical reason is not, therefore, a purely logical principle, a kind of "logical structure" of the practical precepts, but rather already the first principle of practice, and at the same time the first principle of morality.[51] This first principle of practical reason, which St. Thomas Aquinas identifies with the first precept of the natural law, constitutes man jointly as

50. The following is the whole text: "Sicut autem ens est primum quod cadit in apprehensione simpliciter, ita bonum est primum quod cadit in apprehensione practicae rationis, quae ordinatur ad opus: omne enim agens agit propter finem, qui habet rationem boni. Et ideo primum principium in ratione practica est quod fundatur supra rationem boni, quae est, 'Bonum est quod omnia appetunt.' Hoc est ergo primum praeceptum legis, quod bonum est faciendum et prosequendum, el malum vitandum. Et super hoc fundantur omnia alia praecepta legis naturae." The profoundly Aristotelian impress of this text becomes even clearer if one reads it in the light of the commentary of Aquinas on the *De Anima* of Aristotle, where he states that the point of departure of the practical intellect is "the desirable": "ipsum appetibile, quod est primum consideratum ab intellectu practico" (*III De Anima,* lect. 15).

51. I tried to show this, in opposition to the interpretation proposed by L. Honnefelder and by G. Wieland, in chapter 5 of this book. In this chapter my interpretation also differs from that mentioned above advanced by G. Grisez, for whom the first principle is not in all respects a moral principle, but is in some respects pre-moral, a thesis that I have difficulty in fully understanding.

a practical subject and as a moral subject. All the subsequent principles formulated by practical reason (i.e., all of the natural law) will participate in this double function. The natural law, in fact, has this double meaning of being: at one and the same time a principle of practice and a principle of morality. The natural law in its original and deepest meaning is not a norm that from the outside regulates human action. It is, instead, the intrinsic principle itself of human practice, and this in the real meaning of the term: it ensures that man acts. But this human acting is from the outset moral acting, that is to say acting in virtue of the natural law itself it takes place from the outset within the moral difference of "good/evil."

2. The natural law is a practical and preceptive knowing of the human good which unfolds on the basis of the embedding of human reason in the dynamism of the natural inclinations.

The second step of *ST* I-II, q. 92, a. 2 is an explanation of the genesis of the other precepts of the natural law (or the other principles of practical reason). These already have a more specific content. They are not deduced, as has already been observed, from the first principle, but they constitute themselves through a natural and spontaneous process in which practical reason—always under the influence of the "practical copula" which commands doing and pursuing good and avoiding evil—understands the individual goods (ends) of the natural tendencies or inclinations of its own being. This is a genuine experience of the human subject, an experience that is eminently and essentially practical, and that is not derived from any other form of knowledge.[52] It is the originating experience of itself as being moving toward

52. Many induce from the statement to be found in *ST* I, q.79 a.11, sc: "Intellectus speculativus per extensionem fit practicus" (a paraphrase of *De Anima* II, 10, 433a15, to be found in the body of the article correctly quoted as "[intellectus] speculativus differt a practico, fine"), that here we have proof that in fact practical reason depends in its acts on speculative or theoretical reason, denying it thereby its own and independent point of departure. As I sought to demonstrate in *Natural Law and Practical Reason* (24ff.), the quoted statement by St. Thomas refers only to the intellect considered as *intellectual power:* It means that the acts of the practical intellect do not come from *another* intellectual power, but by way of extension from the acting of the same intellect, which is also the speculative intellect. This *extensio,* which refers to the faculty, is not given, however, in the *judgments* of this faculty: the statement that practical reason has its own point of departure refers solely to the *practical* judgments, which, however, as St. Thomas says explicitly, are not derivates from previous theoretical judgments. This does not hinder the maintenance, at the level of the faculty and the being of the person, of the deep unity between theoretical and practical intellect. Moreover, in practical reason itself (the "practical syllogism"), premises are also wanted that are simple statements about reality, that is to say judgments of a "speculative" kind; cf. my analysis in *La prospettiva della morale,* 98ff.

good in the multiplicity of the natural inclinations specific to man, and is, therefore, of a practical and moral character. It is also constitutive of every other experience of specific human nature, just as it is the point of departure for subsequent investigations through theoretical speculation. For this reason the metaphysics of man (philosophical anthropology) presupposes this practical experience of the natural law: the natural law as natural knowing of good is the presupposition of knowledge of human nature.[53]

As a consequence, the natural law is a practical and preceptive knowing of the human good, that good which unfolds on the basis of the embedding of human reason in the dynamism of the natural inclinations. Practical reason has the character of an *imperium:* it is a reason that orders and moves because it is reason that operates within an "inclinational environment."[54] Through practical reason, the natural tendencies and inclinations become a good for reason, they are rationally ordered, and in the order of reason—but only at this intellectual level—they are confirmed as human goods.

In this second step, St. Thomas Aquinas affirms that on the basis of the dynamics of the first practical principle everything that practical reason understands as human good forms a part, as a good to be done or an evil to be avoided, of the precepts of the natural law.[55] On the basis of this formulation, it now becomes clear that the natural law is specifically constituted in

53. I addressed this subject in detail in *Natural Law and Practical Reason,* 22–42. The same approach can be found in John Finnis, *Fundamentals of Ethics* (Washington, D.C.: Georgetown University Press; Oxford: Oxford University Press, 1983), 10ff., 20ff., even though it does not seem to me right to call the Aristotelian doctrine on the "ergon idion" an "erratic boulder" (cf. my criticism in *Praktische Vernunft und Vernünftigkeit der Praxis,* 53ff.). On the other hand, the critical observations made by R. McInerny in *Aquinas on Human Action: A Theory of Practice* (Washington, D.C.: The Catholic University of America Press, 1992), 184ff., seem to me to be based upon a confusion between "ethical reflection" and "practical knowledge" (cf. ibid., 188). "Ethical reflection" already presupposes the practical knowledge from which originally springs the experience of human good and of one's own human nature. The subject of Finnis's (as of my own) analysis is precisely this original practical knowledge of the acting subject, not the subsequent "ethical reflection" based upon it. For this reason, in the exposition by McInerny of the thought of Finnis, that thought is to some extent falsified.

54. Cf. *ST* I-II, q.17 a.1: "Unde relinquitur quod imperare sit actus rationis, praesupposito actu voluntatis." This "imperative" structure applies to practical reason at all levels. Cf. once again the comment on III *De Anima,* lect. 15: "Quia enim ipsum appetibile, quod est primum consideratum ab intellectu practico, movet, propter hoc dicitur intellectus practicus movere, quia scilicet eius principium, quod est appetibile, movet."

55. "[S]o that whatever the practical reason naturally apprehends as man's good belongs to the precepts of the natural law as something to be done or avoided" ("ut scilicet omnia illa facienda vel vitanda pertineant ad praecepta legis naturae, quae ratio practica naturaliter apprehendit esse bona humana").

the process of the deployment of practical reason within the dynamics of the natural inclinations. For this reason, St. Thomas can go on and affirm that "reason naturally grasps everything toward which man has a natural inclination in considering them goods, and as a result as something to pursue with works, and their contrary as an evil to be avoided. Thus, the order of the precepts of the natural law follows the order of the natural inclinations."[56]

St. Thomas begins at this point to speak about the individual natural inclinations—beginning from these inclinations of the precepts of the natural law—without entering further into details about their rational constitution. He does not speak about them, in my opinion, for rather obvious reasons. In the first place, the subject of this article is simply the demonstration that the natural law does not consist solely of a single precept but contains a plurality of them.[57] Having explained that the genesis of the precepts of the natural law is due to the constituent relationship between practical reason and the natural inclinations, and that within man is to be found a plurality of such inclinations, this article has achieved its purpose. In the second place, other aspects that refer to the nature of law in general and the natural law, as well as the fundamental doctrine on reason as a measure and rule of the morality of human acts, have already been addressed in previous articles.[58] However, St. Thomas makes a brief reference to this doctrine in the reply to the second objection. Thus it is that we come to the third point.

3. Grasped by practical reason, the goods and ends of the natural inclinations are understood and affirmed as constituting human good; at the same time, however, these inclinations with their goods and ends are regulated and ordered by reason, that is to say integrated into the whole of the corporeal-spiritual being of the human person, and thereby also transformed. Only as such do they belong to the natural law and are the natural law.

In his answer to the second objection, St. Thomas states that "all the inclinations of any part of human nature, that is to say the concupiscible and iras-

56. "Quia vero bonum habet rationem finis, malum autem contrarii, inde est quod omnia illa ad quae homo habet naturalem inclinationem, ratio naturaliter apprehendit ut bona, et per consequens ut opere prosequenda, et contraria eorum ut mala et vitanda. Secundum igitur ordinem inclinationum naturalium, est ordo praeceptorum legis naturae."

57. The title of article 2, in fact, reads: "Whether the natural law contains several precepts, or one only" ("Utrum lex naturalis contineat plura precepta, vel unum tantum").

58. This is suitably brought out in J. Tonneau, *Absolu et obligation en morale* (Montreal: Inst. d'études médiévales; Paris: J. Vrin, 1965), 89f.

cible parts, as they are regulated by reason, belong to the natural law."[59] The natural inclinations in their pure naturalness are not yet the "natural law." They form a part of it because they are regulated by reason; however, the natural law is formally the judgments of practical reason whose object is the individual goods and specific ends of the natural inclinations. In these practical and preceptive judgments these specific goods and ends become, in the order of reason, judged as what is due, that is to say as ends, goods, and due acts. This is the terminology employed by St. Thomas: in participating through the possession of the *lumen rationis naturalis* in the eternal law—the ordering reason of God—man is not simply guided by the different natural inclinations toward their own acts and ends, but possesses, at a rational level, a specific natural inclination *ad debitum actum et finem.*[60]

This agrees perfectly with St. Thomas's doctrine on the constitution of the moral object by reason. Indeed, the rational constitution of the human good in the sphere of the specific goods and ends of the individual natural inclinations, on the one hand, and the constitution of the moral object, differently from the object in the pure *genus naturae,* on the other, are analogous processes. The similarity is explained by the fact that "in human acts good and evil are determined in relation to reason."[61] This analysis of the constitution of human good also agrees with the statement by Aquinas to the effect that moral acts, in their kind, "are made up of forms because they are conceived by reason."[62] Indeed, reason has a relationship to the natural inclinations—because they are natural—that mirrors that of the relationship between form and matter. Together they form a complex unity (the same applies to the moral object, which is made up of *materia circa quam* and the formal part, which comes from reason).[63] The naturalness of good, as it is formulated in

59. *ST* I-II, q.94 a.2 ad2: "omnes inclinationes quarumcumque partium humanae naturae, puta concupiscibilis et irascibilis, secundum quod regulantur ratione, pertinent ad legem naturalem."

60. Ibid., q.91 a.2.

61. Ibid., q.18 a.5: "In actibus autem humanis bonum et malum dicitur per comparationem ad rationem." That this principle of St. Thomas should be taken seriously was demonstrated years ago with clarity and in a way that is still valid by L. Lehu, *La raison, règle de la moralité d'après Saint Thomas* (Paris: J. Gabalda et Fils, 1930).

62. *ST* I-II, q.18 a.10: "species moralium actuum constituuntur ex formis prout sunt a ratione conceptae" (see also *II Sent.,* d.39 q.2 a.1).

63. Because human acts are voluntary acts, the object is always an object of the will. It is essentially and solely reason, however, that presents the will with its object. For this reason, the goodness of the will, because it depends on its object, specifically depends on reason (*ST* I-II, q.19 a.3). The movement of the will cannot refer itself to something good without this being pre-

the natural law, cannot, however, be reduced to the simple naturalness of the individual natural inclinations and their goods, ends, and acts. Such a reduction would be equivalent to reducing the *genus moris* of an act to its *genus naturae,* to confusing the "moral object" and the "physical object" of a human act. The natural law, as the above-quoted text by Leo XIII affirms, inclines man *ad debitum actum et finem* and thus makes the eternal law itself effective. This would not be possible without the regulating and ordering act of reason.

The Natural Law: Practical and Preceptive Knowledge of Human Good

In this way it becomes possible to do full justice to the preceding statements on the law in general and on the natural law in particular. According to St. Thomas, the law in general is what regulates human acts. This, however, is the task of reason: it is for reason to order to an end. For this reason, the law is *aliquid pertinens ad rationem.*[64] At a more concrete level, by "law" is meant the "universal practical judgments (propositions) of practical reason, ordered to acting."[65] In this sense, the natural law, too, *est aliquid per rationem constitutum,* and, like every judgment, is an *opus rationis.*[66]

To be precise, the natural law is a conjunction of the natural judgments of practical reason, which in a preceptive or imperative way express the good to be done and the evil to be avoided in the sphere of the ends indicated by the natural inclinations. The conjunction of the natural inclinations, ordered by reason, constitutes and defines human identity, and thus also the natural moral order of man. It is thus the natural law that makes "human nature" and that order of reason which is normative for action appear. As a result, the manifestation of the foundations of the objective moral order already presupposes the cognitive presence of the natural law. This last cannot be deduced from such an order since it is the natural law itself that makes this order known.

viously grasped by reason (ibid., ad1). Rightly, the movement toward the due end *(finis debitus)* completely depends on the cognition of the end of which only reason is capable. Furthermore, any object belongs to the *genus moris* and is effective in causing moral goodness in the act of the will exactly to the extent to which it falls under the order or reason: "Ratio enim principium est humanorum et moralium actuum" (ibid., a.1 ad3).

64. *ST* I-II, q.90 a.1.

65. Ibid., ad2: "propositiones universales rationis practicae ordinatae ad actiones."

66. Ibid., q.94 a.1.

The natural law, in concrete terms, is the set of judgments of practical reason that contains what is "by nature reasonable." In truth, within these judgments there is a certain complexity: there are judgments that are immediately evident and carried out with natural spontaneity (the first principles or very common principles, such as the Golden Rule),[67] and others that, through the inventive principle of natural reason, are not deduced from the first but are discursively found in the light of the first principles (the secondary precepts of the natural law, which already refer to types of action such as "respecting other people's property," "don't kill," etc.).[68] These preceptive imperative practical judgments (which those of prudence, at the level of particular judgments, are) move toward acting (or dissuade from acting). In this sense, the precepts of the natural law are not properly "norms" that, when applied by the moral conscience, regulate the freedom of the person and his acting. These practical judgments of natural reason, which form a natural law, are rather the foundation and the point of departure of acting as moral acting. As I have already observed, these judgments or forms of practical knowledge constitute the person as a practical and moral subject, both at a general level and in the various spheres of human action, corresponding to the various moral virtues. For this reason St. Thomas Aquinas can state that "the first orientation of our actions to an end takes place through the natural law."[69] This means that without the natural law there would not be in the least any acting; every acting pursues an end, and without such pursuing, action would not take place.

Conjointly, however, the natural law is a set of judgments about the fundamental goods that should be achieved, the goods that define the order of moral good which is an *ordo rationis*. Therefore, speaking formally and in a proper way, the natural law is not known on the basis of a moral order, or

67. Cf. *In Duo Praecepta Caritatis et in Decem Legis Praecepta, prologus I:* "Nullus enim ignorat quod illud quod nollet sibi fieri, non faciat alteri, et cetera talia."

68. For the *inventio* of the secondary precepts I refer the reader to *Natural Law and Practical Reason,* 267ff. St. Thomas's texts on the primary and secondary precepts of the natural law were helpfully assembled in R. A. Armstrong, *Primary and Secondary Precepts in Thomistic Natural Law Teaching* (The Hague: Martinus Nijhoff, 1966). The *inventio* of the secondary principles, however, is not a deductive and instantaneous process but presupposes concrete experience and takes place in time; that is to say, in a certain sense it possesses a narrative structure. See my "Praktische Vernunft und das 'von Natur aus Vernünftige,'" 511ff.; and *Die Perspektive der Moral,* 253ff. (or *La perspectiva de la moral,* 301ff.).

69. *ST* I-II, q.91 a.2 ad2: "nam omnis ratiocinatio derivatur a principiis naturaliter notis.... Et sic etiam oportet quod prima directio actuum nostrorum ad finem, fiat per legem naturalem."

deduced from it; rather, it is precisely the natural law that constitutes and realizes the moral order as an *ordo rationis*—it is this order that manifests "human nature" in its morally normative meaning. The order of reason, however, is none other than eternal law which is manifested through and in the natural law because the natural law is the eternal law, present in human practical reasonableness.

The Natural Law and the Moral Conscience

It is important to emphasize that the intellect, as a spiritual faculty, has the capacity to reflect in an unlimited way on its own acts. The human intellect reflects on these natural judgments of practical reason, thereby discovering this moral order and this "human nature" as an object of the speculative intellect, as an anthropological reality full of normative meaning. But great care should be employed here: this normativeness is not deduced from or read in a nature that is "in front of" knowing man—on the contrary, it is the original normativeness of practical reason itself which, due to its location within the dynamics of the natural inclinations, explains itself through natural judgments on the human good. These last form an original, irreducible, and fundamental experience. It is an experience in which simultaneously the human being (the anthropological identity of the subject) and the normative aspect of this human identity manifest themselves.

In analyzing the level of reflection on this moral experience, one comes to a second concept of "natural law," not in the formal but in the material sense. This derived concept refers solely to the propositional contents of these judgments of practical reason and the corresponding moral experience, which in a proper and primary sense are the natural law. Through reflection of the intellect on its own practical and ordering acts a *habitus* of forms of normative moral knowledge is formed, which is the natural law as a *habitus* of the principles and foundation of "moral science" (this *habitus* of the first principles is also called synderesis).[70] These forms of knowledge are normative articulations, or moral norms, which, in virtue of the natural way they manifest themselves in the first judgments of practical reason, appear in the conscience as the voice of a truth to which the subject must subject himself, and which are applied to concrete acting through the judgment of the conscience.

70. Cf. ibid., q.94 a.1 ad2: "synderesis dicitur lex intellectus nostri, inquantum est habitus continens praecepta legis naturalis, quae sunt prima principia operum humanorum." Cf. also ibid. I, q.79 a.12.

I will confine myself here to this brief reference to this question, to which I have dedicated a more detailed exposition elsewhere.[71]

The Natural Law and Natural Right

We have seen that the natural law is a combination of the judgments of practical reason which in a preceptive or imperative way express the good to be done and the evil to be avoided in the sphere of the ends indicated by the natural inclinations. These inclinations are many in number and arise from all the other strata of the complex nature of the human person. St. Thomas Aquinas speaks about the inclination to conserve oneself: this is a basic tendency, but when pursued within the order of reason it is pursued in concordance with other needs (e.g., of justice, of benevolence toward one's neighbor, of respect for the common good). "Conserving oneself," as something contained within the natural law, is not only the simple natural inclination in its pure naturalness. Man is also able to sacrifice his own life for the good of others.

The same is applicable to the other example mentioned by St. Thomas: the sexual inclination between a man and a woman. Grasped by reason as a human good and made the content of a practical judgment, the object of this inclination is more than an inclination found in pure nature. It is more than that which, in the words of the Roman jurist Ulpian, "nature has taught all animals."[72] This natural inclination, grasped by reason and pursued in the order of reason—at the personal level—becomes love between two people, love with the requirement of exclusiveness (uniqueness) and of indissoluble faithfulness between persons (i.e., it is not mere attraction between bodies!),

71. Cf. for example *La prospettiva della morale,* 255ff. This approach agrees with the famous passage in Vatican Council II, *Gaudium et Spes* (Pastoral Constitution on the Church in the Modern World, 1965) no. 16: "Deep within his conscience man discovers a law which he has not laid upon himself but which he must obey. Its voice, ever calling him to love and to do what is good and avoid what is evil. . . . For man has in his heart a law inscribed by God." In the encyclical *Veritatis Splendor,* no. 60, the connection between conscience and the natural law is explained further. Natural law is the norm of truth for the conscience: "The judgment of conscience does not establish the law; rather it bears witness to the authority of the natural law and of the practical reason with reference to the supreme good"; and no. 61: "The truth about moral good, *as that truth is declared in the law of reason,* is practically and concretely recognized by the judgment of conscience" (emphasis added).

72. In the first book of his *Institutiones* (D. I, I, I, 3): "Ius naturale est, quod natura omnia animalia docuit." For Ulpian, one example (cited by St. Thomas in *ST* I-II, q.94 a.2) is "maris atque feminae coniunctio, quam nos matrimonium appellamus" (quoted following M. Bretone, *Geschichte des römischen Rechts: Von den Anfängen bis zu Justinian* [2d ed.; Munich: C. H. Beck, 1998], 232, 337).

persons who understand that they are united in the task of transmitting human life. Faithful and indissoluble marriage between two people of different sexes, united in the shared task of transmitting human life, is precisely the truth of sexuality; it is sexuality understood as the human good of marriage. Like all the other forms of friendship and virtue, this specific type of friendship, which is what marriage is, is not found "in nature." It is the property and norm of a moral order, to which man has access through the natural law as an *ordinatio rationis*. What, according to Ulpian, "nature has taught all animals" is certainly a presupposition for human love as well, but it does not yet express adequately the natural moral order to which this love belongs. As a result, in the case of man, what "nature has taught all animals" is not even sufficient to establish any dutifulness or normativity. If the animal does what its nature, endowed with a richness of instincts, prescribes to it, it performs its function. Can the same be said of man?

The most important inclinations, however, arise immediately from the spiritual nature of man. St. Thomas mentions the natural inclination to know the truth, in particular the truth about God, and the natural inclination to live in society. Man naturally flees from ignorance and tries not to offend other men. Indeed, it is the natural law that constitutes the first notions of justice—as of every other virtue—and that also makes possible the notion of "natural right" (i.e., something that is "right by nature"). Any notion of a natural right already presupposes the active presence or the deployment within the subject of the natural law. If the natural law, and with it the *ordinatio* of practical reason, did not form principles of justice, nothing could ever be perceived as something that was "naturally right." Every notion of "right" would be derived from a positive law, whether divine (revealed), or human. The notion of what is "right" would be nothing, as Thrasymachus says, but the self-interest and advantage of the strongest.[73] Not only would the condition of a "natural right" be unthinkable, but so too would be the very concept of "right" as "good" and as "due to somebody."

At times, the terms "natural law" and "natural right" are used indistinctly and as synonyms. This, however, causes a great deal of confusion. For the premodern tradition, the *ius naturale* is the same as *iustum naturale:* a "right" is that which on the basis of a certain fittingness is due to somebody. For example, in the case of an action of buying and selling, every commodity has

73. Plato, *The Republic*, 338E–339A.

its price; while the concrete price, according to St. Thomas Aquinas, can be established in line with convention, the fact that a commodity has a price, and thereby a "commodity-price" relationship, is natural. To pay a price thus corresponds to the *ius naturale*.[74] The modern concept of "right" is semantically somewhat different: it becomes above all else a subjective right, a claim or right "to something."[75] This is what is meant by the rights of freedom and, in general, human rights. The *ius naturale,* as we find it in the Thomistic tradition, is a given fact, a fittingness *secundum naturam,* the foundation of the order of justice. The *ius* is specifically the object of the virtue of justice (which is defined as the "firm and constant willingness to give each person his due"). For this reason as well, the terms "natural law" and "natural right" should be distinguished. The natural law does not refer only to justice concerning acts in relationship with other people; it regulates all the moral virtues, including the acts that concern the agent subject himself, like those that belong to the sphere of temperance or fortitude.

It is, however, of the greatest importance to underline that the notion of "*ius*" is not self-founding and is not even simply "given" in nature. Like all moral notions, the notion of right is constituted specifically within the deployment of the natural law. What is a "natural given fact," which is relevant in some aspects and presupposed for the formation of the natural law, is certain relations of fittingness (such as, for example, the famous *coniunctio maris et feminae* as a natural relation of *adaequatio,* or the relationship between "commodity" and "price," and also many other relations of fittingness and *Sachverhalte,* which are intuitively graspable "from the nature of things," as we are taught by the classic Roman jurists of the epoch of the Principate).[76] Howev-

74. Cf. *ST* II-II, q.57 a.2: "ius sive iustum, est aliquod opus adaequatum alteri secundum aliquem aequalitatis modum. Dupliciter autem potest alicui homini aliquid esse adaequatum. Uno quidem modo, ex ipsa natura rei: puta cum aliquis tantum dat ut tantum recipiat. Et hoc vocatur ius naturale." The second form is that called *ex condicto,* which can be either private or public. The former is held to correspond to the *lex dicta,* known in Roman law and belonging to the *ius privatum,* to be distinguished from the *ius publicum.* The distinction is not in concordance with the modern distinction between public law and private law (cf. G. Dulckeit, F. Schwarz, and W. Waldstein, *Römische Rechtsgeschichte* [Munich: C. H. Beck, 1995], 49f.).

75. In the view of Michel Villey, the genesis of the modern concept of subjective right goes back to Ockham: M. Villey, "Droit subjectif I (La genèse du droit subjectif chez Guillaume d'Occam)," in *Seize Essais de Philosophie de Droit dont un sur la crise universitaire* (Paris, 1969), 140–78. The differences are sometimes exaggerated, however. For a contrasting view see John Finnis, *Natural Law and Natural Rights* (Oxford: Oxford University Press, 1980).

76. Cf. W. Waldstein, "Naturrecht bei den klassischen römischen Juristen," in *Das Naturrechtsdenken heute und morgen: Gedächtnisschrift für René Marcic,* ed. D. Mayer-Maly and P. M. Simons (Berlin: Duncker & Humblot, 1983), 239–53; and see by the same author the de-

er, the normativity of these "relations of fittingness" or *adaequationes* and the very notion of due *(debitum)* come from practical reason, which alone is able to order these relations of fittingness toward the end of virtue, which is the good of the human person. Certainly, these notions come from natural reason, and in this sense are they indeed natural. They are natural in the same sense in which the natural law and the reason that constitutes it are natural. Through it, all these notions that belong to the order of justice are constituted. What St. Thomas states in general regarding the relationship between law and right can also certainly be applied to the relationship between the natural law and natural right, that is to say, "the law is not, in a proper sense, right, but rather that which in a certain sense ensures that what is a right is a right."[77]

A natural right, therefore, is not properly a normativity deduced from nature or "read" in it, but rather the result of a reading of the natural structures in the light of the principles of the natural law. Bearing this in mind is important in order not to fall into a vicious circle or to become guilty of a *petitio principii* when establishing arguments based upon the natural law. Notions such as that of "something due" to one's neighbor, of "not offending," of "not harming," the notion itself of reciprocity (expressed by the Golden Rule) and of equality (of which every form of justice is a determined type) come from this natural inclination to live in society with other men, to communicate with them, to relate to them with acts of exchange and distribution, etc. Without the natural law there would be no notion of "a right" and of "something being right," since every notion of normativeness or dutifulness in relations between men would be absent. At this completely fundamental level, too, "the law is not, in a proper sense, right, but rather that which in a certain sense ensures that what is a right is a right" applies.

Furthermore, the notion of "due" and of "right" *(ius)* as well, which is inherent in every relationship of justice, is not yet sufficient. In order that what is due can fall under the principle of the natural law (*bonum faciendum,* etc.), the "right" must manifest itself as a "good." Indeed, St. Thomas Aquinas says that "to give somebody what is due has the property of a good."[78] One needs, therefore, to trace the notion of right and due back to the notion of good

tailed study "Entscheidungsgrundlagen der klassischen römischen Juristen," in *Aufstieg und Niedergang der römischen Welt: Geschichte und Kultur Roms im Spiegel der neueren Forschung,* ed. H. Temporini and W. Haase, sect. II, Principat, vol. 15, ed. H. Temporini (Berlin and New York: Walter de Gruyter, 1976), 3–100.

77. *ST* II-II, q.57 a.1 ad2: "lex non est ipsum ius, proprie loquendo, sed aliqualis ratio iuris."

78. Ibid., q.81 a.2: "reddere debitum alicui habet rationem boni."

or of *bonum humanum.* Why is the "right" a human good for him who in this way places himself in a relationship with another person? Because of the Golden Rule, which forms part of the first principles of the natural law, and which for its part presupposes the fundamental recognition of another person as being "equal to me." Such a recognition, the foundation of every justice, is once again the work of reason.[79]

Natural Law in the Context of Ethics of the Virtues

I am convinced that from the Thomistic conception of the natural law are derived a multitude of consequences of great importance and fruitfulness for moral philosophy, in terms of both its basic approach and its internal structure.[80] Here I will concentrate on some aspects that appear to me of particular pertinence in the present context.

The Natural Law and the Ethics of the Virtues

Were we to dismiss the rather simplistic idea that the natural law is simply a conjunction of norms to be read in a natural order that is "in front of our eyes" and to realize, instead, that the natural law is specifically something constituted in the natural judgments of the natural reason of each man, we would then understand better that the natural law is really "written and engraved" in the human soul. We would recognize as well the ontological meaning of the natural law, namely, that it is an expression of human nature and the moral order rooted in this nature. Indeed, this law brought forth by the practical reason of the subject is specifically human nature in its normative dynamics: it is simultaneously the self-possession of the subject—a real autonomy, which is participated theonomy—and an objective norm which, in the face of the moral conscience, imposes itself with the force and the authority of truth.

To conceive of the natural law, as St. Thomas Aquinas does, as a set of natural principles of practical reason opens up the road to understanding the intimate connection between the precepts of the natural law and the moral virtues. Indeed, the moral virtues, too, are essentially a type of *ordinatio rationis:*

79. Cf. M. Rhonheimer, "Sins against Justice (IIaIIae, qq.59–78)," in Stephen J. Pope, ed., *The Ethics of Aquinas* (Washington, D.C.: Georgetown University Press, 2002), 290. For the cognitive genesis of the principle of "justice," see also *La prospettiva della morale,* 242ff.

80. Cf. the introduction to *La prospettiva della morale,* and for a more detailed analysis the introduction to the German edition, *Die Perspektive der Moral: Philosophische Grundlagen der Tugendethik* (Berlin: Akademie Verlag, 2001).

as *habitus* they are the order of reason, "sealed and imprinted" in the concupiscible (temperance) and irascible (fortitude) inclinations and in the rational appetite called "will" (justice).[81] Given that man is essentially formed by a rational soul, he has a "natural inclination to act according to reason," and this is to live the virtues whose acts are, therefore, imposed by the natural law.[82] The moral virtues are the fulfillment of the natural law at the level of concrete acting since they are the *habitus* of choosing what is good for man at a concrete level.[83] For this reason, the precepts of the natural law are precisely the principles of prudence.[84] The "truth of subjectivity," of which the natural law at the level of the principles is the foundation, is ultimately guaranteed through the possession of the moral virtues, whose function, as Aristotle taught us, lies in ensuring that there appears as good to the subject that which is also good according to truth.[85] The individual virtues do this by deploying the "appetitive" part of the human being, the sense tendencies, and the will, according to the requirements of reason. In this way, the *secundum rationem agere,*[86] founded in the natural law, is fulfilled in the moral virtues, which also manifest their function of giving full efficacy to the natural law. The intimate nexus between the natural law and moral virtue makes clear why it is that vice is one of the principal causes of the obscuring of the natural law in man. The Thomistic conception thus opens the road to an approach in ethics and moral theology that is centered not simply on the "law" but rather on the virtues.

Permanence of the Natural Law and Contemporary Threats to Human Life

At the present time there is no absence of voices that affirm that the natural law, and with it respect for natural right, has fallen into oblivion or has

81. Cf. *De virtutibus in communi,* q.un., a.9: "virtus appetitivae partis nihil est aliud quam quaedam dispositio, sive forma, sigillata et impressa in vi appetitiva a ratione."

82. Cf. *ST* I-II, q.94 a.3: "Unde cum anima rationalis sit propria forma hominis, naturalis inclinatio inest cuilibet homini ad hoc quod agat secundum rationem. Et hoc est agere secundum virtutem. Unde secundum hoc omnes actus virtutum sunt de lege naturali: dictat enim hoc naturaliter unicuique propria ratio, ut virtuose agat."

83. See Rodríguez Luño, *La scelta etica. Il rapporto fra libertà e virtù* (Milan: Edizioni Ares, 1988).

84. Cf. Rhonheimer, *Praktische Vernunft und Vernünftigkeit der Praxis,* 530ff.

85. Aristotle, *Nicomachean Ethics,* III, 4, 1113a29f.: "The person who is virtuous, in fact, judges every thing rightly and in each thing there appears to him what is true." For the importance of this principle within Aristotelian ethics taken as a whole, see G. Bien, "Die menschlichen Meinungen und das Gute: Die Lösung des Normproblems in der aristotelischen Ethik," in M. Riedel, ed., *Rehabilitierung der praktischen Philosophie* I (Freiburg: Verlag Rombach, 1972), 345–71.

86. Cf. *ST* I-II, q.94 a.3 (quoted above).

become irrelevant both for individuals and for political society and the laws on which that society is based. In this view, the lack of respect for, and even the denial of, the natural law is to be found in the widespread diffusion of contraceptive practices, abortion, and technologies of reproduction (which give rise to the serious problem of human embryos frozen while "waiting" to be used in a "useful" way, the attempts to use them for the attaining of stem cells for medical research, therapeutic cloning, etc.).

In my opinion, this diagnosis is not entirely correct. It seems to me important to test it well in order that the subsequent treatment be well chosen. Indeed, if one were to argue that the natural law is a given fact, which is easily and by self-evidence decipherable in the "nature of things" in such a way that those who are not capable, or deny the existence, of such a "law of nature" would be mere deniers of an evident truth, then the only therapy would be to attempt to overcome them through an insistent affirmation of what they deny. This seems logical: the person who denies what is evident and intuitively knowable should not be answered with arguments but rather with blame, rebukes, and indignation.

I think, however, that things are infinitely more complex. I do not believe that our contemporaries deny what is evident and intuitively knowable. I do not believe, therefore, that they specifically deny the fundamental precepts of the natural law. Indeed, in relation to what is evident (viz., the first precepts of the natural law), there is at the present time a surprising consensus. This consensus bears witness to the presence of the natural law in the consciences of men. Otherwise, the fact that forms of behavior such as killing innocent people, adultery, lying or theft, hating one's neighbor, envy, rash judgments, defamation, and many similar things are generally seen as being dishonest would be incomprehensible. Obviously, this does not change the fact that in reality innocent people are killed, slander is used for private and public purposes, and theft, hatred, and defamation and so many other kinds of injustice are commonplace. But this, because of human wickedness and weakness, has always been the case. Right up until our days, these forms of behavior have always been disapproved of by people who are regarded as being endowed with healthy judgment. Without the effective presence of the natural law in the hearts of men this would not be possible, and indeed the very notions of "adultery," "murder," "lying," "theft," etc., all of which imply that a person possesses a concept of "justice," which itself is a work of the natural law, would not be possible.

It is certainly true that in contemporary culture there exists a widespread tendency to reject, in principle, an "objective" and universal morality. This phenomenon of ethical individualism and subjectivism at a personal level, is, however, linked to another that from certain points of view is in opposition to it: today in public life and in the assessment of both individual and institutional human action in the social, political, and economic fields, more than at any previous time in history, moral norms (under the name of "human rights") which declare themselves to be universal and impose themselves with the force of their objective value, are considered the obligatory point of reference. This seems to be another sign of the fact that the natural law is far from having fallen into oblivion.

On the other hand, even among the many defenders of the existence of a natural law there are discordant opinions as to what its contents really are—that is to say, as to what human reason naturally points out to us as being "good" and "a matter of duty." A consensus exists only at the level of the most important shared and specific precepts. But there exists a whole level of so-called "remote" precepts which, according to St. Thomas, are difficult to understand for most men, and which, in his view, can be understood without error only by "the wisest."[87] Indeed, it is at this level that there exist among believers and non-believers alike great differences of opinion. Issues such as contraception, divorce, even abortion from certain aspects (i.e., when it is practiced with a contraceptive mentality),[88] the prohibition of therapeutic cloning or in vitro fertilization, are, from the point of view of the "natural law," rather remote subjects, whose intrinsic moral quality is at times difficult to perceive. On the other hand, it is easy for everyone, even today, to understand the disordered character of killing, of adultery, of lying and of theft, of hatred for one's neighbor, of envy, of rash judgments, of defamation, etc.—forms of behavior and inner attitudes to which the principal precepts of the natural law refer.

With technological progress the possibilities of intervening in nature—in that which is "given" and presupposed—are constantly increasing. The pow-

87. Cf. ibid., q.100 a.1.

88. Cf. M. Rhonheimer, "Contraccezione, mentalità contraccettiva e cultura dell'aborto: valutazioni e connessioni," in R. Lucas Lucas, ed., *Commento interdisciplinare alla «Evangelium vitae»* (Vatican City: Libreria Editrice Vaticana, 1997), 435–52. See also M. Rhonheimer, "Contraception, Sexual Behavior, and Natural Law: Philosophical Foundation of the Norm of 'Humanae Vitae,'" *Linacre Quarterly* 56, no. 2 (1989): 20–57.

er of man is being extended to what in past periods was simply something to be accepted as "natural" or as "immutable" and that presented itself to man in the form of a destiny to which he had to bend in docile fashion. We now have the power to change—at least in many aspects—the "human condition," to modify it in line with our perspectives (which are not necessarily illicit) of happiness and well-being (one may think here of reproductive technology, genetics, etc.). Finally, in modern society the autonomy of the individual has grown to an extent that it never had before. The identity of persons is not inexorably defined in terms of determined social roles, which are preestablished for insertion into a specific historical, social, or family context. At the level of principle, this process should be regarded as a great gain. But it is logical that this development also renders certain absolute moral prohibitions (at least as regards their social utility) less intelligible. Where the social context no longer predefines determined roles for every individual person or for groups of people (defined, e.g., according to their sex) it becomes more difficult to understand certain moral values and norms which in the past were supported by the processes of socialization and the general configuration of society and by the constrictions imposed by the shared circumstances of life.

Let us take a contemporary example: experimentation on human life for beneficial motives, such as the treatment of illnesses, has always been a dream of men, and not only of scientists. Today it seems that we are able to do this, and the pressure to do so increases not because the natural law is no longer recognized but because the power of man over nature has increased, generating challenges hitherto unknown.

The person who today opts for experimentation on human embryos, and in this context affirms emphatically that an embryo is not yet a being with the dignity and the rights of a human person, does not deny the natural law but specifically (albeit implicitly) confirms it. In fact, he does not want to exploit a human person for a good end, and thus is forced to deny that an embryo has the status of a person. The error here is not connected with the natural law. It is not properly an error of practical knowledge, but is first of all an error of a theoretical kind. The case in question involves an erroneous statement about reality—an error of metaphysical anthropology which certainly causes a grave injustice (viz., the exploitation of certain human individuals for the benefit of other people). Nobody wishes to advocate that the personal dignity of some human beings may be licitly violated in order to benefit the majority; this would clearly contradict the natural law. Instead, one simply denies these human beings the status of a person, so as to "exempt" them from what natural law commands.

In other cases, however, such an error can be due to a real and proper act of discrimination arising from an unjust will which searches above all else for its own well-being, self-determination, or the achievement of personal project—often perhaps licit but pursued at the expense of other people. In this context of injustice, the error of not recognizing the dignity and the rights of unborn human beings, even in the embryonic form of human life, expresses itself as an authentic practical error—that is to say, as injustice.[89] To be habitually involved in such an error causes the obscuring of the natural law in one's own heart, and gradually renders ineffective the light of natural reason in guiding one's own action toward the true good of man.

To appeal to the self-evidence of the natural law, or natural right, cannot be of great help for those people who are in this way involved in evil. At the same time, those who out of good faith or simple ignorance (or the pressures of the environment in which they live) need to be instructed in the truth will find appeals to presumed forms of self-evidence which are not forthcoming (except in certain conditions) insufficient. In other words, very many, perhaps the majority, of the moral problems that are disputed today refer to matters that one would say have to do with precepts of the natural law that are rather "remote." At this level, there is no self-evidence. The inventive process of natural reason can be seriously misled by the concrete forms of conditioning to which the subject is exposed in his social environment, by his biographical or cultural context, and by the pressures and material constraints of the world of work. One may think here, for example, of children and young people who grow up in a society in which divorce and thus "articulated" families ("children with four parents," etc.) have become the norm. In such a situation appeals to self-evidence cannot be of much help. One wants on the one hand arguments, and on the other (for those people who have the grounding to accept it), instruction by means of a recognized authority.

But this is not all. It should also be mentioned that the self-evidence of certain requirements of the natural law can be justified only in the context of Christian faith and with the grace that is conferred within the context of a

89. See M. Rhonheimer, "Fundamental Rights, Moral Law, and the Legal Defense of Life in a Constitutional Democracy: A Constitutionalist Approach to the Encyclical *Evangelium Vitae*," *American Journal of Jurisprudence* 43 (1998): 135–83.

Christian life to live out all the requirements of the natural moral order within the perspective of the mystery of the Cross. This order, even though it is in itself intelligible to everyone, includes for the actual existing man some difficulties and has at times a paradoxical character that renders the human good unintelligible. Only in the light of the faith does the natural law also recover all its intelligibility and humanity. This is not because it is in itself not rationally knowable, but because outside the order of the redemption this intelligibility can often seem illusory and even a burden. It may seem to involve inhuman requirements that are incompatible with the desire for happiness inserted into the human heart.[90] Moreover, for the natural law to reveal itself as a part of that truth which makes us free, what is needed is a patient work of diffusion of good, and of the light of faith, and a subsequent permeation of social structures with the spirit of Christ.[91]

90. On this subject see chapter 1 of this book, originally published as M. Rhonheimer, "Is Christian Morality Reasonable? On the Difference Between Secular and Christian Humanism," *Annales Theologici* 15 (2001): 529–49; "Über die Existenz einer spezifisch christlichen Moral des Humanums," Internationale katholische Zeitschrift *Communio* 23 (1994): 360–72; *Natural Law and Practical Reason,* 547ff.

91. This paper was presented during the eighth General Assembly of the Pontifical Academy for Life (Vatican City, February 25–27, 2002) and published with the title "La legge morale naturale: conoscenza morale e coscienza" in the *Proceedings,* edited by the Libreria Editrice Vaticana.

8

The Perspective of the Acting Person and the Nature of Practical Reason

The "Object of the Human Act" in Thomistic Anthropology of Action

The "Object of the Human Act": In the Perspective of the Acting Subject

The passage in *Veritatis Splendor* no. 78 that clarifies the concept of the "object" of a human act is widely acknowledged as decisive for the central argument of the encyclical, which reaffirms "the universality and immutability of the moral commandments, particularly those which prohibit always and without exception intrinsically evil acts."[1] In accordance with the tradition, but referring explicitly to St. Thomas Aquinas, the encyclical states that "the morality of the human act depends primarily and fundamentally on the "object" rationally chosen by the deliberate will." The text adds: "In order to be able to grasp the object of an act which specifies [an] act morally, it is therefore necessary to place oneself *in the perspective of the acting person.*" By the term "object," the encyclical does not designate "a process or an event of the merely physical order, to be assessed on the basis of its ability to bring about

1. John Paul II, *Veritatis Splendor* (The Splendor of Truth, 1993), no. 115.

a given state of affairs in the outside world." According to *VS*, "objects" of human acts are not mere "givens," that is, "things," realities, or physical, biological, technical, or juridical structures; nor are they bodily movements and the effects caused by such movements; nor is the object of a human act a simple "physical good" or "non-moral good," as is, for example, a human life or a possession. Rather, the "object" of a human act is always the object of an act of the will and, as such, the encyclical affirms, a "freely chosen behavior": it is a type of action, as, for example, "to kill an innocent person" or "to steal."

For this reason, a few lines later the text of the encyclical adds: "[The] object is the *proximate end* of a deliberate decision which determines the act of willing on the part of the acting person." The object of an act must therefore be understood as *the end of an act of the will,* and thus as a practical good, presented by reason to the will. Consequently, in the moral context, no opposition exists between the notions of "object" and "end."[2] The object is, precisely, *a particular type* of end, that is, that toward which, primarily and fundamentally, the act of the will from which an action originates tends: the act of choice or *electio* of an act or of a concrete behavior. This means that it is impossible to describe the object of a moral act without considering it as object and content *of an act of choice of the will,* full of moral significance, or rather as a good toward which the elective act of the will tends. Thus, the object is necessarily already formulated by reason. As the object of an interior act of the will, it is, in the words of St. Thomas, a "good understood and ordered by reason"[3] or, put differently, "the intelligible content that morally specifies a deliberate choice."[4] As a "good understood and ordered by reason," the object also includes in itself an intentional structure, given that it is characteristic of reason to be ordered to an end. Understood in this way, the object of a human act is, precisely, its primary and fundamental intentional content: the object indicates *what* one does when one does something, and for this reason it also indicates, in a basic and fundamental way, *why* one does what one does, given that a human act cannot be understood as a specific kind of act

2. This has been clearly shown by S. Pinckaers in his classic essay "Le rôle de la fin dans l'action morale selon Saint Thomas," in Pinckaers, *Le renouveau de la morale* (Tournai: Casterman, 1964), 114–43 (originally in *Revue des Sciences philosophiques et théologiques* 45 [1961]: 393–421). I am personally very grateful to have found this article, despite the presence of some weaknesses and ambiguities, of which I will later speak.

3. *ST* I-II, q.20 a.1 ad1: "bonum apprehensum et ordinatum per rationem."

4. E. Colom and A. Rodríguez Luño, *Scelti in Cristo per essere santi. Elementi di Teologia morale fondamentale* (Rome: Apollinare Studi, 1999), 127.

without the end to which it is directed: *quantum aliquis intendit tantum facit:* "what someone intends, that he does."[5]

Despite its clear Thomistic character, the notion of the "object" of a human act as I have just described it is not accepted by all adherents of Aquinas's moral theology. Indeed, to conceive the object of a human act in the way expounded above is in contrast with another vision that would also base itself on St. Thomas. It is true that the relevant texts in Thomas are not always clear, and the terminology adopted in them not always coherent. This is because Thomas never treated, in an explicit and systematic way, the question that interests us today: What is a "moral object"? What exactly are we speaking of when we speak of the object of a human act?

Thomas provides us with a systematic exposition of everything that qualifies—at all levels, and not only from a philosophical perspective, but especially theologically—the human act as morally *good* or *evil.* In this context the "object" appears as the element that confers on the human act its primary and fundamental moral specification. As for his theory of action, it essentially serves this ethical-normative purpose. Conversely, he ignores a systematic exposition of certain questions that we today call "meta-ethical." These are not ethical questions, but rather questions *about* ethics, in part pertaining to action theory (e.g., our question regarding the significance of the term "object" of a human act).

One can find various elements for responding to such questions spread throughout St. Thomas's works. His doctrine on the topic is implicit, in the sense that while he certainly employs identifiable meta-ethical presuppositions, he nevertheless does not construct a theory from them: precisely this causes a lack of clarity and at times confusion. One must also admit that, from the *Scriptum super libros Sententiarum* through the *De Malo* to the *Summa Theologiae,* St. Thomas's thought is characterized, if not by contradictions, at least by a notable evolution and maturation. Nevertheless, the *Scriptum* on the Sentences of Peter Lombard is very useful for understanding the genesis and the substructure of the thought—certainly more mature, but also expressed more synthetically—of the *Summa Theologiae.*

It would not seem to me excessive to say that *Veritatis Splendor* itself invites us to further clarify some of these meta-ethical presuppositions of St. Thomas's

5. *De Malo* 2, 2, ad8. For some comments on this passage, cf. John Finnis, "Object and Intention in Aquinas," *The Thomist* 55 (1991): 1–27.

moral theology, and to do so without fearing to affirm things that St. Thomas had not yet said, or to say them in a different way, without ever, of course, ignoring what he actually did say. The encyclical also recommends a direction, that is, that of integrating the point of view of the subject, the perspective of the acting person, more explicitly in the understanding of the human act and the evaluation of its morality. This approach, in a certain sense more "personalistic," means, as we have seen, to understand the object of a human act as an end of the will, as action or behavior inasmuch as it is the object of an elective act of the will. This is what St. Thomas himself does, although to recognize it one must read the texts in the light of questions which for Thomas, at least it seems, did not yet exist.

The Object: A "Thing" or an Action?

The lack of explicitness and clarity on St. Thomas's part regarding what is the object of an act can be illustrated by such typical phrases as "the primary evil in moral actions is that which is from the object, for instance, *to take what belongs to another*,"[6] or "the evil act *ex genere* is that which falls upon inappropriate matter, like *to take that which belongs to another*."[7] We find no effort here by St. Thomas to clarify whether the object, or the referred-to *inappropriate matter*, is the "res aliena," or rather the action itself, "*accipere/subtrahere* rem alienam." According to the perspective we are considering, suggested in *VS* no. 78, we would have to say that precisely *the act* of "to take what belongs to another" would be the object chosen by the will. Nevertheless, it could be objected that the object we are seeking is not *the act* of "to take what belongs to another," but rather the *object of this act* (of the "taking"), that is, the thing itself "which belongs to another." The object of a human act, in this case, would not be an action, but the thing or reality toward which a particular act is directed.[8]

This last interpretation, however, contains difficulties which in my view are not easily overcome. In the first place, the terms "to act," "action," "act," etc. are used throughout the discussion with not a little ambivalence and con-

6. *ST* I-II, q.18 a.2: "primum malum in actionibus moralibus est quod est ex obiecto, sicut *accipere aliena*."

7. *De Malo*, 2, 4, ad5: "actus autem malus ex genere est qui cadit supra indebitam materiam, sicut *subtrahere aliena*."

8. This is what, at first glance, *ST* I-II, q.110 a.1 seems to suggest, as well as the various statements that the "materia circa quam" of the action is identical with its object.

fusion. Are we considering the human act as chosen, willed, and voluntarily carried out? Or those elements of the act which are external and observable behavior? A second difficulty is that a *res aliena* simply cannot, as such, morally qualify a human act. This would be the case, however, if the *res aliena* itself were that which we call "the object of a human act." The confiscation of a stolen item by the police, for example, so as to restore it to its owner, has the same *res aliena* as its "matter" as did the original theft, and yet we are dealing with two acts that are different precisely *because of their object.* The difference seems to derive, therefore, not from the "thing" taken, nor from the fact that it "belongs to another," but from the difference in the act of "taking" of this "thing": from the diversity of will and intentionality, respectively, implicit in the act.

Analogously, "to observe an eagle" and "to kill an eagle" are two different acts because of their objects; this would be inexplicable, however, if the object of the two acts were the eagle itself. In a certain sense it is true that both the *res aliena* and the eagle are "objects," but not of a human act; they are rather the object of bodily movements or the acts of specific organs. But these latter, in themselves, cannot be morally qualified; they are not, in fact, human acts, which always proceed from a deliberate will. The eagle as object of a visual act of the eye, or of a physical movement which causes the destruction of its life, is not considered to be "the object of a human act," but only of a series of events or physical processes. In the act "to kill an eagle," the eagle is certainly the object that specifies the physical act as "eagle-cide"; but this does not further specify it as "just," "unjust," or "indifferent"—that is, it does not specify it *morally.*[9] We, however, are seeking that object which specifies an act morally.

Precisely because we are speaking of the object *of a human act,* this object cannot be isolated from the context of voluntary action, which depends on reason.[10] This is obviously St. Thomas's perspective, as well. When he speaks of the object that morally specifies an act, he always speaks of the object of a moral (i.e., voluntary) act, which is synonymous with "human act."[11] As early as the *Scriptum* on the Sentences it is clear that, just as the acts of natural agents are specified according to the "forms" which are their principles, so

9. Cf. *De Malo,* 2, 4.

10. *ST* I-II, q.1 a.1: "Illae ergo actiones proprie humanae dicuntur, quae ex volunate deliberata procedunt."

11. Ibid., q.1 a.3: "idem sunt actus morales et actus humani."

human acts are specified by their respective "form": this, St. Thomas points out, is a form of the *will.* "The form of the will, however, is the end and the good which is its object and which is what is willed."[12] We must ask ourselves therefore what St. Thomas says when he speaks of the object *of the will:* he does not treat here of simple elements of exterior acts like particular movements of the body or acts of other faculties, even if such an act (for example an act of sexual copulation) possesses a natural finality inscribed in it.

Thomistic theory concerning the will and its object is found in questions 19 and 20 of the *Prima secundae,* which treat of the goodness and evil, respectively, of the interior act of the will (intention, choice) and of the exterior act commanded by it (acts of other powers or organs, or bodily movements, chosen and carried out under the rule of the will).[13] It will be useful here to carry out a more detailed exposition of this theory.

Exterior Act as Object of the Will: St. Thomas (*ST* I-II, 19 & 20)[14]

St. Thomas generally distinguishes the object of the interior act of the will,[14] that is, the end, from that which he sometimes calls the "object of the exterior act."[15] The "object of the exterior act," he says, is to the end as matter is to form. This object of the exterior act is "that on which the exterior action is brought to bear"[16] and which gives to the act its primary good-

12. *In Sent.* II, d.40, 1, 1: "Forma autem voluntatis est finis et bonum, quod est eius obiectum et volitum." Subsequently, in the *Summa Theologiae,* we find the same perspective: I-II, q.1 a.1: "Obiectum autem voluntatis est bonum et finis. Et ideo manifestum est quod principium humanorum actuum, inquantum sunt humani, est finis."

13. The Thomistic notion of "exterior act" is not to be confused with that of an external, visible act carried out with bodily organs. "Exterior acts" are those acts of the will that the will does not carry out by itself, i.e., in an "elicited" way *(velle, intendere, eligere, uti),* but by making use of another power, commanding its act. The exterior act is therefore the action of another power as it is commanded by the will; for example an (voluntary) act of knowing something; or also an act of the will commanded by another act ("elicited") of the will; but, certainly, exterior acts are also properly "external," bodily acts (to walk, to speak, to kill, sexual acts, etc., as commanded by the will). The examples used below will refer exclusively to such external, bodily acts and behaviors, which could cause the impression—which would be mistaken—that these are identical with the "exterior act."

14. For what follows cf. also M. Rhonheimer, *Natural Law and Practical Reason: A Thomist View of Moral Autonomy* (New York: Fordham University Press, 2000) (orig. *Natur als Grundlage der Moral* [Innsbruck-Vienna: Tyrolia-Verlag, 1987]; Italian edition, *Legge naturale e ragione pratica. Una visione tomista dell'autonomia morale* (Rome: Armando, 2001), 396–411; Spanish edition, *Ley natural y razón práctica: una vision tomista de la autonomía moral* (Pamplona: EUNSA, 2000).

15. Cf. *ST* I-II, q.18 a.6.: "id autem circa quod est actio exterior, est obiectum eius"; cf. also ibid., a.7: "obiectum exterioris actus dupliciter potest se habere ad finem voluntatis."

16. Ibid., q.18 a.6: "id autem circa quod est actio exterior."

ness.[17] More decisive, however, is the specification that derives from the end which the will proposes. For this reason "the species of a human act is considered formally with regard to the end, but materially with regard to the object of the exterior act."[18] Thomas then offers an example which shows that he speaks here of an act that is "composed" of the choice of a means, made with the intention of an end. The example demonstrates this: "he who steals that he may commit adultery, is strictly speaking, more adulterer than thief." The result, then, would seem to be as follows: for Thomas, the object of the will is the end; the object of the exterior act, on the other hand, are particular bodily movements or acts of other powers by which one carries out an act, as well as those things to which such bodily movements and acts are directed. A "theft," for example, would be a type of exterior act with its proper object. This object would not be the exterior act itself, but that to which that act is directed; in the case of a theft, the *res aliena.* "To choose to steal" would be precisely to choose particular bodily movements which take a *res aliena* from its owner; and the exterior act of taking would be evil based on its object: the *res aliena.*

This analysis, however, is mistaken, for two reasons. The first is that a *res aliena* as such is neither good nor evil. How then could it alone specify the physical act of taking it as a morally evil act? Some moralists in the past said that the act is morally evil based on a "transcendental relationship" of the physical object to the moral norm, according to which the act is unjust. If this were the case, however, the evil *ex obiecto* would be completely extrinsic, an explicative model being proposed that is more legal than moral, that is, an act would be evil because it is contrary to the moral norm, rather than vice versa. The second reason the analysis is mistaken is that it implies that the exterior act (i.e., the bodily movements in question) would be, immediately and as such, an end of the will. This, however, is simply impossible, and indeed is contrary to one of the most fundamental principles of Thomas's theory of action, that is, the principle that "the will cannot desire a good *that is not previously apprehended by reason.*"[19] This proposed solution, then, ignores the fundamental, constitutive, and normative role of practical reason, which for St. Thomas is the proper, immediate, and intrinsic rule of the goodness and evil of human acts.

17. Ibid., a.2: "prima bonitas actus moralis."

18. Ibid., q.18 a.6.

19. Ibid., q.19 a.3 ad1: "appetitus voluntatis non potest esse de bono, nisi prius a ratione apprehendatur."

Accordingly, Thomas states that the goodness or evil in acts of the will depends generally on the object,[20] because the object is presented to the will by means of reason, which is the principle and the measure of the goodness in human acts.[21] For this reason, he adds, the goodness of the will depends on reason exactly in the measure in which it depends on the object.[22] Indeed, the goodness and evil of acts depend *solely* on the object, because that which specifies the will is the end, but every object of the will is precisely also an end.[23] In other words: any act of the will, and therefore also the act that chooses a concrete action, is specified by that which is called an "object," which is essentially also an *end* of this act of the will. This end, however, is a good rendered present and desirable to the will by means of reason, the principle of human acts.

The coincidence between *objective* determination and *rational* determination of the will, heavily emphasized by St. Thomas, is of decisive importance for the subject we are discussing.

The first important result is that, when human action is considered *formally*—according to that which is of its essence, that is, as action proceeding from a deliberate will[24]—"the object of a human act" is precisely the exterior act itself, or, said with more precision, it is the content, the intelligible significance, of the exterior act of the will. For this reason, the question treated in the (following) 20th question now becomes crucial: *from where does the goodness (or the evil) of the exterior act originate?* Does it originate perhaps from that which, as we have seen, Thomas at times calls the "object of the exterior act,"[25] which then would finally be that object which confers on the human act its primary and fundamental moral specification? Curiously, there is no article in question 20 which asks "if the goodness of the exterior act depends on its object." In fact, in the entire question the term "object of the exterior act" does not appear again. Rather, Thomas states that as the exterior act is ordered, through the intention, to an ulterior end, its goodness

20. Ibid., q.19 a.1: "bonum et malum in actibus voluntatis proprie attenditur secundum obiecta."

21. Ibid., ad3: "bonum per rationem repraesentatur voluntati ut obiectum; et inquantum cadit sub ordine rationis, pertinet ad genus moris, et causat bonitatem moralem in actu voluntatis. Ratio enim principium est humanorum et moralium actuum."

22. Ibid., a.3: "bonitas voluntatis dependet a ratione, eo modo quo dependet ab obiecto."

23. Ibid., a.2: "bonitas voluntatis ex solo uno illo dependet, quod per se facit bonitatem in actu, scilicet ex obiecto"; ibid., ad1: "quantum ad actum voluntatis, non differt bonitas quae est ex obiecto, a bonitate quae est ex fine, sicut in actibus aliarum virtutum."

24. Ibid., q.1 a.1.

25. For example, ibid., I-II, q.18 a.6, a.7.

or evil derives precisely from this act of the will (i.e., from the object of the intention). This corresponds to what had been said earlier.[26] We would now expect the assertion that the goodness or evil of the exterior act, in itself, derives precisely *from its object.* But this is not the case. Thomas continues: "The goodness or malice which the exterior act has of itself, on account of its being about due matter and its being attended by due circumstances, is not derived from the will, *but rather from reason.*"[27] For this reason, adds Thomas, "if the goodness of the exterior act is considered inasmuch as it is ordered and understood ["apprehended"] by reason, it is prior to the goodness of the act of the will."[28] In other words, the goodness of an act of choice, as well as of the voluntary execution of the exterior act (the *usus*), depends on its object, which is the exterior act; the goodness of this latter, however, does not depend, in turn, on an object of its own, but on an "ordinatio et apprehensio rationis" in virtue of which the exterior act becomes properly the object of a human act, a practical good which morally specifies the act of the will, that is, the will's elective act, and along with it the act carried out on the basis of this choice.[29]

It seems significant to me that, in the context of this more analytical discussion, the term "object of the exterior act" does not reappear. From this

26. Ibid., q.18 a.6 (cited above).

27. Ibid., q.20 a.1: "Bonitas autem vel malitia quam habet actus exterior secundum se, propter debitam materiam et debitas circumstantias, non derivatur a voluntate, sed magis a ratione."

28. Ibid.: "unde si consideretur bonitas exterioris actus secundum quod est in ordinatione et apprehensione rationis, prior est quam bonitas actus voluntatis."

29. Precisely in this context, Pinckaers ("Le rôle de la fin dans l'action morale," 135) has fallen into what seems to me a significant contradiction. Initially, he says that the object of the exterior act (according to him, in the case of theft, "the good of another as desirable") confers on the act its first moral specification, "qui le constitue en son essence sur le plan moral." Immediately afterward he adds, however: "Cepandant l'object de l'acte extérieur n'a de valeur morale que si la volonté le prend pour le but de son mouvement." It is not possible, however, that the object of the exterior act confer the first moral specification on the act and, simultaneously, that this act, without it being grasped by the will as an end, not yet possess any moral significance. The cause of what seems a strange contradiction is certainly the failure to include the constitutive function of reason for the object in the analysis. A few pages further on (140) Pinckaers states, surprisingly, that the *finis operis,* which according to him coincides with the *finis proximus* of the will, is not "une donné purement objective," but "déjà une œuvre de la raison humaine." This seems to indicate that Pinckaers, in fact, had not forgotten the constitutive role of reason in the formation of the object. The problem is that at this point Pinckaers asserts that this *finis proximus* (or *finis operis) is not* the object that confers on the human act its first moral specification: "Cet object, c'est la *materia circa quam* qui de soi préexiste et s'impose à l'intention qui dirige l'action; ce sont les matériaux, antérieurement à tout projet de construction." This unfortunate metaphor taken from technology (also used later by Pinckaers in his book *Ce qu'on ne peut jamais faire. La question des actes intrinsèquement mauvais. Histoire et discussion* [Fribourg: Éditions Universitaires; Paris: Éditions du Cerf, 1986], 108ff.) seems, however, to contradict that which the author

perspective, in which the human act is considered as a properly *voluntary*—that is, chosen—act and, therefore, from the perspective of the person who acts, it is precisely the exterior act itself, in its intelligible essence, which shows itself to be "object." What is chosen is not, therefore, the *res aliena,* but *accipere rem alienam:* an intelligible proposal, presented to the will as a good and as a proximate end. And this object is what we call a "theft." In the order of execution, this object—which is a proposal of action, an *intentio voluntatis* directed to a way of acting, conceived by reason—confers on the sum of bodily movements of which the exterior act of the theft is composed its primary and fundamental moral specification as a particular type of act; and chosen in this way, the exterior act of "to take that which belongs to another against his will" causes a disorder in the will of the person who so chooses: it renders him unjust. The object causes such a disorder, obviously, because the *res aliena* is not "appropriate matter" for an act of taking it from someone against his will.[30] We can say that *materially considered* this *res aliena* with all its related circumstances is the object of the act. But an object cannot be understood only materially; its formal part must be included as well. If for St. Thomas the object of an act of seeing is not the thing, but the color which makes it visible,[31] the object of an action such as a theft cannot be properly the "thing which belongs to another," but rather this "thing which belongs to another" taken under its formal aspect of being a practical good, that is,

---

had said on p. 135 (as has been mentioned), i.e., that the exterior act receives from the object of the exterior act, that is from the "materia circa quam," "une spécification morale première." In my opinion, Pinckaers read St. Thomas exactly as I did but is guilty of a significant confusion in terminology. The exterior act or the "materia circa quam"—which St. Thomas identifies with the object that morally specifies the act—is not an aggregate of "preexistent matters" on which the will then confers its moral significance in a "creative" way, an impression that Pinckaers's statements could give, but a "good understood and ordered by reason," presented by reason to the will as an objective datum, a practical proposal or good, already bearing moral significance, but, obviously, "une œuvre de la raison," a "work of reason," a "forma a ratione concepta" (cf. n. 34). If Pinckaers had more closely analyzed St. Thomas's texts regarding on the one hand the relation between "exterior act" / "object" / "materia circa quam," and on the other hand, reason, he would have in my opinion been able to give a more coherent form to his excellent and praiseworthy initial intuition of reevaluating the perspective of the acting subject, of voluntariness, and of finality in the understanding of human action.

30. Cf. *ST* I-II, q.18 a.10: "tollere alienum habet speciem ex ratione alieni, ex hoc enim constituitur in specie furti." The fact that the thing taken is "alien"—or rather the "ratio alieni"—is not the object, but a circumstance, which is understood "a ratione ordinante ut principalis conditio obiecti determinantis speciem actus" (ibid.).

31. Cf., for example *ST* I, q.1 a.7: "sicut homo et lapis referuntur ad visum inquantum sunt colorata, unde coloratum est propium obiectum visus." In other words: the object of the act "to see Peter" is not "Peter," but "Peter under the aspect of his visibility."

a practical aspect, *to be indicated with a verb that expresses an action.*[32] For this reason—and this is the decisive point—only in the context of an action, that is, of an ulterior finalization, can such "matter" appear as "inappropriate" matter. In itself, a *res aliena* is neither "appropriate" nor "inappropriate." It becomes so only in relation to specific desires, choices, and corresponding modes of acting. To establish and to know such a relation is exclusively the work of reason, which in this way informs the will, conferring the moral species on its act. For this reason an object is "evil" which is not in accordance *with reason,* and therefore "to take another's property" is an "object in discord with reason."[33]

Because the morally relevant object of an exterior act is defined not in relation to the material elements to which it refers, but to these elements *as understood and ordered by reason,* St. Thomas says that as "the species of natural things are constituted by their natural forms, *so the species of moral actions are constituted by forms as conceived by reason.*"[34] And in a more general way, Thomas affirms in the *Scriptum* on the Sentences that "the good proper to any human faculty is that which suits it according to reason, because that goodness derives from a certain ordered unification [*commensuratio*] of the act with respect to the circumstances and to the end, *which unification reason performs.*"[35] For this reason it is important to note that when St. Thomas speaks of the goodness or evil "secundum se" of the exterior act, he does not say that this specification comes from its "object," but from its matter and its

32. Cf. Theo G. Belmans, *Le sens objectif de l'agir humain. Pour relire la morale conjugale de Saint Thomas,* Studi Tomistici 8 (Vatican City: Libreria Editrice Vaticana, 1980), 175ff. and passim. I owe much to Belmans's studies. S. Pinckaers, "Le rôle de la fin dans l'action morale," 135, on the other hand, says that the object of a theft is "le bien d'autrui apparu come désirable." This is true in the sense that the aspect of being desirable means to think of the *res aliena* already as the matter of an exterior act insofar as this act is, precisely, an object of the will (and a good or an end for it). For this reason, the object is not the *res aliena* itself, but the action of taking it from its owner.

33. *ST* I-II, q.18 a.5 ad2: "obiectum non conveniens rationi, sicut tollere aliena."

34. Ibid., q.18 a.10: "sicut species rerum naturalium constituuntur ex naturalibus formis, ita species actuum constituuntur *ex formis prout sunt a ratione conceptae.*"

35. *In Sent.,* II, d. 39, 2, 1: "bonum autem cuiuslibet virtutis est conveniens homini secundum rationem: quia talis bonitas est ex quadam commensuratione actus ad circumstantias et finem, *quam ratio facit.*" An explication of the term *commensuratio* as "unification in an ordered way" can be found, e.g., in *ST* III, q.2 a.1 c. Cf. also I-II, q.71 a.6: "Habet autem actus humanus quod sit malus, ex eo quod caret debita commensuratione. Omnis autem commensuratio cuiuscumque rei attenditur per comparationem ad aliquam regulam, a qua, si divertat, incommensurata erit. Regula autem voluntatis humanae est duplex: una propinqua et homogenea, scilicet *ipsa humana ratio;* alia vero est prima regula, scilicet *lex aeterna,* quae est *quasi ratio Dei.*"

circumstances, which, nonetheless, are not *the object,* but the elements from which the object is "understood and ordered" by means of reason.[36]

Our interpretation is confirmed by the response to the first objection of I-II, 20, 1. The objection claims, correctly, that the exterior act is the object of the interior act of the will and for this reason one normally says "to will to commit a theft [to will to take something that is another's property], or to will to give an alms."[37] Thomas's response confirms this, but also makes it more precise. He replies: "the exterior action is the object of the will, inasmuch as it is proposed to the will by reason, *as a good understood and ordered by reason.*"[38] The exterior act, therefore, as the object of the will that chooses it, is a "*bonum apprehensum et ordinatum per rationem.*" For this reason it is not the "object" of the exterior act which is simply the cause of the primary goodness of the act, but rather reason, which forms what is "matter" in this exterior act into an object for the will—its *finis proximus,* on which the morality of human acts depends "primarily and fundamentally." This proximate end is the intelligible content of a concrete way of acting, a "form conceived by reason."

In this precise sense, the goodness of the will is caused by the goodness of the exterior act, which is its object. The exterior act, nevertheless, causes this goodness not as a performed act—not as an external behavior—but precisely as it is the object of an *intentio* of the will, that is, willed,[39] and therefore as the intelligible content of a concrete way of acting. This does not mean that Thomas would want to reduce the objective significance of the exterior act—making it indifferent *in itself*—to that which, in each case, "is willed," thus reducing the object to an intention which is somehow separable from its material conditions.[40] This would be, essentially, Abelard's claim. Such an interpretation loses sight of the fact that the exterior act, as the ob-

36. *ST* I-II, q.20 a.3. We will return to this point briefly later (the relevant texts are cited in notes 49, 50, and 51).

37. Ibid., a.1 arg.1: "Sed actus exterior est obiectum interioris actus voluntatis: dicimur enim velle furtum vel velle dare eleemosynam." As is obvious, "velle furtum" is equivalent to "velle accipere rem alienam." This *velle* is the act of choice, i.e., the *usus,* by which the act is carried out.

38. Ibid. ad1: "actus exterior est obiectum voluntatis, inquantum proponitur voluntati a ratione ut quoddam bonum apprehensum et ordinatum per rationem: et sic est prius quam bonum actus voluntatis."

39. Cf. *In Sent.* II, d. 40, 1, 3: "quia actus exterior comparatur ad voluntatem sicut obiectum, inde est quod hanc bonitatem voluntatis actus interior ab exteriori habet, non quidem ex eo secundum quod est exercitus, sed secundum quod est intentus et volitus."

40. John Finnis, Germain Grisez, and Joseph Boyle use this passage in this way, citing it only partially, however, in their article "'Direct' and 'Indirect': A Reply to Critics of our Action Theory," *The Thomist* 65 (2001): 16.

ject of the interior act of the will, is already a good understood and ordered by reason. For this reason, in the same passage just cited, St. Thomas affirms that the exterior act receives its goodness not from the will, but "from the commensuration of the circumstances, according to which the exterior act is proportioned so as to attain the goal of man."[41] As we know, this *commensuratio* is a work of reason. This being the case, it follows that the "proposal" or proximate end which is "the object" is, certainly, that which is willed, but this willing cannot direct itself to other than what is presented by reason. The measure, therefore, according to which the exterior act is configured as a practical good and chosen by the will is not the will itself, or "that which the agent proposes," but reason. We cannot define or redefine the objective significance of our actions in function of what we propose. Rather, that which an agent can reasonably propose (and consequently choose) in a given situation is understood by reason, not simply as a function of "proposals" or "intentions" that can be freely oriented by the agent, but subject to the concrete circumstances in which the choice is carried out, according to criteria of reasonableness inherent—in virtue of the natural law—in practical reason, criteria which are therefore also objective.[42]

41. *In Sent.* II, d. 40, 1, 3: "actus enim exterior bonitatem habet ex circumstantiarum commensuratione, secundum quam proportionatus est ad finem hominis consequendum."

42. For this reason, *ST* I-II, q.18 a.10 is important (cf. also my *Die Perspektive der Moral. Philosophische Grundlagen der Tugendethik* [Berlin: Akademie Verlag, 2001], 135ff.), where Thomas lays out his doctrine of the formation of the object as "forma a ratione concepta," showing how specific circumstances can at times become a "principalis conditio obiecti rationi repugnans" (cf. also ibid., q.18 a.5 ad4: "circumstantia quandoque sumitur ut differentia essentialis obiecti"). It seems to me that the action theory of Grisez/Finnis/Boyle ignores this decisive aspect of Thomistic doctrine. This becomes evident, for example, in their opinion ("'Direct' and 'Indirect,'" 30f.) that someone who blows up an airplane full of passengers only with the intention of collecting the insurance indemnity for the loss of the airplane, *does not intend and therefore does not choose* the death of the passengers (because this is not his "purpose"—he would do it even if the airplane were empty), but only the destruction of the airplane (proximate end, object), with the ulterior intention of enriching himself; his act, according to these authors, is not therefore an act of "direct killing." The death of the passengers would only be a collateral effect of the destruction of the airplane, an unintentional effect, even if, as the authors add, such a choice would be "gravely wrong," as the collateral effect is foreseen and unjustifiable. I am certain that St. Thomas would not accept such a description of this choice. He would say, rather, that the circumstance of the presence of the passengers in the airplane is a "principalis conditio obiecti rationi repugnans," which causes a "differentia essentialis obiecti": The killing of the passengers, therefore, must be included in the description of the object; indeed, precisely this *would be* the object. The enrichment, on the other hand, would in reality be the ulterior intention for which the massacre of the passengers is chosen and voluntarily carried out. This repugnance to reason does not depend on the will, but is grasped by reason in its function of effecting the *commensuratio* of the various circumstances.

It will be useful to recall that for Thomas Aquinas, the *ratio* is not simply a knowing organ that "discovers" a moral rule, preexistent in nature, so as to then apply it to action. Moral reason—practical reason—is itself a rule: it is "measure" of the morality of human acts, a natural rule, inherent in human nature and a participation in divine reason.[43] Participating in the light of the intellect, reason is not only regulated by the object of its speculative act—the being of things—but, as practical, and primarily as *lex naturalis,* reason itself regulates and directs the "naturalness" of human tendencies and inclinations to their *appropriate* end, an end which comprises part of an order that is not natural, but of reason. This is precisely the order *of reason,* which is the adequate expression of that which is natural for man in a properly *moral* sense. For this reason, as Thomas constantly affirms, morally speaking something is in conformity with man's nature precisely to the degree in which it is in conformity with reason.[44] According to Thomas, this regulating task belongs to

43. Cf. *ST* I-II, q.71 a.6 (full text cited above in n. 35). It is important to understand that the rule on which reason depends is not "nature" but properly the eternal law, which is the divine reason itself. This accords with the Thomistic idea that the natural law—which *is* man's natural reason, distinguishing good from evil—is a participation in the eternal law by the rational creature, an "impressio divini luminis in nobis" (I-II, q.91 a.2). Cf. chapter 5 of this book, or M. Rhonheimer, "The Cognitive Structure of the Natural Law and the Truth of Subjectivity," *The Thomist* 67, no. 1 (2003): 1–44; also in Italian: Rhonheimer, "La legge morale naturale: conoscenza morale e coscienza. La struttura cognitiva della legge naturale e la verità della soggettività," in Juan de Dios Vial Correa and Elio Sgreccia, eds., *Natura e dignità della persona umana a fondamento del diritto alla vita,* Acts of the Eighth General Assembly of the Pontifical Academy for Life (February 25–27, 2002) (Vatican City: Libereria Editrice Vaticana, 2003), 125–58.

44. Cf. *ST* I-II, q.71 a.2: "quod est contra ordinem rationis, proprie est contra naturam hominis inquantum est homo; quod est autem secundum rationem, est secundum naturam hominis, inquantum est homo. Bonum autem hominis est secundum rationem esse . . . Unde virtus humana . . . intantum est secundum naturam hominis, inquantum convenit rationi: vitium autem intantum est contra naturam hominis, inquantum est contra ordinem rationis." Again, in ibid., q.18 a.5: "In actibus autem humanis bonum et malum dicitur per comparationem ad rationem." Cf. also ibid., q.71 a.6 (cit. in n. 35). For a correct understanding of Thomistic doctrine according to which the rule of morality is not "nature" but reason, still useful is Léonard Léhu's book, *La raison, règle de la moralité d'après Saint Thomas* (Paris: Libr. Lecoffre, 1930). Stephen L. Brock, in his review of my book *Natural Law and Practical Reason* (*The Thomist* 66, no. 2 [2002]: 313) has characterized my assertion that, according to St. Thomas, not nature but reason is the measure of morality, as "a disconcerting claim." It is rather this characterization, made by a Thomistic scholar as expert as Brock, that seems to me disconcerting. This can perhaps be explained by the fact that Brock, like not a few other authors, creates a confusion between the question of the *ontological foundation* of the moral order (which is certainly "nature"), and that concerning the *way in which this natural foundation becomes practically effective and regulatory.* This latter is brought about, as St. Thomas never tires of repeating, precisely by means of reason, which, we must bear in mind, is also part of human nature—indeed reason is precisely human nature's most formal determination, and consequently enters into its definition as its specific difference!—and knows the human good in a natural (spontaneous, necessary) way, promulgating

reason for a simple metaphysical or anthropological reason: man is man because he has a rational soul, which is his substantial form. "For that is good for a thing which suits it in regard to its form; and evil, that which is against the order of its form. It is therefore evident that the difference of good and evil considered in reference to the object is an essential difference in relation to reason; that is to say, according as the object is suitable or unsuitable to reason. Now certain actions are called human or moral, inasmuch as they proceed from reason."[45] "Nature," therefore, is not the *rule* of the good and evil of any operation, but only that which determines what this rule of good and evil is in each case. In the case of human nature and human action, this rule is reason (nor is "nature" the rule in the case of "actions" of brute animals, but rather instinct and other sensual drives, which are of course *natural,* as reason, too, is natural for human beings). Thus, nature is not a "norm of morality," but that which establishes this norm, the norm being reason.

The Object of the Human Act: A "Good Understood and Ordered by Reason"

We can summarize the point we have reached thus far with the following four points:

(1) That which morally specifies a human act is, exclusively, the object of an interior act of the will (*electio, intentio,* etc.), and inasmuch as it is such an object.

(2) The primary and fundamental object of the will, which confers on the act its primary goodness, is the exterior act as it is a "good understood and ordered by reason." It is therefore precisely the exterior act as the *intelligible content of a concrete action,* chosen by the will as a practical good, which is "the object of a human act"; for example: "to take from someone that which belongs to him."

---

the *lex naturalis.* Cf. also Brock, *Action and Conduct: Thomas Aquinas and the Theory of Action* (Edinburgh: T&T Clark, 1998) (Italian translation, *Azione e condotta. Tommaso d'Aquino e la teoria dell'azione* (Rome: Edizioni Università della Santa Croce, 2002), where the constitutive role of reason in voluntary action is almost ignored, with the consequence of a certain "naturalization" of human action. (The three passages cited above from *ST* I-II, for example, are not mentioned in Brock's book.)

45. *ST* I-II, q.18 a.5: "Unicuique rei est bonum quod convenit ei secundum suam formam; et malum quod est ei praeter ordinem suae formae. Patet ergo, quod differentia boni et mali circa obiecta considerata comparatur per se ad rationem: scilicet secunudm quod obiectum est ei conveniens vel non conveniens. Dicuntur autem aliqui actus umani, vel morales, secundum quod sunt a ratione."

(3) For this reason, the goodness of the exterior act does not depend, in its turn, on its "object," but, as St. Thomas affirms with emphasis and constancy, *on reason.* This is so because it is precisely reason, and reason exclusively, which proposes the exterior act, in the variety of its components, to the will as an intelligible good, which can then lead to an act of choice and a subsequent action. If one were to further seek an "object" of the exterior act itself as such, he would inevitably fall into physicalism. He would confuse that object on which the primary goodness of the human act depends with a series of natural tendencies, realities, and structures which, though perhaps very significant morally, is not that which, as such, confers its moral species on a human act.

(4) Speaking *materially,* we can say that the various elements that compose the exterior act are like a "materia circa quam," a matter around which the action develops and which specifies it as a particular *type* of action. Considered *formally,* however, that is, as the object of a human act and as an end—as the object, that is, of a voluntary act—this "materia circa quam" is the same exterior act as *bonum apprehensum et ordinatum per rationem.* Only in this way can the *materia circa quam* be understood as a moral object, and only in this way, as St. Thomas explicitly states, does it specify the act *morally.*[46] This shows that the "moral object" is not, for Thomas, properly an "object of the exterior act," but always and exclusively the object of the interior act of the will and, for this reason, a *forma a ratione concepta.*[47]

To call the moral object the "object of the exterior act," as Thomas himself at times does, could therefore cause confusion; it would seem inconsistent with the exposition provided in questions I-II, 19–20.[48] According to

46. Cf. ibid., q.72 a.3 ad2: "obiecta secundum quod comparantur ad actus exteriores, habent rationem materiae circa quam: sed secundum quod comparantur ad actum interiorem voluntatis, habent rationem finium; et ex hoc habent quod dent speciem actui."

47. Cf. ibid., q.18 a.10 (cit. above in n. 34). This "flexibility" of the "materia circa quam" is also explained precisely by the fact that it is not a "materia *ex qua,*" i.e., the matter *of which* something is made (cf. ibid., q.18 a.2 ad2). The "materia circa quam" has different characteristics depending on whether it is considered only materially—in its relation to the exterior act—or as the proximate end of a voluntary act (ibid., q.72 a.3 ad2; cf. previous note); in this latter case, the "materia circa quam" is precisely that which is called the object "et habet quodammodo rationem formae, inquantum dat speciem" (ibid., q.18 a.2 ad2).

48. This problem goes unnoticed even in the accurate and brilliant exposition of St. Thomas's doctrine on this subject by R. McInerny, *Aquinas on Human Action: A Theory of Practice* (Washington, D.C.: The Catholic University of America Press, 1992); for example when the author, although correctly, says: "The external, commanded act of the will can be good because of the kind of act it is, something determined by its object, e.g., giving alms to the poor" (98). "Giving alms to the poor" appears three times in this statement, each with a different meaning: once

that exposition, the exterior act does not properly "have" an "object" (in a moral sense), but the exterior act itself *is* considered to be the object morally, the *finis proximus* of the interior act of the will (i.e., the *electio*), and as such it morally specifies the human act. The expression "object of the exterior act," however, ultimately means—including for St. Thomas—"the exterior act as a good understood and ordered by reason," or "the rational and rationally ordered apprehension of the exterior act" (= of the *materia circa quam*, which as a good understood and ordered by reason is the "form" which morally specifies the act). For this reason, speaking of the good and evil which at times the exterior act possesses *secundum se*, St. Thomas does not say that this derives from its "object," but from its "matter" and its circumstances.[49] These latter are not the object, but precisely the elements that, according to reason, are or are not a "principal condition of the object that determines the action's species"[50] (or an "essential difference of the object"),[51] and which are conceived by reason as the moral species of the action. Precisely this rational comprehension of the exterior act, which contains a rational *ordinatio* of its various material elements, is the object of the act of choice and therefore of a human act.[52]

And this is necessarily so because, as has already been mentioned, it is not possible that the will refer immediately to the constitutive (material, circumstantial) elements of an "exterior act," or to things or to the natural acts

as "exterior act"; then as "object of the exterior act"; and finally as "type of act" (moral species). It is not that this is incorrect but that it requires a further clarification so as to be comprehensible. McInerny's clarification seems correct to me, because it points in the direction of understanding that the object of the external act is precisely this act as its matter and circumstances are understood and ordered by reason, which presents it to the will as a good.

49. *ST* I-II, q.20 a.3: "Quando autem actus exterior habet bonitatem vel malitiam secundum se, scilicet secundum materiam vel circumstantias."

50. Ibid., q.18 a.10: "Et ideo quod in uno actu accipitur ut cicumstania superaddita obiecto quod determinat speciem actus, potest iterum accipi a ratione ordinante ut principalis conditio obiecti determinantis speciem actus." (This is the article that begins with the words, "species moralium actuum constituuntur ex formis prout sunt a ratione conceptae.")

51. Ibid., q.18 a.5 ad4: "circumstantia quandoque sumitur ut differentia essentialis obiecti, secundum quod ad rationem comparatur: et tunc potest dare speciem actui morali. . . . non enim circumstantia faceret actum malum, nisi per hoc quod rationi repugnat."

52. It is correct, therefore, when Tobias Hoffmann, in his article "Moral Action as Human Action: End and Object in Aquinas in Comparison with Abelard, Lombard, Albert, and Duns Scotus," *The Thomist* 67 (2003): 73–94, asserts that the "materia circa quam" is "what the agent is doing," as "uti re sua" or "accipere aliena," which are good or evil objects (or acts) according to their "proportion to reason." It must be added, however, that reason not only judges concerning the goodness of the object, but also formulates or constitutes it cognitively, in the sense that only before reason can it appear as *this kind of* object.

of specific powers, except through the *mediation of reason.*[53] Precisely for this reason the exterior act as such cannot have an "object" from which it receives its moral species—the search for such an object would end in an infinite regression. The "objects" proper to the exterior act (as considered materially, that is, not as an intelligible good for the will) are found at the physical, premoral level (which, to repeat, does not exclude that they be significant and at times decisive for the morality of an act, as, for example, the fact that something belongs to a particular person and a corresponding right of property exists, or that the sexual act is naturally ordered to the procreation of the human species).

Every deliberately chosen human act, on the other hand, already *necessarily* has an object at the moral level, because its object is this exterior act itself, as a "good understood and ordered by reason." To deny this is to fall into physicalism. Traditionally, to avoid this danger, it was customary at this point to resort to the *Deus ex machina* of the mysterious "transcendental relation of the physical object to the moral norm." This solution, however, more juridical than moral, hindered a proper understanding of the *intrinsic* constitution of the moral object, and therefore also of the goodness or evil that human acts intrinsically possess on the basis of their object. To avoid the necessity of recourse to this *Deus ex machina* or—like those who were aware of the inadequacy of this "legalistic" solution and rebelled against it—to avoid ending up in proportionalism or consequentialism (which are nothing other than variations of the same ethical-normative extrinsicism), one must place himself "in the perspective of the acting person," conceiving the object of a

53. Here is where the fundamental error of the so-called "teleological ethics" (consequentialism, proportionalism) is found, all of which assume, in one way or another, that the will can refer in an immediate way to an exterior act and to its elements (to goods, i.e., called "ontic," "non-moral" or "pre-moral," "physical"), without this also implying a moral specification of the will. For example, according to the adherents of "teleological ethics," "to kill a human being" would only be to physically cause the death of a man (to cause a non-moral evil), which, according to the totality of the circumstances and foreseeable consequences, can be considered morally right or wrong. In reality, however, the will chooses the action "to kill a human being" not as though it were simply the (physical) cause of an evil that is equally physical, but as a "good understood and ordered by reason," as the intelligible content of an action that already implies a rational configuration, full of moral significance, of the various "physical goods and evils" implicated in the action. This rational configuration is what morally specifies the act of the will as just or unjust; it specifies it, precisely, independently of the foreseen consequences and of other, perhaps worthy, intentions. I refer here to my book *Die Perspektive der Moral,* which, among other things, is intended as a systematic refutation of so-called "teleological ethics," and to chapter 4 of this book, which appeared earlier as M. Rhonheimer, "Intentional Actions and the Meaning of Object: A Reply to Richard McCormick," *The Thomist* 59, no. 2 (1995): 279–311.

human act as the proximate end of the will, that is, as an "object rationally chosen by the deliberate will" on which "primarily and fundamentally depends" the morality of the human act (*VS* no. 78).

At this point we must state clearly that we have yet to resolve any of the problems of normative ethics, that is, of the argumentative foundation of specific moral norms.

To object, then, that what has been said so far accomplishes nothing, is tautological and, as has been claimed, of "little explanatory value," and that the ethical-normative problem has merely been "put off," would seem to me to express a certain *ignoratio elenchi*, that is, an ignorance of the problem we have been treating so far.[54] We have attempted to clarify the notion of the "object" of a human act as "it causes goodness and evil in the will"; we have not yet, however, spoken of that which is the proper task of normative ethics, that is, how to discern whether this or that act is morally good or evil.

Action theory, which is properly what we have been dealing with to this point, is not asked to resolve normative problems, even if the method of resolving such problems depends in a decisive way on the theory of action one uses to such an end; in the present case it depends on the notion of "moral object," employed in the normative task of ethics.

The theory of action proposed here, firmly based in the thought of Thomas Aquinas, is properly an *anthropology* (or *metaphysics*) of action, and not merely a logical analysis of practical reason. The correct understanding of what is the object of a human act is, moreover, also the key for resolving the difficult question of so-called "intrinsically evil" acts, because what causes problems of comprehension is not so much the objective evil of certain acts, but precisely the notion of their being *intrinsically* evil.

The consequence of what has been shown so far is that to understand the notion of the "object" of a human act, it is necessary to understand the fundamental role—decisive from the anthropological point of view—of practical reason in human action. Whoever looks for an "object of the exterior act" *as an external, observable behavior,* will end by reducing the human act to its non-moral elements, that is, in a crude physicalism that ignores the

54. This is the criticism of my position by Alberto Bonandi, "Dieci anni di teologia morale con *Veritatis splendor*. Aspetti della ricezione dell'enciclia," *La Scuola Cattolica* 131 (2003): 22f. In my opinion, Bonandi in his critique confuses action theory with normative ethics, and he fails to differentiate between their respective tasks; nor does he seem to understand well the importance of the former for the latter.

regulating and morally ordering role of reason. To ignore the decisive role of reason for the constitution of the objective moral significance of human actions flaws not only action theory, but also loses the "moral perspective" itself, that is, that of action guided by a "rational appetite," the will. It forgets that goods and evils in a moral sense are not "ontic" or "physical" goods like "human life," "death," "property," "the conception of a new life," etc., even though these are morally of great importance; but that moral goods and evils are rather *actions* and their corresponding choices, such as "respect human life," "kill an innocent person," "take that which belongs to someone against his will," "transmit human life," etc. The objects that morally specify such actions are not "human life," "another's property," or "the conception of a new life," but precisely the respective actions *inasmuch as they are the intelligible contents of concrete ways of acting,* "goods understood and ordered by reason," and willed as such: in this way these actions are the proximate end, that is, the "object," of the will, and it is precisely this object that confers on the human act its primary and fundamental moral specification.

The perspective set forth here maintains, to return to our earlier example, that an external behavior considered physically (bodily movements like, for example, a sexual copulation, or the act which causes the contents of a safe to disappear) becomes an "object" for the will, and therefore causes moral good or evil in the will, in correlation with certain of the behavior's characteristics which are comprehensible only by reason, such as, for example, the "circumstance" that one is dealing with one's own safe or with that of another. The *res aliena,* or more specifically, the circumstance that the *res* in question is another's property, and the corresponding juridical-moral fact of the existence of the other's right, is in no way "the object" of a theft, but a circumstance that, before reason, shows the *res* to be *indebita* ("inappropriate") with respect to the physical action of taking it from its owner. The characteristic of being *materia debita* or *indebita* does not derive from an ulterior object of the physical act, but from reason in its aspect of being a rule, or, in other words, from the exterior act considered as a "good understood and ordered by reason," that is, from the intelligible content of a concrete type of action.

It is clear that we are speaking of a "reason" that is not a rule only in the formal sense. It is a reason, rather, permeated with axiological content, a content which derives from the fact of reason being a faculty integrated in the being of a human person, constituted in a substantial unity of body and spirit. It is not reason (or the intellect) that knows, but the person who knows *by means of* reason. Even more important, however, is the fact that reason can be the rule of that which is just or unjust because reason itself depends on its own principles, *that is, on the natural law.* This latter, according to St. Thomas, is "the light of natural reason, whereby we discern what is good and what is evil," because it is essentially a "naturalis inclinatio ad debitum actum et finem," "a natural inclination to the *(morally) appropriate* act and end."[55]

To understand the moral configuration of an exterior act, the object of a choice of the acting subject, we must affirm therefore that it does not depend simply on natural acts, but neither does it depend on the will of the subject. Rather, it depends on reason which, as the discursive part of the intellect, is also as intellect and practical reason precisely that cognitive faculty which not only orders our actions, but also fundamentally opens us to the truth of our being, in this way establishing the practical truth of our actions, which is the "truth of the subjectivity" of the person who acts.

Kevin Flannery has raised the criticism that such an emphasis on the contribution of the subject, or rather of the human understanding ("the mind's contribution"), in the constitution of the object of a human act would be "difficult to reconcile with Thomas Aquinas," and that at times would lead to "the exclusion of that which is outside the mind."[56] This objection can be responded to easily using the words of authors who are under no suspicion of subjectivism.[57] Moreover, the criticism seems so odd to me that it may be due to a simple misunderstanding on Flannery's part. This misunderstanding probably consists in the assumption—false, in any case—that what is constituted and ordered by reason is not "objective," is not always rooted in extra-mental reality, and indeed, that it excludes "that which is outside the mind" and depends on the arbitrariness of the subject. In reality things are not this way, and to say so presupposes an anthropology and a conception of the mind different from the Aristotelian concept according to which "the intellect is always correct; the appetite, on the other hand, and the sensible imagination can be either

55. *ST* I-II, q.91 a.2. *Veritatis Splendor* twice cites (nos. 12 and 40) the concise Thomistic formulation of "In duo praecepta caritatis et in decem legis praecepta expositio," Prologus I: "lex naturae . . . nihil aliud est nisi lumen intellectus insitum nobis a Deo, per quod cognoscimus quid agendum et quid vitandum. Hoc lumen et hanc legem dedit Deus homini in creatione." Cf. also the above-mentioned articles (n. 43).

56. K. Flannery, review of my book *Die Perspektive der Moral,* in *Gregorianum* 83 (2002): 592.

57. For example McInerny, *Aquinas on Human Action,* 101f.: "The human voluntary act will be good, insofar as will is measured by reason. . . . Anything that the mind judges to be good, sees as good, is thereby brought under the common formality of goodness. . . . Mind's grasp of the good is the measure of the will's goodness."

correct or not correct,"[58] an anthropology equally reflected in the Thomistic expression according to which, "corrupt reason is not reason."[59]

It is correct, therefore, to sustain that the object of a human act is the act itself. This is not logically contradictory,[60] since it is this act taken precisely as object: as the proximate end of the will, that is, as the intelligible content of a concrete action, a good that can be and is in fact chosen, and not as an act "done" in the order of execution.[61] The object is the exterior act, as the object of the interior act of the will.

58. Aristotle, *De Anima* III, 10, 433a 27–28.

59. *In Sent.* II, d. 24, 3, 3 ad3: "ratio corrupta non est ratio." Cf. on this subject *Die Perspektive der Moral,* 146ff. *("Der anthropologische Primat der Vernunft"),* and in more detail in Rhonheimer, *Praktische Vernunft und Vernünftigkeit der Praxis. Handlungstheorie bei Thomas von Aquin in ihrer Entstehung aus dem Problemkontext der aristotelischen Ethik* (Berlin: Akademie Verlag, 1994), 155–72 and passim. Like not a few Thomists, Flannery apparently works with a somewhat "inverted-Cartesian prejudice" in the sense of dualistically—and in this very sense Cartesian—assuming that the "objective," the "natural," and the "truthful" are equal to what is "outside the mind," whereas what is "inside the mind" (or the mind itself) is "subjective," "non-natural," and the mere representation of truth. Even if such an inverted Cartesianism seems to be a very common neo-Scholastic scheme, I hardly think that it agrees with Aquinas's way of thinking. For him, as for Aristotle (and in another way also for Plato), the human mind—especially the active intellect, which is to intelligible truth as light is to the visibility of things—is part of man's nature and therefore, in a basic ontological way, it *is* "nature" as well. In clarifying the concept of the "natural," both the distinction into intra- and extra-mental reality and that into reason and nature seem to me to be of little use, as well as anthropologically misleading. The intellect and its proper object—intelligible reality—are, for the human person, as natural as any of his natural inclinations are. It is, therefore, strange to assume that the proper objects and goods of *extra*-mental (or non-mental) natural inclinations (such as the natural object and goals of, for example, the sexual inclination or the inclination to self-preservation) should be more "natural" and "objective" than the inclinations, objects, and goods that naturally spring from the mind (or the intellect, or "natural reason"), such as, e.g., the concept of "the just" or "the due" (which, as a concept of the good and formally, is purely "mental," i.e., not to be found in extra-mental reality). Thus, nothing excludes that there is a "mind's contribution," which is both natural and entirely objective, without there being any problematic "subjectivism" or aprioristic transcendentalism. On the contrary, a concept of "naturalness" that excludes the "mind's contribution" would not seem to be an idea of "human naturalness" at all. If we consider the human person both anthropologically and ethically as part of the "outside" or "objective" world, we must include in this consideration the mind and the intellectual powers of man—otherwise such a consideration would reduce man to his pure animality. (We will see later how this bears upon the concept of "natural law" as a moral law.)

60. As Kevin Flannery claims in his review of *Die Perspektive der Moral,* and also Bonandi, 23. Both seem to think that I am saying that the object of an act of choice is the choice itself, which would in fact be absurd.

61. It could be that I have confused Flannery by my statement (somewhat embarrassing, I admit, but marginal) that the object of an act of seeing is not the "thing" that is seen but rather the act of "seeing this thing." This is certainly true if we consider the act of seeing as an exterior act, i.e., as commanded by the will, which is to say as a human act. If we consider it, rather, as a natural act of the vision, it cannot be said that the object of this act of seeing something is the act itself of seeing the thing. The object of the act of seeing would be rather the "thing seen under the formal aspect of its visibility" (for St. Thomas: "the thing as colored"; cf. note 31 above). Flan-

The exterior act itself is a good, known and ordered by reason and as such "presented" to the will, which can also be considered, as such, in abstract. This consideration would be precisely the description of the act in its "objective" significance, that is, at the level of its "object." This significance is not a naturally preexistent "given": it is a species *a ratione concepta,* just as at the universal level the natural law, like every law, is "something constituted by reason," a "work of reason."[62]

Practical Reasonableness and Finality: The Intentional Structuring of the Object

An important consequence derives from the fact that the object of a human act is configured by reason: the exterior act itself, presented by reason to the will as object, as proximate end, and therefore as a practical good, must already include an intentional element which can define it as a "human act" or "human action." An action without its proper and intrinsic finality is inconceivable. Speaking of human acts, "the end is not altogether extrinsic to the act, because it is related to the act as principle or terminus." It is a characteristic property of an act not only that it proceeds from a principle, but also "ut sit ad aliquid," it "tends toward something."[63] It is therefore not possible to dissolve an exterior act into a collection of material elements, devoid of order or finality, without dissolving it, ultimately, as an *action.* The exterior act, as the intelligible content of a concrete action, as the object of the will and a practical good, is precisely a *coherent and unified proposal* which confers significance on a particular aggregation of bodily movements; it is, therefore, precisely that which explains *why one does what one does.* An exterior act, the object of a choice, can be described as such an object only by including an intentional element in the description. It is, in fact, reason's proper task to order something to an end.[64]

---

nery seems to construct his entire criticism around this imprecision, which is entirely marginal to my argument. The argument is based, rather, on the fact that the will refers to extra-mental realities as goods and ends (for example, to another person's watch) only by means of a judgment of reason, and as a "good understood and ordered by reason."

62. *ST* I-II, q.94 a.1: "lex naturalis est aliquid per rationem constitutum, sicut etiam propositio est quoddam opus rationis."

63. Ibid., q.1 a.3 ad1: "finis non est omnino aliquid extrinsecum ab actu; quia comparatur ad actum ut principium vel terminus; et hoc ipsum est de ratione actus, ut scilicet sit ab aliquo, quantum ad actionem, et ut sit ad aliquid, quantum ad passionem."

64. Ibid., q.90 a.1: "rationis enim est ordinare ad finem, qui est primum principium in agendis." The fact that this is equally valid both at the universal level (the law) and at the level of the specification of individual acts is important for the comprehension of the unity of practical reason.

We again see that, in order to be able to describe an object in this way, we must put ourselves in the perspective of the acting person.

Only thus can the object be grasped as the *end* of a choice, and as *a good to be pursued.* Aquinas confirms this when he says that there are exterior acts that can be *"per se"* ordered to the end of the will, such as "to fight" is *"per se"* ordered to "victory"; and there are other acts that are ordered *per accidens* to an end, as when "to rob" is ordered toward "the giving of alms."[65] "To fight" is a series of exterior movements which can be understood as a human act—and as that particular human act—only in virtue of the end of "victory." Indeed, the term "to fight" itself is incomprehensible—it simply doesn't make sense—without a reference to "victory" as its end. The object-basis of the act of fighting is therefore defined by "why one does what one does," that is, by that which the agent intends by what he is doing exteriorly.[66]

To see this more clearly, let us return to our example of the theft. A theft, in the Thomistic tradition, is defined as "taking another's thing secretly."[67] We have already seen that the object of this act *is not* the "res aliena." Moral objects are *practical* goods, and therefore *actions,* and must be expressed linguistically not with a noun, but with a verb (or with the latter's respective nominization). To be able, therefore, to describe the act in question and to identify its object, we must also indicate a primary and fundamental "why" that which is done, is done. This is equally valid for the definition of the theft: in the expression "covert appropriation (or taking)," such a "why" is implicit.[68] This becomes clear by reflection on the term "appropriation" (or "taking"): in fact, from a "physical" or merely "technical" point of view, the act of theft can be carried out in various ways. With the words "appropriate" or "take," however, we are not designating the act at this physical level. Rather, these words signify a *specific way* of "taking" something from another: to

65. Ibid., q.18 a.7: "pugnare per se ordinatur ad victoriam . . . accipere rem alienam per accidens ordinatur ad dandum eleemosynam." Thomas says here that "pugnare" ("to fight") is "the object of the exterior act," which is per se ordered to the end of the will (victory). This mode of expression is a simplification, because to understand the expression "pugnare," we must already include in it the notion of an end (to win), otherwise this "pugnare" would simply not be a "pugnare." Rather than to speak of an object of the exterior act, it would therefore be better to say "the object qua exterior act" (or "the exterior act as object"), which would be the exterior act conceived by reason, ordered to an end, and as such presented to the will as object.

66. Cf. also the well-known example of G. E. M. Anscombe in her book *Intention,* 2nd ed. (Oxford: Basil Blackwell, 1963), 35, of a person lying on a bed. To know "what he is doing," we must know "why" he is doing what we see him do: e.g., to rest, to do yoga exercises, etc.

67. *ST* II-II, q.66 a.3: "occulta acceptio rei alienae."

68. Cf. Anscombe, *Intention,* 34f.

physically take it *for a particular end,* for example, to steal it from someone. "To steal an amount of money from Paul" is more than "to cause the fact that an amount of money pass physically from Paul to John"; it is to cause this fact with the intention of removing the money from the discretional power of Paul, its owner, so as to make it pass into John's discretional power (a complex structure, objectifiable only by reason; according to St. Thomas's expression, this is precisely a "forma a ratione concepta").

With this in mind, let's imagine two different people who, with an artist's skill, remove the watch attached to Mrs. Jones's wrist. One does it merely to entertain the public, or to play a small joke on Mrs. Jones; the other is a pickpocket and commits the same physical action so as to steal the watch from its owner and use it for his own purposes. The two people have performed two acts which, while identical at the physical or natural level, are different at the moral level. The two acts have a different object. Nevertheless, in both acts the watch is identical and, from the point of view of bodily movements or technique, the external act is also identical. The same relationship also exists between the watch and its wearer, that is, it is her legitimate property; for the agent, therefore, it is a *res aliena.* The intentionality implicit in the bodily movements of the agent, however, is different: for this reason, the movements proceed from *different choices.* A simple external observer of this act—without knowing any of the other circumstances—would not be able to distinguish the two actions from the moral and therefore "objective" point of view, since he does not know the content of the agent's choice; from the point of view of an external observer the two acts would be identical. Only by placing oneself in the perspective of the person who acts does it become possible to understand the difference in the acts, which is in fact a difference in choice: the goods pursued in each of the actions are different, as is the *finis proximus.* In other words: only in the perspective of the acting person does the exterior act, the observable behavior, appear also in its significance as the "object" of a human act.

In order to make this fact even more explicit, we must make our definition of the object "a theft" more precise. The object of a theft is to "secretly take something that is another's property *so as to appropriate it.*" It seems obvious, for St. Thomas, that this is understood, given that by the use of the word *acceptio* he certainly does not intend to refer merely to the aggregate of physical movements which cause a local transfer of a thing from its rightful owner to another person. The expression *acceptio* must therefore be understood as including the intentionality to really appropriate the *res aliena* in question—in such a way that it changes owners, against the will and right of the original owner—and not merely to "take it" in a physical sense.[69]

"To place oneself in the perspective of the acting person" means to understand that to *choose* a type of action or behavior—or rather a series of physical or bodily movements—and therefore to carry out a human act, one must *will* this action as a *good.* To describe the object of a human act, therefore, we must also include in the description the *will* with which it is chosen and executed. And given that the action is an end of the *will,* the intervention of reason is necessary, as Aquinas never tires of repeating. It is reason, and only reason, which presents to the will, and therefore also to the act of choice

69. One can object that my description of the act in question is simply mistaken. According to this objection, we must begin from the physical action "to take something from someone," which would then be morally specified by its object: if the object is a *res aliena,* then the taking is illicit and we are dealing with a theft. For this reason, the objection concludes, the object does not include the exterior act but only the thing to which this action is directed, in this case the *res aliena.* The objection does not seem to me, however, to be conclusive. It presupposes that we can describe the action of "taking something from someone" without making reference to an intentional element, i.e., at a merely physical level. This, however, is not possible. *Physically,* the act of taking is no different than, for example, "to cause, by means of a series of bodily movements, the fact that a watch moves from one place to another" (for example, from Mrs. Jones's arm into Mr. Brown's pocket). In this case, however, even if the watch in question were a *res aliena,* we cannot yet say whether we are dealing with a theft or with a trick; indeed, Mr. Brown could even be a policeman who is confiscating the watch—a *res aliena*—which had been previously stolen from Mrs. Smith and is now being retrieved from Mrs. Jones. If we describe, however, the acting of taking not physically but as a human act, then it is impossible to describe it without including the "thing" that is taken. This would mean that to describe "to take something from someone," we must already include the notion that this "something" be a *res aliena;* otherwise the concept of "taking" would automatically fall back to the physical level of simply "causing, by means of a series of bodily movements, the fact that . . ." etc. In this way, the objection falls into a vicious circle. Even if we add to "take something" the element "to appropriate this thing for oneself" we arrive at the same result: the description of the act of "appropriation" includes even more clearly an intentionality. Without this, the act would be, again, nothing other than to "cause, by means of a series of bodily movements, the fact that . . ."; including the intentionality of "appropriating" the thing in question already includes the fact that the thing is a *res aliena.* One could object that it is possible that we are dealing with something that is not (yet) anyone's property, and therefore we are not dealing with a theft (but an act of "original appropriation"). This is true, but it shows that in that case the term "appropriation" is used twice, each time with a different meaning: in the second case it no longer includes the element of "taking of something from someone against his will," etc. With this we arrive at the result, already recognized, that the existence of a *res aliena* is, certainly, an indispensable condition for a concrete action to be a theft, but it is not a sufficient condition. We cannot conclude: since an act of original appropriation, given that there is no *res aliena,* is not a theft, an act of appropriation is a theft *only* because it includes a series of bodily movements that are directed toward a *res aliena* (which would then be the object that morally specifies this act). This is a non sequitur that obscures the circular character of the argument.

(the *electio*), its object.[70] How, then, could it be possible for reason to present a series of bodily movements as a good to the will—such as "to take a watch from Mrs. Jones's arm in a certain way"—if not under the aspect of an end? Indeed, reason must objectivize these movements under the *ratio formalis*—the formal aspect—of a "why one does what one does," for example, "appropriation," or "to entertain an audience." This good is not already "given" with the external behavior, nor is it in some way "included" in the external behavior; the behavior, considered in itself, could have various meanings. It is precisely for this reason that St. Thomas asserts, as has already been mentioned, that the species of human acts are not, like the species of natural things, constituted by natural forms, but by "forms conceived by reason." From this it follows that to describe the object of a human act as chosen by the will, we must describe it in its *rational structure* (as intelligible content at the practical level, as a proposal of action), which, as is obvious, also includes its primary and basic intentionality, which defines it as the object of an *act*.

These statements can be misunderstood, unfairly, as subjectivism leading to arbitrariness, arguing that this perspective makes the moral value of any action depend on the arbitrariness of the person who acts, directing his intentions in each situation toward what he wants. In my opinion, however, this criticism misses the point, since it ignores the decisive fact that every act of the will necessarily depends on reason. Nothing can be willed unless reason presents it to the will as a good, and the judgments of reason regarding the good can be evaluated precisely according to criteria of reasonableness, that is, objectively and therefore not arbitrarily. "Reason is not an arbitrary measure of the will."[71] "To take and appropriate to oneself a watch that belongs to another" is something *objectively* unjust in the sense that it is precisely reason that grasps the necessary relationship of injustice between "another's property" and "taking it from him against his will" so as to appropriate for oneself the thing in question; it is also reason, and reason only, in its speculative as well as in its practical function, which grasps the link between the thing and its owner, that is, the right of property, the difference between "mine" and "yours." Practical reason comprehends all of this, on the basis of its own principles formulated from the natural law, as contrary to justice—for example, as contrary to the Golden Rule—and therefore as an evil to avoid. For this rea-

70. Cf. the texts cited above: *ST* I-II, q.19 a.1 ad3; a.3 c, and ad1; but also q.13 a.1.
71. McInerny, *Aquinas on Human Action*, 102.

son, the intentionality rooted in practical reason does not "create" the injustice of this or that theft; this intentionality only causes that certain movements of the body would be, in fact, a theft. All of this is knowable only by reason, and it is reason that proposes this ordered aggregate of bodily movements and circumstances to the will, as a good to be pursued.[72]

We see therefore how, *for reason,* there exists a non-arbitrary connection between the material elements of the exterior act, its objective moral species as a "theft," and its consequent valuation as "unjust." Equally, there exists, *again for reason,* a non-arbitrary connection between an act of sexual copulation and it specification as good or evil, as, for example, "an act of infidelity" or "an act of conjugal love." This connection is understood by reason on the basis of its natural principles—the natural law—according to which reason orders the act proper to the sexual inclination and its natural end to its morally just end, that is, according to the circumstances that are significant for reason, such as, for example, whether the act is with one's own wife or not.[73]

A possible objection is that the inclusion of a prior—and constitutive for the object—intentionality in the notion of the object of a human act ultimately means to render irrelevant, for the object's description, whatever does not proceed from this intentionality, and is rather "pre-configured" by factors independent of the actor, such as the natural structures and properties of the "things" or realities around which the action is performed. Kevin Flannery, for example, has criticized my assertion that "to swallow X" (where X is, for example, a morphine capsule) is not, as such, a practical good and therefore cannot be understood as the object of an act, precisely because a morphine capsule as such cannot be a good for the will, and therefore cannot even be chosen. To choose "to swallow X," I wrote, it is necessary that there exist a primary and fundamental "why" one does this, as for example "to take a means for alleviating pain."[74] With this, objects Flannery (who seems to want to sustain that it is precisely "to swallow X," as such, that is the object of the act "to swallow X so as to alleviate pain"), the practical sphere would be isolated from the very sphere to which we apply descriptions such as "to swallow X," that is, from the physical sphere, from the nature of things.[75] Which is to say, the con-

72. The first principle of the natural law expresses this structure of the "bonum faciendum et prosequendum"; this is found also at the level of the concrete act, which is always presented to the will as "bonum faciendum et prosequendum"; cf. *ST* I-II, q.94 a.2.

73. Cf. *De Malo,* 2, 4.

74. Cf. Rhonheimer, *Die Perspektive der Moral,* 101.

75. Flannery, review of *Die Perspektive der Moral,* 591.

nection would be lost between the natural properties of morphine (its narcotic effects) and its being a good chosen to the end of alleviating pain.

This criticism, as well, seems to me to express a difficulty that results from failing to notice the constitutive role of reason in the constitution of the moral object, and therefore from a different (or entirely lacking?) anthropology of action. With the assertion, that is, that "to swallow X" is not yet the description of an object of a human act, but that this object is "to swallow X so as to alleviate pain," we in no way separate the realm of praxis from the realm to which we apply the description "to swallow X"—that is, the connection is not severed between the natural properties of the morphine (its narcotic effect) and its being a good chosen for the end of alleviating pain—and this for the simple fact that to be able to choose "to swallow X so as to alleviate pain," reason must understand the link between "X" and "alleviate pain"; it must know that "X," because of its specific (narcotic) effect, is a preparation suitable for alleviating pain. Knowing this identical information, however, it is also possible that one choose "to swallow X" to get high on drugs! This latter act would be different *on the basis of its object,* even though the external act of "to swallow X," as well as the "X" itself, are identical in both cases. This, in my view, proves that "to swallow X" is not the object in the moral sense, but the action considered at a merely physical level, and therefore not as a practical good, that is, not as an object of the will.[76]

At this point, one could nevertheless object that the above example of the taking of the watch is poorly chosen, since the external behavior (the removal of the watch from Mrs. Jones's wrist) can in fact be understood as the object of an act that is morally *indifferent,* which becomes evil only through the successive intention of the unjust appropriation; because of this, according to the objection, my argumentation becomes pointless. This objection seems unconvincing to me, however, given that, as has already been shown, the behavior described in our example can be described as a human act, that is, as an act chosen and voluntarily carried out, if and only if we include a specific intentionality in the description. This makes clear that such an intentionality is not an *ulterior* or *subsequent* intention by which an act, in itself already morally defined on the basis of its proper object, becomes ordered as a

76. This unfolds in what is called a "practical syllogism," in which, by means of theoretical judgments (assertions of facts) one infers, from a higher-level practical judgment, a successive, more-concrete practical judgment, to the point of arriving at the choice of an action, and to the action itself. We will speak of this briefly at the end of this study.

means, but rather it is this basic intentionality that defines the act, precisely, as a *human* act (= an act proceeding from a deliberate will). A different case, and a case of an act which is truly *indifferent "ex obiecto,"* chosen as a means in view of an ulterior end, would be that of one who chooses to "take a walk *with the intention* of preserving his health." "To take a walk" is an act, definable as a human act, which can be considered to be morally indifferent: it is a type of bodily movement or bodily behavior—"walking"—chosen in view of what we typically call a "walk," for example, "to go for a walk"; the term "a walk" itself means: "an act which is the effect of walking without hurry and without fixing a particular destination in advance, so as to move a bit, to enjoy oneself. . . ."[77] Here also the basic intentional element is not lacking in the description of the act and of its objective significance. "To take a walk" is more than simply (physically) "to walk": it is a specific type of "walking," which as intelligible content can be chosen by the will as a good and an end. We can distinguish "to take a walk" from other types of human acts which, from the point of view of the bodily movements involved, are exactly the same, but which are chosen for a different intrinsic end: for example, from the action "to walk to work." One who performs this latter action does not "take a walk with the intention of going to work," for the simple reason that precisely what he does *not* do is "take a walk." Rather, he has chosen, and carries out, a different action: he takes a *trip* (he "walks to work"). "To take a trip" and "to take a walk" are two human acts that are indifferent, but distinguished by their respective objectives; their intelligible content, capable of being chosen by the will, is different. What cannot be done, however, is to describe the external behavior alone—the bodily "to walk"—as a human act, without making reference to an intentionality of the type "take a walk," "take a trip," or something else of this nature (e.g., "make a pilgrimage"). This demonstrates that these bodily movements are not yet the object of a human act, but only the physical elements and requirements of an act, not yet rationally ordered to an end and for this reason not yet morally qualifiable. The same can be said about "to raise an arm,"[78] which is an act of greeting, or one indi-

77. "Atto, effetto di camminare, senza affrettarsi e senza prefiggersi una meta particolare, per fare un po' di moto, svagarsi" (Nicola Zingarelli, *Vocabolario della Lingua Italiana,* 11th ed. [Bologna: Zanichelli, 1988], s.v. "passeggio," 1345). In Italian the word "camminare" indicates the physical act of "walking," while "passeggiare" means "to take a walk."

78. I have used this example, taken from Wittgenstein's "Philosophische Untersuchungen," to illustrate the notion of "intentional basic action," in my judgment very important in *Die Perspektive der Moral,* 96ff.

cating departure, but never simply "to raise an arm." This latter, as such, cannot be chosen. There would not be an intentional basic-action, and therefore no action at all. Nor can it be chosen only so as to falsify the theory of action just proposed, because in that case "to raise an arm" would again be something more than simply "to raise an arm": it would be "to raise an arm so as to demonstrate that my affirmation is in error."

Something similar is valid also for a sexual act: the simple natural end of sexual copulation between a man and a woman—procreation—is not the object that provides such an act with its primary and fundamental *moral* characteristic. I do not want to say here that the moral object of a sexual act has no relation to its natural end. But to grasp the moral object of the sexual union between man and woman, something more is necessary, something that only reason can conceive as a good, and propose to the will as an end to be pursued. "Marriage" is not a "natural" fact or finality, in the sense of being preexistent independently of the ordering act of human reason and of subsequent acts of the will. The objective significance of human sexuality is understood only in the context of the auto-experience of the subject as a being constituted in a unity of body and spirit, of the experience of the other not merely as a body or a "sexual partner," but as a person, "equal to me," and of the sexual act itself as a relationship of love between two *persons.*

It is equally true, however, that between the act "to play a trick" and "to remove another's watch from the arm to which it is attached," or between "to take a walk" and "to walk," there is a different relationship than between "the marriage act" and "the natural end of sexuality." We will speak of this shortly. The only thing I want to point out here is that, just as with "to play a trick," "the marriage act," in its specific configuration (as an act of love and special friendship, of affective union between two persons, open to the transmission of life), is not simply an object "given" by nature, but something in whose configuration also enters the intentionality of the acting person. As an act of love and fidelity between two persons—as an act of persons—sexual union presupposes an intentionality on the part of the persons who perform this act. This intentionality, certainly, assumes the natural finality of the sexual act, but it also transforms, regulates and orders it, in accordance with the requirements of reason, to the end of love between persons and of the procreation of human life. Only within the order of reason can the circumstance that the agents either are, or are not, married—that is, mutually bound in an indissoluble union—present itself as a decisive circumstance for distinguishing, on the basis of their object, the marriage act from an act of fornication. The fact of not being married becomes, therefore, a "principal condition of the object, . . . opposed to reason."[79] Considered, on the other hand, outside of the order of reason, the sexual act cannot be morally qualified as "good" or "evil," even if it fulfills its natural finality of being the cause of the conception of human life.[80]

It would, of course, be equally possible to describe the action of "taking the watch" without making reference to a "why" or to a particular intention of the agent. But in this case, one would be describing this action not as a human act, deliberately chosen and morally qualifiable, but only an event or a physical process. In this case, therefore, the act would not be described from "the perspective of the acting person," and therefore as an act or behavior that is *chosen,* the "proximate end" of an act of the will, informed by reason, which orders the external behavior to this end, presenting it as a (practical) good to the will. If we remain at the merely physical level, we would not be able to understand why *Veritatis Splendor* affirms, in accordance with the entire Thomistic tradition, that the "morality of the act depends primarily and fundamentally" on such an object. We observe, moreover, that *VS* does not say merely that the morality depends on the "object," but that it depends *"on the object rationally chosen by the deliberate will."* With this expression, everything contained in this passage of the encyclical is synthesized at the outset: such an object is the intelligible content of a concrete type of action that is presented by reason to the will as a good, as the proximate end of the will's elective act, that is, of the choice of a concrete action.

The Intentional Constitution of the Object: The "Ethical Context" and the Case of Lying

If we compare no. 78 of *Veritatis Splendor* with the exposition of the *Catechism of the Catholic Church* (CCC), published a year prior to *VS,* on the theme of the "sources of morality,"[81] it is clear that the catechism takes a somewhat different approach on the matter, one based more in the classical tradition of the manuals, with a clear opposition between "objective" and

79. *ST* I-II, q.18 a.10: "principalis conditio obiecti rationi repugnans."

80. Ibid., a.5 ad3.

81. Editor's note: The English edition, originally published in 1994, reflects the same characteristics discussed by the author: *Catechism of the Catholic Church* (hereafter CCC) (Vatican City: Libreria Editrice Vaticana, 1994), no. 1750ff.

"subjective." Compared with the CCC's approach, that of *Veritatis Splendor* seems innovative in various respects, even if there is not yet consensus on the exact meaning and importance of the encyclical's approach.

"The chosen object" of an action is defined by the catechism as "a good toward which the will deliberately directs itself. It is the matter of a human act."[82] To speak, in the Thomistic tradition, of the object as the "matter" of a human act is certainly correct in the sense that the object is called, precisely, "materia circa quam." Nevertheless, we must not forget (as we have seen) that for Aquinas this *materia circa quam* has in a certain sense the character of a form, that is, inasmuch as it confers on the act its species.[83] Human acts, however, receive their species from their end.[84] For this reason Thomas says that the *materia circa quam*—which is the object as exterior act—as it is considered formally, that is, as the object of an interior act of the will (which the act of choice is), possesses the character of an end, *and as such gives the act its species.*[85] It follows that for Thomas the "materia circa quam" is the end and the form of the act.

For precisely this reason, every object is also "matter," in the same sense in which all that is capable of being ulteriorly determined by a form is also "matter." And the object, which confers on the act its first moral species, is susceptible of being informed by successive ends to which this act is ordered by the will, that is, by an "intention" in the strict sense (as distinct from the choice [*electio*] of the means to an end). The object is not, however, "matter" in the sense of a material element of an act which, considered in itself, would as yet be lacking any finalization whatsoever on the part of the subject. This, as we have seen, is not possible, given that the object of the act is the object of an act of the will—the act of choice—and therefore, as voluntary, depends on a previous *ordinatio* on the part of the practical reason of the acting subject: it includes the intelligible content of the constitutive voluntariness of this act.[86]

82. Ibid., no. 1751.

83. *ST* I-II, q.18 a.2 ad2: "habet quodammodo rationem formae, inquantum dat speciem."

84. Ibid., a.6.

85. Cf. yet again *ST* I-II, q.72 a.3 ad2: "obiecta, secundum quod comparantur ad actus exteriores, habent rationem materiae circa quam; sed secundum quod comparantur ad actum interiorem voluntatis, habent rationem finium; et ex hoc habent quod dant speciem actui"; cf. also *De Malo*, 2, 4 ad9: "Finis proximus actus idem est quod obiectum, et ab hoc [actus] recipit speciem"; *ST* I-II, q.73 a.3 ad1: "obiectum, etsi sit materia circa quam terminatur actus, habet tamen rationem finis, secundum quod intentio agentis fertur in ipsum. . . . Forma autem actus moralis dependet ex fine."

86. E. Colom and A. Rodríguez Luño, *Scelti in Cristo per essere santi*, 127.

The distinction between "object" on the one hand and "end" on the other can therefore cause misunderstanding, because the object is the "finis proximus" of the act of choice *(electio),* and the "end" to which the intention tends is the "object" of the act of intention *(intentio).* Nor can it be said that, unlike the end followed by the intention, the object is something that *does not* proceed from the acting person.

In particular, the following statement of the CCC could cause confusion: "In contrast to the object, the intention resides in the acting subject."[87] With this statement, what is valid generally for human action at all levels is attributed to the intention alone. In our example, the difference between the two objects "a trick" and "a theft" is constituted by what the CCC seems to attribute exclusively to the intention: by a different "movement of the will," a different "[orientation to] the good anticipated from the action undertaken."[88] But it is precisely *this*—that is, a particular movement of the will and an intentional orientation toward a good—that we find also at the level of the object of the action itself, and without which we cannot describe this object. Otherwise, we would not be dealing with a human act, morally qualifiable on the basis of its object.

In discussing intrinsically evil acts, however, the *Catechism of the Catholic Church* itself confirms the approach suggested by *Veritatis Splendor* and the interpretation which we have proposed here: to describe, at the moral level, the object of some types of actions which are categorized as morally evil, neither can the CCC do without a reference to an intentional element, constitutive for the object of these actions.

The CCC defines the act of contraception, for example, using the words of the encyclical *Humanae Vitae,* as any "action which, whether in anticipation of the conjugal act, or in its accomplishment, or in the development of its natural consequences, *proposes, whether as an end or as a means,* to render procreation impossible."[89] Masturbation is defined as "the deliberate stimulation of the genital organs *in order to derive sexual pleasure.*"[90] For the description of the act of lying, also traditionally considered to be an intrinsically evil act, the CCC refers to St. Augustine's "De mendacio": "A lie consists in

87. CCC, no. 1752.

88. Ibid.

89. Ibid., no. 2370: "actus qui . . . id tamquam finem obtinendum aut viam adhibendam intendat, *ut procreatio impediatur*" (emphasis added).

90. Ibid., no. 2352: "voluntarium organorum genitalium excitationem, *ad obtinendam ex ea veneream voluptatem*" (emphasis added).

speaking a falsehood *with the intention of deceiving*."[91] The following number adds: "To lie is to speak or act against the truth in order *to lead someone into error*."[92]

It is not possible here to analyze the objects of these types of behavior.[93] It will be useful, however, to further specify some aspects of lying, which will also be important for an exegesis of St. Thomas. It is common opinion that on this point Aquinas differs notably from St. Augustine's position. The difference is, however, not as great as is customarily claimed. For St. Thomas, as well, to tell a lie includes not only to say what is false, but also an *intentio voluntatis* to say what is false, that is, the *voluntas falsi enuntiandi*, the "will to say what is false," which includes the intention to say something that is contrary to what one has in mind.

Thomas expressly says that the act of "manifesting the truth" is an act of reason, which joins a sign to something signified.[94] Even animals, which do not possess reason, manifest something signified by means of signs, but these "do not intend to manifest anything."[95] As the manifestation of the truth is a moral act, Thomas continues, it must be voluntary and depend on an intention of the will.[96] For this reason, he says, the intention of a disordered will can refer either to the declaration of the untruth itself, or to the effect of

91. Ibid., no. 2482: "[enuntiatio falsa] *cum voluntate ad fallendum* prolata" (emphasis added).

92. Ibid., no. 2483: "Mentiri est contra veritatem loqui vel agere *ad inducendum in errorem*" (emphasis added).

93. Concerning contraception, see my analysis in "Contraception, Sexual Behavior, and Natural Law: Philosophical Foundation of the Norm of *Humanae Vitae*," in *Humanae Vitae*, 20 anni dopo. Atti del II Congresso Internazionale di Teologia Morale Roma (Milan: ARES, 1989), 73–113; also published in *The Linacre Quarterly* 56, no. 2 (1989): 20–57; in an expanded version in German as *Sexualität und Verantwortung. Empfängnisverhütung als ethisches Problem*, IMABE Studie Nr. 3 (Vienna: Verlag IMABE/Institut für medizinische Anthropologie und Bioethik, 1995); in Italian in *Sessualità e responsabilità: la contraccezione come problema etico*, in Rhonheimer, *Etica della procreazione. Contraccezione—Fecondazione artificiale—Aborto* (Milan: Edizioni PUL-Mursia, 2000), 15–125; Spanish edition *Ética de la procreación* (Madrid: Rialp, 2004), 27–13. See also my *Contraccezione, mentalità contraccettiva e cultura dell'aborto: valutazioni e connessioni*, in R. Lucas Lucas, ed., *Commento interdisciplinare alla «Evangelium vitae»*, Pontifical Academy for Life, Italian edition ed. E. Sgreccia and R. Lucas Lucas (Vatican City: Libreria Editrice Vaticana, 1997), 435–52.

94. *ST* II-II, q.110 a.1: "est rationis actus conferentis signum ad signatum."

95. Ibid.: "non tamen manifestionem intendunt."

96. Ibid.: "Inquantum tamen huiusmodi manifestatio sive enuntiatio est actus moralis, oportet quod sit voluntarius et ex intentione voluntatis dependens." Although St. Thomas says in the following sentence that the object of the *manifestatio* or *enuntiatio* is "the true or the false," he speaks there of the power moved by the will, and not of the object of the act *qua* a human act. This latter object is the object of the "voluntas falsi enuntiandi," i.e., a "collatio" of a *signum* to a *significatum*, which is properly an act of reason and includes a corresponding intentional structure, without which it could not be an object for the will that chooses this act.

deceiving someone;[97] this second *intentio,* the *intentio fallendi,* according to Thomas, is not part of the *ratio mendacii,* but only of its perfection, which is the effect of deceiving. But even the object of the *ratio mendacii* in the proper sense includes an *intentio voluntatis,* that is, that of declaring what is false. With this, Thomas obviously means that lying is lying merely by the will to say what is false, without there being necessarily an explicit intention to deceive someone. What, however, causes difficulties in Thomas's position—and which seems to make St. Augustine's definition preferable—is to understand how someone could will to lie without also willing to deceive the person to whom one lies. Perhaps St. Thomas would not claim that this is possible; he says only that formally, that is, essentially, lying must be defined without this second intention, and that the first suffices. It seems more logical, however, to include the *intentio fallendi* in the definition of lying or, said otherwise, to consider the will to say what is false and that of deceiving as a single *intentio voluntatis,* constitutive for an act to be a lie according to its object.

In any case, when the CCC says in the following no. 2485 that "by its very nature, lying is to be condemned," which is to say it is *per se* evil and not only due to circumstances or ulterior motivations, this refers to a "nature" of the object which includes a basic intentionality, whether it be to will to deceive (Augustine), or at least the will to intentionally say what is false (Thomas).[98]

The most important point, however, and one that is often ignored, seems to me to be that for St. Thomas, lying by its nature is not only contrary to the nature of linguistic acts and to the truth, but it is also a *violation of justice.* To say what is false so as to mislead is *unjust,* because it violates another's right, that is, that of living in community with one's fellow men on the basis of a mutual trust. By their nature, linguistic acts are communicative acts, the object of the virtue of truthfulness.

97. Ibid.: "Intentio vero voluntatis inordinatae potest ad duo ferri: quorum unum est ut falsum enuntietur; aliud quidam est effectus proprius falsae enuntiationis, ut scilicet aliquis fallatur."

98. It is important to specify "to *intentionally* say what is false," since simply "to say what is false" (a mere *falsiloquium*) would not be a lie even for St. Thomas (even if the "falsiloquium" were voluntary, as in the case in which someone voluntarily says something false, thinking however that it is true: he says what is false, but he does not say it *intentionally*). Also if *ST* II-II, q.110 a.1 says that the "false" and the "true" are *the object* of linguistic acts, then this object is not yet the object that specifies morally. This latter occurs only when "to say what is false" becomes an object of the will. Thomas calls this the "falsitas formalis." We can describe it as "the will to manifest with linguistic acts something that is contrary to what one has in mind." Such a "will to say a falsehood" is necessarily the will to carry out a linguistic act (an exterior act in the material, physical sense) *with the intention to* manifest something that is contrary to what one has in mind. This is already very close to the Augustinian "intentio fallendi," which shows that the differences, in the end, are practically insignificant.

According to Aquinas, the duty to manifest the truth with one's linguistic acts derives from the fact that "it would be impossible for men to live together, unless they believed one another, as declaring the truth one to another."[99] This speaks of a "moral duty" which is based on the fact that human honesty requires that one manifest the truth to others in his use of language,[100] that is, that he not abuse the proper nature of language which consists in the manifestation, by means of words, what one has in mind. This is the virtue of truthfulness, which is part of justice; we can call it "communicative justice."

Contrary to an exegesis that seems to me to concentrate too unilaterally on article 3 of I-II, 110, I believe that for St. Thomas lying is evil, not because it is contrary to the nature of language, but because it is opposed to the virtue of truthfulness, to communicative justice.[101] The fact that words, as Thomas affirms, are by nature signs of what one has in mind is not the reason for which lying is *evil*, but that for which *every* lie is evil.[102] But it is also clear that for Thomas "to say what is false"—a *falsiloquium*—can be a lie (in the moral sense) only inasmuch as it is opposed to the virtue of truthfulness. "Formal untruthfulness" or "the will to tell a falsehood," in which according to Thomas lying consists, is evil precisely because such a will is opposed to the virtue relative to *veritas:* truthfulness.[103] The finality of the virtue of truthfulness constitutes, therefore, the "ethical context" in relation to which lying acquires its objective identity as a particular type of linguistic behavior and, therefore, also its specification as a morally evil act. One who "lies," however,

99. *ST* II-II, q.109 a.3 ad1: "Non autem possent homines ad invicem convivere nisi sibi invicem crederent, tanquam sibi invicem veritatem manifestantibus."

100. Ibid., 3c.: "debitum morale, inquantum scilicet ex honestate unus homo alteri debet veritatis manifestationem."

101. Ibid., q.110 a.1; the virtue of truthfulness is treated in the preceding question, q.109.

102. Ibid., a.3: "malum ex genere."

103. For this reason, article 1 of *ST* II-II, q.110, where lying is defined as "voluntas falsum enuntiandi," bears the title: "Utrum mendacium semper opponatur veritati." This article establishes, therefore, the reason for which lying is a morally evil act. *ST* I-II, q.110 a.3, on the other hand, where Thomas speaks of lying as being contrary to the "nature of language," is entitled: "Utrum omne mendacium sit peccatum." This latter article, therefore, does not deal with the question of what a lie is, and why it is morally evil, but rather why lying is *intrinsically,* always, and without exception, evil: it is the "nature of language" itself—the natural and necessary relationship between *vox* and *signum*—which makes every act of "saying what is false," performed with the will to say what is false, to be a lie, contrary to the virtue of truthfulness, and hence evil. A movement of the hand or an inclination of the head *can* also, according to the situation, be lies, but they are not always, because there is no natural link between a movement of the hand (or an inclination of the head) and that being a sign of a specific mental content. Given that words are *naturally* signs of what one has in mind, to proffer words contrary to what one has in mind is an "actus cadens super indebitam materiam" (ibid.), an act whose matter is (in this case: by nature) inappropriate.

in the context of a scientific experiment so as to test a lie detector, or during a party game in which lying figures as part of the game, clearly does not sin, even if he does do something contrary to the nature of language!

Precisely for this reason the following two cases are completely different: (1) those who told representatives of the Gestapo, searching for Jews so as to deport them, that there were no Jews in the house, and (2) a person, for example, a functionary, a minister, a professor, or a father, who considers that in a particular situation their questioner does not have the right to know what he asks (or, which would be equivalent, that they themselves do not have the right to reveal that which the questioner wants to know) and who therefore thinks that he can licitly mislead his questioner with false answers or by responding "I don't know."[104] In this second case, that is, in the context of normal life, a "communicative community" exists between the people involved in which language fulfills its communicative function, and in which, given a "normal" situation or context, there exists a right that words spoken by one's neighbor be expressions of truth, with a corresponding duty on the part of the neighbor. This is valid also for the case in which someone could, by lying, gain a great advantage or avoid a great disadvantage: a lie remains a lie, even if put forth with good intention. In the first case, on the other hand, a situation of war and aggression exists in which the social significance of linguistic acts is altered; to say what is false becomes an act of self-defense—and of the defense of others—not because "in this case" it is so, but because *objectively* there no longer exists between these persons a communicative community which could be damaged. For this same reason, neither can communicative justice be damaged in such a case. And this latter is the reason why saying what is false, abusing language, is morally evil and is called "lying."

What has been said so far can be summarized in the following two points. First, we cannot understand and define the object of a human act without including in this definition an intentional element that expresses the "why" one does what one (externally) does. Without such a "why" (a basic intentionality which is configured by reason) we would be left with only the material elements of the action, not yet ordered by reason, and therefore incapable of being the "form" of an act of the will and of conferring on it, as an end, its

104. Kevin Flannery arrives at the opposite result—according to my moral intuition in a way that is inadmissible—in his article "The Multifarious Moral Object of Thomas Aquinas," *The Thomist* 67, no. 1 (2003): 95–118: "Thus, all lies are sins, even the notorious lie told to the Nazis who come to the door asking whether there are Jews inside" (109). Cf. also Flannery's critique of my position in his review (cited above) of my book *Die Perspektive der Moral.*

moral species. This basic intentionality which comprises part of the object is, not to forget, Thomistically speaking its "formal" part; as such it is the expression of a good, the "finis proximus" pursued in the action.[105]

Second, I want to accentuate the fact that such a basic intentionality can be formulated and acquire its moral significance only in relation to what we can call the "ethical context." Outside of the context of a proposal to have sexual relations with someone and, for this reason, to want to impede the possible procreative consequences of the act, the ingestion of a contraception would not be, in a moral sense, an act of contraception.[106] It would be, for example, an act of self-defense, if done to prevent the procreative effects of a foreseeable rape; or a therapeutic act, in the case of a woman who intends by doing so to regulate her rhythm; or it could be a measure taken by a woman athlete who wants to impede menstruation during the Olympics. If the ethical context changes, so does the basic intentionality, as well as the object of the act—even if, considered physically, the act is the same in each case. Even lying, as an act contrary to justice, can be defined only in relation to the ethical context of the "communicative community" and therefore as contrary to communicative justice.[107]

105. For this reason it seems strange to me that Jean Porter would assert: "In some cases, the agent's aim forms an essential component which must be taken into account, in order to determine the object of the action" ("The Moral Act in Veritatis Splendor and in Aquinas's Summa Theologiae: A Comparative Analysis," in Michael E. Allsopp and John J. O'Keefe, ed., *Veritatis Splendor: American Responses* [Kansas City: Sheed & Ward, 1995], 288). I do not see why this would be true only in "some cases." Porter maintains this because she thinks that one who commits an act of adultery *does not want to commit an adultery, but to enjoy himself* ("what he wants is not to commit adultery, but to have a good time"), even if, in fact, he commits adultery (cf. ibid.). For Porter, this would be the example of an external action whose object could be determined without reference to what the agent wills. This is false, however: one who (voluntarily) commits an adultery knows that it is in fact an adultery he is committing, *and therefore also wills to commit it,* i.e., he *wills*—intends—"to unite sexually with a woman who is married to another" (even if, obviously, he does not do it "to commit an adultery"). Without the basic intentionality "to will to unite oneself sexually with a woman," the bodily movements, commanded by the will and constitutive of sexual union between a man and a woman, could not be understood as a human act. The fact that the woman is the wife of another is not the object, but a *circumstance,* relevant, however, for the constitution of the object, and therefore to be included in its description. It is, in this case, a "principalis conditio obiecti rationi repugnans" (*ST* I-II, q.18 a.10): It makes the action of uniting sexually with this woman to be morally evil (because it is unjust), and that the action be what is called an "adultery."

106. Cf. M. Rhonheimer, "Minaccia di stupro e prevenzione: un'eccezione?" *La Scuola Cattolica* 123 (1995): 75–90 (reprinted in Rhonheimer, *Etica della procreazione,* 110–25).

107. The notion of "ethical context" does not lead to subjectivism or arbitrarity, at least no more than does the notion itself of the "moral object" of an act. The latter is not simply a "given object," and to know whether it is good or evil, virtuous or opposed to moral virtue, is not always easy, causing debates and at times diverging conclusions; nevertheless, all else aside, the

Objective Evil and Intrinsic Evil: "Intrinsically Evil" Acts

Given that the object of a human act cannot be understood without the inclusion both of a primary and fundamental intentionality and of reference to its specific ethical context, the qualification of an act as "intrinsically evil" also presupposes that it be understood precisely as an intentional act, defined with reference to a specific ethical context. Such ethical contexts are conceivable only by reason, which gives them their specific moral configuration. This "ethical context" is always that of a particular virtue. In the case of lying, the virtue is justice; with contraception and masturbation, chastity. The moral virtues, nonetheless, are not defined without reference to anthropological truth, that is, to human nature, which is made known and imposes itself as a moral rule by means of *reason,* beginning with the natural law, which is the *ordinatio rationis* at the universal level and at the level of principles.

Certainly, in a particular sense of the term "intrinsically," every evil act is *intrinsically* evil, given that it is not evil because it is prohibited, but prohibited because it is evil, that is, precisely on the basis of its intrinsic and specific "moral nature." This meaning of the term "intrinsically evil" is trivial, however, and pleonastic in the context of ethical theory. *Veritatis Splendor*, rather, clarifies the significance of this expression, saying in no. 80 that *intrinsically* evil acts are evil "always and *per se,* in other words, on account of their very object, and quite apart from the ulterior intentions of the one acting and the circumstances." What does this mean?

The notion of "intrinsically evil act" does *not* include, according to the citation from *VS,* the idea that, independent of the person who acts, there would be something evil "*in* the action," considered as a natural datum by itself, and independent of any intentionality on the part of the subject who acts. Rather, according to the encyclical, an act that is "intrinsically evil" is simply an act that is evil when considered *independently of ulterior intentions.* It seems therefore that according to *VS* "intrinsically evil" is equivalent to "evil *ex obiecto*"; what would not be considered "intrinsically" evil would be an action that is evil only because of successive intentions (and perhaps circum-

identification of the object *always* includes a rational valuation. In the same way, an "ethical context" is also an *objective,* non-arbitrary datum, but not in the sense of something given naturally (like, e.g., meteorological facts concerning today's weather), but as something to be ascertained rationally on the basis of the ends of the individual virtues (justice, temperance, courage, etc.), whose rule are the first principles of practical reason, known naturally, which are also called the "natural law."

stances) for which it is done, that is, actions which by their object are good or indifferent, but are made evil by the evil intention with which they are chosen (such as "to give alms with the intention of committing adultery").

For every human action, as *VS* no. 80 affirms, the possibility of distinguishing, in each case, an object *(finis proximus)* from ulterior ends for which this object is chosen is fundamental; and, consequently, to be able to morally qualify this object in a way independent from the *whole* that is the action and all the ulterior intentions. Such a possibility is the basis for refuting every type of "teleological ethics" (e.g., consequentialism or proportionalism), which claims that this distinction is not possible since, according to such an ethics, we can know what a person objectively does only if we take into consideration all ulterior intentions referred to non-moral goods and the consequences that foreseeably derive from the action.[108]

Nevertheless, to read *VS* in this way, that is, in the sense that every act that is "evil on the basis of its object" would also be an "intrinsically evil" act, also seems unsatisfying, because the term "intrinsically evil act" commonly designates something more than simply "evil on the basis of its object." With the words of the CCC cited in no. 78 of *VS*, "intrinsically evil" means that "there are certain specific kinds of behavior that are always wrong to choose, because choosing them involves a disorder of the will, that is, a moral evil." But, to return to our example, the series of bodily movements which cause the watch to disappear from Mrs. Jones's wrist are not a behavior the choice of which is always wrong, because that behavior can also be chosen to play an innocent trick, and therefore as an act that is good or at least indifferent. When, however, this choice is wrong, that is, when it is in fact a theft, then the choice is evil *ex obiecto.* It seems, therefore, that if the argumentation until now put forth is universally valid and applicable to all human acts, then one must deny the existence of certain types of behavior "that it is always wrong to choose," and reduce the notion of "intrinsically evil" to "evil *ex obiecto.*"

This would be a rather awkward conclusion, because the affirmation of the CCC, repeated by *VS*, that "there are certain specific kinds of behavior that are always wrong to choose, because choosing them involves a disorder of the will, that is, a moral evil" seems to indicate the contrary, that is, that the malice of the "intrinsically evil" act is found, not at the level of the choice of a behavior, but rather in the behavior itself that is chosen: *VS* seems to affirm

108. Cf. chapter 4 of this book, or M. Rhonheimer, "Intentional Actions and the Meaning of Object."

that it is precisely this or that type of *external behavior* which causes the disorder in the will. It would be, therefore, precisely the behavior as such, in its pure "physical materiality," which is the cause of the moral evil of the choice of this behavior and, therefore, the object that morally specifies the act.

It is obvious that such an interpretation would contradict not only the entire analysis proposed so far in these pages, but also the text itself of *VS*, which immediately prior had affirmed that the object of an act "is the proximate end of a deliberate choice, which determines the act of willing on the part of the acting person." We must therefore hold, with *VS*, that that which is "always wrong" are not particular kinds of *behavior*, considered in their physical materiality, but particular kinds of *choices of such behaviors*. Even the object of an intrinsically evil act can only be understood "putting oneself in the perspective of the acting person"; it is therefore the object of a choice, and, therefore, the object of a judgment of reason.[109]

The contrary affirmation holds that specific exterior behaviors *as such*, in their "physical materiality" or "natural structure"—for example, bodily movements, including insofar as they produce specific effects, such as "to kill a human being," "to copulate with a human being of the opposite sex," "to utter certain words" ("to speak"), "to walk," "to detach a watch from a wrist," etc.—can *immediately* and as these types of behavior materially considered, be morally wrong and, consequently, are capable of negatively specifying an act of the will, rendering it disordered and evil. We must emphasize here that such a claim would violate one of the basic principles of a Thomistic theory of action. Indeed, it would imply the necessity of formulating a thesis directly contrary to what St. Thomas, as has been shown above, explicitly teaches: that it is always reason which presents to the will its object.[110] An "external behavior," that is, an aggregate of "material" elements such as movements of the body, processes, effects caused by these, etc., cannot influence the will directly; they are not an "object" for the will, except through the mediation of a judgment of reason, as a *bonum apprehensum et ordinatum per rationem*.[111] The material elements of any behavior can be willed as a good and as

109. This is precisely what John Finnis states, with clarity and proficiency, in his study *Moral Absolutes: Tradition, Revision and Truth* (Washington, D.C.: The Catholic University of America Press, 1991), 67ff. What seems to be lacking in Finnis's analysis is an emphasis on the constitutive role of reason in the formation of the object (and therefore of the intentional content of a choice).

110. *ST* I-II, q.19 a.1 ad3; ibid., a.3 ad1 (cf. the text cited in nn. 21 and 19).

111. Ibid., q.20 a.1 ad1 (cf. the text cited in n. 38).

an end only in the measure in which they are presented to the will as a totality ordered by reason,[112] as a *bonum faciendum et prosequendum.*[113] It seems, therefore, that we find ourselves back at the preceding argument. In a certain sense, this is true, but we return to this argument only so as to be able to take a further step forward.

The conclusion is inevitable, in fact, that the "intrinsic evil" we are speaking of is none other than a case of "evil *ex obiecto,*" and that essentially it is precisely this. If this were not the case, we would destroy the fundamental determination of human action on the part of reason, and with that the very voluntariness and freedom of action, given that every voluntary act is specified by its object, and only by its object.[114] This notwithstanding, a difference remains between the act of the theft of a watch or a trick (with the same watch)—and of any theft, for that matter—on the one hand, and a homicide, a lie, or an adultery on the other. This difference, intuitively grasped by all, is that in the case of the watch we are faced with a collection of elements that are in a certain sense accidental, artificial, and man-made (e.g., the watch itself is an artifact; wearing it on the wrist is, though very practical, a human invention; and the relationship of property between Mrs. Jones and the watch is circumstantial and proceeds from the will, e.g., that of Mr. Jones who had bought the watch and given it to his wife—it is not, therefore, a natural and intrinsic characteristic of either the watch or of Mrs. Jones). In the case of lying or of contraception, on the other hand, we are dealing with "material elements" that are more "substantial" and intrinsically linked to the nature of the agent, in the sense that they are less disposable or accidental. They have to do with the "nature of man," the nature of human sexuality, that of human language, and with natural inclinations that spring from the very being of the human person; we are also dealing with the essence of social relationships among people, these in a certain sense also being "natural," that is, not the mere fruit of invention which, while perhaps useful, are more or less arbitrary. We are entering here the realm of specific natural conditionings of human identity, such as life and self-preservation, sexuality and its procreative function, language and its natural communicative function: a "nature" that is not an environment in which we find ourselves and that surrounds us,

112. Ibid., q.19 a.3.

113. Cf. ibid., q.94 a.2.

114. Cf. again ibid., q.19 a.2: "bonitas voluntatis ex solo uno illo dependet, quod per se facit bonitatem in actu, scilicet ex obiecto."

but that nature that each one of us *is,* and which constitutes and delimits the realm of fundamental human goods.

This being the case, I believe it is important to emphasize the following about our approach, according to which 1) the object of an act cannot be understood except by placing oneself in the perspective of the acting person, 2) this object always includes an intentional element, 3) this intentional element must be understood with reference to a precise "ethical context," which is the sphere of a specific moral virtue. Our approach does not exclude two things. First, it does not exclude that between certain natural data, such as are the natural inclinations of the human person and their inherent finality, on the one hand, and the basic intentionality with which these inclinations are pursued, on the other, there exist a necessary and natural connection. Second, inversely, it does not exclude that there be behaviors or ways of acting that it is not possible to choose *reasonably* with *any* intention. One is certainly free to choose the physical act of "laying down on a bed," whether for the end of resting, to do a yoga exercise, or to annoy someone: all of these are different human acts on the basis of their object. The same is not true, however, for a linguistic act: to articulate glottal sounds in the form of words includes, as it were, *in itself* a finality which tends to the expression of what one has in mind, that is, it is an act of communication. To engage in sexual intercourse and pretend that this act has nothing to do with an act that is by nature procreative means to choose and act in an unreasonable manner.[115] There exist natural finalities that form a necessary presupposition for the reasonableness of any intentionality with which the corresponding acts are carried out.

In this regard, the objects of acts such as "to commit a murder," "to lie," "to commit adultery," "to fornicate," "to render infertile one's own freely performed sexual acts," are not formulated in the same way that the object of a theft is constituted. All of these acts have in common the fact that in them there exists a merely "material" plane—the action considered in its *genus naturae*—such as in a murder, the physical act of killing (which perhaps could be licit in a just war),[116] in lying the act of saying what is untrue (which could be licit in the context of a game, in the theater, in an experiment to test a lie detector), in adultery and fornication the sexual act as such (licit in mar-

115. This is valid also for someone who intends to render such an act infertile; he does so precisely because he is dealing with an act that is by nature procreative.

116. On the various types of "killing" in St. Thomas and some problems in this regard, cf. M. Rhonheimer, "Sins Against Justice (IIa IIae, qq. 59–78)," in Stephen J. Pope, ed., *The Ethics of Aquinas* (Washington, D.C.: Georgetown University Press, 2002), 287–303, particularly 292ff.

riage), in a contraceptive act the interference in the hormonal process (licit for example for therapeutic reasons, to regulate a woman's rhythm, to avoid the procreative consequences of a foreseeable rape). But all of these differ from an act of theft by the fact that the "material elements" of a theft have nothing to do with "human nature," they are not elements, structures, or natural data which have a relation to what the human person *is.* They lack a certain anthropological "anchoring."

Even if a quantity of money is another's legitimate property and it would *normally* be a theft to appropriate this money for oneself, it is thinkable that the same action, considered materially—the external "behavior"—could also be chosen licitly in particular circumstances, for example in the case of extreme necessity or to save one's life. In such circumstances, says St. Thomas (in accordance with the theological and canonical tradition of his and later times), everything is common property: even though the right of the owner remains, it becomes relativized in the measure of the neighbor's vital interests; consequently such an act, which normally would be a theft, no longer is, but is rather a licit act of the preservation of one's life.[117] The act of taking a person's property from him against his will is evil due to the fact *that it is unjust,* but not due to the fact that it is (physically) "to take a quantity of money from its owner" (even if against his will); this latter behavior, in other well-defined circumstances (according to criteria of justice, grasped by reason in an objective manner), can also be not contrary to justice. A moral norm which says that "it is not licit to appropriate another's property to oneself" is therefore valid "ut in pluribus"; if it is formulated rather as: "it is illicit to steal," then it is valid *semper et pro semper,* given that it is already implied that some (well-defined) cases of "appropriating another's property" are not theft and, therefore, do not fall under this norm.[118]

Such a *mutatio materiae,* change of matter—not a change of intentionality, but a change of an important circumstance for the object, relativizing the right of property and with that, the significance of the external behavior—is not possible in acts like "to commit a murder," "to lie," "to commit adultery," "to fornicate," or "to practice contraception." Evil, therefore, not only *ex obiec-*

117. This is also due to the fact that the right to property is not absolute, in the sense that it is regulated by the higher principle that the goods of this earth are destined to the use of all.

118. For the validity "ut in pluribus" of the precepts of the natural law cf. *ST* I-II, q.94 a.4. The prohibitive norms, if they are formulated correctly, do not admit of exceptions, and St. Thomas applies validity "ut in pluribus" only to some (positively) prescriptive norms (his example is "deposita sunt reddenda").

to, but *inalterably and always* "ex obiecto," are precisely those evil "ex obiecto" acts whose "materia circa quam" does not permit of alteration, because constituted by something naturally given and constitutive for the nature of the human person, and inasmuch as this "given" is morally significant. A norm of the type "one must never take another's property from him" is not sufficient—rather, one must add "one must never *unjustly* take . . ."; conversely, the norm "one must never have sexual relations with a woman who is married to another man" is valid: the choice of this act, described in behavioral terms, is always objectively an act of infidelity and of injustice, contrary to the nature of conjugal love. What is constitutive for human nature cannot depend on circumstantial facts, as can, alternatively, property rights, because this would mean that the nature of the human person itself could change.

With this we arrive at the conclusion that to affirm the existence of intrinsically evil acts is equivalent to affirming that there exists a nucleus of the human person, called "human nature," which is unchangeable and as such also morally significant, because it formulates the ontological and cognitive presuppositions for the order of reason, which is the moral order.

The Principles of Practical Reason: The Natural Rule of the Objective Significance of Human Action

We have not, however, arrived at the end of the ethical-normative discourse. Indeed, we have yet to begin! The response just given is still inadequate, since, leaving things at this point, such an argumentation would finish in a pure naturalism. "To act against nature" (against the inclination to self-preservation, against the communicative nature of language and the social nature of man, against the natural meaning of sexuality) cannot be considered *morally evil,* as well, simply because it is contrary to something "natural." To this point we have merely found an argument apt to show why some acts, as opposed to others, *and these acts always presupposed to be morally evil,* are so *intrinsically.* But the real ethical-normative question is: how does one know that these are precisely morally *evil?* From where, for example, come our notions of "just" and "unjust," and how do we know if something is not only naturally given and therefore practically important—that is, to be taken into consideration when we act—but also, as natural, *morally* significant? Why are many things that are not "natural," or that even go against nature, such as, for a human being, to swim, to shave one's beard, or to chew gum (frustrating the natural end of the jaws), not morally evil? It is only here that the task of normative ethics begins.

I stated above that, between the intentionality that constitutes the object and certain structures and natural givens, a connection exists that is not at the disposition of the agent. This means that we cannot reasonably choose any behavior we wish with whatever intentionality we wish, even if everything we choose we choose as a proximate end, this latter being precisely the object of the action. It is not rationally possible to chew gum with the end of feeding oneself; nor is it rationally possible to hit someone on the head with the purpose of healing his migraine. To claim to do so would be a sign of irrationality or even of insanity. Nor can two people of the same sex, even if moved by real affection and a bond of friendship, reasonably give fulfillment to their affection and express their friendship by means of acts involving the genital organs, because this would mean to err concerning the nature of the link between love and sexuality. That which we can *reasonably* will as the end of a concrete choice, doing specific things, depends therefore not only on our subjective opinion or on our freedom, but in some cases also on natural preconditions, grasped by reason and understood as human goods.[119]

Even though every "object" is in fact a type of intentionality—a "proposal"—we must not forget that these proposals are also naturally conditioned. The object of an act is not therefore only "what I want" or "what I propose to do"; rather, a materiality proper to the "physical" nature of the act is also present, a materiality which enters into the constitution of the object. In particular cases, this natural matter of the act can have a special importance for reason, due to the fact that we are speaking of a nature that doesn't merely surround us, but that we ourselves *are*.[120]

119. At this point one must speak of the notion of "sin against nature" and the Thomistic doctrine of "nature" as "praesuppositum" of the moral order, a theme amply treated in my *Natural Law and Practical Reason*, 94–109. Jean Porter, in her review of the English edition of this book (in *Theological Studies* 62 [2001]: 851–53), reproves me for having completely ignored St. Thomas's teaching on the "moral significance of pre-rational nature" and on the "peccatum contra naturam." Surprisingly, however, Porter completely fails to mention my ample treatment of the theme. I respond to the objections—unfounded—raised by Porter in my article "The Moral Significance of Pre-Rational Nature in Aquinas: A Reply to Jean Porter (and Stanley Hauerwas)," in chapter 6 of this book, or *American Journal of Jurisprudence* 48 (2003): 253–80.

120. In this sense I agree with what Steven A. Long says in his article "A Brief Disquisition Regarding the Nature of the Object of the Moral Act According to St. Thomas Aquinas," *The Thomist* 67 (2003): 45–71: "The moral object of an act is the act itself—inclusive of its essential matter or integral nature—under the *ratio* of its order to the end sought; it is not solely and simply that *ratio* apart from the essential matter or integral nature of the act" (50). I think, how-

There exists, in fact, a "nature" of language, of sexuality, etc., a "nature" which nevertheless makes itself known, as a human good, only within the *ordo rationis,* which is the order of the moral virtues, which finds its fulfillment in the *ordo amoris.* Likewise, the natural inclination to self-preservation reveals its "nature" as a human good and as part of the *ordo rationis* within the totality of that which is the human person. This nature, of course, can also appear as a simple natural conditioning, as a limit of our human possibilities. But in this latter sense, "nature" is morally ambivalent and does not provide us with a practical orientation: it is natural for a man to walk, and not to fly, yet we can fly artificially, and we do not consider this morally evil, even though it goes against nature. The same is true for the act, also against nature, of having a kidney removed so as to give it to another person who needs one. In other cases, however, "nature" presents itself as a "good," as that which is to be pursued and done, and to act against which would be to err *morally.* The object of the human act is precisely such a good, at the concrete and particular level. It is the task of practical reason to determine this. But practical reason, which is directed to particular goods, is regulated by its own principles. Some of these principles are "natural": they are the principles of natural reason, also called the "precepts of the natural law."

We now arrive at the decisive point: the practical reason which "forms" the object of an act is not a reason which lacks principles of its own. These principles are precisely the precepts of the natural law. The natural law is, simultaneously, the principle of praxis—it impels and motivates the subject to act—and the principle of morality, that is, the rule of the goodness of praxis. Analyzing St. Thomas's exposition on the natural law we discover that, for him, nature and the constitution of this moral law correspond exactly, both at the universal level and at that of principles, to that which we have said about the constitution of the object of a human act. There is a strict parallelism. As the objects and the moral species of human acts are *formae a ratione conceptae,* the natural law is, like every law, *ordinatio rationis,* and as such "something constituted by reason" and a "work of reason."[121] The first precept of the natural law, which is based on the *ratio boni*—its character of being the object of appetite, tendency, and will—commands *"bonum est faciendum et*

ever, that Long has an overly narrow understanding of the significance of the term "intentio" in St. Thomas and, consequently, of the expression "praeter intentionem" (ibid., 62ff.), something which cannot fail to have repercussions on his understanding of the structure of the object.

121. *ST* I-II, q.94 a.1: "lex naturalis est aliquid per rationem constitutum: sicut etiam propositio est quoddam opus rationis."

prosequendum, et malum vitandum."[122] All of the other precepts of the natural law, which correspond to that which the practical reason naturally understands as the human good, are based on this practical principle.[123]

These goods, naturally grasped by the practical reason as human goods, are the ends of the various natural inclinations, not, however—and this is important—as such, but precisely "regulated" by reason. The ends of natural inclinations enter as objects, therefore, in the successive unfolding and specification of practical reason: as objects and "goods of reason" and "for reason," undergoing a respective *commensuratio* of reason itself.[124] Thus, they are understood—in the perspective of the human person who tends to the good and therefore becomes an acting subject, and at the level of the order of reason—as *human,* and not merely natural, goods, inasmuch as they are grasped by reason, as ends and goods of the *voluntas ut natura,* of the natural act of the will.

The natural inclination to self-preservation is, as a human good *apprehensum et ordinatum a ratione,* more than mere self-preservation: it is the will—that is, *rational* desire—to live, which is capable of opening itself to the demands of justice and love of neighbor (to the point, possibly, of giving one's life for him, something which is opposed to the natural inclination as mere *natural* inclination). The sexual inclination, which mutually attracts the sexes to each other, when understood by reason as a human good is more than mere sexuality, which by means of the sexual instinct and its gratification serves to propagate the species: it is love between persons which becomes marriage, mutual donation and affective union, a faithful and indissoluble union in the service of the transmission of human life, which, nevertheless, a person may freely renounce for the sake of pursuing other goods. In the sphere of the natural inclination to live in community with one's neighbors, reason finds language to be a natural and indispensable means of communication, whose use against nature, presupposing the existence of a communicative community, would be an injustice and therefore *in itself* evil (that is, "quite apart from the ulterior intentions of the one acting and the circumstances," as is said in *VS* no. 80,1).

122. Ibid., a.2.

123. Ibid.: "Et super hoc fundantur omnia alia praecepta legis naturae: ut scilicet omnia illa facienda vel vitanda pertineant ad praecepta legis naturae, quae ratio practica naturaliter apprehendit esse bona humana."

124. For the concept of "good of reason" *(bonum rationis)* cf. my systematic study *Praktische Vernunft und Vernünftigkeit der Praxis,* 124–35.

The first practical and moral principles (the precepts of the natural law) develop in reference to these human goods: they are the source of man's self-understanding as human being and moral subject. This self-understanding is the necessary presupposition for every subsequent theoretical and metaphysical comprehension of what we call "human nature." We all know, from our infancy and progressively thereafter, who we are as "human beings" and moral agents; we know this not because we have studied metaphysics and anthropology, but because we possess the reflected experience of our interiority, part of which is the natural law, which is none other than the entirety of the first principles of the practical reason, commanding us to pursue what is good for man and to flee the contrary evils.[125]

These principles provide us with the fundamental notions of the specific virtues and of particular "ethical contexts," without which understanding practical reason would remain without orientation. Therefore it belongs to this "natural law," as well, to be the basis of the understanding of the distinction between "good" and "evil" in human acts. The natural principles of the practical reason—that is, the precepts of the natural law—are therefore like a light that illuminates particular acts, rendering transparent that in them which is objectively good or evil.[126] The analysis of this can be conducted for every area of human action, for example, for the specific areas of sexuality, of truthfulness, and of respect for human life—analyses which I have done in other works to which I refer the reader in the footnote.[127]

The underlying idea in such analyses is to show that some kinds of be-

125. On this topic I refer the reader to my systematic works on the theme: *Natural Law and Practical Reason; Praktische Vernunft und Vernünftigkeit der Praxis;* and *Die Perspektive der Moral.*

126. This is not to be understood in the sense that from the principles it can be deduced how, in each situation, it is good to concretely act. The demands of concrete action, in the variable and complex circumstances in which human life takes place, cannot be deduced from any principle but must be judged by prudence. The principles are, however, the foundation that makes it possible to evaluate the act of prudence and the concrete action according to criteria that are, precisely, moral, and that pertain to the ends of the individual moral virtues. In addition, the principles delineate the limits of the "morally possible," i.e., they determine what one may never do. In this sense, and only in this sense, the principles, formulated as universal prohibitive norms, also regulate concrete action—they are valid *semper et pro semper*—prohibiting the choice of specific concrete behaviors. Cf. M. Rhonheimer, "Praktische Prinzipien, Naturgesetz und konkrete Handlungsurteile in tugendethischer Perspektive. Zur Diskussion über praktische Vernunft und lex naturalis bei Thomas von Aquin," *Studia Moralia* 39 (2001): 113–58.

127. *Die Perspektive der Moral,* 303ff.; *Natural Law and Practical Reason,* 452–90; *Contraception, Sexual Behavior, and Natural Law; Etica della procreazione; Abtreibung und Lebensschutz. Tötungsverbot und Recht auf Leben in der politischen und medizinischen Ethik* (Paderborn: Verlag Ferdinand Schöningh, 2003).

havior can never be reasonably chosen without contradicting some of the first practical principles which order human action to the human good. Such a contrarity consists precisely in a fundamental non-agreement of the practical judgment and the chosen action with correct desire, that is, in a contrarity with respect to practical truth. The fundamental correctness of desire depends, however, on the natural reason, from which emanates the natural law. Precisely in this sense the words cited in *VS* no. 78 are germane, that "there are certain specific kinds of behavior that are always wrong to choose, because choosing them involves a disorder of the will, that is, a moral evil."

The Unity of the Practical Intellect, Subjectivity and Objectivity

At every level, whether at the level of the first practical principles, naturally understood, or at that of concrete acts and of their first moral specification by means of their object, we find the subjectivity and the objectivity of the practical reason intertwined: it is intellective acts which open the subject to the truth that, precisely as truth, is always also objectivity. Moreover, it is the intellect itself which also forms the nucleus of human subjectivity: it is the soul of the will, which is free precisely in the measure in which it is rational. Reason is not only openness to the truth, but also the root and cause of freedom.[128] In this way an objectivity is constituted that, ultimately, is nothing other than the "truth of subjectivity."

The judgments of the practical intellect, nevertheless, should not be understood as simple applications of what is known by the speculative or theoretical intellect. Even if, as St. Thomas says, the intellect becomes practical by its extension to action,[129] this does not mean that practical judgments are extensions and applications of theoretical or speculative *judgments*. It means only that the intellectual *power*—and this is what Thomas speaks of when he speaks of "extension"—which is by its nature originally and *per se* speculative, becomes practical in the extension of its cognitive activity to the realm of action.[130]

This *extensio* is due to the fact that man is a being that tends to the good; in other words, to the fact that the intellect as a power of the soul is always

128. *ST* I-II, q.17 a.1 ad2; *De Veritate* 24, 2.
129. Ibid., q.79 a.11: "Intellectus speculativus per extensionem fit practicus."
130. Cf. for this Rhonheimer, *Natural Law and Practical Reason*, 24ff.

integrated into the totality of the structure of a human person, which is itself a bundle of inclinations and natural tendencies that aim at a variety of goods which this same intellect grasps naturally, rendering them intelligible, as human goods, in the context of the totality of the human person and of the *ordo rationis* which corresponds to him. Because the intellect becomes practical, it is not *theoretical judgments* that are applied to praxis, but it is *the intellect as faculty* that applies itself to the sphere of praxis, generating in this sphere, however, judgments of a particular type—practical judgments—which possess a point of departure of their own. St. Thomas explicitly affirms this: as with the speculative intellect, the practical intellect also has its proper point of departure, its own first principle. Insofar as they are *practical,* practical judgments of the intellect are not derived from judgments of the speculative type.[131]

To affirm that practical reason has its own point of departure and that practical judgments are not derived from theoretical judgments, as though the former were a simple application of the latter to action, is not to say that in the process of practical *reasoning,* composed of a series of judgments—what Aristotle calls the "practical syllogism"—theoretical judgments do not intervene, along with perceptions and experiences of *facts.* In a practical syllogism, the minor premise, indeed, is not practical; but the major premise and the conclusion are.[132] What is important to maintain is that the practi-

131. Cf. *ST* I-II, q.94 a.2.

132. In this sense it is true that: "Practical judgments draw on theoretical insights and theoretical insights motivate practical operations" (Romanus Cessario, *Introduction to Moral Theology* [Washington, D.C.: The Catholic University of America Press, 2001], 160). The example of the fish eaten by the author on the shore of Lake Geneva in the company of his Swiss friend (I confirm the exactness of the account) is also correct. I only want to highlight that a practical judgment is neither an application of a theoretical judgment nor a simple inference from such a judgment. In its practicality it does not derive from any theoretical judgment, even if it can be derived from another practical judgment, of a higher order, *by means of* a theoretical judgment. We can examine his example, putting it in the form of a "practical syllogism": 1) [Major premise, a practical judgment]: "It is good for me (i.e., I want to) to eat a delicious fish." 2) [Minor premise, a theoretical judgment or sensible perception]: "This fish is delicious." 3) [Conclusion, practical judgment and subsequent action]: "It is good for me (i.e., I want to, choose to) eat this fish." The conclusion is not an application of the theoretical judgment "this fish is delicious," but an *inference* from the first practical judgment by means of the theoretical judgment, "this fish is delicious." The process of the practical reason does not derive from an application of theoretical judgments, but is from its beginning practical. Structurally it is based on the first principle of practical reason, "one must do the good and avoid evil," and from the other principles, which are immediately grasped by the practical reason in the totality of the natural inclinations of the human person. For the practical syllogism and the structure of the process of the practical reason, cf. Rhonheimer, *Die Perspektive der Moral,* 108–15.

cality of reason is not reduced to a simple "application," a "practical use" of theoretical judgments (which regard facts, the nature of man, etc.), but that it possesses, as St. Thomas clearly states, its own gnoseological and anthropological point of departure: the *ratio boni.* As being is the first object of the intellect as such, the process of the practical intellect begins with the *apprehensio* of the good (which, certainly, would not be possible without a prior cognition of being).[133] From this moment on, however, the logic of the practical reason follows its own course, with its own logic, an "autonomy" which, to repeat, does not mean *independence* from the theoretical intellect, but precisely "auto"-"nomia." This is clearly demonstrated in the natural cognition of fundamental human goods: they are originally known in the context of the unfolding of practical reason,[134] and only afterwards, in the subject's reflection on this original internal moral experience, do they become the object of the theoretical intellect, which on the basis of this practical original experience progresses in the understanding of "human nature."[135]

The fact that practical reason has its own point of departure means that the natural law, which contains the first principles of practical reason in the form of precepts, is, as has been mentioned, simultaneously both the principle of praxis—that is, stimulus and motivation of the subject toward action—and the principle of morality, that is, the rule of the goodness of praxis. The practical intellect, also, is always *intellect,* that is, a cognitive faculty, although according to the structure of all imperative (or "prescriptive") acts, it would be "located" in an appetitive movement of the will.[136] The latter is in this way directed toward the truth of things. The practical intellect, also, is always the one and same human intellect whose natural object is properly the *truth of being,* even if, as practical intellect, it knows this truth under the "ratio boni," which is to say as an end, that is, the object or the intelligible content of a tendency, a desire or a natural inclination.

133. Cf. *ST* I-II, q.94 a.2: "Sicut autem ens est primum quod cadit in apprehensione simpliciter, ita bonum est primum quod cadit in apprehensione practicae rationis, quae ordiantur ad opus: omne enim agens agit propter finem, qui habet rationem boni. Et ideo primum principium in ratione practica est quod fundatur supra rationem boni, quae est 'Bonum est quod omnia appetunt.' Hoc est ergo primum praeceptum legis, quod bonum est faciendum et prosequen dum, et malum vitandum."

134. Cf. ibid. (cit. in n. 123).

135. In my opinion, *De Veritate,* 1, 9 and 10, 9 is fundamental for this; cf. Rhonheimer, *Natural Law and Practical Reason,* 29f. (and nn. 47 and 48).

136. What St. Thomas says of the act that he calls "*imperare*" ("to command"), which is "actus rationins, praesupposito actu voluntatis" (*ST* I-II, q.17 a.1), generally applies here.

The truth of the practical intellect is a "practical truth." Practical truth is, in the Aristotelian formulation, that truth which consists in the adequation of the judgments of practical reason with a right appetite. These practical judgments have as their object, as Aristotle never tires of repeating, a variable, contingent matter: the sphere of praxis, which is the sphere, not of the immutable order of being, but of that "which could also be differently." Some of these practical judgments, nevertheless, are *natural:* they have the character of *principles,* and as principles they do not refer to and are not measured by any superior appetite (except to that of the good in general). They are goods that refer—as St. Thomas affirms—in a non-derived, spontaneous way to the natural ends of the natural inclinations, grasping their intelligible content as human goods[137] (note the analogy with the object of the human act as "intelligible content of a concrete action"), which implies precisely a regulation on the part of reason: human goods also, grasped by natural reason, are, as the objects of human acts, "goods understood and ordered by reason."[138] The principles of practical reason—the natural law—express that which is "by nature reasonable," a reasonableness which cannot be reasonably founded or ulteriorly demonstrated, precisely because it is the natural law itself which founds all practical reasonableness.[139] Combined in an original way in the natural law, therefore, are the subjectivity of the person who acts and the objectivity of the natural knowledge of human good, a knowledge understood and made explicit by means of a discursive process of the natural reason, to the point of arriving at a knowledge of the species of the concrete acts pertaining to the individual virtues and of acts opposed to them, which latter are therefore evil.[140]

137. Yet again *ST* I-II, q.94 a.2: "ut scilicet omnia illa facienda vel vitanda pertineant ad praecepta legis naturae, quae ratio practica naturaliter apprehendit esse bona humana." And further on: "omnia illa ad quae homo habet naturalem inclinationem, ratio naturaliter apprehendit ut bona."

138. Ibid., ad2: "omnes inclinationes quarumcumque partium humanae naturae, puta concupiscibilis et irascibilis, secundum quod regulantur ratione, pertinent ad legem naturalem."

139. Cf. Rhonheimer, *Die Perspektive der Moral,* 227ff.; Rhonheimer, "Praktische Vernunft und das 'von Natur aus Vernünftige.' Zur Lehre von der Lex naturalis als Prinzip der Praxis bei Thomas von Aquin," *Theologie und Philosophie* 75 (2000): 493–522.

140. In my opinion, what I have expounded in this paragraph was the basic idea, which I agree with completely, of J. M. Finnis, in his book *Fundamentals of Ethics* (Washington, D.C.: Georgetown University Press; Oxford: Oxford University Press, 1983). My objections against Finnis's criticism of the Aristotelian doctrine concerning the *ergon idion* can be found in *Praktische Vernunft und Vernünftgkeit der Praxis,* 53ff. In his debate with Finnis, and more generally against the differentiation between the theoretical and practical use of the intellect, R. McInerny commits the error—in my view significant—of confusing "practical knowledge" (of the moral

"To place oneself in the perspective of the acting person" is necessary therefore not only for comprehending what constitutes the object of a human act, but also for the correct understanding of the principles of practical reason, which we also call the natural law. It is important to emphasize that through the natural law, the human person is constituted simultaneously as a *practical* subject—agent, actor—and as a *moral* subject. In precisely the measure in which the natural law—practical reason at the universal and natural level—is the principle of praxis, it is also the principle of morality. As *ordinatio rationis* it becomes the measure of the goodness of the pursuit of individual natural inclinations, and of all the specific acts which arise from these inclinations.[141]

subject) with "ethical reflection": "Finnis, it seems, wishes to maintain that the end, the good, that guides ethical reflection is known in what he earlier called purely practical knowledge" (*Aquinas on Human Action,* 188). That which McInerny considers to be so fundamentally erroneous is, however, precisely what St. Thomas explicitly teaches in *ST* I-II, q.94 a.2. Speaking, on p. 155, of the "unwisdom of trying to separate as well as distinguish the theoretical and practical uses of the mind," McInerny counters this "incipience" with the argument: "The practical syllogism incorporates speculative truths." Nothing is more true than this, but this is not the question. Here we are speaking of the constitution of the "practicality" itself of a judgment, of the origin of the principles of practical reason and of the constitution of a line of reasoning insofar as it is practical: these cannot be derived from the theoretical or speculative use of the intellect; they do not originate from a simple application of *theoretical judgments* to action. Rather, this process of practical reason is from its origin practical: it begins with the cognition of the precepts of the natural law, which is not only the principle of morality and the moral rule, but also the *principle of praxis,* because it urges and motivates the subject to action within the realm of the intelligibility of fundamental human goods, grasped by practical reason in the subjectivity of the person's natural inclinations. This is St. Thomas's teaching in *ST* I-II, q.94 a.2.

141. Paper partially given at the congress "Walking in the Light: Perspectives for Moral Theology Ten Years after *Veritatis Splendor*" (Pontificia Università Lateranense / Pontificio Istituto Giovanni Paolo II per studi su matrimonio e famiglia, Rome, November 20–22, 2003). Italian text published in the proceedings of the congress Camminare nella luce. Prospettiva della teologia morale a 10 anni da *Veritatis splendor* (Rome: Pontificia Università Lateranense, 2004). English translation by Joseph T. Papa was originally published in *Nova et Vetera* 2, no. 2 (2004):

9

Practical Reason and the Truth of Subjectivity

The Self-Experience of the Moral Subject at the Roots of Metaphysics and Anthropology

Moral Subjectivity and the Question of Its Truth

The fundamental question of every ethics has to do with the truth of subjectivity: is what I do, and what I think to be right and just, *really* right and just? And my conduct in general, as based on interior conviction—is it *truly* right and just? In more precise terms: what must I do or not do in order to be the person I really want to be? Moral questions are questions about the rightness of our will and action. The answers to these questions are founded on principles which emerge from the self-experience of the practical reason of the subject, and that means that in their origin they do not come from metaphysics or some other theoretical forms of knowing. This experience of the self, founded in the anthropological and cognitive primacy of reason, itself possesses an eminently metaphysical dimension. In fact, metaphysics and anthropology presuppose it.

These are the key themes I would like to illustrate here. But first of all, it needs to be made clear that my entire discussion depends on what "subjectivity" means.

I am speaking of the subjectivity of every human being, classically defined as *animal rationale.* It is not the subjectivity of an autonomous will in the Kantian sense, which seeks to affirm its own freedom as an independence from all inclinations and moving forces, as not subject, consequently, to the representations of good that arise from those inclinations, but only to the "ought" as stated categorically by rational imperatives superior to every inclination; instead of this, I am thinking of the subjectivity of a living thing, distinguished by the possession of intellect and reason: the object of which, to the extent that it is *practical* reason, is properly the truth of the realization of its own being. This is precisely the subjectivity of a being whose nature is revealed in its inclinations and instincts, but also in the reason embedded in these inclinations and instincts which that reason regulates and orders; the basis of action and the principle of morality, therefore, is not the "ought" elevated over every good tied to the inclinations; rather, the good, conditioned by the inclinations, but as appearing to the reason, is the foundation of action and principle of morality. "Subjectivity of morality" is equivalent here to the "rationality of morality," and precisely to a species of rationality that in turn consists in the objectivity of the "good-for-man," the objectivity that is precisely the "truth of subjectivity."[1]

Virtue and the Supremacy of Reason in Aristotle

The category "truth of subjectivity" goes back to Aristotle who, in a manner still unsurpassed, located the subjectivity of the moral fact in ethics: the *Nicomachean Ethics* takes up the movements of subjectivity at its very outset. For Aristotle, the agent is fundamentally a being who aims for the good in all possible forms, so that "the good" will be defined as simply that to which everything aims. The very concept of the good as a practical good is the concept of that which is the object of some aim or seeking. This is why human seeking—and the action *(praxis)* which flows from it—are subject to deception. Practical judgments are necessarily conditioned by a pull of forces, which means that the good that we want to do and are able to do is always that which *appears* to us as good. The practical good is thus essentially an "appar-

1. For this position and developments of it see my book *La prospettiva della morale: Fundamenti dell'etica filosofica* (Rome: Armando, 1994); the expanded Spanish edition, *La perspectiva de la moral. Fundamentos de la ética filosófica* (Madrid: Rialp, 2000); and the even more expanded German edition, *Die Perspektive der Moral. Philosophische Grundlagen der Tugendethik* (Berlin: Akademie Verlag, 2001), which is forthcoming in English from The Catholic University of America Press.

ent good" *(phainómenon agathón)*.[2] The *appearance* of the good can deceive us, since what appears to us as good is not always good in reality. The human being can be drawn into deception by the senses, by pleasure, and (only Augustine will explore this in its full profundity)[3] by perversion, by the *curvatio* or "warping" of the will itself.

On the basis of this possible discrepancy between the good that appears and the good that may not *appear* so but really *is* good, there arises not only a program of ethical self-clarification about what is the "good-for-man" in the realm of action but also a program to realize this good in the actions of the subject. This concerns clarifying the conditions for "the apparent good" to be also "the truly good." Or, reversing the terms, this concerns clarifying the conditions for the truly good to appear so to us subjectively, so that we aim for, and carry out in action, what really is right.[4]

And this is Aristotle's answer: this coincidence of seeming and being has for its condition that the reason *(lógos)* or the intellect *(noûs)* be "in charge" within us, so that we act according to reason, since "the intellect is always right, but desire and the images (of the senses) are capable of not being right."[5] The originally Platonic thesis of the anthropological primacy of the intellect and *lógos*—and that includes the thesis of their *cognitive* primacy as well—was based on the conviction that the intellect and the reason—a kind of "god" within us—by nature, and thus infallibly, has truth for its object; it represents that "part" of human nature that characterizes us specifically as human beings. This is not to be understood, at least for Aristotle, in a dualistic sense but in the sense that it belongs only to the "rational part of the animal," the "higher part of the animal," to direct our interior vision to reality in its own truth, and precisely *because* and *to the extent that* in this respect we are dealing with vision by intellect and reason. In fact, the most intimate structure and truth of all "reality" is intelligible, and thereby the natural object of the intellect.

The intellect appears here, then—to use the metaphor that would become

2. Aristotle, *Nicomachean Ethics,* III, 4.

3. This has been rightly emphasized by A. MacIntyre, *Whose Justice? Which Rationality?* (Notre Dame, Ind.: University of Notre Dame Press, 1988), 146–63.

4. As in the first paragraph, I mean the Latin "rectus," which refers not only to the virtue of justice but to all the virtues. Cf. G. Bien, "Die menschlichen Meinungen und das Gute. Die Lösung des Normproblems in der aristotelischen Ethik," in M. Riedel, ed., *Rehabilitierung der praktischen Philosophie* (Freiburg/Br.: I. Rombach, 1972), 345–71.

5. Aristotle, *De Anima,* III, 10, 433a27–28.

operative in neo-Platonism and Thomistic neo-Platonism—as a "light" that, so to speak, makes the colors and contours of reality visible, and thereby reveals reality in its inmost essence. By itself, light illuminates and makes visible, while through what is not itself, and mostly because of other things, it can be clouded, misled, or obscured by the disorder of the senses, sentiment, and the passions, by the deception of false pleasures, by the corruption and "bending" *(curvatio)* of the will.

We have enough here already to establish the "program" of ethics: having ascertained that the *true* "good-for-man" will *appear* such only on condition that our perception of the good is in fact guided by reason and placed under the dominion of intellect, the question spontaneously arises: under what conditions do we will, desire, and act rationally?[6] Plato gave a dualistic answer: on condition that we have known the good with our intellect. When someone does evil, he does so from ignorance. The virtuous person is one who knows: lack of virtue is lack of knowledge, or to be precise, of true knowledge, *epistéme*. The absence of a vision of the essence of the good is a deficiency of *theoria*. Such a defect occurs since the intellect is impeded in its free development through the corporal constitution of man. In such a situation, for the lover of truth—as the *Phaedo* tells us[7]—death, or release from the body, is preferable; only then can there be an undistorted vision of truth.

Aristotle, on the other hand, does not completely refute this reply, but modifies it at a crucial point.[8] He too is of the opinion that someone who does not know the good will not be able to do the good. But he adds that, even though someone knows the good perfectly, the very same person can do evil, because there is another kind of not-knowing: the kind that strikes us at the moment of choice, when impulses and passions obscure reason's judgment and turn it aside. It is possible to have good principles (for example, to know that one ought not to make love to one's neighbor's wife), but nevertheless, overcome by will and passion, such an action here and now may be judged as good and be carried out. In effect, Aristotle observes, the action is done through ignorance, not an ignorance on the level of general princi-

6. This is what I call "the theme of Aristotelian ethics"; cf. *Praktische Vernunft und Vernünftigkeit der Praxis. Handlungstheorie bei Thomas von Aquin in ihrer Entstehung aus dem Problemkontext der aristotelischen Ethik* (Berlin: Akademie Verlag, 1994), 10f., 413ff.

7. Plato, *Phaedo* 63e–69c.

8. On this theme see the classic work of J. J. Walsh, *Aristotle's Conception of Moral Weakness* (1960; New York: Columbia University Press, 1963). Walsh shows that the Aristotelian conception corresponds to a final stage of development of the Platonic doctrine.

ples but on the level of concrete judgment as conditioned by the passions, by reference to what we "here and now" think to be good; a judgment, consequently, that decides on every occasion what we should do or not do. Virtue is "true knowledge" on *this* level: but on this level, true knowing requires the right ordering of our impulses and sentiments.

Ethical or moral perfection—*ethikè areté,* or virtue—is not simply epistemological knowing, but a certain harmony between reason and impulses. Such harmony ensures the efficacy of general ethical knowledge for concrete action and the avoidance of erroneous choice. According to Aristotle, the one who is morally perfected experiences pleasure and its opposite in the right way and manages *not* to be deceived by it, he "judges everything correctly and knows how to discover the true good in every situation," just because he "sees the truth in everything" he will himself become the "rule and measure" for what is truly good.[9]

The ethical problem is resolved when the passions, instincts, inclinations, and impulses—instead of impeding reason—support it, and then, thanks to their being in a good state—moderation, courage, etc.—they really show reason the way. So the Aristotelian program is not the Platonic distancing from bodiliness, from the senses, and from instincts, but rather "appetition according to reason" and "judgment in accord with right appetition."

Aristotelian ethics, therefore, is essentially an ethics of virtue. It vouches for morality not as an observance of rules designed to improve the world, but as a program for improving not only one's own *praxis* but also one's own being. It always poses the question: what type of person will I become if I do this or that, and whether doing it will bring the fulfillment known as happiness. Aristotelian ethics is, however, essentially a *rational* ethics of virtue which connects the well-being of man and his actions with the cognitive conditions of his well-being, and measures the possibilities of being happy according to the criteria of rationality. Right here, however, is where this kind of ethics thinks radically about the "subjectivity of the moral fact": practical reason is planted within the original "aiming" (or seeking, striving) of the subject for the good, and "my reasoning" in every case is not simply the interiorization of rules as if they proceeded from a nature experienced objectively by the subject. In any case the foundation of morality will only be a nature that is presented to the self-experience of the subject as practical, that is,

9. Aristotle, *Nicomachean Ethics,* III, 6, 1113a 29–34.

as practical reason, which comprehends the "naturally rational," that is, the objects of the various virtues.

A Question about the Principles of Practical Reason

It is well known that Aristotelian ethics seems to fall prey to a vicious circle. For the Stagirite, moral virtue depends on practical reason, but at the same time practical reason presupposes the possession of virtue. It is the end which justifies the reasoning of the means, and this end is given by virtue; but virtue, in order to be moral virtue, has need of that reason to which it is supposed to furnish ends. But this "vicious" circle is not unwarranted in Aristotelian ethics; on the contrary, by being part of its essential affirmations, it is really a constitutive part of its truth.[10]

In fact, Aristotle's "vicious" circle describes with precision the practical dimension of the *conditio humana* and is an adequate expression of the subjectivity of the moral fact. One can do good and be good in the proper sense only to the extent one has *intelligentia* (insight, understanding) of the good. Without this type of subjectivity there is no morality. We can talk as much as we want about "objective requirements of morality" and about "objective moral norms" but, without understanding the goodness of what ought to be done there is no possibility, while doing good, of becoming a good person or of making any sense of morality.

On the other hand, the end, and that means the good, appears to each person in conformity to the person's own subjectively motivated constitution: the virtuous person sees virtue as good and desirable, the vicious person sees vice as good and desirable. The unavoidable subjectivity of the moral fact at the same time puts the good radically at risk.

This "vicious" circle leads us precisely to the key question about the principles of practical reason and moral knowledge: is it possible to have a concept of the "good-for-man" even without possessing virtue, that is, understanding the human good in the sense of moral principles or of "norms"? Aristotle elaborated such a doctrine of the principles of ethics only in rough outline. It consists, on the one hand, of recalling the opinions of better and wiser persons about what is good along with their personal examples, such, for example, as Pericles in the context of the Athenian *polis*. On the other

10. Cf. in this regard my books cited above in n. 1, *La prospettiva della morale* and *Praktische Vernunft und Vernünftigkeit der Praxis.*

hand, we find this answer in the *Politics,* to which the final books of the *Nicomachean Ethics* expressly refer: the well-ordered *polis* and its laws are treated as a substitute for the lack of virtue and ethical intelligence of anyone who prefers to follow his own passions rather than reason. Such a man will then be compelled to keep to the good as defined by the laws and sanctions of the *polis.*

Nothing more can be found in Aristotle on this point; and the "subjectivity of the moral fact" in his thinking reaches its limit here. There is a simple reason for this. Aristotle was of the opinion that because the principle of all morality was destroyed in the vicious person, he would also be incorrigible: he whose passions had corrupted what was "the best in him," his reason, would be able to attain to the good only by way of external compulsion. The virtuous person thus becomes an exceptional figure, a member of an elite; for the many, for the mass, the *polis* comes to the rescue with its laws playing the role of the reason, which exists on a generalized level only in this form. In this way ethics becomes the ethics of the *polis.* The truth-power of the reason that appeared so universal to begin with is now reduced to the particularism of a concrete ethos.

The truth of the Aristotelian ethics, and the Platonic heritage preserved in it, only reached its full development through being taken up and integrated within the framework of the creation-metaphysics of Christianity. The Judaeo-Christian revelation would bring to fulfillment those categorical premises by which the Platonic-Aristotelian doctrine of the truth-power of the intellect as "the best in us" could reach its full validity. This secured the subjectivity of the moral fact along with the universality of the moral fact and the reason that was the foundation for both. It would now be possible to break the vicious circle, and bring an end to the essential premise of an ethics of the polis that endangered the subjectivity of the moral fact; for according to this premise only the virtuous man would possess moral intelligence, while the vicious, irreparably lost, would keep to the good only by the constraint of external laws. The Judaeo-Christian revelation brought to pass a certain "democratization" of virtue.

Thanks to the mediation of Judaic neo-Platonism, Biblical and Christian-inspired thought discovered another law, which we carry in our heart, and therefore became known as "the law of nature." Not only Christ, the eternal divine and uncreated *lógos,* but also man's similarity to God led to a transformation of the Stoic doctrine of the *lex aeterna* as a law of the cosmos through which man could realize his own freedom, provided he understood its necessity and subjected himself to it.

The first Christian theologians, or Fathers of the Church, despite all the Stoic influences, were radically detached from the Stoic mode of looking at the world.[11] In fact, for them as Christians the image of God was not to be found in the cosmos and the eternal law is not the *lógos* that rules this cosmos; the image of God in this world is the human soul alone, which now stands above the order of the cosmos. Consequently the eternal law of God, by which everything is ordered, is not a *lógos* of nature, and the participation in the eternal law is not the Stoic *oikeíosis,* or natural assimilation to the order of nature, a kind of *inhabitatio* in it and submission to its necessity. The eternal law, which underlies all nature, is instead the wisdom of God the *transcendent* Creator of all nature. Man participates in this wisdom and not simply because he is "nature" but because of his own reason, which is nothing other than participation in the divine light of the Creator's wisdom. The Christian Ambrose of Milan wrote in the fourth century—all the Stoic elements having been removed—that the natural law would be the "voice of God" written in our hearts, thanks to which "we understand that what is evil is naturally to be avoided and that what is good is naturally commanded to us" *(id quod malum est naturaliter intelligimus esse vitandum et id quod bonum est naturaliter nobis intelligimus esse praeceptum).*[12]

So then, while Cicero wrote of the natural law in a fully Stoic manner as *ratio summa, insita in natura*[13] (the highest reason, planted in nature) or as *recta ratio naturae congruens*[14] (right reason, in agreement with nature), which we "draw from nature,"[15] for Ambrose, the natural law is a natural manner of knowing; not, as for Cicero, a "voice of nature," but rather a "voice of God" in us, which makes itself heard *via* the natural knowledge of the reason.

The Platonic-Aristotelian theme of the *noûs* and *lógos* as "god in us" and as "the ruling part of the soul" returns here in Christian form, and correspondingly energized. The intellect is represented as the basic capacity of the human being to direct himself to the "human good," and precisely through a rationality that is secured not only by the possession of moral virtues, but also by a

11. Cf. M. Spanneut, "Les normes morales du stoïcisme chez les Pères de l'Église," in S. Pinckaers and C. J. Pinto de Oliveira, eds., *Universalité et permanence des lois morales* (Fribourg: Éditions Universitaires; Paris: Éditions du Cerf, 1986), 114–35.

12. Ambrose, *De Paradiso,* 8, 39.

13. Cicero, *De Legibus,* I, 6, 18.

14. Cicero, *De re publica,* III, 22, 33.

15. Cicero, *Pro Milone,* IV, 10 *(lex . . . quam . . . ex natura . . . hausimus).*

"light of reason"; through this "light" being proper to human nature *insofar as it is nature,* and thereby indefectibly present, and through this light the "subjectivity of the moral fact" is confirmed in a new form, and remains unsurpassed. Therefore, according to Thomas Aquinas, the "law of nature" is not a law of the cosmos but—as he explains in the Prologue to his commentary on the Decalogue—the law of nature "is nothing other than the light of the intellect infused in us by God"; thanks to this, "we know what should be done and should be avoided. God gave us this light and this law in creating us."[16]

At the distance of almost a thousand years from Ambrose, this specifically Christian perspective of the Patristic period is still current in the thought of Thomas Aquinas. Only a few centuries later (under the influence of modern natural science and of the "natural laws" discovered by it, for example, Kepler's planetary laws, Newton's laws of motion, Galileo's laws of gravitation, etc.), people would begin to speak about "natural laws" in the sense of "regularity" and "normativity," even within the realm of ethics. By falling back into a Stoic perspective, they tended to reduce the rational to the natural, and to reconceive the natural law in the ethical sphere in a Stoic sense, as a species of "natural normativity."

By contrast, the Thomist elaboration of the doctrine of the *lex naturalis* (in part along Aristotelian lines, but in another respect anchored in the metaphysics of creation) is nothing other than a doctrine of the principles (absent in Aristotle) of the practical reason.[17] The same *lex naturalis* is now the capacity of every human being to realize the "truth of subjectivity," and thereby the subjectivity of the moral fact. It demonstrates further what I have called the "democratization of virtue."

The "Light of the Natural Reason" and Its Normative Function

In order to avoid an erroneous understanding of the Thomistic doctrine of the natural law as an *ordinatio rationis* and to keep before our minds its *cognitive* function, we must read it in its Platonic-Aristotelian context.[18] We

16. Aquinas, *In duo praecepta caritatis et in decem legis praecepta Prologus.*

17. This is one of the central themes of *Praktische Vernunft und Vernünftigkeit der Praxis.*

18. See chapter 5, "The Cognitive Structure of the Natural Law and the Truth of Subjectivity," also published in *The Thomist* 67, no. 1 (2003): 1–44, and (originally) as "Natural Moral Law: Moral Knowledge and Conscience. The Cognitive Structure of the Natural Law and the Truth of Subjectivity," in *The Nature and Dignity of the Human Person as the Foundation of the Right to Life,* Proceedings of the Eighth Assembly of the Pontifical Academy for Life (February 25–27,

will misunderstand it if we consider reason only as an *organ* for knowing a nature that is conveyed to the reason in an object-like manner, as a norm that is "legible," so to speak, from nature, and knowable by the theoretical reason. This would be false, because the intellect and the reason are not organs for knowing a moral norm, but *are themselves the moral norm,* and precisely because they too are *nature:* the nature of man, a part of his being, in Aristotelian terms the "leading part of the soul," the "god in us." The intellect opens up a view for us on the intelligible truth of the good, to which we, insofar as we are human beings, always aim by nature with our instincts, inclinations, and desires; the end remains hidden to these latter, however, since they are merely nature not guided by reason.

Reason, as a discursive explication of the intellect, is therefore a *rule* and measure of morality, and precisely because the nature of the human being is formed from an essentially rational soul: this is, consequently, the essential and vital principle of the human being. The metaphysical and anthropological constitution of man is what founds the naturally normative function of the reason. Precisely because the "rationality" in man *is* his "nature," not simply "nature" but "reason" is the parameter for what is good-for-man. This good is essentially the "good of the reason," *bonum rationis.*

This is clarified when Thomas defines the natural law as "participation in the eternal law."[19] But this definition becomes obscure, ambiguous, or simply incomprehensible without reference to the Platonic-Aristotelian doctrine of the anthropological and cognitive primacy of the intellect, and of the "light function" of the reason. The definition does not constitute a limitation of the reason, but on the contrary, the very foundation and empowering of its central position. This is true because, if we prescind from revelation, we know the eternal law of God thanks only to *our* reason, "which derives from the divine spirit as its image."[20]

This is why Thomas so often cites the question of the Psalmist in the Fourth Psalm, "*Many say, Who will show us good things?*" In the Psalmist's re-

---

2002), ed. Juan de Dios Vial Correa and Elio Sgreccia (Vatican City: Libreria Editrice Vaticana, 2003), 123–59. A more systematic presentation can be found in M. Rhonheimer, *Natural Law and Practical Reason: A Thomistic View of Moral Autonomy* (New York: Fordham University Press, 2000) (German original: *Natur als Grundlage der Moral. Eine Auseinandersetzung mit autonomer und teleologischer Ethik* [Innsbruck: Tyrolia; Vienna: Verlag, 1987). Important for the theme and very useful are also the studies of G. Abbà, *Lex et virtus. Studi sull'evoluzione della dottrina morale di San Tommaso d'Aquino* (Rome: LAS, 1983), and *Felicità, vita buona e virtù. Saggio di filosofia morale* (Rome: LAS, 1989).

19. *ST* I-II, q.91 a.2.

20. Ibid., q.91 a.4 ad3um.

ply: *Lord, the light of Your countenance shines upon us,* Thomas sees a scriptural confirmation of the fact that "the light of the intellect, by which we distinguish good from evil—and this is precisely the sphere of the natural law—is nothing other than the light of the divine within us" *(impressio divini luminis in nobis.)*[21] Could there be any clearer expression than this of the Platonic-Aristotelian doctrine of the anthropological and cognitive primacy of the intellect and of the "natural reason," and its integration within the perspective of the Christian theology of creation?

The Thomistic teaching of the reason as norm, rule, and measure of morality (many Thomists attenuate it or avoid it as if they saw the reason merely as an organ for knowing, but not as a norm in itself), once it has been shorn of compromises, does not assume that the natural reason forms the good out of nothing, as it were "creating" it out of itself; rather, it does this insofar as it is the reason of a living being, constituted in a corporeal/spiritual unity. It "regulates" and therefore needs "something" to be regulated. The reason regulates the reality that we are, insofar as we are beings that move by nature to the good; it regulates, that is to say, what Thomas calls the *naturales inclinationes,* which, as the nature that we ourselves *are,* we cannot have at our free disposal; but they are still not moral norms, even if, as Thomas emphasizes, they pertain to the natural law to the extent that they are ordered by reason.

These natural inclinations are not a simple and formless "raw material," but a structure that is already *in*-formed according to nature, in which function and finality are inherent; the reason is not able to dispose of these inclinations at its whim, without failing to be the reason of a being that is naturally constituted in an essential soul/body unity. On the other hand, the natural law is not simple natural inclination, but rather the natural inclination *ordered* according to the requirements of reason. The natural law, like every law, is an *ordinatio rationis*[22] and *aliquid per rationem constitutum* and an *opus rationis*[23] (an "ordering of the reason," "something constituted by reason," a "work of reason"), hence the moral order, established by that reason in acts of the will, is a "rational order" (*ordo rationis,* "an order of reason").[24] Both, then—the naturally given inclination and the reason—are in relation to each other as matter and form, founding an essential unity. This removes any anthropological dualism.

21. Ibid., q.91 a.2.
22. Ibid., q.94 a.2 ad2um.
23. Ibid., q.90 a.4.
24. Ibid., q.94 a.1.

To make it clear with an example: it is only on the horizon of the reason that the sexual instinct—directed toward the body of another person along with all the connected emotional experiences—becomes the human good of conjugal love. This is a love of reciprocal self-giving at the service of friendship—a benevolence that refers to the whole person—and a love of indissoluble fidelity at the service of the transmission of life. This conjugal love is the truth of human "sexuality" which takes shape only on the level of reason. "Sexuality" insofar as it is nature only receives *at the level of reason* that configuration which distinguishes it as a fundamental human good, and only in this order does the relation between sexuality and love become rightly understood in its personal and thus human meaning. Purely as nature, sexuality is concerned, at most, with procreation and satisfaction of pleasure, and not with friendship, love, giving, and fidelity. Thus no command of the law of nature can be referred only to sexuality understood in this purely naturalistic sense; such a command would offer no *moral* guidance or instruction to human action.

The *Lex naturalis:* A Work of Practical Reason and the Subjectivity of the Moral Fact

We have arrived at a first and decisive consequence: just because the natural law is an *ordinatio rationis,* the reason is that-which-orders as the *practical* reason. What is the practical reason? With reference to the *faculty,* this is not a reason any different from the speculative or theoretical reason, but only an *extension* of the same intellectual capability in the realm of action.[25] It is the one human reason, capable of understanding truth and reality, which is displayed in the context of natural inclination, and principally and fundamentally in the context of that absolute tending ("seeking," "aiming," or "striving") toward the good that is the foundation of all other goods. At the very place where he speaks of the point of departure of the process of practical reasoning and its first principle,[26] Thomas cites—and not by chance—the sentence that opens the *Nicomachean Ethics:* "The good is that to which all things aim."[27]

The good appears originally in the context of aiming (= Latin *appetere,* "to seek after" or "tend to"; cf. Ital. *tendere,* or "striving," cf. Ger. *Streben*),

25. Ibid., q.79 a.11.

26. Ibid., q.94 a.2.

27. Aristotle, *Nicomachean Ethics,* I, 1, 1094a 3.

or inclination, desire, and will. Only in this context does the reason become practical and instigate action. The human being is not only a being who comprehends in a theoretical, epistemological, or speculative manner, referring to the fundamental law of being, according to which that which *is* cannot at the same time and in the same respect *not be;* the human being is also one who aims toward the good. But right here rationality begins with a first principle and does not derive from another higher principle: "the good is to be pursued and the evil is to be avoided."[28] This is the first principle of the *lex naturalis* upon which are founded in succession all the other practical principles (or commands) known by the reason in a natural manner.

The principles of the practical reason have as their object "the good-for-man" in its fundamental and universal form: not yet, of course, as concretely actualized action, but as a normative principle of the goodness of every concrete action. This good is by its essence the good as known and ordered by the reason; it is a *bonum rationis* that in its original form unfolds to human view in the self-experience of practical reason.

The originality of the Thomistic doctrine of the *lex naturalis* lies in the way it consistently takes the subject as its point of departure. Again, this is not the Stoic law of the cosmos, thanks to which man finds his liberty, provided only that he understands its necessity and subjects himself to it—as Hegel would maintain—but it is, rather, an active participation in the reason of divine providence, through which the human being becomes *providentiae particeps, sibi ipsi et aliis providens* ("sharing in providence, providing for oneself and others").[29] It is only by way of reason that what is good-for-man becomes "visible" to him, and only by reason do the instincts, inclinations, and tendencies of every kind lead to what we call the "human act," that is, an action guided by a rational will. This is why the reason is the *radix libertatis,* or "root of liberty," according to Thomas.[30]

This carefully thought-out subjective perspective of the Thomistic *lex naturalis* also results from the fact that the natural law is at the same time principle of *praxis* and principle of the morality of this *praxis.* By the natural law, the subject is constituted at one and the same time as an acting subject *and* as a moral subject, since this law is at the same time principle of action and principle of morality: it *moves* the subject "to pursue and carry out the

28. *ST* I-II, q.94 a.2.
29. Ibid.
30. Ibid., q.17 ad2um; also *De Veritate,* 24, 2.

good, to avoid the evil," and at the same time is the norm of the morality of this action. Insofar as they are principles of practical reason, the precepts of the *lex naturalis* are precisely those intelligible impulses that move us to action but, at the same time, always place this action under the distinction between "good" and "evil," and thereby confer a personal and moral dimension upon it.[31]

The teaching of the encyclical *Veritatis Splendor* on this theme (no. 43) can serve as a summary statement of what has been said so far: "But God provides for man differently from the way in which he provides for beings which are not persons. He cares for man not 'from without' through the laws of physical nature, but 'from within,' through reason, which, by its natural knowledge of God's eternal law, is consequently able to show man the right direction to take in his free actions."

The Priority of the Self-Experience of the Practical Reason and the Relation between Ethics and Metaphysics

A certain neo-Scholastic interpretation of Thomas that is still very widespread conceives the *lex naturalis* as, above all, a "law of nature" in the sense of a "normativity on the part of nature," or a conformity to the laws that are planted in "nature" perceived as an "objective reality" external to the human mind; such conformity to the laws is understood and carried out as a kind of "moral code." Practical reason would be nothing other than this "application" of the good recognized in nature by the use of the theoretical reason.

This is not the place to analyze the difficulties and the contradictions inherent in this conception, nor to show how it is virtually impossible to remedy them through reference to St. Thomas. It is opportune, however, to show here how this conception, which we could call the "naturalistic" interpretation, involves at least three errors.

Ontological Foundation versus Cognitive and Normative Validity

In the first place, the naturalistic interpretation of the natural law does not take into any account the special anthropological position within human nature of the intellect and the reason, and erroneously interprets nature it-

31. Cf. M. Rhonheimer, "Praktische Vernunft und das 'Von Natur aus Vernünftige.' Zur Lehre von der Lex naturalis als Prinzip der Praxis bei Thomas von Aquin," *Theologie und Philosophie* 75 (2000): 493–522 (English translation in chapter 5 in this book).

self, since the nature in question is *human* nature. In fact, the "subject" itself and subjectivity are also this "nature," as manifested in its rationally guided openness to reality.[32]

Now the objection that not reason but nature is the rule and measure of moral good is without force. This misses the very point of the dispute insofar as it does not distinguish between two distinct questions.

The first question, of a *metaphysical* character, considers the foundation of the "good-for-man." Such a foundation is nothing but the "nature of man." And this nature is what formulates the ends and thereby the perfection of human existence. Thus, in an ontological sense, it is the measure of human good and of the goodness of human actions.

32. Not a few Thomists appear to adhere to a certain "inverse Cartesianism" in the sense of supporting in a dualistic, and in this sense precisely Cartesian, manner the view that the "objective," the "natural," and the "true" would be equivalent to what is "found outside the mind," while what is in the mind (or the mind itself) would be "subjective," "non-natural," and a mere representation of the truth. Even if such "inverse Cartesianism" appears to be a very common neo-Scholastic conception, I do not believe that it accords with the thought of St. Thomas. For Thomas, as for Aristotle (and in another way for Plato as well), the human mind—especially the active intellect, which stands in relation to intelligible truth as light to the visibility of things—is part of human nature, and, therefore, in an ontological and fundamental way, the mind too is "nature." Both distinctions—between intra-mental reality and extra-mental reality and between mind and nature—seem to me to be of little use for clarifying the concept of the "natural," and misleading as well from the anthropological perspective. The intellect and its proper object—intelligible reality—are something natural for the human person, just as are the natural inclinations. It is thus strange to think that the objects and goods of the natural inclinations that are *extra*-mental (or non-mental)—as for example the objects and natural ends of the sexual inclination or the inclination toward self-preservation—would be more "natural" and "objective" than the inclinations, objects, and goods that rise in a natural way from the mind (or from the intellect or "natural reason"), as for example the concepts of the "just" or the "obligatory" (insofar as they are concepts of a good, and formally speaking are purely "mental," which is to say they are not found in extra-mental reality). We can, therefore, without hesitation maintain that there exists a "contribution of the mind" that is natural and entirely objective, without falling into an unsupportable "subjectivism" or aprioristic transcendentalism. On the contrary, a concept of the "natural" that excludes the contribution of the mind does not appear to be a concept of *human* nature. If we think, in an anthropological or ethical perspective, of the human person as a part of the "exterior" or "objective" world, we must include the mind and the intellectual faculty of man in this consideration—for otherwise we would be reducing man to his mere animality. (This note has been taken from chapter nine, *The Perspective of the Acting Person and the Nature of Practical Reason: The "Object of the Human Act" in Thomistic Anthropology of Action,* originally published in the Acts of the Congress Camminare nella luce. Prospettive della Teologia morale a 10 anni dalla *Veritatis Splendor,* held at the Pontifical University of the Lateran [November 20–22, 2003]; the note refers to K. Flannery's criticism of the action theory espoused in my book *Die Perspective der Moral.*) In his criticism, Flannery maintains that my emphasis on the contribution of the subject or the human intention ("the mind's contribution"), in the constitution of the object of a human act, would be "difficult to reconcile with Thomas Aquinas," and that it would sometimes lead to "excluding what exists outside the mind." Cf. K. Flannery, review of *Die Perspective der Moral* in *Gregorianum* 83 (2002): 591–94, esp. 592.

But the second question is put in the following terms: how does this demand of nature become valid at the cognitive and practical-regulative level? To this *ethical* question—which really concerns the moral norm—we reply by saying that it is only on the horizon of reason that the natural given is revealed in its "goodness-for-man": only by the light of reason—that is, insofar as it is rational—does nature become normative. Only under the guidance and regulation of reason can the ends of the instincts and the natural tendencies be—in a natural way—a "good-for-man." And this is precisely why the moral order *is* founded on nature, but on the nature of a *rational* being.

These ends are not recognized by the reason simply as normative facts that are then transformed in praxis, but they show their normative content only *insofar* as they are objects of the reason. These ends become visible in their intelligible content only through their objectivization by way of the reason and, with that, they become integrated within the higher order of reason. That reason does indeed play this role follows from the fact that it is itself part—the dominant part—of the natural entity to which "nature" is related as a measure. I want to emphasize that this follows directly from the fact that human nature is the ultimate foundation, and in this sense also "norm" (or "meta-norm"), of moral good.

Consequently, as Thomas constantly affirms, in moral terms anything is conformable to the nature of the human being just insofar as it conforms to reason.[33] According to Thomas, this regulating function belongs to reason by a simple metaphysical or anthropological consideration: man is man because he has a rational soul, because his soul is his substantial form. "What is good for every thing is what conforms to it according to its form; what is evil is what is alien to the order of its form. Therefore it is evident that to this extent

33. Cf. *ST* I-II, q.71 a.2: "quod est contra ordinem rationis, proprie est contra naturam hominis inquantum est homo; quod est autem secundum rationem, est secundum naturam hominis inquantum est homo. Bonum autem hominis est secundum rationem esse . . . unde virtus humana . . . intantum est secundum naturam hominis, inquantum convenit rationi: vitium autem intantum est contra naturam homini, inquantum est contra ordinem rationis." The same conception is found at q.18 a.5: "In actibus autem humanis bonum et malum dicitur per comparationem ad rationem." Cf. even q.71 a.6: "Habet autem actus humanus quod sit malus, ex eo quod caret debita commensuratione. Omnis autem commensuratio cuiuscumque rei attenditur per comparationem ad aliquam regulam, a qua, si divertat, incommensurata erit. Regula autem voluntatis humanae est duplex: una propinqua et homogenea, scilicet ipsa human ratio; alia vero est prima regula, scilicet lex aeterna, quae est quasi ratio Dei." For a correct understanding of the Thomistic teaching according to which the rule of morality is not "nature" but reason, the book by L. Lehu is still useful: *La raison, règle de la moralité d'après Saint Thomas* (Paris: Libr. Lecoffre, 1930).

the difference between good and evil, when it comes to the object, is determined with reference to the reason: that is to say, this difference depends on whether the object is suited or not suited to the reason. In fact, some acts are called human or moral, insofar as they proceed from reason."[34]

The distinction between asking about the (ontological) *foundation* of the moral order (which is certainly "nature") and asking about *how this natural foundation becomes practically effective and regulative* seems to me to be fundamental. We do not use the terms "*moral* norm," "*moral* rule," or "measure" for an *ontological* fact like "human nature," but we do use them for a *practical function of the intellect* (pertaining to this human nature), for measuring or determining the good and the bad in the acts of our will and, with that, in human acts. This is expressed in Thomas's statement: "In human actions, good and bad are spoken of with reference to the reason." *(In actibus humanis bonum et malum dicitur per comparationem ad rationem).* He says that it is this way because this corresponds to human nature; and this means that "nature" is not the norm, but always and only the reason.[35]

34. *ST* I-II, q.18 a.5: "Unicuique rei est bonum quod convenit ei secundum suam formam; et malum quod est ei praeter ordinem suae formae. Patet ergo, quod differentia boni et mali circa obiecta considerata comparatur per se ad rationem: scilicet secundum quod obiectum est ei conveniens vel non conveniens. Dicuntur autem aliqui actus humani, vel morales, secundum quod sunt a ratione."

35. In his review of my book *Natural Law and Practical Reason* (English translation of *Natur als Grundlage der Moral*) in *The Thomist* 66, no. 2 (2002): 313, Stephen L. Brock states that my affirmation that according to Thomas not nature but reason is the measure of morality is "a disconcerting claim." In a paradoxical fashion Brock refers to *ST* I-II, q.18 a.5, which is supposed to prove that according to Thomas not reason but nature is the norm of morality. I cannot explain this objection of Brock except as a misunderstanding (a classic, but rather anachronistic one, as can be seen from a reading of the work by L. Lehu cited in n. 33 above) of the distinction between the practical-regulative function of a "moral norm" and the ontological foundation that determines to which element in a determinate nature this practical-regulative role pertains. Once again: human nature is not the norm, but that which specifies what the norm is for the being in question! This is precisely what Thomas is saying in *ST* I-II, q.18 a.5; given that the (substantial) form of man and consequently his nature is of a rational kind, the rule of good and evil in his own actions is the reason. This rule is not the "substantial form" (an ontological principle) but the reason as faculty, and more precisely: the practical universal judgments of this faculty; judgments that are not referred to single actions as the judgments of prudence, but certain *types* or *species* of actions, some of which, namely the precepts of the natural law, are natural, and with that, really principles of the practical reason and a rule or "law" for all the acts of the practical reason. It seems strange and nonsensical to me that the "substantial form" functions as a "moral norm," and that in order to know what we should do, we must, so to speak, "consult" or "follow" our *substantial form!* Rather, it is precisely because we are beings of a rational nature that we ought to follow our reason: the moral norm is, time after time, the *practical judgment* of our reason (a *dictamen rationis,* or "enunciation of the reason" of a universal kind, as I have said, which refers to a species of action), and it is regulated, I emphasize once again, by those practical judgments that are natural and perform the function of practical principles: the precepts of

In no operation is "nature" the *rule* (or norm) of good and evil: rather, the nature of a being is what determines what this rule is in each case. In the case of human nature and human acts, this rule is the reason (not even in the case of animals is their "nature" the rule, but rather instinct and the other sensible impulses which, to be sure, are *natural,* as the reason is natural for human beings). Therefore (human) nature is not the "norm" of morality, but the intrinsic ontological principle that determines reason to be this norm.

The Self-Experience of the Practical Reason: Its Cognitive Primacy

We now arrive at the second error—closely connected with the first—concerning the naturalistic interpretation of the natural law. It has to do with the origin of our moral concepts, and above all our conception of the "good-for-man"; it regards, therefore, the genesis of practical and moral self-experience and the relationship between theoretical and practical reason. Misled by this erroneous interpretation, we think we know "human nature" before anything else, and that we think of the "good-for-man" by way of this knowledge and, as a final phase, carry it out in actions. But to think in this way is to negate the originality of the comprehension of the "good-for-man," and to *reverse* the relationship between "knowledge of good and evil" and "knowledge of human nature."

In reality, we are able to interpret human nature adequately only if we already possess an idea of the "good-for-man." Without the self-experience of the instincts and inclinations of the subject and of the "order of reason" established in us by way of the reason, we would not be able in fact to comprehend the nature of man as a simple object of external observation. The nature of non-rational living beings, which conduct themselves according to "the laws of nature," can be adequately described and defined to a certain extent—just as Aristotle does in the eighth chapter of the second book of the *Phys-*

---

the natural law. We need only recall that moral virtue comes into existence so that the reason can carry out its role as a moral norm—so it can be *recta ratio*—even if the normative role of the natural law is realized independently of the possession of moral virtue. This doctrine implies, I would like to emphasize, the Platonic-Aristotelian doctrine reaffirmed by Thomas, according to which the intellect in itself is an infallible light of truth, and likewise of the truth about good, and is distorted only by "exterior" influences such as the passions, the will, ignorance, prejudices of various kinds (this is why Aristotle says that "the intellect is always right, but appetition and sensory imagination are not necessarily so" [*De Anima* III, 10, 433a 27–28]); and according to Thomas (*In Sent* II. D. 24, 3, 3 ad3um), "ratio corrupta non est ratio" ("corrupted reason is not reason"); cf. the same text referred to at n. 55 here. This implies as well (and what is really the basis of the doctrine) that the reason and intellect insofar as they are mental realities pertaining to man *are nature* (cf. above, n. 32).

ics—observing what happens normally and regularly. But for this purpose a *Historia animalium* would suffice, that is, an empirical description and classification. Disciplines like natural science and biology would be enough, and there would be no need for ethics.

On the other hand, the nature of a being that possesses a spiritual soul and therefore is rational and free is not accessible to this kind of observation, because in a free entity, the regular and normal case is not by itself the criterion of what is adequate and good for man *insofar as he is man* (and not merely a living organism, for example). The distinction between what I "see" by observing and what I experience in my interior life as "myself," is precisely the difference between the nature of a highly developed mammal and the nature of a *rational animal,* that is to say, of an organism whose vital principle is a soul endowed with spirit. "Rationality," "spirituality," also "freedom," and in short, "personhood" are not observable objects, but more than anything else are only *experienced* as a "self."

As Thomas teaches us, the essence of "things, in themselves" is unknown to us; we only know them from their operations.[36] But the acts of those powers of the soul that are specific to man we can observe "originally," so to speak, only as they exist in ourselves: only here is fully revealed the "nature" of a living entity endowed with rationality and acting in freedom. Only on the basis of this experience and in the ongoing reflection upon it do we succeed in adequately interpreting nature—and the nature of human beings—by recognizing them as equal to ourselves and placing them in an analogy with ourselves.

And it is just for the same reason that the self-experience of the "good-for-man" does not really derive from "theoretical principles" about human nature, but is originally a *practical* fact.[37] We can form the theoretical principles for it only afterwards. Now, this does not mean that this self-experience is arbitrary, artificially constructed, or merely "at our disposal." To say that this flows from a genuinely *practical* act of the intellect only means that it flows from a mode of knowing that from the outset and in a natural way—and we cannot remove ourselves from it—is inserted within the dynamism of appetition and is cognitively referred to that same dynamism. For this reason,

36. *De Veritate,* 10, 1.

37. Cf. J. Finnis, *Fundamentals of Ethics* (Oxford: Clarendon Press, 1983), 10ff. and 20ff. I think that J. Maritain had already understood this correctly: *Neuf leçons sur les notions premières de la philosophie morale* (Paris: Tequi, 1951).

in his commentary on the Aristotelian work *De Anima*[38] Thomas not only says that the practical intellect "observes truth for the sake of action" *(speculatur veritatem propter operationem)* but he also says that it does this because, insofar as it is intellect, it becomes practical when it is referred to an object of an appetition ("seeking" or "aiming"), since "that at which the appetition aims, namely the 'appetible' or 'seekable' is the principle of the practical intellect" *(illud cuius est appetitus, scilicet appetibile, est principium intellectus practici)*. The text proceeds as follows: "Precisely because the object of the seeking [the *appetibile*]—the first object known by the practical intellect [*quod est primum consideratum ab intellectu practico*]—*moves,* we also say that the practical intellect moves insofar as its own principle, the object of the seeking, is to move."

The intellect is practical, then, to the extent that it operates in the context of appetition. Its point of departure is the object of the appetition, whether this be of a sensible or even intellective nature, such as the tendency of the will, and not a theoretically known entity. And the point of departure simply has to be natural seeking, that is, that which nature herself produces and what the process of the practical reason originally generates. This is precisely, once again, the *lex naturalis* and its commands or principles which refer to fundamental human goods.

Now this does not mean that such knowing—the *speculatio veritatis propter operationem* (observation of the truth for the purpose of action) mentioned above—does not refer to being, to reality, to *res naturae* or that it does not depend on that, since the tendencies and the inclinations are real being. The same *regula rationis humanae* derives from the "created reality that man knows in a natural manner."[39] It means only that here "entity," "being," and "nature" are being understood from the outset in the practical dimension and hence as correlated to an appetition, and that is to say objectified as good. This is precisely what Thomas is explaining in the famous statement: *bonum est quod omnia appetunt*[40] ("The good is what all things seek"). The fundamental human goods are comprehended in a natural way by the practical intellect, such that "everything that ought to be done or avoided pertains to the precepts of the natural law, which practical reason grasps in a natural way as human goods."

38. *In Aristotelis librum De Anima commentarium* III, lect. 15.
39. *ST* I-II, q.74 a.7.
40. Ibid., q.94 a.2.

Consequently, also, the practical reason grasps reality and knows truth: the truth of the *appetitum* or "object sought," the truth of the good, or Aristotle's "good in reality."

Practical and Theoretical Reason: Their Parallelism and Interaction

Practical judgments (even those primary ones which, as precepts of the *lex naturalis,* form the principles of the practical reason and constitute the human being as a practical and moral subject) are not deductions or applications of theoretical judgments. This does not mean, as the critics of this conception often object, that the sphere of *praxis*—the sphere of practical judgment about the good to be realized in action—would be disconnected from the sphere in which we make judgments about natural and practically relevant properties of things, their structures, or capacities, etc. It may be objected, for example, that someone who wants to heal others would need knowledge concerning the natural properties of medicinal substances and their suitability for this or that disease, and that these are instances of theoretical knowledge only subsequently put to use in practical applications. This would prove that practical judgments by definition are nothing but applications of the theoretical judgments about something that possesses this or that property, capacity, suitability, quality, or convenience. In an analogous way we would first recognize the nature of man, in order, afterwards, to conform to this nature by applying the theory to the world of action.

But this objection rests on a confusion between practical *judgment* on the one side and the entire process of discursive practical reasoning on the other, which is what Aristotle called the "practical syllogism." To affirm, as I have been doing here, that practical judgments are not formed by deriving them from theoretical judgments or by "applying" them, and that the practical reason in general is not taken to be derived from the theoretical use of the reason, does not mean to deny the presence of theoretical judgments in the discursive process of practical reasoning, that is to say, judgments about facts and their corresponding evaluations.

The practical syllogism, as presented by Aristotle in its classic form, as a structural and discursive pattern of practical reflection, consists of a *sequence* of judgments, of which the first, or *major,* premise is necessarily a practical judgment which, imbedded within an "aiming" or "seeking," moves the subject to action, and this would be of the type: "it is good (for me) to pursue and do this or that," where the phrase "it is good for me" indicates a judgment that does not affirm some given fact, but rather expresses a determined willing, an intention, such as: "I am pursuing the end of healing." In seeking the modes of realizing the practical syllogism there is need of a second premise, the *minor* premise, which emerges from sense perception, or is a judgment of theoretical reason which establishes a fact: "this medicine has this or that property, and is adapted to producing these or those effects," and so on. This is then followed by the *consequence* that in its own turn is again *practical* (Aristotle says it is "the action itself"): "it is good (for me) here and now to take this medicine"; this is the judgment that underlies the choice of action or the action itself.

Decisive for this structure is the fact that the practicality—that is, the moving force—of the ultimate judgment, the very thing that triggers the action, does not come from the minor theoretical premise, but only and exclusively from the practical major premise of the syllogism. Nothing practical or relevant for the praxis of a concrete subject would come about *only* from the minor premise ("this is a medicine meant for alleviating a headache") *if this judgment were not already inserted within the process of practical reasoning.* The conclusion of such reasoning and the consequent actions are not practical "applications" of the theoretical judgment of the *minor* premise about the suitability of the medicine, but rather a concretization of the *major* premise, already of a practical character, which first set the discursive process in motion and received its own practical character from one of the first principles of practical reason.

Nothing practical follows from a theoretical judgment as such (e.g., nothing practical follows from the judgment "this is a good medicine against headache"); instead, something does follow from the previous practical judgment—the intention—which by its lack of concreteness is not immediately operative; but this of course is *by way of* the theoretical judgment. Theoretical judgments consequently do have practical relevance, precisely because they exist within the context of a practical syllogism, which is to say they are integrated into the process of practical reasoning. The ascertainment of facts is not such as directly to generate something practical, but is the *means whereby* something practical can be carried out, that is, the concrete and practical judgment about what conduces to an end.

The ever-repeated objection[41] that this affirmation of a parallelism of

41. A prominent example is R. McInerny, *Aquinas on Human Action: A Theory of Practice* (Washinton, D.C.: The Catholic University of America Press, 1992), 184ff.

theoretical and practical reason each with its own gnoseological normativity would disconnect "reasoning about actions" from "reasoning that grasps being" may appear as a rather benign misunderstanding. After all, is it not the unity of reason that makes a connection possible between the intelligible ends of appetition and the theoretically intelligible structures of reality?

Despite the seemingly harmless nature of the disagreement, however, a crucial point is at issue for a true understanding of ethics and the human person as a moral subject. The defense of the parallelism of the practical and theoretical reasons and of the autonomy and non-derivability of the principles of practical reason leads us to an adequate understanding of the subjectivity of the moral fact and thereby to the truth that man is not a natural being just like other living things.

In fact, man is a natural being which, insofar as he is rational, is "nature" not to the same standard as the other natural beings, but in a way that brings with it the principle of its own regulation and measurability, not only as a natural inclination built into him in a passive way, but, as Thomas Aquinas expressly maintains, in an active way as well, since man is to a certain degree "a law unto himself." Only that which has been regulated and put into order by the reason is "human nature," where this active principle of order, the practical reason, belongs to this nature as its dominant part. The theoretical reason is not in fact called to regulate or put into order, but, insofar as it is human reason, is always and only referred to what has already been regulated by nature, to then take it up into itself, to accept and observe it. Such knowing would become practical only to the extent to which it enters into the process—constituted independently—of discursive practical reasoning (the "practical syllogism"), that is, in the natural intellective appetition or "aiming" of the human being toward the good and toward that ultimate fulfillment we call happiness.

In this way the practical reason is a mode of reason not reducible to any other type of knowing. If practical reason is reduced to a pure application of theoretical judgments in the practical sphere, human nature would be "naturalized" or objectivized in an improper way, and man himself would be reduced to a simple object: the subjectivity of the moral fact, if not quite completely lost to view, would be weakened and undervalued as pure "subjectivism." But human *persons* would be nothing other than objects in nature for moral reasoning, and not subjects whose nature comes to light only on the horizon of rationality and with the self-experience of the good. In fact, the good is not comprehensible from the perspective of the third person, but only and always from that of the first person, insofar as it is correlated to our own striving, as guided by reason toward the good.

The Relationship between Ethics and Metaphysics/Anthropology

We now have arrived at the third problem with the "naturalistic" interpretation of the *lex naturalis,* which is a misunderstanding of the relationship between ethics on the one hand and metaphysics—or anthropology—on the other. Thomists and Catholic moral theologians are accustomed to say that ethics is founded on metaphysics and that no ethics is possible without this. Although I am very far from calling such a view mistaken, a few qualifications are needed.

In fact, what has been discussed so far is nothing other than anthropology and in this sense metaphysics as well. Even before we pose any questions about the relations between ethics and metaphysics, these two are already in existence. By beginning with metaphysics or by dedicating ourselves to the study of the human person with philosophical-anthropological intentions, we already presuppose that which constitutes ethics as a philosophical discipline: the self-experience of the human person as an acting and moral subject, and that is to say the existence of the subjectivity of the moral fact along with the inseparable experience of the "good-for-man." And *this* is even less deducible from theoretical reason in general, or from metaphysics or anthropology.

It is significant that Aristotelian metaphysics begins with the statement: "All men by nature desire to know." Even if "knowing" or "understanding" are acts of the theoretical intellect, *aiming* toward this knowing and *knowing* that the "good-for-man" is in question here are both eminently practical by nature. Without knowledge of the good that consists in "desiring to know" (Thomas refers to it as one of the natural inclinations within the context of which the *lex naturalis* takes shape), there would be no metaphysics or science at all.

But even the *object* of metaphysics, insofar as it concerns man, is something that is revealed to us especially and in an authentic way in the self-experience of the practical reason, as we have described above. If metaphysics, according to Plato, is the question regarding the "nature of being," or if, according to Aristotle, it is the inquiry into "being as being," then the being that man is cannot be adequately visualized without the self-experience of the practical reason. If metaphysics is supposed to say something about the human being that it cannot say about *any* natural entity, then it would need at the outset to have this concept of man that discloses itself to us only by way of the self-experience of the practical reason as the "good-for-man," and that is likewise the point of departure for ethics.

We can conclude from this that ethics does not derive from metaphysics, and equally so, that metaphysics does not derive from ethics. As philosophical disciplines with their own proper mode of knowing and as distinct systematic reflections on reality, they constitute themselves, rather, in a truly reciprocal fashion, supporting and illuminating each other. Of course, we should not operate under the deception that reality is structured according to philosophical disciplines or to the academic canon of subject matters; it is a great and complex unity of which we human beings can only know some aspects, and it shows itself to our theoretical reflection not only as *being* but also as *good,* as the object of the practical intellect.

Ethics is a reflection upon our self-experience insofar as we are acting subjects, with the end of making sure that our action is right. This self-experience is already an experience of being. The question is not simply *whether* ethics is founded simply on metaphysics, but *under what aspect* it is so founded. We can reply to such a question only when we have understood where our knowledge about being human and about "the-good-for-man" originally comes from. But we have already replied to this question, that it originates, in fact, from the self-experience of the "good-for-man" insofar as it is an original object of the practical reason (that is, of reason working in the context of / "embedded" in desire, striving, aiming). This means that ethics is not subalternate to metaphysics, that is, subordinated or "posterior" to it, that it is not in a relationship of derivation from it, but possesses its own principles, taken directly from the reality of the self-experience of man all along, as a practical and moral subject.[42]

Now, I do not intend to assert that metaphysics—by some kind of role reversal—takes its first principles, for example, from practical reasoning. This would be a gigantic error, since the first principle of the speculative intellect is the principle of contradiction, which is given immediately with the original act of comprehending being as such, an act that without any doubt precedes every act of the practical reason. That being is the supreme object of all

42. I would like to refer here to the classical treatment of this problem that begins in W. Kluxen, *Philosophische Ethik bei Thomas von Aquin* (Hamburg: Meiner, 1964, 1984, 1998).

knowing cannot be doubted. On this is founded the priority of the speculative use of the reason over the practical use.

But this priority does not imply that the practical reason is reduced to the function of applying speculative judgments to the practical realm. And this is not in contradiction with the fact that metaphysics, to the extent that it is relevant for ethics—and that means as philosophical anthropology—should not already be in possession of the object of ethics which cannot be derived from metaphysics. The "good-for-man" and the corresponding interpretation of "human nature" are not founded by metaphysics or by philosophical anthropology, but on the contrary: it is really the knowledge of such things that lends those disciplines their very objects, to the extent that they affirm something true about human nature.

However, metaphysics permits us to penetrate this object more deeply and illuminate it. We may reflect as follows: even if the "good-for-man" is originally object of the practical reason, which receives its own principles in response to it, this original experience will be in need of deeper interpretation, in a reflection that can only be of the "theoretical" kind. Different forms of such interpretations are conceivable and are in fact well known: we can understand the experience of the self psychologically as the "superego" simply inculcated by education, or as a sociological phenomenon produced by socialization. The human sciences offer us a vast quantity of data and possible interpretations which will continue to be subject to evaluation and interpretation on the basis of moral criteria. But behind the moral content of this self-experience we can also discover the demands of a "nature" that incites us to the realization of potentialities that lie hidden within it, and this would itself be an example of genuinely metaphysical reasoning. Furthermore, behind the "voice of reason" that is clearly manifested within us, we can also hypothesize about the "voice of God" instead of a "superego."

This clarifies again how we cannot fail to take a little metaphysical journey when we consider the human being as a practical and moral subject. The Platonic and Aristotelian thesis that affirms the anthropological and cognitive primacy of the reason and the corresponding understanding of the practical reason as the origin of our consciousness of the "good-for-man," not to speak of the connected knowledge of the "subjectivity of the moral fact," is already a significant piece of philosophical anthropology.

It would be difficult to establish at every point where "ethics" begins and where "metaphysics" ends; both possess their own autonomy, and each is dependent on the other. Nevertheless, this is the decisive point: to know what is "the-good-for-man" and to know that we are moral subjects does not require a study of metaphysics and anthropology. If that were the case, the *lex naturalis* would not have any use: its function as law or as an *ordinatio* of practical reason is precisely that of authentically showing us the "good-for-man" and of directing our striving and our actions, as we constitute ourselves as acting and moral subjects.

But this last mentioned fact would not be possible if we had to study metaphysics first. It is not necessary to teach children what "justice" is: if they do not know what it is after a certain age—say, when they reach the age of "the use of reason"—then any particular instruction intended to explain why this or that is just or unjust would be a waste of time, since they would be deprived of the very concept of what is just or unjust. That is a concept that develops naturally as a principle of the practical reason, as for example the Golden Rule. The principles are really *principia,* that is, starting points, points of departure (Greek *archai*)—which penetrate and dominate everything that follows. If they are not already present, they will not even be capable of being grasped by way of instruction or study, since these latter presuppose something superior, something prior to the principle itself which, as we see in the natural course of things, cannot be given. Whoever has not experienced the sexual attraction of another person, or whoever has not experienced friendship, will never succeed in understanding the goods that are implanted there, just as someone blind from birth will never understand color, or a deaf person music.

Education and training presuppose the subjectivity of the moral fact, and are addressed to persons who already understand themselves as moral subjects prior to any instruction. This also holds for the human being who is going to accept any revealed moral teaching: he will accept revelation as *moral* instruction only to the extent that he is already a moral subject.

Empowerment of Reason by the Theology of Creation: Cognitive Autonomy and "Participated Theonomy"

One essential consequence of the Platonic-Aristotelian doctrine concerning the anthropological and cognitive primacy of the intellect and of reason is the concept of a normative authority of the reason and rationality as empowered by the theology of creation, and also a specific conception of autonomy as *cognitive* autonomy. Autonomy at the cognitive level, in the perspective of the theology of creation, means that man knows the good as established by God, and is able by his natural reason to distinguish between good and evil. This autonomy is in reality "participated theonomy," the cognitive possession of that which corresponds, within man, to the wisdom of divine providence. In the "natural law" the eternal law becomes known, and the divine will along with it. The eternal law is recognized and ratified in the human reason in just the degree to which the latter distinguishes between good and evil.

If we prescind for a moment from the possibility of revealed moral instruction, man would certainly be "thrown back" in a way upon himself. Thanks to this hypothesis, once again it becomes clear how Thomas likewise is thinking radically about the "subjectivity of the moral fact." Once again it is a question of a subjectivity oriented toward rationality, the legitimacy of which is connected for its own part to rational criteria. It is a subjectivity which knows that it is linked to a higher subjectivity, the creative subjectivity of God.

There is, consequently, a need for practical rationality to be alert against being deceived, and to remain in the truth. Even if, as Aristotle says, the intellect is "always right," the human intellect is nevertheless the intellect of a living being composed of a body and soul, affected because of this by instincts and passions, a being whose free will can rebel against what corresponds to reason, by "turning back" against itself. Subjectivity will have to be concerned with the "objectivity" which I referred to at the beginning as the "truth of subjectivity." We learn from Aristotle that this truth is guaranteed on condition that the inclinations of the human person are brought within the state we call "moral virtue."

In this way an ethics of the anthropological primacy of reason and of the autonomy of reason becomes virtue ethics. Thomas repeats this in the treatise on law: since man is by nature a rational being, he possesses as well the natural inclination to act according to reason; this is to act in conformity with virtue so that it is proper to virtue to make us adhere to the natural law.[43] However, theologians normally speak rather of the "moral law" than of virtue; and they do this for various reasons. I would like to mention the most important of these.

43. *ST* I-II, q.94 a.3.

It is self-evident that Christian theology, being rooted in biblical revelation, is bound up with the category of law. But even the divine law of biblical tradition and of God as Legislator are understood through the analogy of the experience of law and human legislation. God as "Legislator" and the order of His Providence as "law" are obviously anthropomorphisms based on the experience of human arrangements regulated by laws, an experience that also becomes for the God of Israel the means of making *intelligible* His moral instructions and the Tables of the Covenant. The discourse about the "natural law" is also understood in this sense: in Thomas this results from his intention to locate a doctrine of the practical reason of definitively Aristotelian inspiration within the framework of a Christian theology, and to formulate it accordingly as a "law" that is not "divine" but "natural."

It is important to understand this not only to avoid distorting discourse about "natural law," but also to understand the concept of autonomy correctly. Certain currents of post-conciliar moral theology have in fact misunderstood this autonomy in an anthropological sense—so-called "theonomous autonomy"—and they conceive it as a species of independence, or of "delegated competence for one's own affairs," and of divine "authorization" for the sake of a normative creativity that is subject to continuous revision in light of the changing conceptions of the human sciences.[44] Human autonomy is not, in any case, a type of "delegated competency for one's own affairs," but rather participation in the competency proper to God, the very same "participation of the eternal law," or "participated theonomy." In other words, human autonomy is not a "free space" for the creation of norms that man possesses over against God, but rather, it is *within* human autonomy—the cognitive autonomy of the decisive, "dominant" function of reason—that theonomy establishes itself: the eternal law, the *ratio* of divine wisdom that guides all things to their end.[45]

Looking at the matters in this light can re-establish the "radical subjectiv-

44. Cf. among others F. Böckle, *Fundamentalmoral* (Munich: Kösel, 1977), and the book by his student K.-W. Merks, *Theologische Grundlegung der sittlichen Autonomie. Strukturmomente eines 'autonomen' Normbegründungsverständnisses im lex-Traktat der Summa Theologiae des Thomas von Aquin* (Düsseldorf: Patmos, 1978).

45. Cf. J. Finance, "Autonomie et Theonomie," in M. Zalba, ed., *L'Agire Morale,* Atti del Congresso Internazionale (Rome-Naples, April 17–24, 1974), *Tomasso d'Aquino nel suo settimo centenario* 5 (Naples, 1974), 239–60. I have treated this theme fully in *Natural Law and Practical Reason* (see above, nn. 18, 35). Cf. also Rhonheimer, "Autonomia morale, libertà e verità secondo l'enciclica Veritatis Splendor," in G. Russo, ed., *Veritatis Splendor. Genesi, elaborazione, significatio,* 2nd ed. (Rome: Edizioni Dehoniane, 1995), 193–215.

ity of the moral fact" in terms of the theology of creation, as well as the anthropological and cognitive primacy of the reason. But this primacy is that of a reason that does not understand itself as the *origin* of truth; rather, it is a reason that comes to know truth and always has to pose to itself the question about its own rationality. Or better: *the subject,* to which this rationality pertains, will have always to pose to itself the old fundamental question of ethics. This is the point of departure, according to Aristotle, for our reflections: Is what appears to us as good *truly* good? Is the appearance of the good joined with the truth of the good?

As we have seen, this is what brought Aristotle to the concept of moral virtue, referred to in his *Eudemian Ethics* as the "intellect's organ" *(tou nou organon):*[46] virtue is that state of the subject in which reason, by governing, is able to affirm its own needs and, to be precise, not *in spite of,* but *with the help of* the inclinations (which in themselves are *not* rational), so long as these latter are being ordered in conformity with the reason. The Thomistic conception of the *lex naturalis* provides the doctrine of the principles of the practical reason (a doctrine that is missing in Aristotle)[47] but without compromising the Aristotelian approach to *praxis;* by which it differs from science in not being directed toward what is eternal but "to what can be otherwise,"[48] meaning to what is contingent and situationally conditioned and particular.

It is at once evident that an ethics that is biblically founded, whose principles are constituted by a divinely revealed law—the *lex divina*—and not by the reason of the moral subject, is not necessarily in contradiction with what has just been proposed. To the contrary, it is sustained by a conception of participative/cognitive autonomy, as expounded in Thomas's doctrine of the anthropological and cognitive primacy of the reason. It is just through this that the human reason, insofar as it is an image of the divine reason, becomes a law as well, to be precise the "law of nature," and man becomes understood as a moral subject in conformity with the divine law. But it is just this also which at the same time preserves the divine law from false interpretations of a legalistic, morally positivistic, or nominalistic character.

It therefore appears clearly again that the divine revelation of moral norms, just like any instruction and education, always has recourse to sub-

46. *Eudemian Ethics,* VIII, 2, 1248a 29.

47. Cf. once again my contribution to this discussion in *Praktische Vernunft und Vernünftigkeit der Praxis,* esp. part V.

48. Aristotle, *Nicomachean Ethics* VI, 3, 1140a1.

jects that are already constituted as *moral* subjects. For example, the commandment not to kill would not be understood if the concepts of good, obligation, just, and unjust were not already present in those to whom the commandment is addressed. Even when it imparts commandments that are contained in the natural law, the divine law would not be understood as *moral* instruction without the previous presence of the *lex naturalis* in the subject to whom the divine law is addressed.

Because moral revelation is not a surrogate for the subjectivity of the moral fact, it can always be understood only as a help and support to this subjectivity, as a support, therefore, for the "truth of subjectivity." Moral revelation is directed to beings who are moral subjects thanks to reason, for otherwise it would not be able to achieve its purpose of *moral* instruction, but would only be an instrument of dominion of the superior over the naturally inferior.

Conclusions: The Inescapable Authority of Reason and Its "Salvation" by Way of Faith

I would like to conclude with two important consequences that follow from what I have presented. First: moral autonomy is understood as a cognitive autonomy that is not *limited by,* but *supported and empowered by,* revelation. In a certain sense, revelation and faith are really "the salvation of reason."[49] By the light of biblical revelation we know that the reason's condition, as contested by instincts and disordered inclinations, is a fallen condition: Thomas describes for us how the primeval state of the first human beings was a condition of full possession of moral virtues in which reason had its own power intact for directing man to the good. Precisely *because* this was reason's proper role, that is, in virtue of the anthropological and cognitive primacy of the reason, a revelation directed to rational beings is not a diminution but an empowering of their autonomy.[50]

And this is the second consequence: even under the divine law, subjectivity of the moral fact remains. Above all, the relationship between freedom

49. J. Ratzinger, "Christliche Orientierung in der pluralistischen Demokratie? Über die Unverzichtbarkeit des Christentums in der modernen Gesellschaft," in H. Bürkle and N. Lobkowitz, ed., *Das Europäische Erbe und seine christliche Zukunft,* Veröffentlichungen der Hanns-Martin-Schleyer-Stiftung 16 (Cologne-Bachem: Hanns-Martin-Schleyer-Stiftung, [1985]), 20–35, esp. 31ff.; reprinted in J. Ratzinger, *Kirche, Ökumene und Politik. Neue Versuche zur Ekklesiologie* (Einsiedeln: Johannes Verlag, 1987), 183–97.

50. See the first essay in this collection, "Is Christian Morality Reasonable? On the Difference between Secular and Christian Humanism," originally published in *Annales Theologici* 15, no. 2 (2001): 529–49.

and truth can be understood only by way of the reason. It is true that only the truth makes us free, but it can do so only as truth *known* to be such in the subjectivity of one's own cognitive process. To desire a stable bond between freedom and truth that dislodges or degrades the anthropological and cognitive primacy of the reason would really mean the *instability* of this very relationship (between truth and freedom) and would put servitude in place of freedom, sheer "legalism" in place of morality. Thomas expresses this in a statement unique in its kind: "He who avoids evil not because it is evil but because it is prohibited by God is not free; he who avoids evil because it is evil is free."[51] This affirmation looks to the conception of Aristotle, according to which he alone is virtuous who does what is virtuous because it is virtuous, and not because others have commanded it, such as happens, for example, when we follow the advice of a medical doctor for a certain cure, without having to know medical science ourselves.[52] Along the same lines is Thomas's teaching that one sins by going against one's own conscience, even if the conscience is erroneous: "A will not in accord with reason is bad, whether the reason is right or mistaken."[53]

The authority of the reason is inescapable,[54] and this brings certain consequences to man in terms of obligation and responsibility. He is not only condemned to freedom, but also to that which forms its root, that is, rationality, even if what is rationally proposed does not lead us all to the same opinion. But this has to do much less with the principles of the natural law as with its applications.

Is it naïve or simply an exaggeration to say that reason shows us what is good in reality, and without any deception? No; because this does not mean that we are incapable of making mistakes in using our reason, but that reason as such (or rather, the intellect) cannot err, that if it errs it does not do so *insofar as* it is reason. Error is always in some sense a *lack* of reason, brought about through various causes: passionate-emotive conduct, ignorance, cultural conditioning, prejudice. As Thomas puts it in lapidary style: *Ratio corrupta non est*

51. Thomas Aquinas, "Super secundam epistolam ad Corinthios lectura" II, lect. 3, in *S. Thomae Aquinatis, super Epistulas S. Pauli Lectura*, ed. R. Cai (Turin-Milan: Marietti, 1953, Editio 8a revisa), 464: "Ille ergo qui vitat mala non quia mala, sed propter mandatum Domini, non est liber; sed qui vitat mala, quia mala, est liber."

52. Aristotle, *Nicomachean Ethics* VI, 13 1143b28, 33.

53. *ST* I-II, q.19 a.5.

54. Hence the affirmation of Spaemann: "One cannot want to hear reason instead of having to listen to reason" ("Man kann nicht Gründe hören wollen dafür, dass man auf Gründe hören soll"). Cf. R. Spaemann, *Glück und Wohlwollen. Versuch über Ethik* (Stuttgart: Klett-Cotta, 1989), 11.

ratio ("Corrupted reason is not reason"), just as a false syllogism is not a syllogism.[55] The aim of ethical self-clarification is always to help reason have its way. The reason that makes us grasp what is truly good without deception—*orthòs lógos, recta ratio*—is the reason of the wise, that is, the fully virtuous person,[56] a reason, that is, that has not been deviated by impulses and emotion.

On the other hand, on the plane of fundamental principles, there is a surprising consensus among people about the imperatives of the natural law: the killing of innocents, adultery, lying, theft, slander, envy, and hatred toward one's neighbor are generally considered evil. The point is simply that we are not able to understand these moral concepts without the efficacy of the natural law, even if we do not agree on how to apply them in the concrete. But it is on the plane of application and not on the plane of principles that emotional dispositions, cultural conditioning, and the cognitive level of the subject play a determinative role in leading the practical reason astray. For just this reason ethical discourse exists, which is always a discourse about reason and in the interests of reason.

Even faith cannot remove itself from this "inherent rationality," since faith does not replace intellect but is an empowerment of intellect and an act of the human intellect. But an act that for its part stands under the power of the will as moved by grace can consent to divine revelation only in virtue of this grace, which it does insofar as it is a *human* intellect.[57] Its subjectivity is not destroyed but safeguarded and empowered. This in turn stands in the line of the ultimate empowering of the subjectivity of the moral fact, the *lex nova* ("New Law") which consists above all in the grace of the Holy Spirit which acts interiorly, by the power of which man—only on the supernatural plane—receives the ultimate interior connaturality with the good not only in its abstract and reflective form, but also concretely and originally, in the Trinitarian personhood of God. In this way the question about what is good brings us to the question concerning the *summum bonum* (and also concerning the One Who "alone is Good" in the Gospel) as the creator of every other good.[58]

55. *In Sent.* II, D. 24, 3, 3, ad3um.

56. Aristotle, *Nicomachean Ethics,* VI, 4, 1140b5.

57. *ST* II-II, q.2 a.9.

58. This essay was translated by Gerald Malsbary from the Italian, "Ragione practica e verità della soggettività: l'autoesperienza del soggeto morale alle radici della metafisica e dell'anthropologia," which was prepared from the German original for a February 2004 conference sponsored by the faculty of philosophy at the Pontifical University of the Holy Cross. It was chosen over the German version as the basis for our translation because it is a later text, with footnotes expanded beyond those of the original.

10

Review of Jean Porter's *Nature as Reason*

A Thomistic Theory of the Natural Law

In her new book on natural law, which I have been invited to review,[1] Jean Porter intends to "develop a theological account of the natural law which takes its starting points and orientation from the concept of the natural law developed by Scholastic jurists and theologians in the twelfth and thirteen centuries" (5). This view, Professor Porter asserts, is an alternative to "the modern and contemporary insistence on the universality and rationally compelling force of the natural law, considered as a set of moral norms" (5). Porter recognizes in what she calls in a summary way "the Scholastics" a kind of understanding of natural law which is bound to its religious, theological, cultural, and social context and thus "did not attempt to construct theories of the natural law on the basis of purely rational—that is to say, non-theological—starting points and arguments" (27). It rather acknowledged that rational inquiry cannot be purified from historical contingencies because it "can *only* take place within some context of culturally specific practices, mores and traditions" (29). Therefore, the Scholastic idea of natural law is opposed to "most contemporary natural law theorists" who "would agree that it is possi-

1. Jean Porter, *Nature as Reason: A Thomistic Theory of the Natural Law* (Grand Rapids, Mich.: Eerdmans, 2004). I thank Professor Porter for her generosity in having accepted the following exchange, and I thank both her and the editor of *Studies in Christian Ethics* for giving me the opportunity to reply to her response to my review.

ble to establish a natural law morality through rational reflection alone, without any necessary reference to particular religious or other traditions" (28f.).

Porter's aim is to "develop a fresh construal of the natural law tradition" (45). She does not want to call her own method a Scholastic one—this would, she says, be "anachronistic"—but only "a friendly approach to the Scholastics" (46), though she believes that the account of the natural law that she develops "is an authentic expression of the Scholastic concept, admittedly an expression which they could not have developed in their own day." Moreover, Porter insists that she does not claim that her account of the natural law "represents the views of any one of the Scholastic authors," though she adds that her "own theory of the natural law *is* in its essentials that of Aquinas," yet "developed and extended in a contemporary context" (46f). Her account, thus, "should be regarded as a Thomistic account of the natural law," but "not as a straightforward presentation of Aquinas's own views" (47).

As these assertions invite us to assume, Porter actually intends to present a theory of her own, yet faithful to the spirit of Thomism. In what follows, I will try to substantiate my view as clearly as possible in order to facilitate the debate. In particular, I will argue that Porter's theory of the natural law is not only "not a straightforward presentation of Aquinas's own views" as she admits, but also far from "Thomistic" in any possible sense. For sure, Porter's book offers a wide variety and richness of outlooks on different aspects of the subject. Her learning is extensive and her arguments often subtle. Moreover, her book has the merit of putting Aquinas's doctrine of natural law into its proper context: the quest for happiness and the virtues. She rightly acknowledges that natural law does not simply "provide us with a system of ethical norms" (5) deduced from some rational principles, but has to be integrated with a conception of the overall human good expressed in an ideal of the virtuous life. Porter also considers fundamental problems of action theory, notably the topic of the basic moral evaluation of human acts (the theme of the "moral object"). She says important things about the moral virtues and shows how a species-concept of human nature is not invalidated by the result of evolutionary biology. At the end, she even offers an original and surprising theory of natural rights.

But in all this, Professor Porter seems to promote an agenda of her own which, rather than being Thomistic, points in the direction of a theologically warranted kind of moral relativism under the name of "moral pluralism." Porter disregards the core of Aquinas's concept of natural law. She also fails to consider key texts of Aquinas that do not fit into her agenda. In the following, I will concentrate on substantiating this charge which, of course, concerns the most central aspect of her book.

Porter starts with discussing natural law as being rooted in what she calls "premoral nature," the teleological conception and the intelligibility of which she defends against modern biology. There is, she affirms, continuity between created reality—"human nature"—and natural law, though it is not possible to move directly from nature to moral conclusions. The natural law "reflects the teleological orientation of the creature considered as a whole, rather than the teleological orientation of particular inclinations. . . . Hence, the cornerstone of a Thomistic theory of the natural law will be an account of happiness, understood as the final end and ultimate perfection of the human creature" (322). Yet, as is explained in chapter 3, happiness is not to be simply equated to the practice of the virtues. Basic human inclinations are directed toward non-moral goods and the intelligible structures of these inclinations "give rise to certain ideals of virtue and render them naturally desirable and admirable" (323). However, as Porter accentuates, virtues and moral reasoning related to them have to be analyzed on the basis of corresponding types of action (e.g.—the following examples are mine—for moral reasoning it is not sufficient to refer to general principles and ideals of virtue like "one ought to be just" or "one ought to avoid injustice"; notions like "just" and "unjust" have to be related to types of action like "one ought to give back what one has borrowed," "one ought not to take away another's property against his will," "one ought not to kill the innocent"). Only in this way is one able to formulate moral norms which are "overriding rules for action" (ibid.) such that there is "an intrinsic connection between paradigms of particular virtues and the ideal of reasonableness governing all the virtues" (194). So, also a conception of practical reason is needed. Practical reason, Porter rightly stresses, "never operates in isolation from the intelligibilities informing prerational nature, nor can the normative force of reason be understood apart from its grounding in wider forms of intelligibility" (232). With this Porter tries to do justice to the idea of the important twelfth-century canonist Huguccio that natural law springs from reason and that human reason is properly law "which yields authoritative precepts binding us to compliance" (233).[2]

2. Regarding the Scholastic canonists, Porter refers to Brian Tierney's landmark studies, first published as a book in 1997, *The Idea of Natural Rights: Studies on Natural Rights, Natural Law and Church Law 1150–1625* (Grand Rapids, Mich.: Eerdmans, 2001). As I will argue later on, however, Tierney's book does not support Porter's argument.

Yet, in her development of essential points of a theory of practical reason, including a new stance on the issue of the "moral object" of the human act,[3] Porter finally arrives at the result that "the Thomistic theory of the natural law offered here . . . does not offer a comprehensive and substantive set of moral rules which are universally valid and can be recognized as such" (325). Porter rather stresses the fact that natural law is from the point of view of both nature and rationality, always *underdetermined.* Although natural law reflects universal aspects of human nature, Porter thinks it needs concretization by a cultural context and social practices, and that it can only be fully understood in theological terms. Therefore, Porter concludes, there is not *one* natural law ethics, but a plurality of them. She endorses without reservation Jacques Dupuis's understanding of religious pluralism as developed in his 1997 book *Towards a Christian Theology of Religious Pluralism* to affirm analogously "the diversity of moral traditions" which "reflect a providential way of preserving distinctive forms of human goodness" (378). Not surprisingly, at the end of its complex and sometimes tortuous argument, the final theological perspective of the book results in the breakdown of the idea of natural law. According to Porter's concluding view, "natural law" no longer exists in the sense of a *moral* law, a universal standard of moral truth which transcends cultural and religious frontiers and expresses the fundamental moral exigencies of acting morally as a human being. "Nature as reason" turns out to be neither "nature" nor properly "reason," but a kind of mere ground for common moral discourse which, depending on cultural contexts, can generate different normative results. "Even though we cannot provide a convincing foundationalist justification for a universal morality, which would be specific enough to be practically useful and yet would be rationally compelling to all persons of good will, we can nonetheless identify certain recurring aspects of moral practices, which do seem to cut across cultural and historical lines" (363). These, Porter adds rather vaguely, "reflect species-specific patterns of behavior, which provide an indispensable basis for morality and as such provide one touchstone for evaluating moral theories" (ibid.).

3. On 277ff., she asserts having abandoned the views held by her in the past that the "object" is the *outcome* of an evaluative process "dependent on a global assessment of intention and circumstances," while she now thinks that it must be "a distinctive and irreducible component of analysis," which on 299f., however, she defines in an eventist and physicalist way. For this, she somewhat surprisingly now draws upon authors who tend to exclude reason from nature and, therefore, toward a more "naturalistic" understanding of the moral object, such as Stephen L. Brock and Steven A. Long.

I fully agree with the assertion that, independently of culture and a societal environment, natural law is not sufficient to generate in a univocal manner—as a "universal morality"—concrete practical orientation. Yet, this is only as true as saying that prudence cannot generate universal norms or that, conversely, moral principles alone are not yet sufficient for making out concrete choices. However, in the context of her critique of contemporary attempts to renew the natural law tradition, she rejects (on p. 80) the core assumption of the natural law tradition. This is the idea that "natural law," rooted in some way in natural inclinations of human beings, expresses a fundamental basis of moral normativity which is independent of concrete cultural and social concretization and serves as a standard for evaluating them. In contrast, Porter asserts that the account of natural inclinations and natural law as given by "the Scholastics," including Aquinas, is an "account of what life considered as a whole should look like" (77). As it is explained later, this is something very much dependent on "social practices" and "communal reflection," thus on sociological, cultural, and historical factors. These, in turn, are interpreted in the last chapter in a theological key which, as announced on page 5 of her book, transforms Porter's theory, into a "theological account of the natural law," and not only of natural law, but also of human nature (56). The outcome is stated on page 339: "For this reason we cannot speak of *the* natural law at the level of determinate norms, but must rather speak in terms of natural law moralities in the plural."[4]

For a philosopher, and especially for one who has worked on Aquinas's idea of natural law, this sounds rather puzzling. Without going into all the details of Porter's argument, one of its main flaws is that it is worked out without referring to, let alone discussing, key texts of Aquinas himself on natural law. Moreover, she rarely quotes the texts of Aquinas literally, but instead includes only general references to their location. On the other hand, she generously quotes and draws on two rather trivial texts by Philip the Chancellor and Albert the Great where the concept of "nature as reason" *(natura ut ratio)* opposed to "nature as nature" *(natura ut natura)* appears. The typically Thomistic concept of "natural reason" *(ratio naturalis),* which—inversely—corresponds instead to "reason as nature," does not figure in her vocabulary. With this Porter continues a long and in my view unfortunate tradition of opposing in moral theory "reason" to "nature," a pair of opposites

4. The text says only "natural moralities"; according to parallel texts I have added "law," supposing that this is a typo.

alien to Aquinas's understanding of morals thanks to its profoundly Aristotelian inspiration. The most central text on natural law from the *Summa Theologiae* (*ST* I-II, 91, 2), where the concept of "natural reason" is prominent, is quoted by Porter only incompletely (without mentioning the omission). Moreover, and surprisingly, besides insignificant exceptions, Porter exclusively concentrates on texts from the *Summa Theologiae,* neglecting an analysis of the commentary to Aristotle's *Nicomachean Ethics* and *De Anima* (a key text for understanding Aquinas's Aristotelian concept of practical reason). She also neglects analysis of Aquinas's scriptural commentaries (most importantly, those on the Gospel of St John and St Paul's Epistle to the Romans), the *Summa contra Gentiles* (with its treatise on law and the idea of *bonum rationis*) and of most relevant passages of the *Quaestiones disputatae,* mainly those on the virtues.

Porter's misleadingly selective use of Aquinas's texts begins on page 48 with what she calls the "starting point" of her account: *ST* I-II, 91, 2. This actually is *the* key text of the *Summa Theologiae* on natural law, which contains its definition. Now, the question is where in this article the definition is to be found. Porter quotes its first part in which Aquinas asserts that natural law is participation in God's eternal reason through which human beings become participants of God's providence and have a natural inclination of directing themselves to the due act and end. Yet, it is the omitted portion of text which makes explicit what I will call Aquinas's "core doctrine of the natural law." This text contains a succinct definition of natural law that first summarizes what has been previously presented and then says:

> Hence the Psalmist . . . says: "The light of Thy countenance, O Lord, is signed upon us": thus implying *that the light of natural reason, whereby we discern what is good and what is evil, which is the task of the natural law, is nothing else than an imprint on us of the Divine light.* It is therefore evident that the natural law is nothing else than the rational creature's participation of the eternal law. (emphasis added)

These lines contain not only the proper theological, but also the decisive metaphysical and anthropological, perspective for what, according to Aquinas, natural law is:[5] it is the eternal law, but the eternal law *in us,* that is, it is the eternal law itself, but, in virtue of creation—on the level of secondary causes—participated in by human beings. This includes not only being "sub-

5. The portion of text omitted by Porter occupies also a central place in the exposition of the doctrine of natural law in John Paul II's encyclical *Veritatis Splendor* (The Splendor of Truth, 1993), no. 42. Strangely, Porter never mentions that encyclical.

ordinated" to or ruled by the eternal law (this also applies to irrational creatures), but also participating in the proper law-giving reason of divine wisdom. This is why natural law can be properly called a "law," that is, a "law of nature." A Thomistic theory of natural law must therefore be a theory of moral knowledge and of its principles. It is essential to such a theory that "natural reason"—which is "reason as nature," that is, reason working like nature: spontaneously and necessarily[6]—has a truth-attaining, illuminating power: it is like a "light" intrinsic to our soul, an expression of the fact that human persons are created in the image of God. The core definition of natural law according to Aquinas, thus, says: *the natural law is the light of natural reason, whereby we discern what is good and what is evil.* This definition is never even mentioned in Porter's book, though Aquinas uses it constantly.[7]

Aquinas typically quotes the words of Psalm 4:6–7 when he pronounces this core doctrine of natural law. He also quotes them when he mentions only "natural reason" and does not refer explicitly to natural law as, for example, in *ST* I-II, 19, 4 (emphasis is added):

It is from the eternal law, which is the Divine Reason, that human reason is the rule of the human will, from which it derives its goodness. Hence it is written (Psalm 4:6,7): "Many say: Who showeth us good things? The light of Thy countenance, O Lord, is

6. In Aquinas, the term "reason as nature" *(ratio ut natura),* as distinguished from "reason as reason" *(ratio ut ratio),* is seldom used (four times in *Super Sent.* and three in *De Veritate*), and in different senses (see, e.g., *Super Sent.,* lib.3 d.15 q.2 a.3 qc.2 co.: "ratio ut natura dicitur secundum quod judicat de eo quod est secundum se bonum vel malum, naturae conveniens vel noxium"). It never occurs in the *Summa Theologiae,* although it would perfectly fit with *voluntas ut natura* in the sense of what is "naturally known" by the intellect and, therefore, becoming "naturally desired" by the will. The term *ratio naturalis,* on the other hand, sometimes means "natural" reason in the meaning of reason unaided by supernatural revelation. It also, however, refers to the *natural mode* of reason's grasping of reality, that is, the *intelligere* as distinct from the *ratiocinari.* For Aquinas's doctrine about *ratio naturalis* and the *lumen naturale* see my *Natural Law and Practical Reason: A Thomist View of Moral Autonomy* (New York: Fordham University Press, 2000), 257–74. The terms "nature as nature" and "nature as reason" (used by Porter) never occur in Aquinas, according to the *Index Thomisticus.*

7. That natural law is the "rational creature's participation of the eternal law" is not properly a definition of the essence of natural law, but only a characterization of its relation to eternal law (as when we say "man is the image of God in the material world," this is not a definition of the essence of man but rather a characterization of the relation of his nature to God's nature; a definition of the essence of man would be "man is a rational animal"). Aquinas's definition of the natural law, which is "natural law is the light of natural reason, whereby we discern what is good and what is evil" (a definition that exactly evidences what this "participation in the eternal law" consists in), appears each time he treats the subject, while the characterization "rational creature's participation of the eternal law" just appears in the *ST* I-II, q.91 a.2, to put the doctrine of natural law into the context of the logic of its treatise on law (after the article on "eternal law"). Notice that according to I-II, q.93 a.3, all laws, including human law, insofar as they are true law, derive from the eternal law!

signed upon us": *as though to say: "The light of our reason is able to show us good things, and guide our will, in so far as it is the light* [i.e., derived from] of Thy countenance."

In the answer to the third objection of the same article, Aquinas states the connection between the truth-attaining light-character of natural reason and the image of God in us:

Although the eternal law is unknown to us according as it is in the Divine Mind: nevertheless, it becomes known to us somewhat, either by natural reason which is derived therefrom as its proper image; or by some sort of additional revelation.

Not surprisingly, this doctrine about natural reason can be found in Aquinas's commentary on Psalm 4.[8] The same doctrine is present when Aquinas speaks on natural law in his explication of *naturaliter faciunt quod sunt legis* (the "natural way" in which the Gentiles accomplish the moral precepts of the Mosaic law) in the commentary on St. Paul's Epistle to the Romans.[9] "*Naturaliter,*" Aquinas says, can be understood as referring to human nature insofar as it is renewed by grace, or to natural law which, as Psalm 4:7 says, "shows us what to do," natural law being "the light of natural reason in which is the image of God."[10] The same can be found in the commentary on the Gospel of St. John,[11] where not only Christ is called the "light" which illumines the human soul, but prior to that and on the level of creation, this property of being "light" is attributed to the human intellect itself. Once again, Aquinas refers to Psalm 4.[12]

8. *Super Psalmos, "The light of Thy countenance, O Lord, is signed upon us:* as if to say that the natural reason which has been put into us teaches us to discern good from evil; and this is why he says *The light of Thy countenance, O Lord, is signed upon us, et cetera.* God's countenance is that by which God is known, as man is known by his countenance, and that means God's truth. From this truth of God, a semblance of his light shines in our souls. And this is like a light, and it is signed upon us, because it is something higher within us, and is like a sign upon our faces, *and by means of this light we can know the good*" (last emphasis added).

9. *Ad Rom.*, c. 2, lect. 3.

10. Ibid., "Vel potest dici *naturaliter,* id est per legem naturalem ostendentem eis quid sit agendum, secundum illud Ps. IV, 7 s.: *multi dicunt: quis ostendit nobis bona? Signatum,* etc., quod est lumen rationis naturalis, in qua est imago Dei." Aquinas adds that this refers to *knowledge,* but that in order to *accomplish* what natural law commands, grace is still necessary *(ad movendum affectum),* so that Pelagianism is excluded. Russell Hittinger, in his *The First Grace: Rediscovering the Natural Law in a Post-Christian World* (Wilmington, Del.: ISI Books, 2003), 10, quotes only the first of the two meanings and affirms, strangely and in contradiction to the text, that "any other interpretation, Thomas warns, would be Pelagian."

11. *Super Ioannem,* c. 1, lectio 3.

12. "We would never be able to recognize this Word and this light except by participating in the light which is actually in the human being, and which is the superior part of our soul, that is

What is perhaps the most concise formulation of Aquinas's core doctrine of the natural law—which exactly corresponds to the portion of text of *ST* I-II, 91, 2 that is omitted in Porter's book—is to be found in the *Proemium* of his Commentary on the Decalogue, where it is said that the "natural law is nothing other than the light of the intellect implanted in us by God, whereby we understand what must be done and what must be avoided," a light given to man by God at his creation.[13] And also here, Thomas immediately adds the standard quotation of Psalm 4 which, as he asserts, contains the truth that nobody can ignore what he should do, because the "light of the intellect" shows it to him.[14]

Textual evidence, thus, suggests that the focal meaning of natural law in Aquinas is founded in a doctrine of creation and participation in which "natural reason" appears as *lumen,* as a *light* by which the human person is capable of distinguishing good and evil according to what is established in the eternal law. "Natural law," thus, is properly a law. It comes from God, but in the human person, natural reason cognitively establishes in the natural inclinations a first and basic order of what one ought to do and what one ought to avoid. "Natural reason" has this power, because it is nothing other than the active presence of eternal law in human beings, and is the way God *naturally* (apart from supernatural aids) leads human persons to their end.[15]

Obviously, to point out the "core" or "focal" meaning of natural law is not yet to provide a complete Thomistic theory of natural law; it only shows the

---

to say, the light of the intellect about which Ps. IV:7 speaks: *The light of Thy countenance, O Lord, is signed upon us,* that is, the light of your Son, who is your face, by which you are manifested." In *Super Ioannem,* c. 1, lect. 5, Aquinas stresses the participated character of the illuminating power of natural reason: "[A]ll human beings coming into this sensible world are illuminated by the light of natural knowing by participating in this true light, from which is derived whatever light of natural cognition they share in."

13. *In duo praecepta, Prologus,* he writes, "lex naturae . . . nihil aliud est nisi lumen intellectus insitum nobis a Deo, per quod cognoscimus quid agendum et quid vitandum. Hoc lumen et hanc legem dedit Deus homini in creatione." This text is quoted more than once in *Veritatis Splendor;* e.g., nos. 12, 40.

14. "But many who do not observe this law believe they are excused by ignorance. Against those, however, the prophet says in Psalm IV:6: *Many say: Who showeth us good things?* As if they did not know what they ought to do. But the Psalmist replies in verse 7: *The light of Thy countenance, O Lord, is signed upon us,* that is, the light of the intellect, by which we know what we ought to do."

15. As we will see, Aquinas calls "natural law" sometimes the reason itself insofar as it distinguishes the good to be done from the evil to be avoided, sometimes the *propositions* (judgments) that spring from natural reason and express these distinctions. Of course, "law" in the most proper sense is the propositions, applied to actions, though the reason as well is called "law," because it is the way eternal law is participated in by the human person.

way to proceed. Jean Porter goes in nearly the opposite direction. The point of the doctrine of participation expressed in this core doctrine is, as Aquinas explicitly says in *ST* I-II, 19, 4 ad 3 (quoted above), that the eternal law in itself is unknown to us. Apart from revelation, it only comes to be known through the ordering judgments of natural reason—the practical judgments to "do this" and "shun that"—which themselves have the character of a "law." So, apart from revelation, human beings have to rely on their own regulative judgments of practical reason. Yet, the analogy with "light" makes it clear enough that the reason, as natural reason—that is, "reason as nature"—really *illuminates* and is a truth-attaining power. The light analogy has to be taken seriously: as light by its proper nature "renders visible" what it illuminates—light cannot do otherwise—so natural reason makes visible both the intelligible goods inherent in our natural inclinations and the corresponding evils that oppose them. Insofar as natural reason is not impeded by some cause external to it, it works without fail.[16] Also in this respect Aquinas follows the Aristotelian doctrine of *De Anima* (III, 10 433a 27–28) that on the level of principles the intellect *qua* intellect cannot err and is always right, though it can be misguided by the senses and by the will, which is free to resist what reason presents as good. Thus, Thomas calls the propositions of "natural reason"[17] the primary precepts of natural law by which human acts receive their *prima directio.*[18] These propositions simultaneously are the principles of practical reason. As such, they constitute the human person not only as a *moral* subject, but also as a *practical* (acting) subject, because practical principles are principles of motion and *praxis* is a kind of motion. In *ST* I-II, 94, 2, Aquinas famously and concisely expounds how this "reason as nature" works in the practical domain, where it is embedded in the dynamics of the natural inclinations such that it both understands and regulates them.

Yet, ironically, one of the central aims of Porter's argument is to polemicize against a concept of natural law which stresses the *rational* character of it. She tries to de-legitimize such a claim, mainly by attacking the Grisez/

16. This is also the doctrine of the *Summa contra Gentiles* III, chap. 129.

17. "Natural" here is not simply in the sense of "belonging to human nature," but of "reason as nature" *(ratio ut natura)*, which grasps in the inclinations what is "naturally reasonable." For a detailed discussion, see the fifth essay of this collection, "Practical Reason and the 'Naturally Rational': On the Doctrine of the Natural Law as a Principle of Praxis in Thomas Aquinas," originally published as "Praktische Vernunft und das, von Natur aus Vernünftige'. Zur Lehre von der Lex naturalis als Prinzip der Praxis bei Thomas von Aquin," *Theologie und Philosophie* 75 (2000): 493–522.

18. See *ST* I-II, q.91 a.2 ad2.

Finnis version of it (the so-called "new natural law theory"). Not being of that school, I do not intend to defend this theory here. Yet Porter presents it in a way which hides its true nature and merits. Natural law theories which stress the rational character of natural law, including the Grisez/Finnis theory and my own reading of Aquinas, do not disregard what Porter calls "pre-rational" nature nor do they deduce the content of natural law from a set of purely rational imperatives. Rather, they understand themselves as a kind of explication of *how we come to understand our nature:* we originally come to understand many aspects of our being through the practical reason's grasping of the fundamental human goods in the natural inclinations (some of which spring from the pre-rational, that is, in themselves non-rational, or not yet rational, strata of human nature). This, again, is what Aquinas expounds in *ST* I-II, 94, 2.[19] Here also Porter, in my view, fails to adequately distinguish between the epistemological and the ontological level and the different kinds of questions corresponding to these different levels, as I have already explained in my response to her review of my *Natural Law and Practical Reason.*[20]

The extent to which Porter passes over Aquinas's explicit and repeated teaching on natural law is somewhat surprising. Certainly, she does notice in her brief discussion of *ST* I-II, 94, 2 (262ff.) that Aquinas here establishes "the necessary starting point for all practical reasoning." She also correctly underlines that these "first principles of practical reason are nothing other than the rational creature's grasp of the intelligibilities inherent in created existence," and she accurately remarks that these first principles are "natural principles of motion" (264). Yet, for Porter they are still "morally underdetermined," and this is why she thinks that "the basic principles of intelligibility constituting the natural law must be translated into social norms though a process of communal reflection, in order to be practically effective" (267). It is of course true, and trivial, that the practical principles which form the natural law are under-

19. In this Finnis and I agree: See John M. Finnis, *Fundamentals of Ethics* (Oxford: Clarendon Press, 1983), 10ff., 20ff.; M. Rhonheimer, *Natural Law and Practical Reason,* translated from the 1987 original *Natur als Grundlage der Moral* by Gerald Malsbary, 1–57; *Praktische Vernunft und Vernünftigkeit der Praxis* (Berlin: Akademie Verlag, 1994), 51f., 53ff. (where I expound my differences with Finnis); *Die Perspektive der Moral. Philosophische Grundlagen der Tugendethik* (Berlin: Akademie Verlag, 2001), 163ff., 227ff.

20. Porter's review was published in *Theological Studies* 62 (2001): 851–53; I have responded to her in the sixth essay of this collection, "The Moral Significance of Pre-Rational Nature in Aquinas: A Reply to Jean Porter (and Stanley Hauerwas)." (On p. 188, n. 53, Porter refers to this article; as she says, she unfortunately had not the time to incorporate it into the discussion of my views, which I regret.)

determined for making choices of concrete acts. Yet, they are not, as Porter suggests, *morally* underdetermined—having not yet reached the level of morality—but they are only *practically* underdetermined: in order to determine what one ought to do in each case a judgment of prudence is required. Principles and even moral norms are universal; as negative precepts they can determine what one ought never to do, but they cannot yet determine and guide actions in a *positive* way. So, by natural law one knows that one ought never tell a lie; but by natural law alone one does not know whether, how, and to what extent—here and now—one ought to speak the truth. It is also true that only on the level of becoming an *ethos,* a concrete moral tradition including the political, cultural, and religious dimension, that natural law gains momentum as a shaping force of a whole society. The ethos of solidarity between children and parents may be shaped in different cultures by different norms of behavior, though embodying the same principle of natural law. Yet, what Porter says is different: she actually contends that the principles of practical reason, that is, the natural law, are not yet really *moral* principles; that is to say that they become *moral* principles and *moral* norms only when they are "translated into social norms though a process of communal reflection." This is why—by confusing "being *practically*" and "being *morally* underdetermined"—she in reality asserts that there is no natural law which could be properly called a *moral* law showing us the good to do and the evil to avoid.

Against my emphasis on the importance of Aquinas's core doctrine of natural law as a cognitive reality, someone might object that—for a theory of natural law—such a doctrine is of little avail, because it does not help us to make out criteria for resolving questions about what belongs to natural law, and what does not. One might refer to disagreements about natural law which imply that it cannot act as a common ground of rational consensus. Porter's approach seems to happily overcome such difficulties because she draws on Alasdair MacIntyre's central idea that rational inquiry and practical reason are dependent on tradition and do not exist *as such.* In this way at least the problem of intercultural disagreement disappears (not as disagreement, of course, but as a problem). By stressing the cognitive disagreements and difficulties in applying natural law to "hard cases," Porter concludes that according to different traditions and cultures there must be also a *plurality* of diversified natural law moralities. She even says that this is a theological view, because such a pluralism is "part of God's plan for humanity" (377) and "the diversity of moral traditions reflect a providential way of preserving distinctive forms of human goodness"

(378) which even extends to the suggestion that "we cannot claim without qualification that the Christian way of life represents God's unique will for humanity" (ibid.). Admittedly, these formulations are sufficiently indistinct that there must be some truth in them; but in this context, they serve to de-legitimize the idea that there really exist universally valid norms of natural law which in principle can be universally known by natural reason (which, of course, is a consequence of the truth-attaining power of natural reason). Disagreement about natural law and cultural diversity, and with this moral pluralism, becomes for Porter part of the proper *theological* dimension of natural law as a manifestation of God's will. Yet, I have difficulties in recognizing such a view as a valid or even possible revitalization of the Scholastic, let alone the Thomistic, tradition of natural law.

The reference to disagreement and diversity has always been a weak argument against the truth claim of universality of the natural law. As I have written elsewhere,[21] it is certainly true that a consensus concerning natural law exists only at the level of the most important shared and specific precepts. There exists a whole level of so-called "remote" precepts which, according to St. Thomas as well, are difficult to understand for most human beings, and which, in his view, can be understood without error only by "the wisest" (cf. *ST* I-II, 100, 1). But apart from these, disagreement on natural law is not so dramatic as to entitle us to affirm that there is no general agreement on most of its content. We are sometimes so much focused on certain very special moral problems predominant in our society that we tend to overlook the obvious: that there exists a widely shared set of moral principles. For example, not only is it easy for everyone to understand, but most people (except the morally perverse) in fact do understand, the disordered character of killing one's neighbor, of adultery, of lying (especially when it causes damage) and of theft, of hatred for one's neighbor, of envy, of rash judgments, of defamation, etc., forms of behavior and inner attitudes to which the principal precepts of the natural law refer. It is important not to overlook the fact that the very notions which underlie these norms, and even the notion of "justice" itself, testify to the working presence of natural law in the human person. The very fact that all of us have a shared sense of justice and use notions of the kind just mentioned, though we often disagree about how to ap-

21. See the seventh essay of this collection, "The Cognitive Structure of Natural Law and the Truth of Subjectivity," especially 189ff.

ply them, proves that the natural law does exist and that it guides us in distinguishing good from evil.

This is why it is so important to understand the proper cause and nature of disagreement and diversity. Porter's answer, which is directed toward a "moral pluralism," inscribed in the plans of God, seems to me to be no answer at all. In any case, the answer of the Christian tradition is different: it affirms that disagreement in questions of natural law is caused by sin, which obscures the light of reason. Aquinas's—and, of course, "the Scholastics'"—solution belongs to this tradition; Porter dramatically departs from it. Now, what does "obscuring by sin" mean in the context of a Thomistic natural law theory? For Aquinas, who is an Aristotelian, it means the disorder which is opposed to moral virtue. It is not surprising that Porter's book is silent about "sin" and "vice." Her theory of natural law does not contain a critical analysis of moral disagreement or of the "corruption" or "obscuring" of natural law in a human person's heart. It does not even put forward or analyze the notion of moral evil. Such an analysis however is an essential part of Aquinas's theory of natural law. Of the six articles of question 94 on natural law, two of them—articles 4 and 6—analyze the causes of disagreement and of corruption of natural law. This is also treated elsewhere, such as in *ST* I-II, 91 on the *fomes peccati,* and in the different treatises on virtues and vices. The analysis of these two articles highlights, on one side, the influence on moral knowledge of distorted social practices, and on the other, the disorder of the passions and the will. More generally, they highlight *vice,* which is the opposite of moral virtue, which results in the obscuring of natural moral knowledge.

Porter does deal extensively with moral virtue, but her treatment fails to notice the anthropological dimension of the classical doctrine of virtue. This dimension, as clearly present in Aquinas with its Platonic and Aristotelian roots,[22] includes the central teaching that the possession of "moral virtue" is the condition under which human persons are truly reasonable. It is only the virtuous person whose natural reason infallibly illumines and correctly distinguishes good from evil. The possession of moral virtue, to some degree, is thus the condition under which natural law works as it should, though its basic principles are always present in the human mind. Therefore, a truly Thomistic "natural law morality" at the end must be an ethics of the virtues including a theory of vice and moral evil.

22. See for this my *Praktische Vernunft und Vernünftigkeit der Praxis.*

Porter actually does present her theory as linked to virtue ethics, but she ignores the central features of Thomistic virtue ethics just mentioned. Of course, I agree with Porter on the importance of analyzing virtues in association with specific kinds of actions by showing "that there is an intrinsic connection between paradigms of particular virtues and the ideal of reasonableness governing all the virtues" (194).[23] I would not want to assert that her contribution to this is without any merit, because, as I have mentioned earlier, it shows that natural law theory needs to be integrated into an account of the virtues, the overall human good, and happiness. However, while for Aquinas there is a clear correspondence between the ends of the different virtues and the principles of natural law, Porter's theory of the virtues seems to me to finally collapse into her master idea that, as with the contents of natural law, so too the rationale of the virtues cannot be identified independently of social practices and cultural contexts. Thus, according to her, virtue is also to be understood in a "pluralistic" way. Of course, in a sense virtues are by their very nature "pluralistic": they adapt to circumstances, and the virtuous "mean," according to reason, of the virtues of temperance and fortitude are a mean *quoad nos,* "according to us," that is, they are subject-related. But this does not exclude the idea that their very rationale is linked to basic intelligible human goods which *define* the ways of virtue and the boundaries of the morally possible—the domain of so-called "moral absolutes"—that is, they are linked to natural law *as such.*

Upon closer examination, we can detect that most disagreement on natural law is not properly disagreement about moral principles, but about their application to concrete cases. The reason why such errors occur may be ordinary difficulties of knowledge and judgment, sometimes due to prejudice or culturally caused bias, but also disordered self-interest of widely differing kinds (which may lead to discriminating against others) or the striving for power, glory, success, well-being at any price, and similar things. With such a discourse, we have properly entered the domain of (classical) virtue ethics. According to Aquinas, what is opposed to the virtues obscures the light of natural reason and thus corrupts the natural law in us. Conversely, natural law commands us to live the virtues. Whoever actually engages in such a discourse cannot be a moral "pluralist" in the proper sense, because he imme-

23. Contrary to what Porter asserts, this is exactly what I have treated in various articles, and it is one of the central concerns of my book, of which she appears to be unaware, *Die Perspektive der Moral* (cited above).

diately enters the battlefield of talking about "moral good" and "moral evil," and finally about the difference of true and erroneous conscience, subjects strangely avoided in Porter's theory of natural law.

Jean Porter's approach makes her also overlook another key aspect of Aquinas's theory of natural law: its being a theory of practical reason in the Aristotelian tradition. As I have tried to demonstrate at length,[24] Thomas's doctrine of natural law takes the place and has the systematic function of a doctrine of the principles of practical reason, alluded to by Aristotle in his *Nicomachean Ethics, Posterior Analytics,* and *De Anima.* In my view, thus, Aquinas's theory of natural law fills a real gap in a virtue ethic of an Aristotelian type.

Certainly, such a view may be challenged,[25] but I regret that Porter simply ignores it or represents it in a way which renders it unintelligible.[26] Only the Aristotelian background of Aquinas's conception of practical reason explains why for him the natural law is truly a *law,* though it is called a law in an analogous way. As the comprehensive definition of law in *ST* I-II, 90, 4 shows, for Aquinas "law" in the first, proper, and full sense is the *lex humana,* that is, the positive civil law.[27] But in all these cases there is a common *ratio legis* which

24. See my *Praktische Vernunft und Vernünftigkeit der Praxis.*

25. As it was done by D. J. M. Bradley, in his impressive and stimulating work *Aquinas on the Twofold Human Good: Reason and Human Happiness in Aquinas' Moral Science* (Washington, D.C.: The Catholic University of America Press, 1997). I think, however, that his critique is founded on a misunderstanding; see my *Die Perspektive der Moral,* 29f., n. 60.

26. In my view this is the case on page 189. Porter plays speculative reason off against practical reason. Like many interpreters of Aquinas, however, she fails to recognize what Aquinas explicitly asserts in *ST* I-II, q.94 a.2: that it is not speculative but practical reason that *originally and naturally* grasps the intelligibility of the goods inherent in the natural inclinations in a way that also generates the precept of pursuing them and avoiding corresponding evils. Only *in actu signato,* that is, reflecting on the natural acts of practical reason, does speculative reason come to a theoretical concept of "human nature." The self-experience of practical reason is the very part of "nature" over which the theoretical intellect then reflects. It is significant how Porter tries to rule out the possibility that the "intelligibilities of nature" are a natural and immediate object of the practical reason, which, of course, makes them enter directly into the realm of morality. (This Porter absolutely excludes, because for her the "intelligibilities of nature" are morally underdetermined and need to be "translated into social norms through a process of communal reflection" [267].) Notice too that practical reason is also an act of the intellect; thus it is a *cognitive* act, but embedded in the striving dynamics of the natural inclinations and therefore truly practical (moving to *pursuing* the good and to *avoiding* the opposed evil). In this context, Aquinas's commentary on the third book of Aristotle's *De Anima* is of crucial importance (esp. *In De Anima* III, lectio 15). Here Thomas asserts that the practical intellect also knows truth, but it does so for the sake of action; and that "what is desired" is the starting point of the practical intellect.

27. "Thus from the four preceding articles, the definition of law may be gathered; and it is nothing else than *an ordinance of reason for the common good, made by him who has care of the community, and promulgated.*"

is expressed by the fact that "law is a rule and measure of acts, whereby man is induced to act or is restrained from acting"; because "the rule and measure of human acts is the reason, which is the first principle of human acts" and "since it belongs to the reason to direct to the end, which is the first principle in all matters of action . . . it follows that law is something pertaining to reason" (*ST* I-II, 90, 1). More specifically, Aquinas adds, laws are "universal propositions of the practical intellect that are directed to actions" (ibid. ad 2).

If therefore natural law is properly a "law," it must be such a set of "universal propositions of the practical intellect that are directed to actions." That Aquinas actually extends to natural law what he says about the nature of law in general is shown by his remarks in *ST* I-II, 94, 1 where he affirms "that the natural law is something constituted by reason *(aliquid a ratione constitutum),* just as a proposition is a work of reason *(opus rationis).*" This is, as Aquinas had said before, why "the participation of the eternal law in the rational creature is properly called a law, since a law is something pertaining to reason" (*ST* I-II, 91, 2 ad 3). A clear application of this doctrine can be seen in *ST* I-II, 94, 2 where Aquinas affirms that "whatever the practical reason naturally apprehends as man's good (or evil) belongs to the precepts of the natural law as something to be done or avoided." So, in Aquinas's theory of natural law, the doctrines about (1) the principles of practical reason (the object of what Aristotle in the last chapter of the second book of his *Posterior Analytics* called the *nous tōn archōn* or *intellectus principiorum*),[28] (2) the ends of natural inclinations, and (3) the precepts of natural law are integrated into one coherent conception. Aquinas's doctrine of natural law, hence, is simultaneously a doctrine of the principles of practical reason. This is also confirmed in a later question (*ST* I-II, 100, 1) where Aquinas affirms about the natural knowledge of the moral precepts of the Mosaic law that "as every judgment of speculative reason proceeds from the natural knowledge of first principles, so every judgment of practical reason proceeds from principles known naturally, as stated above: from which principles one may proceed in various ways to judge of various matters." This again reveals the twofold nature of natural law, that is to say, that it is both a principle of motion (*praxis,* action) and a principle of morality. Because of this, we can say that the natural law originally constitutes the person at the same time as a *practical* and as a *moral* subject.

28. *In Post. Anal.*, II.

What in this way is generated is properly a "law of nature" springing from natural reason's truth-attaining capacity. Notice, as has been already mentioned, that for Aquinas the term "natural law" is used for both the reason insofar as it naturally distinguishes good from evil and the propositions thus established by reason containing that distinction. Natural law in this second sense is a set of propositions of the practical reason which ordain our actions to the true human good; these propositions, as Aquinas says, are "the work of reason," they are, as quoted above, *aliquid a ratione constitutum* (*ST* I-II, 94, 1). Of course, the "reason" Aquinas talks about is the human reason with its truth-attaining capacity. In this sense, natural reason is properly—though in an analogous sense—a "legislator," but it is so only by participation, because the law established by natural reason is nothing other than the eternal law preexisting in "eternal reason," the mind of God, and which "God instilled into man's mind so as to be known by him naturally," which, Aquinas asserts, is tantamount to its "promulgation" (*ST* I-II, 90, 4).[29]

Therefore, although natural reason owes its illumining and action-guiding power to nothing other than its being a participation in the light of eternal reason, on the level of the creature and of secondary causes it is precisely the work of natural reason itself to constitute a law, in the sense of a regulative judgment or dictate of reason, and the corresponding obligation. It is reason which imposes its requirements and its order on the will and the sensual drives (the "lower part of the soul"). The moral precepts of the old law (which are all precepts belonging to natural law) do not, Aquinas says, originally oblige because of being divinely revealed, but they "derive their binding force from the dictate of reason itself, because natural reason dictates that something ought to be done or to be avoided. These are called 'moral' precepts: since human morals

29. In Russell Hittinger's *The First Grace,* quoted above, the question about the law-character of natural law according to Aquinas (chapter 2) seems to me to be answered in an unsatisfactory way, because the law-character of natural law, according to Hittinger, is due to the fact that it springs from a "divine legislator." Aquinas, however, never uses the term "legislator" for natural law, nor for eternal law; in this context he only speaks about *gubernatio.* "Legislator" is used only for designating the source of positive (human and divine) law. Therefore, according to Aquinas, natural law is not properly dependent on a divine "legislator," but it is the *participation* of the eternal law and, thus, possessed *as law* by the rational creature (see for this again *ST* I-II, q.91 a.2 ad3: "the participation of the eternal law in the rational creature is properly called a law, since a law is something pertaining to reason, as stated above"). The point is that irrational animals are also subject to the rule of the eternal law and in this sense participate in it, but being irrational they do not participate in it as a *law.* This is why in my *Natural Law and Practical Reason* I have widely spoken about "participated autonomy" (which has its origin and fundament in participation of theonomy).

are based on reason" (*ST* I-II, 104). This again shows how natural reason is really a kind of lawgiver and that its universal practical judgments have the characteristic of law.

In fact,[30] Aquinas compares reason to a kind of "ruler" in the realm of human actions, which again proves that he sees natural reason as having a properly governing and "legislative" role in the human soul. So he asserts—again referring to the moral precepts of the ancient law which are precepts of natural law—that "the reason, which is the guiding principle of moral matters *(principium moralium),* holds the same position, in human beings, with regard to things that concern them, as a prince or judge holds in the state" (in *ST* I-II, 104, 1 ad 3). This also recalls Aristotle's expression in the *Nicomachean Ethics* (VII, 9 1152a 20–24) that the unrestrained person, who does possess the good principles of reason but by weakness does not follow them, "resembles a state which passes all the proper enactments and has good laws, but which never keeps its laws," while the viciously intemperate man, who has corrupted principles, "is like a state which keeps its laws but whose laws are bad."[31]

This closes the circle. Porter's "Thomistic theory of natural law" seems to be far away from such a doctrine, which combines a profoundly metaphysical perspective with a doctrine of practical reason and of moral virtue, both solidly rooted in classical anthropology. Porter's version of a Thomistic theory of the natural law systematically disregards Aquinas's doctrine on the illuminating power of natural reason. It equally fails to notice the underlying doctrine about the light of natural reason which reflects the *imago,* the image of God in the soul of his rational creatures, a doctrine which theologically opens unexpected perspectives of bringing together nature and grace, a possibility left unexploited in Porter's final chapter on this question (which instead sets forth a rather surprising theory on "natural rights").

Ironically, Porter's theory of natural law contradicts what, as she repeatedly asserts, is one of her most important sources of Scholastic natural law teaching, that is to say, the eminent twelfth-century canonist Huguccio, according to whom "the natural law, that is, reason, constrains one to do those

30. In this, he follows Aristotle's well-known doctrine of the "political rule" of the reason over the other parts of the soul.

31. See also Aquinas's idea of human self-government by reason as a constituent part of God's government of the world, as it is most famously expressed in the *Summa contra Gentiles* III, chap. 113.

things which are contained in it, and one is obliged to those things by reason."[32] Aquinas's theory of natural law, which is a theory of moral knowledge and of the illuminating power of "reason as nature," definitely belongs to this Scholastic tradition which after all goes back to the Fathers (see, e.g., Saint Ambrose's *De Paradiso* 8, 39). Porter's account of natural law dramatically departs from both the Patristic and the Scholastic tradition, which has always expressed belief in the truth-attaining power of the human intellect as God's *imago* in the human mind.[33]

Admittedly, there remain many open questions. One is how from the precepts of natural law we arrive at concrete moral judgments and how to resolve the sometimes difficult questions of applying natural law precepts to concrete cases. Porter addresses these questions, but perhaps influenced by the prejudice that the whole field of moral action is determined by natural law, she confounds it with the question about natural law *as such.* Porter is certainly right in saying that in Aquinas no unique "natural law ethics" in the sense of a complete set of moral norms can be found. As a matter of fact, for him the proper realm of natural law is more restricted; its task is to open and to preserve the way to moral virtue. Considered as a whole, Thomistic moral theory is not a "natural law ethics" but a virtue ethics.[34] But Porter's conclusion (335) that therefore there must be a plurality of such natural law ethics is to throw out the baby with the bath water. There are of course a plurality of different cultural configurations of the natural law, some of them deficient or

32. This is from his commentary on Gratian's *Decretum,* quoted by Porter on p. 15 of her book, according to Odon Lottin, *Le droit naturel chez saint Thomas d'Aquin et ses prédécesseurs,* 2nd ed. (Beyart: Bruges, 1931), 110.

33. Porter affirms that she draws on Brian Tierney's *The Idea of Natural Rights* (cited above). Tierney actually shows how the Scholastic canonists had, in Porter's words, a concept of natural law "which regards an interior power or capacity for moral discernment" (348). To Porter, however, this seems to be nothing else than the power to "free self-direction" (351), which, in her book, ends up in her already mentioned pluralistic view of "natural law moralities." "Natural rights" become, in fact, "local mores . . . expressed, so to speak, within a framework set by the broad patterns of behaviour characteristic of us as a species" (363). Such formulations could be entirely acceptable as parts of a Thomistic theory of natural law, if they were not pronounced on the background of the denial of what is exactly most characteristic of the Scholastic idea of natural law, that is, the illuminating power of natural reason that gives every human being access to moral *truth.* Contrary to Porter's use of it, Tierney's book demonstrates magnificently that such a concept of natural law and natural right was that of the Scholastics, not only for Huguccio, but also for other canonists such as Rufinus, Odo of Dover, Simon of Bisignano, and Sicardus (see Tierney, *The Idea of Natural Rights,* 62ff.).

34. See the Prologue to *ST* II-II, where Aquinas characterizes the program of his moral theology as "totam materiam moralem ad considerationem virtutum reducere."

distorted, but not necessarily; and there is also the plasticity of moral virtue regarding which moral norms are underdetermined, not morally, but practically, because they do not yet determine what concretely has to be done. But despite this plurality of *ethos* and the variety of goodness according to moral virtue, there still is the *natural law* with its task of moral guidance on the level of principles; there is still natural law, that is, as a universal standard of the practical truth—that is, conformity with right desire and principle—of human acts and of the existing ethos. Natural law itself as a basic standard of moral truth rooted in anthropological truth, disappears in Porter's account, which collapses into a form of moral pluralism that seems to be very close to moral relativism.

On the other hand, Porter's treatment of some concrete questions of normative ethics seems to me to be still too much dominated by a "third person" approach typical of the post-Tridentine manualist tradition of moral theology and of casuistry. The beneficial effect on her of authors like Stephen Brock and Steven Long seems to be to have driven her away from her earlier views about the "moral object" of a human act. Unfortunately, however, these authors, who tend to exclude reason from nature, have led her now into the direction of a more "naturalistic," non-moral understanding of the "object." While according to her earlier theory, the "object" necessarily was already the outcome of a moral evaluation "dependent on a global assessment of intention and circumstances" (277), her new, naturalistic solution now permits her to state that also the "object" of a human act is something "morally underdetermined." This, of course, supports the same kinds of conclusions as the theory she has abandoned, and it even provides additional plausibility to her moral pluralism.

Recent attempts to retrieve and actualize the natural law tradition have, conversely, generally gone in the direction of a "first person" approach in moral philosophy in the sense of what *Veritatis Splendor* calls "the perspective of the acting person."[35] It is normally linked with a virtue ethics approach and gives, in my view, a more adequate answer to questions of normative ethics, an answer, moreover, which does justice to the varieties of goodness

35. No. 78. Cf. G. Abbà, *Quale impostazione per la filosofia morale?* (Rome: LAS, 1996). A recent contribution to this attempt (including a short critique of Porter's earlier views on the "moral object") is found in the eighth essay of this collection, "The Perspective of the Acting Person and the Nature of Practical Reason: The 'Object of the Human Act' in Thomistic Anthropology of Action." See n. 105 on Porter.

proper to moral virtue. Furthermore, contrary to what Porter suggests and independent of concrete religious and social contexts, an account of natural law is *in principle* possible. Yet, such an account of natural law must simultaneously include a theory of moral disagreement over natural law principles, that is, it must contain as a constitutive part an account of the causes of the non-functioning or ill-functioning of natural law. In the classical tradition, the theory of the virtues provides such an account because it sees moral virtue as the condition for human beings to be fully reasonable, while recognizing truth-attaining reasonableness as the natural human endowment. Such an approach centered in the virtues, then, opens also the way to the truly theological dimension (faith, hope, and especially charity) which is the final completion—grace which presupposes nature—of the image of God in the human soul.

One might object: even if all this is true, one nevertheless needs a context of tradition, special practices, and religious faith in order to correctly grasp the truth to which natural reason is directed. Nothing is truer than that. It is in fact an empirical truth that traditions and social practices—as well as religious faith—decisively support moral knowledge rooted in natural law, and to some extent, as the Catholic Church actually teaches, this support is even necessary. But for Porter, it will be impossible to espouse such a view, because it implies that there are traditions, social practices, and religious faiths which are truth-supporting and others which are not. This, however, in Porter's theology is an impossibility, because also on the level of truth, she opts for religious and corresponding moral pluralism so that for her a tradition or social practice cannot be properly called "truth-supporting," but only, in the best case, adequate to "species-specific patterns of behavior, which provide an indispensable basis for morality" (363). Yet, as she repeats throughout her whole book, this basis is morally underdetermined and, thus, nothing like a "moral law."

We cannot here address the question of whether—and to what extent—the natural law is fully intelligible to unredeemed human nature without the help of revelation and grace.[36] At any rate, from a *Christian* and *theological* point of view, any natural law theory will be only the torso of an account of moral principles, let alone of the moral life. For Christian ethics and moral theology, the Christological perspective is indispensable.[37] Such a perspec-

36. I have tried to answer this question in the first essay of this collection.
37. Cf. my *Natural Law and Practical Reason*, 545–53.

tive, however, is absent from Porter's book. Admittedly, a "theory of the natural law" need not include a Christological perspective. But Porter's theory of natural law claims to offer a *theological* and a *Christian* theory of natural law. Yet, in consonance with her pluralistic ethical outlook and following Jacques Dupuis's idea of religious pluralism, in her theology there is no privileged place for Christology anymore. Porter speaks abundantly about "God" and his plans, and about "grace," but she cannot anymore speak about the incarnated Word—the true *imago*—of God, which is Christ, and of *Christ's* grace. So, in her *theological* account of natural law, Christ, the plenitude of truth about man and the true light which illuminates his mind, is absent; what remains is the plurality of religions which, according to this view, all in a way express God's will. Therefore, in Porter's theory not only does natural law disappear (as a consequence of her forgetting about the image of God in human beings), but also the law of Christ vanishes (because she forgets about the incarnation of the true image of God the Father) and with this vanishes a properly *Christian* ethics in the context of a specifically Christian theology.

One can—and many people actually do—speak about the *reality* of natural law and argue according to its logic without using the *term* "natural law" while entirely upholding its central meaning of a truth-attaining, natural rational power in us distinguishing good and evil. Paradoxically, Professor Porter sticks very much to the *term* "natural law"—as to terms like "Thomistic" and "Scholastic"—giving up, however, key aspects of the *reality* and *meaning* of natural law. This, I think, is what renders Jean Porter's "Thomistic theory of natural law" so perplexing.

Bibliography

Abbà, Giuseppe. *Lex et virtus. Studi sull'evoluzione della dottrina morale di San Tommaso d'Aquino.* Rome: LAS, 1983.

———. *Felicità, vita buona e virtù. Saggio di filosofia morale.* Rome: LAS, 1989.

———. *Quale impostazione per la filosofia morale?* Rome: LAS, 1996.

Annas, J. *The Morality of Happiness.* Oxford: Oxford University Press, 1993.

Anscombe, G. E. M. *Intention.* 2nd ed. Oxford: Basil Blackwell, 1963.

———. *Contraception and Chastity.* London: Catholic Truth Society, 1975.

Armstrong, R. A. *Primary and Secondary Precepts in Thomistic Natural Law Teaching.* The Hague: Martinus Nijhoff, 1966.

Bastit, M. *Naissance de la loi moderne: La pensée de la loi de saint Thomas à Suarez.* Paris: P.U.F., 1990.

Belmans, Theo G. *Le sens objectif de l'agir humain. Pour relire la morale conjugale de Saint Thomas.* Vatican City: Libreria Editrice Vaticana, 1980.

Bien, G. "Die menschlichen Meinungen und das Gute: Die Lösung des Normproblems in der aristotelischen Ethik." In *Rehabilitierung der praktischen Philosophie* I, edited by M. Riedel. Freiburg: Verlag Rombach, 1972.

F. Böckle, *Das Naturrecht im Disput.* Düsseldorf: Patmos-Verlag, 1966.

———. "Natürliches Gesetz als göttliches Gesetz in der Moraltheologie." In *Naturrecht in der Kritik,* edited by F. Böckle and E.-W. Böckenförde. Mainz: Matthias Grünewald, 1973.

———. *Fundamentalmoral.* Munich: Kösel, 1977.

———. "Was bedeutet 'Natur' in der Moraltheologie?" In *Der umstrittene Naturbegriff. Person—Natur—Sexualität in der kirchlichen Morallehre,* edited by F. Böckle. Düsseldorf: Patmos-Verlag, 1987.

Bonandi, Alberto. "Dieci anni di teologia morale con *Veritatis splendor.* Aspetti della ricezione dell'enciclia." *La Scuola Cattolica* 131 (2003): 22f.

Bonelli, Johannes, ed. *Der Mensch als Mitte und Massstab der Medizin.* Vienna/New York: Springer-Verlag, 1992.

Bormann, F. J. *Natur als Horizont sittlicher Praxis. Zur handlungstheoretischen Interpretation der Lehre vom natürlichen Sittengesetz bei Thomas von Aquin.* Münchner philosophische Studien, Neue Folge, vol. 14. Stuttgart/Berlin/Cologne: Verlag W. Kohlhammer, 1999.

Bradley, D. J. M. *Aquinas on the Twofold Human Good: Reason and Human Happiness in Aquinas' Moral Science.* Washington, D.C.: The Catholic University of America Press, 1997.

Braine, D. *The Human Person: Animal and Spirit.* Notre Dame, Ind.: University of Notre Dame Press, 1992.

Bretone, M. *Geschichte des römischen Rechts: Von den Anfängen bis zu Justinian.* 2nd ed. Munich: C. H. Beck, 1998.

Broad, C. D. *Five Types of Ethical Theory.* London: Routledge & Kegan Paul, 1930.

———. "Some of the Main Problems of Ethics." *Philosophy* 21 (1946). Reprinted in *Broad's Critical Essays in Moral Philosophy,* edited by D. R. Cheney. London: Allen & Unwin; New York: Humanities Press, 1971.

Brock, Stephen L. *Action and Conduct: Thomas Aquinas and the Theory of Action.* Edinburgh: T&T Clark, 1998. Italian translation: *Azione e condotta. Tommaso d'Aquino e la teoria dell'azione.* Rome: Edizioni Università della Santa Croce, 2002.

———. Review of *Natural Law and Practical Reason* by Martin Rhonheimer. *The Thomist* 66 (2002): 313ff.

Bruch, R. "Das sittliche Gesetz als Gottes- und Menschenwerk bei Thomas von Aquin." *Zeitschrift für Katholische Theologie* 109 (1987): 294–311.

Bubner, Rüdiger. *Handlung, Sprache und Vernunft.* 2nd ed. Frankfurt/M: Suhrkamp, 1982.

Cahill, Lisa Sowle. "Accent on the Masculine." *The Tablet,* December 11, 1993, 1618–19.

Carrasco de Paula, Ignacio. "El estudio y la enseñanza de la moral fundamental, hoy. Reflexiones en torno al quehacer teológico." *Scripta Theologica* 32, no. 3 (2000): 919.

Cessario, Romanus. *The Moral Virtues and Theological Ethics.* Notre Dame, Ind.: University of Notre Dame Press, 1991.

———. *Introduction to Moral Theology.* Washington, D.C.: The Catholic University of America Press, 2001.

Colom, E., and A. Rodríguez Luño. *Scelti in Cristo per essere santi. Elementi di Teologia morale fondamentale.* Rome: Apollinare Studi, 1999.

Danto, A. C. "Basic Actions." *American Philosophical Quarterly* 2 (1965): 141–48.

Diels, Hermann. *Die Fragmente der Vorsokratiker.* Revised by Walther Kranz. 6th ed. Berlin: 1952.

Di Noia, J. A., and Romanus Cessario, eds. *Veritatis Splendor and the Renewal of Moral Theology.* Princeton, N.J.: Scepter; Huntington, Ind.: Our Sunday Visitor; Chicago: Midwest Theological Forum, 1999.

Dulckeit, G., F. Schwarz, and W. Waldstein. *Römische Rechtsgeschichte.* Munich: C. H. Beck, 1995.

Elm, Ralf. *Klugheit und Erfahrung bei Aristoteles.* Paderborn: F. Schöningh, 1996.

Elsässer, A. Response to "Wer hat wofür Verantwortung? Zum Streit um deontologische oder teleologische Ethik," by Robert Spaemann. *Herder Korrespondenz* 36 (1982): 509ff.

Finance, J. "Autonomie et Theonomie." In *L'Agire Morale,* edited by M. Zalba. Atti del Congresso Internazionale (Rome/Naples, April 17–24, 1974). *Tomasso d'Aquino nel suo settimo centenario,* vol. 5 (Naples: Edizioni Domenicane Italiane, 1974), 239–60.

Finnis, John. *Natural Law and Natural Rights.* Oxford: Clarendon, 1980.

———. *Fundamentals of Ethics.* Washington, D.C.: Georgetown University Press, 1983.

———. *Moral Absolutes: Tradition, Revision, and Truth.* Washington, D.C.: The Catholic University of America Press, 1991.

———. "Object and Intention in Moral Judgments According to Aquinas." *The Thomist* 55 (1991): 1–27.

———. "Reason, Relativism and Christian Ethics." *Anthropotes* 9, no. 2 (December 1993): 211–30.

Finnis, John, Germain Grisez, and Joseph Boyle, "'Direct' and 'Indirect': A Reply to Critics of our Action Theory." *The Thomist* 65 (2001): 1–44.

Flannery, Kevin. *Acts Amid Precepts: The Aristotelian Logical Structure of Thomas Aquinas's Moral Theory.* Washington, D.C.: The Catholic University of America Press, 2001.

———. Review of *Die Perspective der Moral* by Martin Rhonheimer. *Gregorianum* 83 (2002): 591–94.

———. "The Multifarious Moral Object of Thomas Aquinas." *The Thomist* 67 (2003): 95–118.

Forschner, M. *Die stoische Ethik: Über den Zusammenhang von Natur-, Sprach- und Moralphilosphie im altstoischen System.* Stuttgart: Klett-Cotta, 1981.

Frankena, William K. *Ethics.* Englewood Cliffs, N.J.: Prentice Hall, 1963.

Fuchs, J. *Natural Law: A Theological Investigation.* Translated by H. Reckter and J. Dowling. New York: Sheed and Ward, 1965.

———. "The Absoluteness of Moral Terms." *Gregorianum* 52 (1971). Reprinted in *Readings in Moral Theology No. 1: Moral Norms and Catholic Tradition,* edited by Charles E. Curran and Richard McCormick. New York: Paulist Press, 1979.

———. "'Intrinsece malum': Überlegungen zu einem umstrittenen Begriff." In *Sittliche Normen: Zum Problem ihrer allgemeinen und unwandelbaren Geltung,* edited by Walter Kerber. Düsseldorf: Patmos, 1982.

———. "Das Problem Todsünde." *Stimmen der Zeit,* February 1994.

———. "Die sittliche Handlung: das instrinsece malum." In *Moraltheologie im Abseits? Antwort auf die Enzyklika "Veritatis Splendor,"* edited by Dietmar Mieth. Freiburg: Herder, 1994.

Geach, Peter. "Good and Evil." *Analysis* 17 (1956): 33–42. Republished in *Theories of Ethics,* edited by Philippa Foot. Oxford: Oxford University Press, 1967.

George, Robert P., and Hadley Arkes. "The Splendor of Truth: A Symposium." *First Things,* January 1994.

Grisez, Germain. "The First Principle of Practical Reasoning: A Commentary on the *Summa Theologiae,* 1–2, Question 94, article 2." *Natural Law Forum* 10 (1965): 168–201. A slightly abridged version is in *Aquinas: A Collection of Critical Essays,* edited by A. Kenny. Garden City, N.Y.: Anchor Books, 1969.

———. "A New Formulation of a Natural-Law Argument Against Contraception." *The Thomist* 30, no. 4 (1966): 343f.

———. *The Way of the Lord Jesus.* Vol. 1: *Christian Moral Principles.* Chicago: Franciscan Herald Press, 1983.

Grisez, Germain, Joseph Boyle, and John Finnis. "Practical Principles, Moral Truth, and Ultimate Ends." *American Journal of Jurisprudence* 32 (1987): 99–151.

Hall, P. M. *Narrative and the Natural Law: An Interpretation of Thomistic Ethics.* London/Notre Dame, Ind.: University of Notre Dame Press, 1994.

Hauerwas, Stanley. *Sanctify Them in the Truth.* Nashville, Tenn.: Abingdon, 1998.

Heller, Agnes. *Beyond Justice.* Oxford: Basil Blackwell, 1987.

Hirschberger, J. "Naturrecht oder Vernunftrecht bei Thomas von Aquin?" In *Gegenwart und Tradition. Strukturen des Denkens (Festschrift für Bernhard Lakebrink),* edited by C. Fabro. Freiburg i. Br.: Rombach, 1969.

Hittinger, Russell. *A Critique of the New Natural Law Theory.* Notre Dame, Ind.: University of Notre Dame Press, 1987.

———. "The Pope and the Theorists." *Crisis* 11 (December 1993): 31–36.

———. *The First Grace: Rediscovering the Natural Law in a Post-Christian World.* Wilmington, Del.: ISI Books, 2003.

Hoffmann, Tobias. "Moral Action as Human Action: End and Object in Aquinas in Comparison with Abelard, Lombard, Albert, and Duns Scotus." *The Thomist* 67 (2003): 73–94.

Honnefelder, L. "Praktische Vernunft und Gewissen." In *Handbuch der Christlichen Ethik* 3. By A. Hertz, W. Korff, T. Rendtorff, and H. Ringeling. Freiburg/Basel/Vienna: Herder, 1982.

———. "Die Begründbarkeit des Ethischen und die Einheit der Menschheit." In *Die Welt für morgen. Ethische Herausforderungen im Anspruch der Zukunft,* edited by G. W. Hunold and W. Korff. Munich: Kösel, 1986.

———. "Wahrheit und Sittlichkeit. Zur Bedeutung der Wahrheit in der Ethik." In *Wahrheit und Einheit in der Vielheit,* edited by E. Coreth. Düsseldorf: Patmos-Verlag, 1987.

———. "Die ethische Rationalität des mittelalterlichen Naturrechts. Max Webers und Ernst Troeltschs Deutung des mittelalterlichen Naturrechts und die Bedeutung der Lehre vom natürlichen Gesetz bei Thomas von Aquin." In *Max Webers Sicht des okzidentalen Christentums,* edited by W. Schluchter. Frankfurt am Main: Suhrkamp, 1988.

———. "Absolute Forderungen in der Ethik. Im welchem Sinn ist eine sittliche Verpflichtung absolut?" In *Das absolute in der Ethik,* edited by W. Kerber. Munich: Kindt Verlag, 1991.

———. "Natur als Handlungsprinzip. Die Relevance der Natur für die Ethik." In *Natur als Gegenstand der Wissenschaften,* edited by L. Honnefelder. Freiburg/Munich: K. Alber, 1992.

Höver, Gerhard. *Sittlich handeln im Medium der Zeit. Ansätze zur handlungstheoretischen Neuorientierung der Moraltheologie.* Würzburg: Echter Verlag, 1988.

Janssens, Louis. "Ontic Evil and Moral Evil." *Louvain Studies* 4 (1972): 114–56.

Keenan, J. F. "Die erworbenen Tugenden als richtige (nicht gute) Lebensführung: Ein genauerer Ausdruck ethischer Beschreibung." In *Ethische Theorie praktisch,* Festschrift K. Demmer, edited by F. Furger. Münster: Aschendorff, 1991.

———. *Goodness and Rightness in Thomas Aquinas's "Summa Theologiae."* Washington, D.C.: Georgetown University Press, 1992.

Kenny, Anthony, ed. *Aquinas: A Collection of Critical Essays.* London and Melbourne: Macmillan, 1969.

———. *Action, Emotion and Will.* 5th ed. London: Routledge & Kegan, 1976.

Kluxen, W. *Philosophische Ethik bei Thomas von Aquin.* Hamburg: Felix Meiner, 1964.

———. "Menschliche Natur und Ethos." *Münchener Theologische Zeitschrift* 23 (1972): 1–17.

———. *Ethik des Ethos.* Munich: K. Alber, 1974.

———. "Anmerkungen zur thomistischen Naturrechtslehre." In *Staat, Kirche, Wissenschaft in einer pluralistischen Gesellschaft,* Festschrift Paul Mikat, edited by D. Schwab, D. Giesen, J. Listl, and H.-W. Stratz. Berlin: Duncker & Humblot, 1989.

Knauer, Peter. "The Hermeneutic Function of the Principle of Double Effect." In *Readings in Moral Theology No. 1,* edited by Charles E. Curran and Richard McCormick. New York: Paulist Press, 1979.

Korff, W. "Der Rückgriff auf die Natur. Eine Rekonstruktion der thomanischen Lehre vom natürlichen Gesetz." *Phil. Jahrbuch* 94 (1987): 285–98.

Léhu, Léonard. *La raison, règle de la moralité d'après Saint Thomas.* Paris: J. Gabalda et Fils, 1930.

Locke, John. *The Reasonableness of Christianity, as deliver'd in the Scriptures.* London: Awnsham and John Churchill, 1695.
Long, Steven A. "A Brief Disquisition Regarding the Nature of the Object of the Moral Act According to St. Thomas Aquinas." *The Thomist* 67 (2003): 45–71.
Lottin, Odon. *Le droit naturel chez saint Thomas d'Aquin et ses prédécesseurs.* 2nd ed. Beyart: Bruges, 1931.
Luño, Angel Rodríguez. *La scelta etica: Il rapporto fra libertà e virtù.* Milan: Edizioni Ares, 1988.
———. *Etica.* Florence: Le Monnier, 1992.
MacIntyre, Alasdair. *After Virtue.* 2nd ed. Notre Dame, Ind.: University of Notre Dame Press, 1984.
———. *Whose Justice? Whose Rationality?* Notre Dame, Ind.: University of Notre Dame Press, 1988.
———. "How Can We Learn What *Veritatis Splendor* Has To Teach?" *The Thomist* 58 (1994): 171–95.
Maritain, J. *Neuf leçons sur les notions premières de la philosophie morale.* Paris: Tequi, 1951.
May, William E. *Moral Absolutes: Catholic Tradition, Current Trends, and the Truth.* Milwaukee, Wis.: Marquette University Press, 1989.
McCormick, Richard A. *Doing Evil to Achieve Good.* Edited by Richard McCormick and Paul Ramsey. Chicago: Loyola University Press, 1978.
———. "Document Begs Many Legitimate Moral Questions." *National Catholic Reporter* 29, no. 44 (October 15, 1993): 17.
———. "Killing the patient." *The Tablet,* October 30, 1993, 1410–11.
———. "Some Early Reactions to *Veritatis Splendor.*" *Theological Studies* 55 (1994): 481–506.
———. "Geburtenregelung als Testfall der Enzyklika." In *Moraltheologie im Abseits? Antwort auf die Enzyklika "Veritatis Splendor."* Freiburg: Herder, 1994.
McInerny, Ralph. "The Principles of Natural Law." *American Journal of Jurisprudence* 25 (1980): 1–15.
———. *Ethica Thomistica: The Moral Philosophy of Thomas Aquinas.* Washington, D.C.: The Catholic University of America Press, 1982.
———. *Aquinas on Human Action: A Theory of Practice.* Washington, D.C.: The Catholic University of America Press, 1992.
Merks, K.-W. *Theologische Grundlegung der sittlichen Autonomie. Strukturmomente eines "autonomen" Normbegründungsverständnisses im lex-Traktat der Summa Theologiae des Thomas von Aquin.* Düsseldorf: Patmos-Verlag, 1978.
———. "Naturrecht als Personrecht. Überlegungen zu einer Relektüre der Naturrechtslehre des Thomas von Aquin." In *Naturrecht im ethischen Diskurs,* Schriften des Instituts für Christliche Sozialwissenschaften 21, edited by M. Heimbach-Steins. Münster: Aschendorff, 1990.
Messner, J. *Das Naturrecht.* Innsbruck-Vienna: Tyrolia Verlag, 1966.
Müller, Anselm W. "Radical Subjectivity: Morality versus Utilitarianism." *Ratio* 19 (1977): 115–32.
Müller-Goldkuhle, P. Response to "Wer hat wofür Verantwortung? Zum Streit um deontologische oder teleologische Ethik," by Robert Spaemann. *Herder Korrespondenz* 36 (1982): 606ff.

Murphy, William F. "Martin Rhonheimer's *Natural Law and Practical Reason.*" *Sapientia* 56, no. 210 (2001): 517–48.

Nagel, Thomas. *The View from Nowhere.* Oxford: Oxford University Press, 1986.

Nelson, D. M. *The Priority of Prudence: Virtue and Natural Law in Thomas Aquinas and the Implications for Modern Ethics.* University Park: Pennsylvania State University Press, 1992.

Newman, John Henry. *Apologia pro Vita Sua.* London: J. M. Dent; New York: E. P. Dutton, 1912.

Pinckaers, Servais. "Le rôle de la fin dans l'action morale selon Saint Thomas." *Revue des Sciences philosophiques et théologiques* 45 (1961): 393–421. Reprinted in Pinckaers, *Le renouveau de la morale.* Tournai: Casterman, 1964.

———. *Les sources de la morale chrétienne. Sa méthode, son contenu, son histoire.* Fribourg: Editions Universitaires de Fribourg, 1985.

———. *Ce qu'on ne peut jamais faire. La question des actes intrinsèquement mauvais. Histoire et discussion.* Fribourg: Éditions Universitaires; Paris: Éditions du Cerf, 1986.

Porter, Jean. "The Moral Act in Veritatis Splendor and in Aquinas's Summa Theologiae: A Comparative Analysis." In *Veritatis Splendor: American Responses,* edited by Michael E. Allsopp and John J. O'Keefe. Kansas City: Sheed & Ward, 1995.

———. *Natural and Divine Law: Reclaiming the Tradition for Christian Ethics.* Ottawa: Novalis; Grand Rapids, Mich.: Eerdmans Publishing Company, 1999.

———. Review of *Natural Law and Practical Reason* by Martin Rhonheimer. *Theological Studies* 62 (2001): 851–53.

———. *Nature as Reason: A Thomistic Theory of the Natural Law.* Grand Rapids, Mich.: Eerdmans Publishing Company, 2004.

Purger, F. Response to "Wer hat wofür Verantwortung? Zum Streit um deontologische oder teleologische Ethik," by Robert Spaemann. *Herder Korrespondenz* 36 (1982): 603ff.

Ratzinger, Joseph. "Christliche Orientierung in der pluralistischen Demokratie? Über die Unverzichtbarkeit des Christentums in der modernen Gesellschaft." In *Das Europäische Erbe und seine christliche Zukunft,* Veröffentlichungen der Hanns-Martin-Schleyer-Stiftung 16, edited by H. Bürkle and N. Lobkowicz. Cologne-Bachem: Hanns Martin Schleyer-Stiftung, 1985. Reprinted in Ratzinger, *Kirche, Ökumene und Politik. Neue Versuche zur Ekklesiologie.* Einsiedeln: Johannes Verlag, 1987.

Ricken, F. "Naturrecht I." *Theologische Realenzyklopädie,* vol. 24. Berlin/New York: W. de Gruyter, 1994.

Rhonheimer, Martin. "Moral cristiana y desarollo humano." In *La Misión del Laico en la Iglesia y en el Mundo.* VIII Simposio Internacional de Teología de la Universidad de Navarra, edited by A. Sarmiento, T. Rincón, J. M. Yanguas, and A. Quirós. Pamplona: Ediciones Universidad de Navarra EUNSA (1987): 919–38.

———. "Contraception, Sexual Behavior, and Natural Law. Philosophical Foundation of the Norm of *Humanae Vitae.*" "*Humanae Vitae*": *20 anni dopo. Atti del II Congresso Internazionale di Teologia Morale Roma* (November 9–12, 1988). Milan: ARES, 1989, 73–113. Also published in *The Linacre Quarterly* 56, no. 2 (1989): 20–57. An expanded German version is published as "Sexualität und Verantwortung. Empfängnisverhütung als ethisches Problem." *IMABE,* no. 3. Vienna: Institut für medizinische Anthropologie und Bioethik, 1995. In Italian as "Sessualità e responsabilità: la contraccezione come problema etico," in *Etica della procreazione. Contraccezione—Fecondazione artificiale—Aborto,* by Rhonheimer. Milan: Edizioni PUL-Mursia, 2000. In Spanish in *Ética de la procreación.* Madrid: Rialp, 2004.

———. "Menschliches Handeln und seine Moralität. Zur Begründung sittlicher Normen." In *Ethos und Menschenbild. Zur Überwindung der Krise der Moral,* Sinn und Sendung 2, by Martin Rhonheimer, Andreas Laun, Tatjana Goritschewa, and Walter Mixa. St. Ottilien: EOS Verlag, 1989.

———. "Perché una filosofia politica? Elementi storici per una risposta." *Acta philosophica* 1, no. 2 (1992): 233–63.

———. "Zur Begründung sittlicher Normen aus der Natur" and "Ethik-Handeln-Sittlichkeit." In *Der Mensch als Mitte und Massstab der Medizin,* edited by Johannes Bonelli. Vienna/New York: Springer-Verlag, 1992, 49–94 and 137–74.

———. "'Ethics of Norms' and the Lost Virtues: Searching the Roots of the Crisis of Ethical Reasoning." *Anthropotes* 9, no. 2 (1993): 231–43. A revised version of this paper appears in chapter 2 of this book.

———. *La prospettiva della morale. Fundamenti dell'etica filosofica.* Rome: Armando Editore, 1994. Expanded and updated edition in Spanish: *La perspectiva de la moral.* Madrid: Rialp, 2000. There is also a substantially enlarged and updated edition in German: *Die Perspektive der Moral. Philosophische Grundlagen der Tugendethik.* Berlin: Akademie Verlag, 2001. An English translation tentatively titled *The Perspective of Morality: Philosophical Bases of Thomistic Virtue Ethics* is forthcoming from The Catholic University of America Press.

———. *Praktische Vernunft und Vernünftigkeit der Praxis. Handlungstheorie bei Thomas von Aquin in ihrer Entstehung aus dem Problemkontext der aristotelischen Ethik.* Berlin: Akademie Verlag, 1994.

———. "'Intrinsically Evil Acts' and the Moral Viewpoint: Clarifying a Central Teaching of *Veritatis Splendor.*" *The Thomist* 58 (1994): 1–39. Reprinted as chapter 3 of this book, and in J. A. Di Noia and Romanus Cessario, eds., *Veritatis Splendor and the Renewal of Moral Theology* (Princeton, N.J.: Scepter Publishers; Huntington, Ind.: Our Sunday Visitor; Chicago: Midwest Theological Forum, 1999), 161–93.

———. "Über die Existenz einer spezifisch christlichen Moral des Humanums." Internationale katholische Zeitschrift *Communio* 23 (1994): 360–72.

———. "Autonomia morale, libertà e verità secondo l'enciclica Veritatis Splendor." In *Veritatis Splendor. Genesi, elaborazione, significatio,* 2nd ed., edited by G. Russo. Rome: Edizioni Dehoniane, 1995, 193–215.

———. "Intentional Actions and the Meaning of Object: A Reply to Richard McCormick." *The Thomist* 59, no. 2 (1995): 279–311. Reprinted as chapter 4 of this book, and in *Veritatis Splendor and the Renewal of Moral Theology,* edited by J. A. Di Noia and Romanus Cessario. Princeton, N.J.: Scepter Publishers; Huntington, Ind.: Our Sunday Visitor; Chicago: Midwest Theological Forum, 1999.

———. "Morale cristiana e ragionevolezza morale: di che cosa è il compimento la legge del Vangelo?" In *Gesù Cristo, legge vivente e personale della Santa Chiesa,* edited by G. Borgonovo. Casale Monferrato: Piemme, 1996.

———. "Contraccezione, mentalità contraccettiva e cultura dell'aborto: valutazioni e connessioni." In *Commento interdisciplinare alla "Evangelium vitae,"* edited by R. Lucas Lucas. Vatican City: Libreria Editrice Vaticana, 1997.

———. "Lo Stato costituzionale democratico e il bene comune." In *Ripensare lo spazio politico: quale aristocrazia?,* edited by E. Morandi and R. Panattoni. Padua: Il Poligrafo, 1998.

———. "Fundamental Rights, Moral Law, and the Legal Defense of Life in a Constitutional Democracy: A Constitutionalist Approach to the Encyclical *Evangelium Vitae.*"

American Journal of Jurisprudence 43 (1998): 135–83. An initial version, in Italian, of this article was published in *Annales Theologici* 9 (1995): 271–334.

———. *Natural Law and Practical Reason: A Thomistic View of Moral Autonomy.* Translated by Gerald Malsbary. New York: Fordham University Press, 2000. German original: *Natur als Grundlage der Moral. Eine Auseinandersetzung mit autonomer und teleologischer Ethik.* Innsbruck/Vienna: Tyrolia Verlag, 1987. Italian edition: *Legge naturale e ragione pratica. Una visione tomista dell'autonomia morale.* Rome: Armando, 2001. Spanish edition: *Ley natural y razón práctica: una vision tomista de la autonomía moral.* Pamplona: EUNSA, 2000.

———. "Praktische Vernunft und das, 'von Natur aus Vernünftige'. Zur Lehre von der Lex naturalis als Prinzip der Praxis bei Thomas von Aquin." *Theologie und Philosophie* 75 (2000): 493–522. English translation by Gerald Malsbary in chapter 6 of this book.

———. *Etica della procreazione: Contraccezione, Fecondazione artificiale, Aborto.* Mursia, Milan: Edizioni PUL, 2000.

———. "Praktische Prinzipien, Naturgesetz und konkrete Handlungsurteile in tugendethischer Perspektive. Zur Diskussion über praktische Vernunft und lex naturalis bei Thomas von Aquin." *Studia Moralia* 39 (2001): 113–58.

———. "Is Christian Morality Reasonable? On the Difference Between Secular and Christian Humanism." *Annales Theologici* 15 (2001): 529–49. Reprinted as chapter 1 of this book.

———. "Sins against Justice (Iia–IIae, qq. 59–78)." In *The Ethics of Aquinas,* edited by S. J. Pope. Washington, D.C.: Georgetown University Press, 2002.

———. "The Cognitive Structure of the Natural Law and the Truth of Subjectivity." *The Thomist* 67, no. 1 (2003): 1–44. In Italian: "La legge morale naturale: conoscenza morale e coscienza. La struttura cognitiva della legge naturale e la verità della soggettività." In *Natura e dignità della persona umana a fondamento del diritto alla vita,* Acts of the Eighth General Assembly of the Pontifical Academy for Life (February 25–27, 2002), edited by Juan de Dios Vial Correa and Elio Sgreccia. Vatican City: Libreria Editrice Vaticana, 2003. Reprinted in chapter 7 of this book.

———. "The Moral Significance of Pre-Rational Nature in Aquinas: A Reply to Jean Porter (and Stanley Hauerwas)." *American Journal of Jurisprudence* 48 (2003): 253–80. Reprinted in chapter 6 of this book.

———. *Abtreibung und Lebensschutz. Tötungsverbot und Recht auf Leben in der politischen und medizinischen Ethik.* Paderborn: Verlag Ferdinand Schöningh, 2003.

———. "The Perspective of the Acting Person and the Nature of Practical Reason: The 'Object of the Human Act' in Thomistic Anthropology of Action." Italian text in the proceedings of the Congress, *Camminare nella luce. Prospettiva della teologia morale a 10 anni da "Veritatis splendor,"* held at the Pontificia Università Lateranense / Pontificio Istituto Giovanni Paolo II per studi su matrimonio e famiglia, Rome, November 20–22, 2003, edited by L. Melina and J. Noriega. Rome: Pontificia Università Lateranense, 2004. Translated by Joseph T. Papa in *Nova et Vetera* 2, no. 2 (2004): 461–516. Reprinted as chapter 8 of this book.

———. "Ragione practica e verità della soggettività: L'Autoesperienza del soggeto morale alle radici della metafisica e dell'anthropologia." Given at a February 2004 conference sponsored by the faculty of philosophy at the Pontifical University of the Holy Cross. Translated by Gerald Malsbary in chapter 9 of this book.

Ross, W. D. *The Right and the Good.* Reprint. Oxford: Clarendon Press, 1965.

Scheeben, M. J. *Die Mysterien des Christentums,* Gesammelte Schriften, vol. 2, edited by J. Höfer. Freiburg: Herder (1951): 200–59.

Schockenhoff, E. *Naturrecht und Menschenwürde. Universalethik in einer geschichtlichen Welt.* Mainz: Matthias-Grunewald-Verlag, 1996. In English: *Natural Law and Human Dignity: Universal Ethics in an Historical World.* Washington, D.C.: The Catholic University of America Press, 2003.

Scholz, Franz. *Wege, Umwege und Auswege der Moraltheologie. Ein Plädoyer für begründete Ausnahmen.* Munich: Bonifatius, 1976.

Schönberger, R. Review of *Praktische Vernunft und Vernünftigkeit der Praxis* by Martin Rhonheimer. In *Zeitschrift für philosophische Forschung* 49 (1995): 629–32.

Schörer, C. *Praktische Vernunft bei Thomas von Aquin,* Münchener philosophische Studien. Neue Folge 10. Stuttgart-Berlin-Cologne: W. Kohlhammer, 1995.

Schüller, Bruno. "Various Types of Grounding for Ethical Norms." In *Readings in Moral Theology No. 1: Moral Norms and Catholic Tradition,* edited by Charles E. Curran and Richard A. McCormick. New York: Paulist Press, 1979.

———. *Die Begründung sittlicher Urteile. Typen ethischer Argumentation in der Moraltheologie.* 2nd ed. Düsseldorf: Patmos, 1980.

———. "Eine autonome Moral, was ist das?" *Theologische Revue* 78 (1982): 103–6.

———. "Die Quellen der Moralität. Zur systematischen Ortung eines alten Lehrstückes der Moraltheologie." *Theologie und Philosophie* 59 (1984): 535–59.

Schuster, J. *Moralisches Können. Studien zur Tugendethik.* Würzburg: Echter, 1997.

Spaemann, Robert. "Wer hat wofür Verantwortung? Zum Streit um deontologische oder teleologische Ethik." *Herder Korrespondenz* 36 (1982).

———. "Nochmals: deontologische oder teleologische Moralbegründung?" *Herder Korrespondenz* 37 (1983): 79–84.

———. *Glück und Wohlwollen. Versuch über Ethik.* Stuttgart: Klett-Cotta, 1989.

Spanneut, M. "Les normes morales du stoïcisme chez les Pères de l'Église." In *Universalité et permanence des lois morales,* edited by S. Pinckaers and C. J. Pinto de Oliveira. Fribourg: Éditions Universitaires; Paris: Éditions du Cerf, 1986.

Tierney, Brian. *The Idea of Natural Rights: Studies on Natural Rights, Natural Law and Church Law 1150–1625.* Grand Rapids, Mich.: Eerdmans, 2001.

Tonneau, J. *Absolu et obligation en morale.* Montreal: Inst. d'études médiévales; Paris: J. Vrin, 1965.

Trapé, A. "L'universalità e l'immutabilità delle norme morali e l'oggettività del giudizio morale secondo i Padri latini, in particolare secondo Sant'Agostino." In *Universalité et permanence des lois morales,* edited by S. Pinckaers and C. J. Pinto de Oliveira. Fribourg: Éditions Universitaires; Paris: Éditions du Cerf, 1986.

Utz, A. F. "Wonach richtet sich das Gewissen? Die neue Ordnung." *Heft* 2 (1988): 155.

Villey, Michel. "Droit subjectif I (La genèse du droit subjectif chez Guillaume d'Occam)." In *Seize Essais de Philosophie de Droit dont un sur la crise universitaire,* by M. Villey. Paris: Dalloz, 1969.

Virt, Gunter. "Epikie und sittliche Selbstbestimmung." In *Moraltheologie im Abseits? Antwort auf die Enzyklika "Veritatis Splendor,"* edited by Dietmar Mieth. Freiburg: Herder, 1994.

Waldstein, W. "Entscheidungsgrundlagen der klassischen römischen Juristen." In *Aufstieg und Niedergang der römischen Welt: Geschichte und Kultur Roms im Spiegel der neueren Forschung,* edited by H. Temporini and W. Haase. Sect. II, Principat, vol. 15, edited by H. Temporini. Berlin and New York: Walter de Gruyter, 1976.

———. "Naturrecht bei den klassischen römischen Juristen." In *Das Naturrechtsdenken heute und morgen: Gedächtnisschrift für René Marcic,* edited by D. Mayer-Maly and P. M. Simons. Berlin: Duncker & Humblot, 1983.

Walsh, James. *Aristotle's Conception of Moral Weakness.* New York: Columbia University Press, 1963.

Westberg, D. *Right Practical Reason: Aristotle, Action, and Prudence in Aquinas.* Oxford: Clarendon Press, 1994.

Wieland, G. "Secundum naturam vivere. Über das Verhältnis von Natur und Sittlichkeit." In *Natur im ethischen Argument,* Studien zur theologischen Ethik 31, edited by B. Fraling. Freiburg: Herder, 1990.

Williams, Bernard. "A Critique of Utilitarianism." In *Utilitarianism: For & Against,* by J. J. C. Smart and Bernard Williams. Cambridge: Cambridge University Press, 1973.

Wittgenstein, Ludwig. *Philosophical Investigations.* Translated by G. E. M. Anscombe. Edited by G. E. M. Anscombe and R. Rhees. Oxford: Basil Blackwell, 1958.

Wolbert, Werner. *Ethische Argumentation und Paränese in 1 Kor 7.* Düsseldorf: Patmos, 1981.

———. "Naturalismus in der Ethik. Zum Vorwurf des naturalistischen Fehlschlusses." *Theologie und Glaube* 79 (1989): 234–67.

———. "Die 'in sich schlechten' Handlungen und der Konsequentialismus." In *Moraltheologie im Abseits? Antwort auf die Enzyklika "Veritatis Splendor,"* edited by Dietmar Mieth. Freiburg: Herder, 1994.

Wright, R. *The Moral Animal: Why We Are the Way We Are.* London: Vintage, 1995.

Zingarelli, Nicola, ed. *Vocabolario della Lingua Italiana.* 11th ed. 1988.

Martin Rhonheimer's Publications

Books

Politisierung und Legitimitätsentzug. Totalitäre Kritik der parlamentarischen Demokratie in Deutschland. Reihe Praktische Philosophie, vol. 8. Freiburg/Munich: Karl Alber Verlag, 1979.

Familie und Selbstverwirklichung. Alternativen zur Emanzipation. Cologne: Verlag Wissenschaft und Politik, 1979.

Natur als Grundlage der Moral. Die personale Struktur des Naturgesetzes bei Thomas von Aquin: Eine Auseinandersetzung mit autonomer und teleologischer Ethik. Innsbruck-Vienna: Tyrolia-Verlag, 1987.

La prospettiva della morale. Fondamenti dell'etica filosofica. Rome: Armando, 2006. (Updated edition of 1994 original.)

Praktische Vernunft und Vernünftigkeit der Praxis. Handlungstheorie bei Thomas von Aquin in ihrer Entstehung aus dem Problemkontext der aristotelischen Ethik. Berlin: Akademie Verlag, 1994.

Sexualität und Verantwortung. Empfängnisverhütung als ethisches Problem. Institut für medizinische Anthropologie und Bioethik, no. 3. Vienna: Verlag IMABE, 1995.

Absolute Herrschaft der Geborenen? Anatomie und Kritik der Argumentation von Norbert Hoersters "Abtreibung im säkularen Staat." Institut für medizinische Anthropologie und Bioethik, no. 4. Vienna: Verlag IMABE, 1995.

La filosofia politica di Thomas Hobbes. Coerenza e contraddizioni di un paradigma. Rome: Armando, 1997.

Derecho a la vida y estado moderno. A propósito de la "Evangelium vitae." Madrid: Rialp, 1998.

Etica della procreazione. Contraccezione—Fecondazione artificiale—Aborto. Milan: Edizioni PUL-Mursia, 2000.

Natural Law and Practical Reason: A Thomist View of Moral Autonomy. New York: Fordham University Press, 2000. (English translation of *Natur als Grundlage der Moral,* 1987.)

La perspectiva de la moral. Fundamentos de la ética filosófica. Madrid: Rialp, 2000. (Spanish translation of *La prospettiva della morale,* 1994.)

Ley natural y razón práctica. Una visión tomista de la autonomía moral. Pamplona: EUNSA, 2000. 2nd ed. 2006. (Spanish translation of *Natur als Grundlage der Moral,* 1987.)

Legge naturale e ragione pratica: una visione tomista dell'autonomia morale. Rome: Armando, 2001. (Italian translation of *Natur als Grundlage der Moral,* 1987.)

Die Perspektive der Moral. Philosophische Grundlagen der Tugendethik. Berlin: Akademie Verlag, 2001. (Expanded and updated edition of 1994 original.)

Abtreibung und Lebensschutz. Tötungsverbot und Recht auf Leben in der politischen und medizinischen Ethik. Paderborn: Verlag Ferdinand Schöningh, 2003.

Ética de la procreación. Madrid: Rialp, 2004.

Verwandlung der Welt. Zur Aktualität des Opus Dei. Cologne: Adamas Verlag, 2006.

The Perspective of the Acting Person: Essays in the Renewal of Thomistic Moral Philosophy, ed. William F. Murphy Jr. Washington: The Catholic University of America Press, 2008.

Contributions to edited collections

"Konservatismus als politische Philosophie." In *Die Herausforderung der Konservativen,* edited by Gerd-Klaus Kaltenbrunner. Herderbücherei Initiative, no. 3. Freiburg/Br.: Herder, 1974, 104–28. (Italian translation: "Il conservatorismo come filosofia politica." In *La sfida dei conservatori,* edited by Gerd-Klaus Kaltenbrunner. Rome: Giovanni Volpe, 1977, 115–41.)

"Die Entdeckung der Familie." In *Familie—Feindbild und Leitbild,* with N. Lobkowicz, J. Fontes, and B. Hassenstein. Cologne: Adamas Verlag, 1977, 11–44.

"Sozialphilosophie und Familie. Gedanken zur humanen Grundfunktion der Familie." In *Familie—Herausforderung der Zukunft.* (Familiensymposium der Universität Freiburg/Schweiz, November 1981.) Edited by B. Schnyder. Freiburg: Freiburger Universitätsverlag, 1982, 113–40.

"Die Konstituierung des Naturgesetzes und sittlich-normativer Objektivität durch die praktische Vernunft." In *Persona, Verità e Morale. Atti del Congresso Internazionale di Teologia Morale* (Rome, April 7–12, 1986). Rome: Città Nuova, 1987, 859–84.

"Moral cristiana y desarollo humano." In *La Misión del Laico en la Iglesia y en el Mundo.* VIII Simposio Internacional de Teología de la Universidad de Navarra. Edited by A. Sarmiento, T. Rincón, J. M. Yanguas, and A. Quirós. Pamplona: EUNSA, 1987, 919–38.

"Gut und böse oder richtig und falsch—was unterscheidet das Sittliche?" In *Ethik der Leistung* (Lindenthal-Colloquium 1987), edited by Hans Thomas. Herford: Busse-Seewald, 1988, 47–75.

"Contraception, Sexual Behavior, and Natural Law: Philosophical Foundation of the Norm of *Humanae Vitae.*" In *"Humanae Vitae": 20 anni dopo. Atti del II Congresso Internazionale di Teologia Morale* (Rome, November 9–12, 1988). Milan: ARES, 1989, 73–113.

"Menschliches Handeln und seine Moralität. Zur Begründung sittlicher Normen." In *Ethos und Menschenbild: Zur Überwindung der Krise der Moral,* by M. Rhonheimer, A. Laun, T. Goritschewa, and W. Mixa. Sinn und Sendung, vol. 2, 45–114. St. Ottilien: EOS-Verlag, 1989.

"Zur Begründung sittlicher Normen aus der Natur. Grundsätzliche Erwägungen und Exemplifizierung am Beispiel der I.v.F." In *Der Mensch als Mitte und Maßstab der Medizin* (Medizin und Ethik, vol. 1), edited by J. Bonelli. Vienna: Springer-Verlag, 1992, 49–94.

"Ethik—Handeln—Sittlichkeit. Zur sittlichen Dimension menschlichen Tuns." In *Der Mensch als Mitte und Maßstab der Medizin* (Medizin und Ethik, vol. 1), edited by J. Bonelli. Vienna: Springer-Verlag, 1992, 137–74.

"Die Instrumentalisierung des menschlichen Lebens. Ethische Erwägungen zur In-Vitro-Fertilisierung." In *Fortpflanzungsmedizin und Lebensschutz* (*Veröffentlichungen des Internationalen Forschungszentrums für Grundfragen der Wissenschaften Salzburg,* Neue Folge vol. 55), edited by F. Bydlinski and T. Mayer-Maly. Innsbruck-Vienna: Tyrolia-Verlag, 1992, 41–64.

"Autonomía y teonomía moral según la encíclica *Veritatis splendor.*" In *Comentarios a la "Veritatis splendor,"* edited by G. del Pozo Abejón. Madrid: Biblioteca de Autores Cristianos, 1994, 543–78.

"L'uomo, un progetto di Dio." In *Lettera enciclica "Veritatis splendor" del Sommo Pontefice Giovanni Paolo II. Testo e commenti.* Vatican City: Libreria Editrice Vaticana, 1994, 186–91.

"Autonomia morale, libertà e verità secondo l'enciclica Veritatis Splendor." In *Veritatis splendor. Genesi, elaborazione, significato.* 2nd edition, updated and expanded. Edited by G. Russo. Rome: Edizioni Dehoniane, 1995, 193–215.

"Morale cristiana e ragionevolezza morale: di che cosa è il compimento della legge del vangelo?" In *Gesù Cristo, legge vivente e personale della Santa Chiesa. Atti del IX Colloquio Internazionale di Teologia di Lugano sul Primo capitolo dell'Enciclica "Veritatis Splendor"* (Lugano, June 15–17, 1995), edited by G. Borgonovo. Casale Monferrrato: Edizioni Piemme, 1996, 147–68.

"Anticoncepción, mentalidad anticonceptiva y cultura del aborto: valoraciones y conexiones." In *Comentario interdisciplinar a la "Evangelium vitae,"* edited by R. Lucas Lucas. Madrid: Biblioteca de Autores Cristianos, 1996, 435–52.

"Contraccezione, mentalità contraccettiva e cultura dell'aborto: valutazioni e connessioni." In *Commento interdisciplinare alla "Evangelium vitae."* By Pontificia Accademia per La Vita, Italian edited by E. Sgreccia and R. Lucas Lucas. Vatican City: Libreria Editrice Vaticana, 1997, 435–52.

"L'immagine dell'uomo nel liberalismo e il concetto di autonomia: al di là del dibattito fra liberali e comunitaristi." In *Immagini dell'uomo. Percorsi antropologici nella filosofia moderna,* edited by I. Yarza. Rome: Armando, 1997, 95–133.

"'Intrinsically Evil Acts' and the Moral Viewpoint: Clarifying a Central Teaching of *Veritatis splendor.*" In "*Veritatis Splendor" and the Renewal of Moral Theology,* edited by J. A. Di Noia and Romanus Cessario. Reprint. Princeton: Scepter; Huntington: Our Sunday Visitor; Chicago: Midwest Theological Forum, 1999, 161–93.

"Intentional Actions and the Meaning of Object: A Reply to Richard McCormick." In "*Veritatis Splendor" and the Renewal of Moral Theology,* edited by J. A. Di Noia and Romanus Cessario. Reprint. Princeton: Scepter; Huntington: Our Sunday Visitor; Chicago: Midwest Theological Forum, 1999, 241–68.

"Sins Against Justice (IIa IIae, qq. 59–78)." In *The Ethics of Aquinas,* edited by Stephen J. Pope. Washington, D.C.: Georgetown University Press, 2002, 287–303.

"Der selige Josemaría und die Liebe zur Welt." In *Josemaría Escrivá. Profile einer Gründergestalt,* edited by C. Ortiz. Cologne: Adamas Verlag, 2002, 225–52.

"La imagen del hombre en el liberalismo y el concepto de autonomía: más allá del debate entre liberales y comunitaristas." In *Más allá del liberalismo,* edited by Robert A. Gahl. Madrid: EIUNSA, 2002.

"La legge morale naturale: conoscenza morale e coscienza. La struttura cognitiva della legge naturale e la verità della soggettività." In *Natura e dignità della persona umana a fondamento del diritto alla vita* (Atti dell'ottava assemblea generale della Pontificia Accademia per la vita, February 25–27, 2002), edited by Juan de Dios Vial Correa and Elio Sgreccia. Vatican City: Libreria Editrice Vaticana, 2003, 125–58.

"Natural Moral Law: Moral Knowledge and Conscience. The Cognitive Structure of the Natural Law and the Truth of Subjectivity." In *The Nature and Dignity of the Human person as the Foundation of the Right to Life* (Proceedings of the Eighth Assembly of the Pontifical Academy for Life, February 25–27, 2002), edited by Juan de Dios Vial Correa and Elio Sgreccia. Vatican City: Libreria Editrice Vaticana, 2003, 123–59.

"La realtà politica ed economica del mondo moderno e i suoi presupposti etici e culturali. L'enciclica Centesimus annus." In *Giovanni Paolo teologo. Nel segno delle encicliche,* edited by Graziano Borgonovo and Arturo Cattaneo, Preface by Camillo Cardinal Ruini. Rome: Edizioni Arnoldo Mondadori, 2003, 83–94.

"Katholischer Antirassismus, kirchliche Selbstverteidigung und das Schicksal der Juden im nationalsozialistischen Deutschland. Das 'Schweigen der Kirche' zur Judenverfolgung im NS-Staat: Ein Plädoyer für eine offne Auseinanderssetzung mit der Vergangenheit." In *Unterwegs nach Jerusalem. Die Kirche auf der Suche nach ihren jüdischen Wurzeln,* edited by Andreas Laun. Eichstätt: Franz-Sales-Verlag, 2004, 10–33.

"Il rapporto tra verità e politica nella società cristiana. Riflessioni storico-teologiche per la valutazione dell'amore della libertà nella predicazione di Josemaría Escrivá." In *Figli di Dio nella Chiesa. Riflessioni sul messaggio di San Josemaría Escrivá. Aspetti culturali ed ecclesiastici* (*La grandezza della vita quotidiana.* Atti del Congresso Internazionale, January 8–11, 2002, vol. 5/2), edited by Fernando de Andrés. Rome: Pontificia Università della Santa Croce, 2004, 153–78.

"El hombre como sujeto de la experiencia moral. El primado antropológico y cognitivo de la razón y la verdad de la subjetividad." In *Teología Moral.* Actas del Congreso Internacional, November 27–29, 2003. Murcia: Universidad Católica San Antonio de Murcia, 2004, 31–64.

"La prospettiva della persona agente e la natura della ragione pratica. L'oggetto dell'atto umano' nell'antropologia tomista dell'azione." In *Camminare nella luce. Prospettive della Teologia morale a partire da "Veritatis Splendor,"* edited by L. Melina and J. Noriega. Rome: Pontificia Università Lateranense, 2004, 169–224.

"Ragione pratica e verità della soggettività: l'autoesperienza del soggetto morale alle radici della metafisica e dell'antropologia." In *Ripensare la metafisica. La filosofia prima tra teologia e altri saperi,* edited by Luis Romera. Rome: Armando, 2005, 73–104.

"Thomas von Aquin: Das ewige und das natürliche Gesetz (Summa Theologiae, I-II Q. 90, 91, 94)." Introduction. In *Ethik Lehr- und Lesebuch,* edited by Robert Spaemann and Walter Schweidler. Stuttgart: Klett-Cotta Verlag, 2006, 68–76.

"Thomas von Aquin: Das Gewissen (Über die Wahrheit Q. 17)." Introduction. In *Ethik Lehr- und Lesebuch,* edited by Robert Spaemann and Walter Schweidler. Stuttgart: Klett-Cotta Verlag, 2006, 175–86.

Articles in journals and encyclopedias

"Politik, Vernunft und Entscheidung. Anmerkungen zu Theorie und Geschichte der konservativen Intelligenz." *Criticón* 26 (1974): 259–65.

"Edmund Burke—Klassiker des Konservatismus?" *Criticón* 28 (1975): 81–87.

"Sozialisation oder Erziehung? Die neue Bedrohung der Familie." *Die politische Meinung* 175 (1977): 39–58.

"Das kleinere Übel?" *Neue Zürcher Zeitung,* September 8, 1977, 29.

"Wo der Mensch das Menschsein lernt. Die Familie als Magd der Gesellschaft?" (review of *Feindbild Familie. Krise und Therapie,* edited by F. Reitze [Cologne: Sonderdruck, 1978]). *Rheinischer Merkur* 3: 15–17.

"Politisierung und Demokratiekritik. Anmerkungen zur Geschichte des Politisierungsbegriffes." *Archiv für Begriffsgeschichte* 29 (1985): 138–46.

"Die praktische Vernunft als Gegenstand philosophischer Ethik. Vorbereitende Überlegungen für eine 'Rekonstruktion' der Lehre vom Naturgesetz bei Thomas von Aquin." *Forum Katholische Theologie* 2 (1986): 97–119.

"'Natur als Grundlage der Moral': Nichts als Spiegelfechterei? Anmerkungen zur Stephan Ernsts 'Marginalien.'" *Theologie und Glaube* 79 (1989): 69–83.

"Contraception, Sexual Behavior, and Natural Law: Philosophical Foundation of the Norm of *Humanae Vitae.*" *Linacre Quarterly* 56, no. 2 (1989): 20–57.

"Der anspruchsvolle Weg zum Glück." *Rheinischer Merkur / Christ und Welt,* 29 (1989): 22.

"Politisierung." In *Historisches Wörterbuch der Philosophie,* edited by J. Ritter and K. Gründer. Vol. 7. Basel: Schwabe-Verlag, 1989, 1075–79.

"Perché una filosofia politica? Elementi storici per una risposta." *Acta philosophica* 1, no. 2 (1992): 233–63.

"L'uomo, un progetto di Dio. La fondazione teonomica dell'autonomia morale secondo l'Enciclica *Veritatis Splendor.*" *L'Osservatore Romano,* November 5–6, 1993, 1–4.

"Freiheit ist an Wahrheit gebunden." *Katholische Internationale Presseagentur KIPA,* October 5, 1993, 8–10.

"*Veritatis splendor:* veniamo al dunque. Il legame tra libertà e verità è ciò che interessa al Papa." *Giornale del Popolo,* December 11–12, 1993, 24.

"'Ethics of Norms' and the Lost Virtues: Searching the Roots of the Crisis of Ethical Reasoning." *Anthropotes* 9, no. 2 (1993): 231–43.

"'Intrinsically Evil Acts' and the Moral Viewpoint: Clarifying a Central Teaching of *Veritatis Splendor.*" *The Thomist* 58, no. 1 (1994): 1–39.

"Über die Existenz einer spezifisch christlichen Moral des Humanums." *Internationale katholische Zeitschrift 'Communio'* 23 (1994): 360–72.

"Neuevangelisierung und politische Kultur." *Schweizerische Kirchenzeitung* 162 (1994): no. 44, 608–13; no. 45, 622–27.

"Sittliche Autonomie und Theonomie gemäss der Enzyklika *Veritatis splendor.*" *Forum Katholische Theologie* 10, no. 4 (1994): 241–68.

"Minaccia di stupro e prevenzione: un'eccezione?" *La Scuola Cattolica* 123 (1995): 75–90.

"Empfängnisverhütung, Sexualverhalten und Menschenbild. Wider die angebliche Unbegründbarkeit der Lehre von *Humanae vitae.*" *Imago Hominis* 2, no. 2 (1995): 145–52.

"Intentional Actions and the Meaning of Object: A Reply to Richard McCormick." *The Thomist* 59, no. 2 (1995): 279–311.

"Diritti fondamentali, legge morale e difesa legale della vita nello stato costituzionale democratico. L'approccio costituzionalistico all'enciclica *Evangelium vitae.*" *Annales Theologici* 9 (1995): 271–334.

"Ethik als Aufklärung über die Frage nach dem Guten und die Aristotelische 'Perversion des ethischen Themas.' Anmerkungen zu W. Pannenbergs Aristoteleskritik." *Anthropotes* 13, no. 1 (1997): 211–23.

"Lo Stato costituzionale democratico e il bene comune." In *Ripensare lo spazio politico: quale aristocrazia?* Edited by E. Morandi and R. Panattoni. *Con-tratto—Rivista di filosofia tomista e contemporanea,* 6 (1997). Padua: Il Poligrafo, 1998, 57–122.

"Sulla fondazione di norme morali a partire dalla natura." *Rivista di Filosofia Neo-Scolastica* 89 (1997): 515–35.

"Contrattualismo, individualismo e solidarietà: per rileggere la tradizione liberale." *Per la filosofia* 16, no. 46 (1999): 30–40.

"Fundamental Rights, Moral Law, and the Legal Defense of Life in a Constitutional Democracy: A Constitutionalist Approach to the Encyclical *Evangelium Vitae*." *American Journal of Jurisprudence* 43 (1998): 135–83.

"Die sittlichen Tugenden. Anthropologische und praktisch-kognitive Dimensio." *Imago Hominis* 7, no. 2 (2000): 103–14.

"Praktische Vernunft und das 'von Natur aus Vernünftige.' Zur Lehre von der Lex naturalis als Prinzip der Praxis bei Thomas von Aquin." *Theologie und Philosophie* 75 (2000): 493–522.

"Autoritas non veritas facit legem: Thomas Hobbes, Carl Schmitt und die Idee des Verfassungsstaates." *Archiv für Rechts- und Sozialphilosophie* 86 (2000): 484–98.

"Praktische Prinzipien, Naturgesetz und konkrete Handlungsurteile in tugendethischer Perspektive. Zur Diskussion über praktische Vernunft und lex naturalis bei Thomas von Aquin." *Studia Moralia* 39 (2001): 113–58.

"Is Christian Morality Reasonable? On the Difference between Secular and Christian Humanism." *Annales Theologici* 15, no. 2 (2001): 529–49.

"Christliches soziales Lehren und Handeln." *Schweizerische Kirchenzeitung* 170, no. 5 (2002): 54–59.

"La legge morale naturale: conoscenza morale e coscienza. La struttura cognitiva della legge naturale e la verità della soggettività." *Ars Interpretandi* 7 (2002): 47–85.

"Warum schwieg die Kirche zu dem Vernichtungskampf? Gedanken zum Brief Edith Steins an Pius XI.: Der Papst sollte nicht nur den Nationalsozialismus verurteilen, sondern gegen die Verfolgung der Juden protestieren." *Die Tagespost,* March 22, 2003, 5.

"The Cognitive Structure of the Natural Law and the Truth of Subjectivity." *The Thomist* 67, no. 1 (2003): 1–44.

"Laici e cattolici: oltre le divisioni. Riflessioni sull'essenza della democrazia e della società aperta." *Fondazione Liberal,* no. 17 (2003): 108–16.

"Nur Personen entwickeln die Eigenschaften von Personen. Die Befürworter der verbrauchenden Embryonenforschung benutzen häufig versteckte metaphysische Argumente." *Die Tagespost,* April 18, 2003, 10.

"Das Gewissen reinigen: Sich erinnern, wie es wirklich war." *Die Tagespost,* June 28, 2003, 9–10.

"The Holocaust: What Was Not Said." *First Things,* November 2003, 18–27.

"The Moral Significance of Pre-Rational Nature in Aquinas: A Reply to Jean Porter (and Stanley Hauerwas)." *American Journal of Jurisprudence* 48 (2003): 253–80.

"Correspondence: 'The Church and the Holocaust,' Martin Rhonheimer responds." *First Things,* February 2004, 2–5.

"The Truth About Condoms." *The Tablet,* July 10, 2004, 10–11.

"Mel Gibsons Passionsfilm: Antisemitisch?" *Schweizerische Kirchenzeitung* 33–34 (2004): 600–602; 613–15.

"Eine heilsame Provokation, bewusst verkannt, zu Unrecht verrissen. Ein Plädoyer für Gerechtigkeit im Umgang mit Mel Gibsons umstrittenem Jesus-Film." *Die Tagespost,* August 28, 2004.

"Nicht Zerstörung, sondern Verhinderung der Metaphysik. Kants 'Kritik der reinen Vernunft' ist eine faszinierende Konstruktion mit falschen Prämissen, vor der die katholische Theologie kritische Distanz wahren sollte." *Die Tagespost,* September 25, 2004.

"Eine neue Form der Rechtfertigung des Tötens." *Neue Zürcher Zeitung,* October 27, 2004, 15.

"The Perspective of the Acting Person and the Nature of Practical Reason: The 'Object of the Human Act' in Thomistic Anthropology of Action." *Nova et Vetera,* English edition, 2, no. 2 (2004): 461–516.

"Mel Gibson's 'The Passion of the Christ': A Plea for Fairness." *Logos* 8, no. 1 (Winter 2005): 13–27.

"On the Use of Condoms to Prevent Acquired Immune Deficiency Syndrome (Reply to Benedict Guevin)." *National Catholic Bioethics Quarterly* (Spring 2005): 40–48.

"Das Recht, geboren zu werden." *Die Tagespost,* July 7, 2005.

"Cittadinanza multiculturale nella democrazia liberale: le proposte di Ch. Taylor, J. Habermas e W. Kymlicka." *Acta Philosophica* 15, no. 1 (2006): 29–52.

"The Political Ethos of Constitutional Democracy and the Place of Natural Law in Public Reason: Rawls' 'Political Liberalism' Revisited." *American Journal of Jurisprudence* 50 (2005): 1–70.

Forthcoming

La prospettiva della morale. Fondamenti dell'etica filosofica. 2nd edition, enlarged. Rome: Armando.

The Perspective of Morality: Philosophical Bases of Thomistic Virtue Ethics. Washington, D.C.: The Catholic University of America Press.

"Can Political Ethics Be Universalized? Human Rights as a Global Project."

"Christian Secularity and the Culture of Human Rights."

Voce "Consenso," *Dizionario di Filosofia,* Bompiani.

Index

The Perspective of the Acting Person: Essays in the Renewal of Thomistic Moral Philosophy was designed and typeset in Minion by Kachergis Book Design of Pittsboro, North Carolina. It was printed on 60-pound House Natural Smooth and bound by Sheridan Books of Ann Arbor, Michigan.